PATTERNS OF DISCIPLESHIP
IN THE NEW TESTAMENT

McMaster New Testament Studies

The McMaster New Testament Studies series, edited by Richard N. Longenecker, is designed to address particular themes in the New Testament that are of concern to Christians today. Written in a style easily accessible to ministers, students, and laypeople by contributors who are proven experts in their fields of study, the volumes in this series reflect the best of current biblical scholarship while also speaking directly to the pastoral needs of people in the church today. *Patterns of Discipleship in the New Testament* is the first volume in the series.

Patterns of Discipleship in the New Testament

Edited by

Richard N. Longenecker

WILLIAM B. EERDMANS PUBLISHING COMPANY
GRAND RAPIDS, MICHIGAN / CAMBRIDGE, U.K.

© 1996 Wm. B. Eerdmans Publishing Co.
255 Jefferson Ave. S.E., Grand Rapids, Michigan 49503 /
P.O. Box 163, Cambridge CB3 9PU U.K.
All rights reserved

01 00 99 98 97 96   7 6 5 4 3 2 1

Library of Congress Cataloging-in-Publication Data

Patterns of discipleship in the New Testament /
edited by Richard N. Longenecker.
p.   cm.
ISBN 0-8028-4169-4 (pbk.: alk. paper)
1. Bible. N.T. — Criticism, interpretation, etc.
2. Christian life — Biblical teaching. I. Longenecker, Richard N.
BS2545.C48P38   1996
248.4′09′015 — dc20   96-26062
                                               CIP

Contents

II. PAULINE LETTERS

III. OTHER WRITINGS

Contributors

DAVID E. AUNE   Professor of New Testament and Early Christianity, Loyola University, Chicago, Illinois, USA

LINDA L. BELLEVILLE   Associate Professor of Biblical Literature, North Park Theological Seminary, Chicago, Illinois, USA

PETER H. DAVIDS   On-Site Study Center Director, Schloss Mittersill Study Center, Mittersill, Austria

TERENCE L. DONALDSON   Professor of New Testament and Biblical Languages, College of Emmanuel and St. Chad, Saskatoon, Saskatchewan, Canada

GERALD F. HAWTHORNE   Professor Emeritus of Greek, Department of Foreign Languages, Wheaton College, Wheaton, Illinois, USA

MELVYN R. HILLMER   Principal Emeritus and Adjunct Professor of New Testament, McMaster Divinity College, Hamilton, Ontario, Canada

LARRY W. HURTADO   Professor of New Testament Language, Literature, and Theology, University of Edinburgh, Edinburgh, Scotland

L. ANN JERVIS   Associate Professor of New Testament, Wycliffe College and Trinity College, University of Toronto, Toronto, Ontario, Canada

MICHAEL P. KNOWLES   Assistant Director of the Institute of Evangelism and Assistant Professor of New Testament, Wycliffe College, University of Toronto, Toronto, Ontario, Canada

WILLIAM L. LANE   Professor of Biblical Studies, Department of Religion, Seattle Pacific University, Seattle, Washington, USA

RICHARD N. LONGENECKER   Distinguished Professor of New Testament, McMaster Divinity College, McMaster University, Hamilton, Ontario, Canada

J. RAMSEY MICHAELS   Professor Emeritus of Religious Studies, Southwest Missouri State University, Springfield, Missouri, USA

JEFFREY A. D. WEIMA   Associate Professor of New Testament, Calvin Theological Seminary, Grand Rapids, Michigan, USA

Preface

With the present volume we inaugurate the McMaster New Testament Series, sponsored by McMaster Divinity College, Hamilton, Ontario, Canada. The series is designed to address particular themes in the New Testament that are (or should be) of crucial concern to Christians today. The plan is to prepare and publish annual symposium volumes, with contributors selected because of their proven expertise in the areas assigned and their known ability to write intelligibly for readers who are not necessarily academics. Each article included in the symposium volumes, therefore, will evidence first-class biblical scholarship, but will also be written in a manner capable of capturing the interest of intelligent laypeople, theological students, and ministers. In purpose, the articles will be both scholarly and pastoral. In format, they will be styled to reflect the best of contemporary constructive scholarship, but in a way that can be understood by alert and intelligent people in the church today and can speak to their needs.

This first symposium volume is on "Patterns of Discipleship in the New Testament" and is designated McMaster New Testament Series number 1. It deals with a subject that lies at the heart of all Christian thought, life, and ministry. This subject has often been treated, both popularly and academically. We believe, however, that it needs better biblical rootage than it usually receives in the popular press and better personal application than it usually receives in scholarly writings. Our prayer, therefore, is that this first volume will prove to be of significant help to many earnest Christians who seek to be better disciples and followers of Christ, and so have a positive impact on the Christian church at large.

Our heartfelt thanks are expressed to Dr. William H. Brackney, Principal and Dean of McMaster Divinity College, and to the faculty, administration, and boards of the college for their encouragement and support of the entire project. We also express our deep appreciation to the family of Herbert Henry Bingham, B.A., B.Th., D.D., a noted Canadian Baptist minister and administrator of the previous generation, which has generously funded the "H. H. Bingham Colloquium in New Testament" at McMaster Divinity College, held during June 12-13, 1995. It was at that colloquium that the authors of the present volume presented their papers and received criticism from one another, from the editor, and from others in attendance, before then reworking and polishing their papers, as necessary, prior to final editing and the normal publication process. Most heartily, however, we thank those who have written articles for this volume, for they have taken time out of busy academic schedules to write in a more popular fashion — in many cases, distilling from their academic publications material of pertinence for the Christian church generally. We also thank Dr. Allan W. Martens and Dr. John W. Simpson, Jr., for their expert editorial assistance. And we thank Bill Eerdmans and the Wm. B. Eerdmans Publishing Company for their support of the present volume, which was offered at a most propitious time.

THE EDITOR

Abbreviations

GNB	Good News Bible (Today's English Version)
JB	Jerusalem Bible
KJV	King James Version
LB	Living Bible
LXX	Septuagint (a Greek translation of the Hebrew Scriptures used in the early church)
NAB	New American Bible
NASB	New American Standard Version
NEB	New English Bible
NIDNTT	*New International Dictionary of New Testament Theology,* ed. C. Brown. Three vols.; Grand Rapids: Zondervan, 1975-78
NIV	New International Version
NKJV	New King James Version
NRSV	New Revised Standard Version
par.	and parallel passages
REB	Revised English Bible
RSV	Revised Standard Version
TDNT	*Theological Dictionary of the New Testament,* ed. G. Kittel and G. Friedrich, tr. G. Bromiley. Ten vols.; Grand Rapids: Eerdmans, 1964-76

Introduction

Discipleship has been for centuries a way of thinking and speaking about the nature of the Christian life. Today, in fact, the topic of discipleship recurs repeatedly in both scholarly biblical writings and the popular Christian press. The expression "following Christ" is usually used synonymously.

But what is meant by Christian discipleship? And what is meant by following Christ? These terms, of course, can mean different things to different people. All too often, Christians have developed various deviant teachings and aberrant lifestyles — all in the name of "Christian discipleship" or on the pretext of "following Christ." What is needed for most of our theories about Christian discipleship, however, is a firmer rootage in the biblical materials. And what is needed for our practice is a clearer grasp of the patterns of discipleship set out in the New Testament.

1. Discipleship and Following Christ in the New Testament: A Linguistic Overview

The earliest self-designation of Christians seems to have been "those of the Way" (Acts 9:2; 19:9, 23; 22:4; 24:14, 22), with "the Way" *(hē hodos)* referring to the salvation revealed by God in the ministry and person

1

of Jesus of Nazareth. It was only first at Syrian Antioch that believers were called "Christians" *(Christianoi)*, that is, "those of the household of Christ" or "Christ-followers" (Acts 11:26). Probably the name was originally given by others to distinguish believers in Jesus residing at Antioch, who were both Jews and Gentiles, from Jews who were not believers in Jesus. It was perhaps first given in derision. Evidently, however, it soon became accepted by the believers in Jesus themselves, being used to express the essence of their own self-consciousness (cf. Acts 26:28; 1 Pet 4:16; Josephus, *Antiquities* 18.64 [18.3.3]).

The most common designation in our canonical Gospels and Acts for one committed to Jesus — that is, for one who accepted his teachings and sought to be identified with him — is "disciple" *(mathētēs,* literally "pupil"/"learner," from the verb *manthanein,* "to learn"). Jesus' associates are called disciples in the Gospels; the (eleven) disciples are commanded to "make disciples of all nations" in Matt 28:19; and believers generally are called disciples throughout Acts. The verb "to follow" *(akolouthein)* and the adjectival participle "those who follow" *(hoi akolouthountes)* appear regularly in the Gospels to identify the crowds who thronged around Jesus. But they are also used in the Gospels to identify the "disciples" as those committed to Jesus (cf. also their use in connection with "the 144,000" of Rev 14:4 and "the armies of heaven" of Rev 19:14).

"Disciple" and "follower" were common expressions in the secular parlance of antiquity. Yet they seem not to have been widely used with religious significance in Jesus' day. "Disciple" *(mathētēs)* appears at most only three times in the LXX (possibly at Jer 13:21; 20:11; 46:9, though with variant readings in each case in important manuscripts). The Hebrew equivalent for "disciple" *(talmid,* "pupil"/"learner," derived from the verb *lamad,* "to learn") occurs only once in the Old Testament (1 Chron 25:8, of a student among the temple musicians), with its substantive participle "one who is taught" *(limmud)* appearing in this manner, at best, only a small handful of times (Isa 8:16; probably also Isa 50:4; 54:13). The words for "disciple," "pupil," or "learner" (whether *talmid* or *limmud* or their cognates) have not been found, to date, in the Aramaic or Hebrew texts of the Dead Sea Scrolls, even though great stress was placed on instruction and various degrees of learning in that community.

On the other hand, "disciple" *(mathētēs)* was used in many of the Greek philosophical schools of the classical and koine periods for one who learned from and became a follower of a particular teacher. True, Socrates (470-399 B.C.), Plato (427-347 B.C.), and Aristotle (384-22 B.C.), as well as the historian and essayist Xenophon (430-356 B.C.), for both philosophical and sociological reasons, never wanted to be addressed as "teacher" *(didaskalos)* and refused to allow their associates to call themselves their "disciples" *(mathētai)*. Among the Sophists, Cynics, Stoics, Epicureans, and many other philosophical schools, however, particularly where Socrates' theory of innate knowledge was rejected or his personal influence was not strong, there developed master-disciple relationships that not only highlighted the features of learning, companionship, and imitation, but also verged on veneration in an almost quasi-religious sense.

Likewise in the Talmud (i.e., the Mishnah and the Babylonian Gemaras) and the other rabbinic writings (e.g., the Tosephta, the Palestinian Gemaras, the Midrashim, and the Sayings of various individual rabbis) — which, though composed later, are essentially codifications of the Oral Torah of earlier times and so may be assumed to reflect in large measure the thought and language of the Jewish world of Jesus' day — the Hebrew word for "disciple" *(talmid)* is used a number of times for one who takes instruction from and is a follower of a particular rabbi. For example, Mishnah Pirke Aboth ("The Sayings of the Fathers"), the earliest tractate of rabbinic lore, begins as follows:

> Moses received the Law from Sinai and committed it to Joshua, and Joshua to the Elders, and the Elders to the Prophets; and the Prophets committed it to the men of the Great Synagogue. They said three things: "Be deliberate in judgment; raise up many disciples [*talmidim*]; and make a fence around the Law" (1:1).

"To follow" *(akolouthein)* also appears seldom in the LXX in a religious context. Usually it occurs in the mundane sense of physically following someone (cf. Num 23:20; 1 Kgs 16:22; Ruth 1:14; Isa 45:14; Hos 2:5; also Sirach prologue 2 and Judith 12:2) or of accompanying someone as an attendant (cf. 1 Sam 25:42; also Judith 15:13). Yet in 1 Kgs 19:20 Elisha is depicted as offering to "follow after" *(akolouthēsō opisō sou)* his predecessor Elijah in the religious sense of being his disciple. Likewise, in 2 Maccabees 8:36 Jews are spoken of as those who "followed" the laws of God; while in *Testament of Asher* 6:1 the patriarch is portrayed as exhorting his children to "take heed to the commandments of the Lord, following the truth with singleness of face" (see also Judith 2:3, which refers to people who "followed not" the laws of Nebuchadnezzar, the quasi-divine king of the Assyrians; and Judith 5:7, which speaks of Ammonites who were "not minded to follow the gods of their fathers").

Both "disciple" and "follower," therefore, while common in secular parlance, seem also to have had some currency in the religious language of Jesus' day. The rabbinic writings, which codify earlier Jewish teachings and situations, reflect such a currency. And the increased frequency of these terms in our canonical Gospels and (to some extent) in Acts vis-à-vis their appearance in Paul's letters, which were written earlier, seems to suggest that this religious usage was increasing during the time the New Testament was written.

So in our canonical Gospels, followers of Jesus are frequently referred to as his "disciples" (mathētai) — 67 or 68 times in Matthew, 44 times in Mark, 34 times in Luke, and 73 times in John. In addition, there are references to the "disciples" of John the Baptist (Matt 9:14; 11:2; 14:12; Mark 2:18; Luke 5:33; 7:18-19; 11:1; John 1:35, 37; 3:25; 4:1), to "disciples" of the Pharisees (Matt 22:16; Mark 2:18), to "disciples" of Moses (John 9:28), and to relationships between disciples and teachers generally (Matt 10:24-25/Luke 6:40). In Acts "disciple" appears in the masculine gender some 28 times, almost always in a broad, inclusive manner to refer to believers in Jesus, both men and women, at some particular locale (e.g., 6:1-2, 7; 9:1, 19, 25, 26, 38, and passim), though also three times with reference to a particular believer (9:10: Ananias of Damascus; 16:1: Timothy of Lystra; 21:16: Mnason of Jerusalem). Only in Acts 9:36 is the feminine form of "disciple" (mathētria) used, there of Tabitha of Joppa, whom Peter raised from the dead. The verb "to be/become a disciple" (mathēteuein) occurs three times in Matthew (13:52; 27:57; 28:19) and once in Acts (14:21).

The verb "to follow" (akolouthein) and its participle "those who follow" (hoi akolouthountes), of course, appear frequently in the Gospels with reference to the crowds who traipsed after and thronged around Jesus (e.g., Matt 4:25; 8:1; 12:15; 14:13; Mark 5:24; 10:32; 11:9; Luke 7:9; 9:11; John 6:2). But they are also used some 14 times by the evangelists in the religious sense of following Jesus as his disciple (Matt 8:19; 9:9; 19:21, 27, 28; Mark 1:18; 2:14 [twice]; 8:34; Luke 5:11, 27, 28; John 1:40, 43). And the participle is used with similar significance in the Apocalypse of John of the 144,000 who "follow the Lamb wherever he goes"

4

(14:4; cf. also the use of the verb in association with "the armies of heaven" who follow "the Rider on the White Horse" in 19:14).

Outside the four Gospels, the Acts, and the one or two instances in the Apocalypse, however, "disciple" and "follower" are conspicuously absent in the rest of the New Testament. Rather, what we have elsewhere in the New Testament are (1) statements regarding the nature of authentic Christian existence, (2) exhortations urging that the truths of these statements be put into practice (often in Paul's letters, though also in 1 and 2 John, using the verb *peripatein*, "to walk about" or "to conduct one's life"), and (3) calls (either explicit or implied) for believers to be "imitators" *(mimētēs*, or with the verb *mimeomai)* and/or to reflect in their lives the "example" or "pattern" *(typos, hypotypōsis)* of the apostle Paul, of Jesus Christ, or even of God himself. At times, as well, there are calls to imitate or reflect the example of an apostolic emissary or another church or churches. But in every case — whether through the use of the expressions "disciple," "to be/become a disciple," or "to follow," the concepts of imitation, example, or patterning, or statements and exhortations regarding authentic Christian existence — teachings regarding Christian self-understanding and practice are to the fore. And in every case, whether in the Gospels and Acts or in the other writings of the New Testament, those teachings are set in quite specific contexts, both historically and ideologically. So it is important to interpret the New Testament presentations of Christian self-understanding and practice in terms of both their universal qualities and their specific situational features, of both their overlapping agreements and their differences.

2. Patterns for Christian Self-Understanding and Practice: A Working Hypothesis

Our English dictionaries define "pattern" as "Anything proposed for imitation; an archetype; exemplar; that which is to be, or is fit to be, copied or imitated" (Webster) or "1. A design, plan, model, etc., from which a thing is to be made; 2. An original to be imitated; an exemplar, a model" (Oxford). All of these definitions have some relevance for the subject at hand, though, obviously, those pertaining more to persons than things and to behavior than mechanics have greater cogency. By the use of the plural "patterns" we mean to suggest that in the New Testament can be found a number of varied portraits, depictions, and

5

presentations that speak directly to issues of Christian self-understanding and living — or, stated more concisely, to the theory and practice of Christian discipleship.

The overarching thesis of the articles in this volume is that each of the New Testament writers presents the concept of Christian discipleship in a manner related to his own ideological background and perspectives, the perceived needs and understanding of his audience, and the specific details of the situation addressed. An author may, when writing to different audiences in differing circumstances, even express himself somewhat differently on the same subject, conditioning what he writes by what he perceives to be his audience's needs. That means that while there is a certain "sense of center" among the presentations of the various New Testament authors, each of their writings will also have its own unique and characteristic way of portraying authentic Christian existence.

Diversity within continuity, therefore, is the working hypothesis of the present volume. Various components found within the portrayals of the different New Testament authors will be highlighted, without any attempt at reductionism. And various patterns will be set out and urged, without any claim for a strict exclusivism. It is hoped that, by a fuller and better presentation of the biblical data on the subject, a deeper, broader, and truer understanding of Christian discipleship will emerge. And what is prayed for is that by such a truer understanding, a better and more effective practice of the Christian religion will take place.

3. A Word about Style and Focus

What follow, then, are attempts by a number of first-rate New Testament scholars to address a topic that is (or should be) of crucial concern to Christians today, and to do so in a manner that will be understood by intelligent laypeople, theological students, and ministers. Each chapter has a "Selected Bibliography" for further study, with many of the works cited being foundational for the various articles themselves. But the articles will be devoid of footnotes containing discussions of competing positions or subsidiary materials. Documentation is held to a minimum and is set in abbreviated form in parentheses in the text when felt to be absolutely necessary.

Likewise, scholarly discussion of a host of critical matters and interpretive methodologies that have to do with the study of the New Testament is kept to a minimum. Such matters are not unimportant, but the purpose of this volume is to explicate how the various New Testament writers have portrayed Christian discipleship, not to be a learned treatment of the critical issues or methodologies that may be associated with that topic. Admittedly, no topic of any significance in the New Testament can be treated without taking certain critical stances and adopting certain interpretive methods. The authors of the articles in this volume know that well, and so have been quite up-front in their handling of the crucial issues and in their proposals regarding various methods of interpretation. What they have attempted to do is to use traditional designations (e.g., as to authorship), common parlance (versus the developed jargon of the academic world), and standard methods — building on the fruits of contemporary biblical scholarship and giving basic reasons for positions taken, but not endeavoring to interact extensively with other views or to nuance their own positions in a highly academic fashion.

Unabashedly, the authors of this volume have taken certain critical stances and used a variety of interpretive methodologies in their respective treatments. The only criterion they have followed in doing so is that of greatest compatibility with the material being studied. It is expected that their academic expertise will be evident in what they write. More than that, however, it is hoped that through their efforts the message of the New Testament on Christian discipleship — both in its common features and in all of its diversity — will be explicated.

THE EDITOR

Following Jesus in the Gospel of Mark — and Beyond

LARRY W. HURTADO

The Gospel of Mark is manifestly a narrative about Jesus. It is also, however, about Christian discipleship, or what it means to be a follower of Jesus. Two types of material in Mark are generally recognized as reflecting this latter concern: (1) teaching on discipleship that is directed to the disciples/readers and (2) the portrayal of the Twelve, which seems also to have a strongly didactic purpose behind it. Furthermore, as we will argue later, in his portrayal of Jesus the evangelist was concerned to clarify the nature of discipleship. So the themes of "christology" and "discipleship" in Mark's Gospel go closely hand in hand.

1. Teaching on Discipleship

The whole of Mark's Gospel was undoubtedly intended by its author to be instructive for its readers as they lived out their lives as Christians — both its narrative portions and those materials more directly presented as teaching. The portrayals of the Twelve were probably meant to teach by example important points about following Jesus. But certain teaching sections of Mark also seem intended to address (or at least to include) the readers directly with instructions about being Jesus' disciples. And it is to this material that we turn first, beginning with those passages (1) where the behavior of the disciples triggers criticism and

9

(2) where Jesus' response to that criticism seems intended by Mark to inform his readers.

The Controversy Stories of 2:1–3:6

The collection of controversy stories in 2:1–3:6, where Jesus defends his disciples against their critics, provides a number of examples of teachings on discipleship. For in this section, Jesus justifies his calling of "sinners" (2:17, where the term is probably used with a touch of sarcasm) — those who do not fast according to the practices of some Jewish groups (2:18-22) and do not keep the sabbath according to the scruples of the Pharisees (2:23-28) — on the basis of their eschatological awareness and his authority to exempt them from certain religious regulations. All of this amounts to teaching the readers of Mark's Gospel that true followers of Jesus are those who base their behavior on an understanding of eschatological fulfillment and on Jesus' authority — in the light of which their religious practices are justified, even if criticized as insufficiently observant by the religious authorities.

Likewise, in 3:31-35 Jesus identifies his followers seated around him as his true family, with the "whoever" of verse 35 opening the circle to include Mark's readers as well. So here again discipleship is presented as an obedience to God that has Jesus as its focus and that includes an ever-widening circle of Jesus' followers as his family.

Criticism of the disciples' eating habits elicits from Jesus both defense and teaching in 7:1-23. And his response includes both counter-polemics against scribal authorities (vv 6-13) and programmatic teachings on what Jesus' true followers are to understand as constituting real defilement (vv 14-23).

Jesus' reply to the scribe's question about the chief commandment (12:28-34) was also likely intended by Mark to be appropriated by his readers. For here Jesus puts total love for God first and links to it love for one's "neighbor." And the scribe's affirmation of Jesus' statement moves Jesus to affirm the scribe's nearness to the kingdom of God, which in biblical language is the sphere of discipleship.

In a first-century setting, these episodes would undoubtedly have been seen as having great significance for the subject of Christian discipleship, defining it over against other definitions (particularly Jewish) of religious responsibility. Even more significant for our purposes, however, are two rather sizable bodies of teaching material that appear to have been intended to instruct, in a rather direct manner, the readers of Mark's Gospel about discipleship: 8:22–10:52 and 13:5-37.

The Passion Predictions in 8:22–10:52

In 8:31–10:52 extensive teaching about discipleship is linked to three predictions by Jesus of his own sufferings, death, and resurrection. This material forms the larger part of the central section of Mark's Gospel, which consists of 8:22–10:52, begins with the healing of a blind man (8:22-26), concludes with the healing of blind Bartimaeus (10:46-52), and includes accounts of Jesus' questioning of his disciples, Peter's confession, and Jesus' call for secrecy (8:27-30).

After the first passion prediction (8:31-33), Jesus announces to both the crowd and his disciples that "anyone" who would be his follower must be prepared for total commitment — a commitment that involved even death, and that as patterned after Jesus' coming crucifixion (8:34-37). The open-ended warning in verse 38 widens the circle of those addressed to include the evangelist's readers and so makes Jesus the object of devotion and the eschatological witness who will speak against "whoever is ashamed of me and of my words." After the second passion prediction (9:30-32), Jesus' teaching to the Twelve about service to others is again couched in terms that open out to include the readers ("anyone who would be first," v 35; "whoever," v 37).

The third passion prediction (10:32-34) — the longest and most detailed, suggesting, therefore, its climactic placement among the three passion predictions in Mark — is also immediately followed by a scene of Jesus teaching on discipleship (10:35-45). And in this scene earlier themes on discipleship appear again. For it is *Jesus'* cup and *Jesus'* baptism that James and John must partake of, probably referring to Jesus' own sufferings as the index of their commitment. The references to Jesus' cup and baptism, found only in Mark, probably allude to the two widely practiced rites of early Christians, the Lord's supper and baptism (cf. Hurtado, *Mark* 177). If so, the intention may have been to teach readers to associate these rites with Jesus' sufferings and therefore to make participation in these rites represent commitment to Christian discipleship. The "whoever" in verses 43-44, however, again seems intended to extend the circle of addressees to include the readers, with

11

Jesus' admonition serving to point away from the domineering models proposed by the disciples to the self-sacrificing service exemplified by the Son of Man (cf. v 45). Furthermore, the explicit congruence between discipleship and Jesus' fate demanded in 8:34, after the first passion prediction, comes to the fore again in 10:43-45 after this final passion prediction.

In addition to the linkage of teaching on discipleship with the three passion predictions, another feature is to be found in 8:31–10:52. After each passion prediction and immediately before each unit of teaching on discipleship, some misguided and self-interested behavior on the part of the disciples is depicted and thus functions as a contrasting foil for Jesus' own fate and for the teaching Jesus is giving. One of the widely recognized features of Mark's Gospel, of course, is its portrayal of the Twelve in a more negative light than the other Gospels. Later we will ask why Mark does this. Here, it is sufficient to identify this motif in this section, suggesting its import for the readers' understanding of discipleship.

In 8:32-33, Peter recoils from Jesus' prediction of his approaching violent death, and Jesus rebukes Peter for his purely human reaction. But Peter's revulsion over Jesus' death sets up Jesus' demand that anyone who would follow him must, in fact, make a commitment to him that includes just such a death. In 9:33-34, rivalry among the Twelve introduces and contrasts with Jesus' teaching about mutual service among his followers, with that teaching being expressed both verbally and in an action-parable with the "little child" in 9:35-37 (and amplified further in 9:38-49). And in 10:35-37, the request of James and John for powerful positions, coupled in 10:41 with the jealousy of the others, forms a stark background for Jesus' teaching about proper community life among the disciples in 10:42-45. In short, each of the three situations has three components: (a) a passion prediction, (b) an account of misguided behavior on the part of one or more of the Twelve, and (c) Jesus' corrective teaching on the true nature of discipleship, which in each case links discipleship with his own ministry and commitment.

These three complexes of material — each braiding together a passion prediction, an account of misguided behavior, and Jesus' corrective teaching — form the key portions in the central section of Mark's Gospel. Yet all the material in this central section is related, in one way or another, to the topic of discipleship. The story of the blind man in 8:22-26 and the account of the healing of blind Bartimaeus in 10:46-52 probably function as the frame for this section, reflecting an ancient literary device referred to by scholars as *inclusio*, in which the beginning and end of a body of material are designed to correspond to each other in some way. Here, the two healings of blind people probably signal that the material framed by these accounts deals with insight into Jesus' mission and what it means to follow Jesus. Moreover, the first story of a blind man involves a two-stage healing and may have been intended to prefigure the behavior of the Twelve, who evidence enough insight into Jesus and their calling to lead them forward, but not enough to keep them from certain misguided statements or behavior. We are probably to see in the final statement in the story about Bartimaeus, "he followed him [Jesus] on the way" (v 52), a confirming indication that this whole central section of Mark, in its teaching about discipleship, was intended to speak to the evangelist's readers, who were themselves "on the way" in their lives of discipleship.

Furthermore, in 9:2-8, after Jesus is transfigured in glorious form, the divine voice from heaven proclaims Jesus' status as that of God's "Beloved Son" and commands Peter, James, and John to "listen to him" *(akouete autou)* — an expression likely intended to have force for the readers as well. And after the discussion of Elijah in 9:9-13, which reveals the disciples' dim-sighted response to Jesus' predictions about his mission, is the more extensive passage dealing with the healing of the demoniac boy in 9:14-29. This latter narrative combines a demonstration of Jesus' power, references to the shortcomings of Jesus' disciples, and exhortations about the importance of faith and prayer that are directed to them — and, probably, also to the readers (esp. vv 18b-29, 23, 28-29; cf. 11:20-26, where Jesus again urges faith and gives teaching on the importance of forgiving others as a condition underlying the effectiveness of prayer).

In its present context, as noted earlier, 9:38-50 seems to function by amplifying and illustrating the teaching given in 9:33-37 on the interpersonal relations that are to be cultivated among Jesus' disciples. The reference to an unnamed exorcist in 9:38 leads to Jesus' rather inclusive statement about those who are to be recognized as his followers and as fellow disciples (or, at least, as potential disciples): "Whoever is not against us is for us!" — which certainly leaves the door open to anyone who does not oppose Jesus and his cause (cf. Luke 9:50: "against you"). And the references to healing and hospitality in Jesus' name (vv 39, 41) set out illustrations of how people might show their interest in

Jesus without first being formally counted among his disciples (cf. Matt 12:30/Luke 11:23, which sets a reverse version of this maxim in contexts dealing with conflict and opposition to Jesus). The lesson likely intended for Mark's readers is that they should not close the circle of fellowship too tightly, but should be open to a variety of ways by which people might begin to register their devotion to Jesus. In Mark's Gospel, in fact, both here and elsewhere, a positive attitude toward Jesus is the crucial marker and common factor identifying those who are to be regarded as disciples.

It is striking that in 10:1-31 the human relationships of marriage (vv 1-12) and adults and children (vv 13-16) are strongly affirmed and linked with the will of God, whereas there also appear stern warnings against the dangers of riches for disciples (vv 17-27). Jesus' disciples cannot exercise the freedom to divorce their spouses at will, as was claimed by some. Nor can they disdain children, but are to see them as a figure of the humble position that disciples are to take in view of the coming kingdom of God. In contrast, the episode of the rich man and Jesus' stark words about riches serve to warn readers that the love of possessions poses a real hindrance to entering God's kingdom.

Demonstrating that these passages are to be taken as directed to Jesus' followers, both his immediate disciples and those beyond, the discussion about riches is immediately followed in 10:28-31 with words of assurance to those who must sacrifice possessions or lose family relationships for the sake of Jesus and his gospel. For Jesus promises that in the fellowship of his disciples, they will find physical sustenance and new family relationships that will offset — but not spare them from — persecutions and the cost of discipleship, while they await the eschatological gift of eternal life. Jesus' promise of surrogate family relationships in 10:29-30 should be read in the light of 3:31-35, where Jesus claimed for himself similar surrogate family relationships in the circle of his disciples — his natural family being pictured negatively in 3:20-35 with, in particular, tension between them and Jesus reflected in 3:31-35 (cf. Hurtado, *Mark* 66-67).

In sum, the whole of 8:22–10:52 is concerned with discipleship. Through a combination of didactic narrative episodes and Jesus' sayings, this central section of Mark's Gospel emphasizes (1) that discipleship is shaped by Jesus himself, his death being the benchmark of commitment, his self-sacrificing service the pattern, and allegiance to his name the marker of the fellowship of his disciples; (2) that the circle of disciples

14

is to be open and inclusive, with a concern to promote mutual care more than rank and competition; and (3) that, though marriage and children are affirmed, the love of possessions is another matter entirely, with disciples needing to be prepared to forfeit everything for Jesus' sake and to find in the fellowship of Jesus' disciples such caring relationships as will compensate for whatever losses they experience.

The Olivet Discourse of 13:5-37

In 13:5-37 we have one of two discourse-size blocks of sayings material in Mark that are concerned with the proclamation of the gospel in the face of adversity, the other being the collection of parables in 4:1-34. The four parables in chapter 4 are all on the effects of the message of the kingdom of God (which 1:14-15 tells us was the focus of Jesus' proclamation). Though the Twelve and the crowd are the only ones explicitly addressed, it is likely that Mark's readers were also expected to associate themselves with the proclamation of the kingdom of God and so to take exhortation and encouragement from these parables as well. There are implicit exhortations in the warnings about unproductive seeds (4:14-19) and hiding one's light (4:21-22). But more dominant are the notes of encouragement regarding the marvelous yield of the good seed (4:20) and the images of a shining lamp (4:21), harvest (4:26-29), and a large mustard shrub (4:30-32; cf. Hurtado, *Mark* 71-85, on these notes of encouragement).

We will concentrate here, however, on 13:5-37, because the "Olivet Discourse" quite transparently addresses the continuing concerns of disciples beyond the more immediate situation of Jesus and the Twelve. Jesus' discourse begins in response to a question from members of the Twelve (v 4), and so addresses the Twelve. But it is likely that readers also were intended to take direction for their lives as disciples from what is reported here. For one thing, this discourse is predictive prophecy, a form of speech that invites subsequent readers to seek application to their own situations. Readers are, in fact, explicitly addressed in the aside in verse 14 about the "desolating sacrilege": "Let the reader understand." And the discourse concludes in verse 37 with a saying that generalizes those addressed: "What I say to you, I say to all: Watch!"

Moreover, the contents of the discourse suggest that it was intended for continuing application in the lives of Mark's readers, who

15

are to include themselves in the plural "you" of those addressed. A major emphasis of the discourse is to redirect misguided eschatological excitement that is vulnerable to deception and easily discouraged when things do not seem to go as hoped (13:5-8, 13, 21-23, 32-37). The troubles that might be thought of as signs of the immediacy of the end are denied that significance (vv 7-8). Rather, they are downgraded to the level of unavoidable woes and only early symptoms ("but the beginning of the birth pangs") of the coming divine deliverance of the world. Even the "desolating sacrilege" itself (using the language of Dan 12:11 to refer to the destruction of the Jerusalem temple) and its accompanying hardships, though terrible in scope (vv 14-20), do not signal the eschatological moment, and disciples are warned about deceptive claims to the contrary (vv 21-23). All this would be especially meaningful for first-century readers who were situated far enough after Jesus' time to wonder about the apparent delay of the end, and who may have been in danger of deception or discouragement.

Instead of offering an eschatological timetable or speculative calculation on the basis of a checklist of eschatological woes, Mark 13 focuses on the responsibility of proclaiming the gospel and the opposition that such proclamation receives (vv 9-13). The worldwide progress of the gospel message is the key eschatological necessity. It is the condition that "must" be fulfilled "first" for the eschaton to appear (v 10). Disciples of Jesus who persevere in the face of opposition directed against their allegiance and their witness to Jesus will receive salvation at the eschatological "end" (v 13). When put on trial for their proclamation, they are not to concentrate on defending themselves but are to use the opportunity to witness in the words given by the Holy Spirit (v 11).

As for the time of the eschatological denouement, 13:24-37 seems to place that final outcome or climax of God's redemptive working at some general time "after that suffering" (v 24, perhaps referring back to v 19) — with an emphasis on the impossibility of any specific calculation, even by Jesus himself (vv 32-37; cf. Hurtado, *Mark* 222-23, where "these things" in v 30 are treated as referring to the events of vv 5-23, not to the end itself)! Three verbs are used in verses 33-37 — "beware" *(blepete)*, "keep alert" *(agrypneite)*, and "keep awake" *(grēgoreite)* — that command alertness and commitment to one's duty, without encouraging attempts to determine the time of the end. Mark 13, in fact, discourages attempts to calculate the end. Rather, the discourse warns against deceivers who may use eschatological excitement for their own advantage, emphasizes as of central importance faithful witness and steadfast endurance in the face of opposition, and summons "all" disciples to wakeful duty (v 37).

2. The Portrayal of the Twelve

The second type of evidence that is commonly pointed to as being relevant to understanding Mark's view of discipleship is his treatment of Jesus' disciples, particularly his portrayal of the Twelve. Jesus' group of disciples, of course, extends beyond the Twelve. But the Twelve, while given special status, seem to represent in Mark's Gospel the larger circle of disciples as well. And their failures are also representative of the failures of that larger group. Thus no distinction between the Twelve and the larger circle of disciples as to blameworthiness need be postulated in Mark, and no attempt need be made to play off the Twelve against another group of disciples that might represent alternative factions of early Christians. Female disciples are treated more positively (see the discussion of 16:8 later in this chapter), but they do not seem to represent any particular faction of early Christianity.

Nearly every scholarly analysis recognizes the negative way in which the Twelve are treated in Mark's Gospel. But there are two sharply different views about what to make of that treatment. A few scholars insist that Mark was written with a strongly polemical purpose that involved discrediting the Twelve as representatives of a type of Christianity and/or a christology that the author of Mark regarded as heretical. In this view a "divine man" christology, in which Jesus was basically a wonder-worker and the cross was little understood, is what Mark opposes. Furthermore, it is alleged that the early Christian group or groups holding this "divine man" christology revered the Twelve and pointed to them as founding figures. Consequently, Mark allegedly conducts a "vendetta" against the Twelve as a major strategy for refuting this heretical christology (cf. esp. T. J. Weeden, *Mark — Traditions in Conflict* [Philadelphia: Fortress, 1971]).

The most recent defense of this general position is that of Werner Kelber ("Apostolic Tradition," 1985). Kelber implicitly acknowledges that the once-touted "divine man" category has been shown to be a modern imaginative construct and so he redefines the heresy that was the supposed object of Mark's polemics as a christology that emphasized the resurrection of Jesus! But neither Kelber's assertion regarding the nature of Mark's polemics nor his exegesis of the larger literary pattern of Mark's Gospel has been found persuasive (for a critique of the approach to Mark as polemics and for a more cogent treatment of Mark's view of Jesus, see Kingsbury, *Christology of Mark's Gospel* 25-45).

Other scholars, who comprise the clear majority, view Mark's purpose as being more didactic than polemical, and so see the Twelve as functioning to provide the readers with lessons in discipleship. In the view of these scholars, the failures of the Twelve emphasized in Mark are not intended to invalidate them as fellow disciples with whom the readers are to associate themselves, but function as warning examples for the readers. The debate has been extensive in scholarship on Mark during the past few decades, and it is impossible in the present article to interact in any adequate manner with the scholarly literature on this matter. Suffice it here to say that we are in agreement with this latter, majority approach. And rather than attempt to debate the issues, we will concentrate in what follows on passages in Mark that have relevance to the subject of discipleship, reflecting, in the process, the work of such scholars as Ernest Best, Clifton Black, Philip Davis, David Hawkin, Jack Kingsbury, Elizabeth Malbon, and Robert Tannehill (see "Selected Bibliography").

The Prominent and Positive Role of the Twelve

The first thing to say about the role of the Twelve in Mark's Gospel is that it is a prominent one. After the introductory statement of Jesus' Galilean ministry in 1:14-15, the next incident that Mark relates is the calling of the first four members of the Twelve (1:16-20). Thereafter, Mark portrays Jesus as operating characteristically with his disciples. This emphasis in Mark even manifests itself philologically. For one of the distinguishing linguistic features of Mark's Gospel is its frequent use of plural verbs ("they") that bring together Jesus and his disciples in accounts of their movements and activities (e.g., 1:21; 5:1-2, 38; cf. C. H. Turner, "Marcan Usage: Notes, Critical and Exegetical, on the Second Gospel," *Journal of Theological Studies* 26 [1925] 225-31).

It will, perhaps, suffice here to cite only a few more examples of the prominence of the disciples in Mark. Three of the five controversy stories in 2:1–3:6, as noted earlier, concern Jesus' disciples (2:13-17, 18-22, 23-28). The account of Jesus' appointment of the Twelve in 3:13-19 contains a threefold definition of their station that is fuller than what is found in the Synoptic parallels (Matt 10:1; Luke 6:13): (1) to be specially associated with Jesus *(met' autou)*, (2) to be sent out as his emissaries *(apostellein)* to proclaim his message, and (3) to exercise his authority *(exousia)* in expelling demons (vv 14-15). In 3:20-35, the scribes and Jesus' family are implicitly likened to each other in their failure to grasp the validity of Jesus' ministry, with, then, Jesus pointing to his disciples as those who do the will of God in following him (v 35). In 6:7-13, Jesus sends out the Twelve equipped with his supernatural authority over demons, and these disciples extend Jesus' ministry in word and powerful deed. And 6:14 even suggests that the mission of the Twelve on behalf of their Master was what helped to bring Jesus to the attention of Herod. All of this, of course, gives the Twelve a very high and generally positive role in Mark's Gospel, and the evangelist probably expected Christian readers to identify with these disciples.

Negative Criticism of the Twelve

Yet even as he relates the appointment of the Twelve to responsibilities and position in Jesus' ministry in 3:13-19, Mark also subtly introduces a complexity or ambivalence in how the readers are to view the Twelve when he refers in v 19 to Judas's betrayal of Jesus. This reference to Judas "prepares us for a story involving not only a division between critics and supporters of Jesus but also a testing and crisis for those who became his followers" (Hurtado, *Mark* 60). And this ambivalence regarding the nature of the Twelve continues in 4:10-13, 33-34. For on the one hand, the disciples are those to whom "the secret of the kingdom of God" is given, as distinguished from those "outside" (v 11); moreover, to the disciples Jesus "explained everything," whereas the crowd received only parables (vv 33-34). On the other hand, Jesus' statement in verse 13 hints that the disciples did not show the level of understanding that Jesus desired of them.

The first sea-miracle story in 4:35-41 has the first of a number of explicitly negative references to the Twelve. Here they panic (v 38) and Jesus speaks critically of their fear and lack of faith (v 40). And though they have witnessed a miracle of theophanic significance, they are unable to rise above the awe and puzzlement that characterizes the reactions of the crowds (v 41).

The second sea-miracle story, where Jesus comes to his disciples by walking on the water (6:45-52), underscores the critical portrayal of the Twelve. For in their terror, they mistake him for a malevolent spirit (vv 49-50). Matthew's parallel to this story concludes with the Twelve worshiping Jesus as the Son of God (cf. Matt 14:22-33). In Mark's Gospel, however, the reponse of the disciples is merely astonishment, which the evangelist attributes to a lack of understanding of the miracle of the "loaves" (in the immediately preceding account of the feeding of the five thousand) on account of their "hardened hearts" (vv 51-52). The expression "hardened hearts" is particularly negative, implying a spiritual failure to perceive the revelation of God. A similarly critical picture of the Twelve appears in 8:14-21, where the disciples' misunderstanding of Jesus' warning about "the leaven of the Pharisees and of Herod" introduces severe statements about their "hardened hearts" and their general failure to understand the significance of what they have witnessed.

In our earlier examination of the passion predictions in chapters 8–10, we noted how each passion prediction is immediately followed by some act of obtuseness by one or more of the Twelve, which Jesus then must correct in his teaching on the subject of discipleship. Jesus' rebuke of Peter in 8:33, after the first passion prediction, is especially negative, labeling as satanic Peter's response to Jesus' coming sufferings. It is also appropriate to mention again the transfiguration scene in 9:2-8, where the disciples are depicted as being dumbfounded and terrified. Also of significance in Mark's negative portrayal of the Twelve is their puzzlement and question in 9:9-13, which reflected their dullness, and their inability to deal with the demoniac boy in 9:14-29 (see esp. vv 18-19, 28).

But surely the most negative treatment of the Twelve in Mark's Gospel is in the passion narrative in chapters 14–15. One of the Twelve, Judas, betrays Jesus (14:10-11, 43), and the rest forsake Jesus in cowardice (14:50). Their failure is all the more glaring in light of their bravado after Jesus' prediction of their desertion in 14:26-31. The depth of their failure is set out in Mark's detailed account of Peter's threefold denial of Jesus in 14:66-72. For, as has often been suggested, Peter's cursing in 14:71 (anathematizein) is probably to be taken as directed against Jesus himself, with Peter's "anathema" being the nadir of this shameful epi-

20

sode (cf. G. W. H. Lampe, "Church Discipline and the Interpretation of the Epistles to the Corinthians," in *Christian History and Interpretation: Studies Presented to John Knox*, ed. W. R. Farmer, C. F. D. Moule, and R. R. Niebuhr [Cambridge: Cambridge University Press, 1967] 358; K. E. Dewey, "Peter's Curse and Cursed Peter [Mark 14:53-54, 66-72]," in *The Passion in Mark*, ed. W. H. Kelber [Philadelphia: Fortress, 1976] 96-114).

Though all four canonical Gospels have negative features in their treatment of the Twelve, Mark's portrayal is undeniably more severe than the others. But to take this as a simple "vendetta" against the Twelve and to understand Mark's intent as discrediting some other faction within early Christianity requires one to read the data much too selectively. It evidences, in fact, a dullness of perception like that of the Twelve themselves in several incidents of the narrative! For there is no hint in Mark of factions among Jesus' disciples. Several characters in particular vignettes of Mark's narrative are praised for their faith and are treated positively — for example, the paralytic's friends (2:1-5), the Gerasene demoniac (5:19-20), the woman with the hemorrhage (5:24-34), the Syrophoenician woman (7:24-30), Bartimaeus (10:52), the scribe (12:34), the woman with the ointment (14:3-9), women disciples at the crucifixion (15:40-41), and Joseph of Arimathea (15:43). But there is no indication that these characters are to be taken as representing an alternative group of Christians whom Mark favored and wanted to promote in some kind of ecclesiastical struggle, whether over christology or over leadership authority.

The Two Roles of the Twelve

If we do justice to all the evidence regarding the Twelve in Mark's Gospel, we must conclude (1) that Mark portrays them as having two roles, both positive and negative, and (2) that it is in this duality that the evangelist's purpose is served and disclosed (cf. Hawkin, "Incomprehension of the Disciples"; Tannehill, "Disciples in Mark"). The dominantly positive treatment throughout 1:1–6:44 cannot be ignored. This material makes most sense if it is seen as promoting an initially positive attitude toward the Twelve. That is, Mark's readers were likely expected to see the Twelve as representative of the Christian calling to follow Jesus and to participate in the mission of the gospel. Thus readers were to be disposed by this initial information to identify themselves with Jesus' disciples and the Twelve.

But what were readers expected to make of the critical treatment of the dullness and failures of the Twelve? In light of the overall story line narrated and projected in Mark, it seems best to conclude that the failures of the Twelve were portrayed for didactic reasons and not for polemical purposes. The dullness or incomprehension of a disciple or student was a frequent feature in ancient didactic narratives and was intended to serve as a foil to allow the teacher to make more emphatic and clear the points that he or the narrator sought to promote.

More specifically, the failures of the Twelve highlight the very dangers that Mark wanted to warn his readers about. Showing such failures was far more dramatically effective than simply listing prescriptions against them. Indeed, to warn readers of the terrible possibility of failure in discipleship by portraying the failures of the very disciples with whom they were to identify themselves and whom they knew as their "forebears" in the faith — and so to generate determination to avoid such failures — was a bold and dramatically effective decision on the part of the evangelist.

This view of the role of the Twelve is confirmed by their continued status as Jesus' designated associates and followers, right through to the end of the narrative and beyond it. In Mark 13, well after their incomprehension and other shortcomings have been introduced, the Twelve, on behalf of subsequent Christian disciples, receive instructions about the future mission that Jesus' followers are to pursue in taking the gospel to all nations. The warnings about false teachers and teachings in 13:5, 21-22 can hardly be taken (contra Kelber) as directed against the Twelve. Rather, the Twelve, along with all subsequent readers, are warned about such dangers from others — with the seamless connection in 13:37 between the Twelve ("you") and all subsequent readers ("all") making it more than likely that Mark pursued a didactic/representative purpose, not a polemical one, in his handling of the Twelve.

It is also very important to note how the desertion of Jesus by the Twelve in 14:26-28, though no less heinous for it, is clearly bracketed in the account at both ends and set within a divine purpose that is greater than the failure of the Twelve as disciples. For their forsaking of Jesus, Mark presents Jesus as declaring, was foreseen by God in Scripture (quoting Zech 13:7) and will be overcome in the restoration of the Twelve by the risen Jesus, despite their cowardice and his own terrible death. By any literary logic that includes the significance of a "reliable voice" in a story, Jesus' solemn promise of his resurrection and their restoration in 14:28 must be taken as authoritative. Jesus' promise also has the effect of projecting the story line out beyond the end of Mark's written narrative and into the post-Easter life of the church. That is, the events in Mark, including the failures of the Twelve, are intended to be interpreted within the context of a larger story that both (1) precedes Mark's narrative in divine foreknowledge and prophecy (e.g., 1:2-3), and (2) extends beyond Mark's account to include both the restoration of the Twelve and the discipleship of Christian readers. Jesus' prediction to James and John in 10:39 that they will face a fate like his functions similarly, for it anticipates their future faithfulness beyond their immediate cowardice narrated in chapters 14–15.

The Witness of the Women in 16:7-8

The directive to the women in 16:7 explicitly recalls Jesus' assurance of the restoration of the Twelve in 14:28. It is a serious mistake, however, to take 16:8 as indicating that the women's fright nullified the divine purpose. Had Mark intended to portray the women as disobeying the directive given in 16:7, a conjunction expressing contrast ("but," Greek *alla* or *de*) would have been appropriate. Instead, we have a simple connective (*kai*, translated variously, e.g., "and" [RSV] or "so" [NRSV]), which hardly seems adequate to express the complete contrast that many interpreters assume between what the women were commanded to do and what they did. Moreover, since early Christian tradition (e.g., 1 Cor 15:5) views the Twelve as influential witnesses to Jesus' resurrection and as leaders in the early church, it is difficult to imagine how Mark could have expected first-century readers to see 16:8 as indicating that the Twelve were never informed of Jesus' resurrection. (This amounts to a change in my own understanding of 16:8 from that reflected in my commentary [p. 283], where I took the verse as indicating that the women temporarily disobeyed what the "young man" commanded.)

Kelber's idea that 16:8 represents Mark's way of explaining why the Twelve were never restored to fellowship with the risen Jesus requires the strange conclusion that it was really not the failure of the Twelve that prevented their restoration, but the disobedience of a small group of frightened women. But this hardly amounts to much in the way of a condemnation of the Twelve. Furthermore, it goes against the otherwise consistently positive portrayal of Jesus' female followers in Mark's Gospel, which always presents them as role models of faith (e.g., 5:34), insight (7:29), prescient devotion (14:3-9), and faithfulness (15:40-41). In reality, interpreters who read 16:8 as telling of the women's failure may be saying more about their own cultural stereotypes of "weak women" than about the evidence of this verse.

It is a far more reasonable reading of 16:8 to see it as indicating that the women said nothing to anyone other than the ones to whom they were sent, thereby explaining why news of Jesus' resurrection did not become public until it was proclaimed through the witness of the Twelve and of others who were chosen by the risen Jesus for this task. Elizabeth Malbon has defended a somewhat similar view of how 16:8 is to be read ("Fallible Followers" 45), though without giving the same explanation for the verse's function. She points to the similarity between "they said nothing to anyone" *(oudeni ouden eipan)* in 16:8 and "say nothing to anyone" *(mēdeni mēden eipēs)* in 1:44, which obviously refers to "anyone" other than the priest to whom the cleansed leper was sent. So in 16:8, she argues, the phrase must mean that the women did not speak to "anyone" other than those to whom they were sent.

Mark 16:8 is there, it seems, to explain to readers why it was that the women, who were the first to learn of Jesus' resurrection, did not become the ones who bore witness publicly to that event. It tells Mark's readers that it was because of the women's (quite understandable) agitation that they did not "go public," leaving that role to the Twelve and to other "official" witnesses whom Mark's readers would have known about from early tradition.

Conclusions

In sum, Mark's Gospel takes its readers beyond the written account and beyond the failures of the Twelve, into their restoration and the subsequent mission of the church and the progress of the gospel. The role of the Twelve is to represent for readers the responsibility to which disciples are called, but also to portray the dangers that they must avoid. Yet even more boldly, Jesus' promise of the restoration of the Twelve — even after their desertion and denial — is the message that Mark holds out to readers who, like Peter, may have failed under threats but may still experience forgiveness and restoration. In a first-century setting, where opposition from relatives and neighbors or intimidation from Jewish and Roman authorities might have led some Christians to compromise their witness, this hope would have been very meaningful.

3. Jesus as the Model of Discipleship

As John Donahue has said, "The story of Jesus is also to be the story of his followers" ("Jesus as the Parable of God" 377-78). In Mark's account, Jesus is both the basis for and the pattern of discipleship. His death is the salvific ransom (10:45), the covenant-making sacrifice (14:24), the index of commitment for his disciples (e.g., 8:34), and the servant-pattern that they are to follow (10:43-45). In fact, Mark makes Jesus the only adequate model of discipleship.

Mark's posing of Jesus as the positive model of discipleship permits him the freedom to portray the Twelve in such a critical way. Ernest Best explains the more critical treatment of the Twelve in Mark in comparison with Matthew and Luke on the basis of what he terms Mark's more "epiphanic" christology (*Disciples and Discipleship* 116). In our view, however, Mark's christological emphasis falls more on the cross as the disclosure of the meaning of Jesus, which is why an accurate understanding of Jesus is withheld from all human characters in Mark's Gospel until the crucifixion. This cross-emphasis in Mark's view of Jesus' mission coheres with his emphasis on Jesus' crucifixion as the paradigm of faithful discipleship. The shortcomings of the Twelve and the positive example of Jesus together form major components in Mark's literary and didactic plan — the Twelve functioning as warning examples of the dangers that readers must avoid and Jesus' example functioning to show what faithful discipleship looks like. Discipleship, Mark emphasizes, means *following* Jesus, with the story of Jesus serving as the paradigm.

Presenting Jesus as the model of discipleship also accords with Mark's christology, which highlights Jesus as the unique and central divine agent whose crucifixion is an essential disclosure of his significance and purpose. Discipleship, Mark emphasizes, means following *Jesus*, with no rival, no distraction, and no competition for the allegiance of his disciples. Although the Twelve are called to participate in Jesus' assault on the demonic (3:14-15; 6:7-13), the account of their exorcistic failure and Jesus' success in 9:14-29 emphasizes *Jesus'* example and authority. James and John are warned that they will, in fact, face sufferings on account of Jesus and will be associated with his fate (10:39; 14:36). But Mark's portrayal of Jesus as progressively more isolated and then completely abandoned by the Twelve emphasizes that Jesus leaned on no one, and so was the unique pathfinder whom his disciples are to follow.

Mark's conflated account of the interrogation of Jesus and the questioning of Peter (14:53-72) presents Jesus as the only proper role model for Christian disciples who may be interrogated before councils, synagogues, governors, and kings (13:9). In contrast to Peter's negative example, and exhibiting the pattern commanded in 13:9-11, Jesus makes no defense before the Jewish council. Rather, he speaks only the oracular confession of 14:62 and endures his sufferings as the faithful witness. And in his interrogation before Pilate, Jesus' behavior evidences the courageous reserve that he urged on his disciples in 13:9-11.

As Philip Davis has suggested ("Christology, Discipleship, and Self-Understanding"), Jesus' role in Mark as the paradigm for discipleship is probably the best explanation for the overall shape of Mark's story, which, in comparison to the shape of Matthew's and Luke's accounts, seems to have "omissions." There is no infancy narrative in Mark. Instead, Jesus first appears at his baptism. And if 16:8 represents the original ending of Mark's Gospel (as we believe), there is no appearance of the risen Jesus. Instead, Mark sets out several authoritative predictions of Jesus' resurrection (8:31; 9:9, 31; 10:34; 14:28) and then says that it has been accomplished (16:6-7). What we have, then, is a story of Jesus that "can be read as a blueprint for the Christian life: it begins with baptism, proceeds with the vigorous pursuit of ministry in the face of temptation and opposition, and culminates in suffering and death oriented toward an as-yet unseen vindication" (Davis 109).

It would be a simplistic argument from silence to conclude that the apparent absence of a birth narrative is the result of Mark having nothing to report. Mark begins with Jesus' baptism because baptism is where the life of discipleship begins. Mark's story of Jesus then concentrates on his mission (with less space given to Jesus' teachings than in the other Gospels) because the disciple is called to follow Jesus' example.

The absence of a resurrection appearance is likewise probably a direct reflection of Mark's concern to focus on Jesus as the sole model for discipleship. From other New Testament accounts, we see that reports of resurrection appearances served to certify the witnesses as authoritative figures (cf., e.g., 1 Cor 9:1; 15:3-11; Matt 28:16-20; Luke 24:48-49; John 20:21-23). In Mark's Gospel, however, the unique significance of Jesus is preserved right through to the end of the narrative. Jesus' resurrection is sure. But no attention is distracted from Jesus to any Christian authority figure through the relating of an appearance story. The last word in Mark's Gospel to readers is that given to the Twelve: to continue following Jesus beyond the pages of the narrative (16:7). There they will see Jesus — that is, in the course of their response to his summons to join him in his mission (i.e., "into Galilee").

If we recognize that Mark intended to present Jesus as the true model of Christian discipleship and that Mark's narrative was shaped to make the story of Jesus the blueprint for the lives and ministry of all his disciples, then we have probably only grasped what was staring us in the face all along in the caption to the Gospel in 1:1. "The beginning *(archē)* of the gospel of Jesus Christ" is probably to be taken as referring to Mark's entire account of Jesus. That is, Jesus' ministry is the "beginning" of the message and mission to which all future disciples are summoned — the source, ground, first cause, or foundation from which the mission and preaching of the Christian church proceeds and by which all its activities are to be measured. (For a recent discussion of 1:1, see M. E. Boring, "Mark 1:1-15 and the Beginning of the Gospel," *Semeia* 52 [1990] 43-81, who takes a somewhat similar view of this verse. Cf. also R. A. Guelich, *Mark 1–8:26* [Dallas: Word, 1989] 5-10.)

Conclusions

Mark's story of Jesus is vitally concerned with discipleship. There is ample sayings material in which Jesus instructs and inspires the Twelve and subsequent disciples. Jesus' disciples, especially the Twelve, are memorably presented in a complex role as representing the calling and equipping of Jesus' followers for discipleship, and as demonstrating the difficulties and failures to which disciples are subject. Mark also boldly and dramatically counterposes the shortcomings and failures of the Twelve to Jesus' exemplary behavior in order to portray the demands of discipleship, with Jesus himself as the object and paradigm of discipleship. Jesus' authoritative promise of the restoration of the Twelve to fellowship after their shameful collapse makes Jesus' calling the sole basis of the Christian life and offers paradigmatic hope to subsequent disciples who may fail their Master.

Finally, embedded within Mark's explicit narrative are pointers and invitations to participate in a continuation of the narrative in the post-Easter fellowship of Christian disciples, who, like the Twelve, are summoned to mission, witness, servant dedication, and faithfulness empowered by the Holy Spirit.

Selected Bibliography

Barton, S. C. *Discipleship and Family Ties in Mark and Matthew.* Cambridge: Cambridge University Press, 1994.

Best, E. *Disciples and Discipleship: Studies in the Gospel according to Mark.* Edinburgh: T. & T. Clark, 1986.

———. *Following Jesus: Discipleship in the Gospel of Mark.* Sheffield: JSOT Press, 1981.

Black, C. C. *The Disciples according to Mark: Markan Redaction in Current Debate.* Sheffield: Sheffield Academic Press, 1989.

Davis, P. "Christology, Discipleship, and Self-Understanding in the Gospel of Mark," in *Self-Definition and Self-Discovery in Early Christianity: A Case of Shifting Horizons. Essays in Appreciation of Ben F. Meyer from his former Students,* ed. D. Hawkin and T. Robinson. Lewiston: Mellen, 1990, 101-19.

Donahue, J. R. "Jesus as the Parable of God in the Gospel of Mark," *Interpretation* 32 (1978) 369-86.

Hawkin, D. J. "The Incomprehension of the Disciples in the Markan Redaction," *Journal of Biblical Literature* 91 (1972) 491-500.

Hurtado, L. W. *Mark.* New International Biblical Commentary, Peabody: Hendrickson, 1989.

Kelber, W. H. "Apostolic Tradition and the Form of the Gospels," in *Discipleship in the New Testament,* ed. F. F. Segovia. Philadelphia: Fortress, 1985, 24-46.

Kingsbury, J. D. *The Christology of Mark's Gospel.* Philadelphia: Fortress, 1983.

Malbon, E. S. "Disciples/Crowds/Whoever: Markan Characters and Readers," *Novum Testamentum* 18 (1986) 104-30.

———. "Fallible Followers: Women and Men in the Gospel of Mark," *Semeia* 28 (1983) 29-48.

Meye, R. P. *Jesus and the Twelve: Discipleship and Revelation in Mark's Gospel.* Grand Rapids: Eerdmans, 1968.

Stock, A. *A Call to Discipleship: A Literary Study of Mark's Gospel.* Wilmington: Glazier, 1982.

Schweizer, E. "The Portrayal of the Life of Faith in the Gospel of Mark," *Interpretation* 32 (1978) 387-99.

Tannehill, R. C. "The Disciples in Mark: The Function of a Narrative Role," *Journal of Religion* 57 (1977) 386-405.

Guiding Readers — Making Disciples: Discipleship in Matthew's Narrative Strategy

TERENCE L. DONALDSON

There are two ways in which we might approach the theme of discipleship in Matthew's Gospel. More broadly, we could attempt to discern how Matthew views the nature of Christian existence in the period between the resurrection and the "end of the age," as the era of the church is delimited in the closing verses of his Gospel. Alternatively, we could look more narrowly at the evangelist's portrayal of Jesus' disciples and their place in the story of Jesus. In the final analysis, however, these two ways are intertwined. For in the commissioning scene with which Matthew's Gospel concludes, the (eleven) disciples are commanded to "make disciples *(mathēteusate)* of all nations" (28:19). This indicates that "disciple," while used by Matthew in the first instance to refer to followers of the earthly Jesus, is also his preferred term for "Christian." So by telling the story of the disciples in their experience with Jesus, Matthew is, in fact, also guiding his readers to an understanding of what discipleship will mean for them. Thus a study of discipleship, narrowly considered, will, of necessity, lead as well to an understanding of Matthew's contribution to the broader theme of the nature of Christian existence.

Until recently, such a study would probably have been carried out using the methods and tools of redaction criticism, an approach that seeks to identify the various literary tendencies and theological emphases that are characteristic of an evangelist by comparing his Gospel

30

with its putative sources (in this case Mark and Q). But the theme of discipleship in Matthew's Gospel has been rather fully studied from this perspective already (e.g., Barth, Deutsch, Luz, Wilkins). Scholarly study, of late, has been enriched and enlivened by a different approach, one that takes seriously the narrative character of the Gospels and sets out to examine them as stories. In what follows, therefore, our intention will be to make use of the insights of narrative criticism in order to explore the role of the disciples in Matthew's story of Jesus.

This is not the place to present an analysis of narrative theory or to discuss in detail the various features of narrative criticism. A fine introduction can be found in the book by Mark Powell, *What Is Narrative Criticism?* For our purposes, the following simple definition of narrative will suffice: a narrative consists of a story, told in a particular way in order to produce a desired effect in the reader. Simple though it may be, this definition nevertheless provides the framework for a comprehensive and fruitful pattern of interpretation that comprises three areas of analysis: (1) the Story — that is, the characters, settings, and events, combined in such a way as to produce a plot; (2) the Telling (or the Discourse) — that is, the way in which the narrator unfolds the elements of the story, establishes the normative point of view necessary for a proper understanding, and guides the process of reading; and (3) the Reading — that is, the actual experience of reading, as a reader submits to the narrator's guidance and experiences the story as it unfolds in a sequential manner. While each element could be discussed at length, this is perhaps enough of an introduction — most of us having at least an intuitive sense of how stories work — to set the stage for our more particular discussion. Additional comments of a theoretical nature will be made as needed along the way.

1. The Role of the Disciples in Matthew's Story

The Characters in the Story

In addition to Jesus, most of the characters in Matthew's story fall into four or five main categories: the disciples, the crowds, the Gentiles, the Jewish leaders, and (perhaps) the "supplicants" who come to Jesus for healing, though these could be seen simply as representative members of either the crowds or the Gentiles. Of these groups, the disciples are, of course, closest to Jesus, appearing in the first scene of Jesus' public ministry (4:18-22) and present with him — with the notable exception of their desertion at his arrest — through to the end (28:16-20).

This categorization is not simply a product of abstract analysis. Matthew, the narrator and implied author, tends to view these characters as collective entities. In particular, the disciples — even when all due recognition is given to the place of specific individuals in the story — appear in the great majority of instances as an undifferentiated group. Most frequently they are referred to as "his disciples" or "the disciples," occasionally "the twelve disciples" (but rarely "the Twelve"). Call narratives aside (i.e., 4:18-22; 8:21-22; 9:9), none of the disciples is presented as an individual character in any scene prior to Peter's walking on the water in 14:28-32. And while there is more individual activity in the remainder of the narrative, for the most part it has to do with Peter, either on his own or with James and John. Except for the frequently discussed statement in 16:17-19, where he is associated with the rock on which the church is to be built, Peter's role is tightly connected with that of the disciples as a whole — that is, as their speaker, leader, or representative figure (cf. Wilkins, *Concept of Disciple* 173-224). The only other individual disciples identified by name in the context of specific incidents are James and John, who desire special status in the kingdom (20:20-23), Judas, who betrays Jesus (26:14-16, 20-25, 47-50; 27:3-10), and Joseph of Arimathea — the only one to appear in a positive light — who claims Jesus' body for burial (27:57-60).

While it is true that Mary Magdalene and several other women appear in the narrative as followers of Jesus, Matthew does not identify them as disciples (a point to which we will return later). Yet discipleship is not restricted to the Twelve. On several occasions other followers of Jesus are so identified (cf. 8:21; 27:57; perhaps also 10:42). Nevertheless, when Matthew speaks simply of "his disciples," he generally has only the Twelve (or the eleven) in view (e.g., 28:7, 16).

Despite the importance of the term "disciple" for Matthew, it is not in and of itself a specifically Christian designation. The evangelist can also speak of disciples of John the Baptist (9:14; 11:2; 14:12) and disciples of the Pharisees (22:16). Furthermore, he assumes that his readers will know what the term means without any special guidance. Without fanfare, "his disciples" appears for the first time in 5:1. The only possible disciples in the story to this point were the four fishermen of 4:18-22, who left their nets in response to Jesus' call and followed him. But they are not designated in the narrative as disciples. Rather, readers are simply expected to know that "disciple" denotes the adherent of a teacher and so to identify as such those called by Jesus in that earlier passage.

From all this it can be seen that the distinctive character of discipleship for Matthew is determined by (1) the person to whom disciples give their allegiance and (2) the nature of the relationship established between disciples and teacher. At this point it would be possible to investigate Matthew's distinctives further by carrying out a study of the disciples as characters in the narrative. In the interests of economy, however, we will be content to let this come out in other contexts, turning our attention now to the plot of the story.

The Plot of the Story

As recognized by everyone from Aristotle to contemporary structuralists, stories unfold on the basis of a three-part structure that consists of a beginning, a middle, and an end. The function of a story's beginning is, generally, (1) to establish some lack or desideratum (i.e., something needed and desired) and (2) to introduce a protagonist who will undertake to supply what is missing or desired or to restore things to a state of equilibrium. The middle of a story consists of a number of stages through which the action moves forward, with the goal becoming clarified or complicated, with various obstacles or opponents encountered, with various accomplishments achieved or setbacks experienced, and so on. Finally comes the end, where the story reaches its resolution in the establishment of a new state of equilibrium. Thus the plot of a story can be defined as the connected sequence of events by which the story moves from its beginning to its final resolution.

Plots will vary, of course, according to the differing patterns of change that are effected between the beginning and the end. To enter into a general discussion of plot types would take us too far afield. Even to discuss the plot of Matthew's Gospel in any thorough fashion is too complicated a matter for our present treatment (for a more extensive treatment, see my "Mockers"; also Powell, "Plot and Subplots").

One useful approach, however, is that proposed by the French linguist A. J. Greimas, which is called "actantial analysis" and works from the identification of the "actants" in a story (for an English summary, see Patte, *Structural Exegesis*). Described in simplest fashion (as il-lustrated by the story of Little Red Riding Hood), this type of analysis speaks of six elements at work in most stories: (1) a sender (Little Red Riding Hood's mother) wants to send (2) some object (a basket of food) to (3) a receiver (the grandmother); this task is to be carried out by (4) a subject (Little Red Riding Hood), who is often distinct from the sender; the subject, however, cannot complete the task without over-coming obstacles presented by (5) some opponent (the big bad wolf), and so is assisted in crucial ways by (6) a helper (the woodcutter). In longer narratives, this actantial analysis can be applied both to the story as a whole and to smaller subunits within it. The structure can be represented schematically as follows:

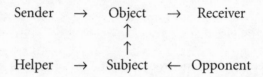

The beginning of Matthew's story (in Greimas's terms, the "Initial Sequence") comes into view in two mandating statements made about Jesus in the first two chapters. The first is given by an angel of the Lord and so is completely to be trusted: "You are to name him Jesus, for he will save his people from their sins" (1:21). The second, though spoken by the Jewish leaders in response to a question by King Herod, is, nonetheless, a quotation from Scripture, and so is equally reliable: "From you [Bethlehem] shall come a ruler who is to shepherd my people Israel" (2:6). The story begins, then, with Israel — those who are both God's people (2:6) and Jesus' people (1:21) — in exile (1:1-17, esp. v 17), suffering the consequences of their sins, in need of a shepherd and a savior. In Greimas's terms, our initial impression as readers is that the story will have to do with the way God (the sender) accomplishes salvation (the object) for Israel (the recipient) through Jesus (the sub-ject), who has been sent by God to deliver his people from their state of sin and exile. Jesus accepts this mandate for himself by identifying with the repentant members of Abraham's family in being baptized by John (3:1-17). Then after his acceptance is put to the test in the temp-tation (4:1-11), Jesus sets off to fulfill his mandate (4:12-17), announc-ing the reversal of Israel's plight in the imminent appearance of the kingdom of heaven (4:17).

As we move into the middle part of the story (Greimas's "Topical Sequence"), our impression is that salvation will consist of — or be produced by — Jesus' ministry of preaching, teaching, and healing. These are the terms in which Jesus' activity is summarized (in almost identical ways) in 4:23 and 9:35, and almost everything in between these two verses consists of detailed examples of precisely these activities. Jesus' ministry of healing in 9:2-8 is even linked with the forgiveness of sins, pointedly recalling the terms of the mandate in 1:21.

Throughout the middle part of the story, the recipients of Jesus' saving activity (and thus the "receivers" in Greimas's terms) appear, for the most part, in the form of great crowds who throng around him (cf. 4:25; 5:1; 7:28-29; 8:1, 18; 9:8, 33, 36). While the story of one Gentile supplicant is included (8:5-13), the crowds are described in specifically Jewish terms: "like sheep without a shepherd" (9:36) — so being identified with the "lost sheep of the house of Israel" who are the specific focus of Jesus' ministry (cf. 10:5-6; 15:24). This is, of course, in keeping with Jesus' original mandate to be the shepherd of God's people Israel (2:6). Yet a kind of narrowing or further definition is also taking place. For throughout this section the crowds are sharply differentiated from the Jewish leaders (7:28-29; 9:3-8, 33-34), Israel's ostensible shepherds. Thus Jesus' shepherding activity is directed not at Israel as a whole, but at a smaller subgroup within it. And as for the Jewish leaders, right from the beginning of the narrative they appear in the role of Jesus' opponents (2:3-6; 3:7; 9:3, 11, 34), their opposition reaching something of a first plateau only a little later in their decision to try to find a way to destroy him (12:14).

The Role of the Disciples in the Plot

The initial appearance of a character is often important, for it creates expectations that readers carry with them into the rest of the story. Thus on the assumption that Matthew expects his readers to associate the disciples of 5:1 (at least in part) with the followers called in 4:18-22, the reader's first impression of the disciples is that they will function as Jesus' "helpers" — that is, that the purpose of their call is that they might "fish for people" (4:19). And by the time the reader gets to the mission discourse of chapter 10, this impression has been fully confirmed. For in chapters 5–7 the disciples are identified as the recipients of Jesus'

35

teaching about the kingdom of heaven; indeed, they are spoken of at the outset of these chapters as being salt and light and are called on to act in such a way that others will give glory to God (5:13-16).

Furthermore, in the montage of Jesus' ministry in chapters 8–9, the disciples are referred to with sufficient frequency (8:14, 23; 9:10, 37) that we must assume their presence with Jesus as he "went about all the cities and villages, teaching in their synagogues, proclaiming the good news of the kingdom, and curing every disease and every sickness" (9:35). Thus we are fully prepared for it when Jesus not only asks his disciples to pray for more workers (9:37), but also sends them out to engage in that same ministry of healing and preaching (though, interestingly, not yet of teaching) that he himself has been carrying out from the outset (10:1-8) — thereby making them the answer to their own prayers even before they had time to pray! And so, by the time the reader reaches the mission discourse of chapter 10, the impression is firmly established that the disciples will play the role of "helpers," assisting Jesus as he carries out his mandate of being both shepherd (cf. 2:6) and savior (cf. 1:21) of the "lost sheep of the house of Israel" (9:36; 10:6).

But then a curious thing happens in the story. For unlike the other Synoptic evangelists, Matthew tells us nothing about the disciples' mission. He narrates neither their departure nor their return. The disciples receive their marching orders, but they march nowhere. In fact, though they have been called to fish for people, to bring in the harvest, and to gather the flock, in the rest of the story they do precious little fishing, harvesting, or shepherding. Where they do appear in ministry situations with the crowds, they are ineffectual: wanting to send the needy away (14:15; 15:23; 19:13-15), uncertain of what is to be done (15:33), or even — in the only instance where they take initiative on their own — failing miserably (17:14-20). In addition, in their relationship with Jesus, while some positive factors are mentioned, for the most part the emphasis in Matthew's Gospel falls on the slowness of the disciples to understand (15:12-20; 16:5-12), on their fear (14:26, 30), and on their lack of faith (14:31; 16:8).

When all of this regarding the ineffectiveness, denseness, and failures of the disciples is taken into consideration vis-à-vis the growing emphasis beginning in chapters 11 and 12 on the powerful opposition to Jesus, one comes to the end of the next section of the story (16:20) with the impression that the features proposed by Greimas in the analysis of a story are distressingly lopsided. For Jesus' opponents seem to be much more effective in their roles than his disciples could ever hope to be in theirs.

Admittedly, in 11:1–16:20 the disciples do not appear in a completely negative light. They recognize Jesus as Messiah and Son of God (14:33; 16:16); they are identified as the true family of Jesus (12:46-50); they are blessed with special revelation (13:11-17; cf. 11:25-27); and, while they are slow to understand, they nevertheless come to understand things eventually as a result of Jesus' teaching (13:51; 16:12). Though none of this serves to eliminate the puzzlement or to clarify their role, their continuing importance for Jesus signals their continuing importance for the story being told about Jesus. Most importantly, this section comes to a close with Jesus' reference to the future — that is, to the building of the church and Peter's special role in it (16:17-20).

To make sense of this unexpected turn in the story of the disciples, we need to see it in connection with a major turn in the larger story of Jesus, which begins to be apparent at 16:21: "From that time on, Jesus began to show his disciples that he must go to Jerusalem, undergo great suffering, be killed, and on the third day be raised." From this point in the story it becomes apparent that salvation from sin is to be accomplished not simply by means of Jesus' preaching, teaching, and healing, but more particularly through his death and resurrection. Saving his people from their sins (cf. 1:21) is to be accomplished, Matthew tells his readers, through Jesus' "blood of the covenant, which is poured out for many" (26:28). For only after being struck down himself (26:31) will the shepherd-leader receive authority to rule (cf. 2:6; 28:18).

This shift in the means by which Jesus is to accomplish his mandate occasions a startling shift in the actantial structure of the story (cf. Powell, "Plot and Subplots"). For in plotting Jesus' death, the leaders — in a kind of irony — function no longer as Jesus' opponents, but now as his unwitting helpers. Indeed, if Jesus is to fulfill his mandate through death, then nothing working toward that event can be construed as opposition. Rather, opposition takes the form of attempts to turn Jesus aside from the path of redemptive suffering — which is the role played by Satan (4:1-11) and his surrogates Peter (16:22-23) and the mockers at the cross (27:38-44).

Likewise, with such a shift in the story the identity of the recipients changes as well — though in a manner not yet clearly explicated. Initially in Matthew's Gospel, the "people" who were to be the beneficiaries of Jesus' saving activity were identified as Israel (2:6; cf. 1:1-17). Very

37

quickly, however, as we have seen, a narrowing takes place in Matthew's story. Some (particularly the leaders) who thought of themselves as members of Abraham's family (3:7-10) and heirs of the kingdom (8:12) are excluded; and while Jesus always limits his task to saving the lost sheep of the house of Israel, those sheep seem to be more and more identified with the crowds (9:35-38). But as Matthew's story of Jesus reaches its climax, the crowds join their leaders in calling for Jesus' death (27:20-26). So while Jesus' blood is to be poured out for "many" (26:28; cf. 20:28), the identity of those "many" is left somewhat undetermined.

But what of the disciples as the story moves to its climax? Again, the picture is mixed and ambiguous. The section begins on a negative note, with Peter's blunt rejection of Jesus' message of suffering and Jesus' equally blunt rebuke of Peter's alignment with Satan (16:22-23). The final glimpses of the disciples in this section are of their desertion of Jesus at his arrest (26:56) and Peter's subsequent denial (26:69-75). Indeed, in almost every scene where the disciples initiate or engage in activity of one kind or another, they are cast in a negative light. Only in 21:1-7 and 26:17-19, where they successfully carry out Jesus' instructions to fetch a donkey and arrange for the Passover meal, do they provide Jesus with any concrete assistance, and this of only the most mundane kind. Otherwise, as helpers they are failures, both with respect to Jesus' ministry with the crowds (as already noted: 17:14-20; 19:13-15) and with respect to Jesus' journey to the cross. In their rebuke of the woman who anoints Jesus (26:8-9), their inability to stay awake with Jesus in Gethsemane (26:36-46), their attempt to jockey for position with each other (20:20-28), and, ultimately, their desertion of the one they have been called to follow, they fail to support Jesus as he struggles with the cup he has been given to drink (20:22-23; 26:39). On two occasions, in fact, they even attempt to turn Jesus aside from his path: in Peter's rebuke (16:22-23) and in the halfhearted attempt to prevent Jesus' arrest by force (26:51).

Nonetheless, as Jack Kingsbury has observed (*Matthew as Story* 129), the disciples' actions in Matthew's Gospel do not affect the unfolding of the plot to any great extent. The disciples provide Jesus with very little help and are even drawn into Satan's role on one or two occasions. But they cannot really be identified as Jesus' opponents, at least in Greimas's sense of that term. Even their desertion, when it comes, has little impact, since Jesus has already pointed beyond it to their reunion in Galilee (26:31-32).

This anticipation of a future gathering of the scattered "flock," however, leads the readers into the other side of the portrayal of the disciples in this section. For while the disciples may seem to be irrelevant to the story in the present, discipleship continues to be an important theme in Jesus' teaching. Furthermore, there are many indications in this section of a significant role for the disciples in the future — in that state of affairs that will emerge on the far side of the cross. The section begins with Peter's rebuke (16:22-23). But this simply provides Jesus with an opportunity to teach his disciples more about the way of discipleship (vv 24-26) and to promise that some of them will see the coming of the kingdom (vv 27-28). And in the material that follows, the disciples' status as disciples is confirmed: they understand when Jesus explains things (17:13); they, like Jesus, are sons of the kingdom (17:24-27); they are commended for their sacrificial commitment to Jesus (19:27-30). Moreover, the remaining discourse material deals to a significant extent with the nature of discipleship: both chapter 18, on life in the kingdom community, and chapters 24–25, on life until Christ's "coming and the end of the age," are addressed to the disciples. Even the scathing denunciation of the scribes and Pharisees in chapter 23 contains some teaching in passing about the contrasting nature of the community of the Messiah (cf. vv 8-12).

Most important, however, is the series of statements that point to a significant role for the disciples in the future: they will tell others about the transfiguration vision after the resurrection (17:9); they will have authority in the church to bind and to loose (18:18-20); they will "sit on twelve thrones, judging the twelve tribes of Israel" (19:28); and they (presumably) will be the ones proclaiming the gospel of the kingdom throughout the world (24:14). But the most striking anticipation of the future mission of the disciples is to be found in the highly ironic passage with which this section ends. For in 27:62-66 the Jewish leaders ask Pilate for a guard at the tomb; "otherwise," they say, "his disciples may come and steal the body and tell the people, 'He has been raised from the dead,' and this last deception will be worse than the first" (27:64). Matthew, of course, has already provided his readers with enough information to recognize the fundamental futility of such a course of action. Guard or no guard, Jesus will indeed be raised from the dead (16:21; 17:9; 20:19; 26:32). Yet attentive readers will also be able to perceive a second level of futility and so to anticipate a time when the disciples will carry out a successful mission among the people. Thus throughout this section appear various indications that despite their weakness and failure, the disciples will eventually be cast into a helping role after all — with 27:62-66 also suggesting that in the postresurrection period, the Jewish leaders would continue on in their role as opponents (cf. 10:17-18).

The story of Jesus reaches its final resolution in chapter 28 (Greimas's "Final Sequence"). Having resisted all temptations to turn aside from the way of the cross (26:39; 27:38-44) and so having fulfilled his saving mandate, Jesus is vindicated in resurrection (28:1-10) and endowed with universal sovereignty (28:18). This makes possible (cf. the Greek particle *oun*, "therefore," in 28:19) the creation of a new community of salvation. Thus the "people" whom Jesus "saves from their sins" (cf. 1:21) is now identified as a community drawn from all nations, bound to Jesus through baptism and adherence to his commands (28:19-20).

The end of Jesus' story brings the story of the disciples to an end as well. Two things are to be noted. First, the disciples are the ones through whom Jesus will create this new community. Their desertion does not seem to have affected their status at all. Rather, without any reference back to their failings or desertion, the risen Jesus calls the disciples his "brothers" (28:10). And so the worst fears of the Jewish leaders are realized: the disciples, who are sent out by the risen Jesus himself, are to spread this "deception," not only among the Jewish "people" (the use of *laos* in 27:64 is significant; cf. 1:21) but also among the Gentiles. Jesus' reception of universal authority, in fact, makes it possible for his disciples to carry out the helping role for which they were initially called — with the one important difference being that now that task is described in terms not of fishing, but of making disciples. This "making disciples," in turn, is defined in terms of baptizing and (for the first time; cf. 10:1-8) teaching.

A second significant point about the role of the disciples in chapter 28, however, needs also to be noted. For in 28:19 the community that Jesus came to save is described as a community of disciples: "Go and make disciples *(mathēteusate)* of all nations." The disciples gathered around Jesus on the Galilean mountain are called to replicate themselves. Thus Jesus' first disciples function not only as the means by which his community of salvation is to be created, but also as the model of what membership in that community is all about.

All this puts their role in the story of Jesus into proper perspective. For to the extent that they are the means by which the new community is brought into being, their role is unrepeatable; the story of the disciples is the story of their preparation as the founding missionaries. But to the extent to which they are the model of community membership, their portrait in the Gospel is of ongoing significance.

Within the story of Jesus, the disciples function primarily as a model of what is involved in being a member of Jesus' "people." Readers of Matthew's Gospel learn what it means to be a disciple by following the disciples' own story under the narrator's guidance — that is, in identifying with them, in learning from their successes and failures, and, above all, in joining with them as they listen to Jesus' teaching. The disciples have little impact on the plot of the story of Jesus itself, emerging as significant agents only after that story comes to its narrated end. Their presence in the story, however, is far from insignificant. They serve the important function, both positively and negatively, of showing the readers of the Gospel just what is involved in being a follower of Jesus and a beneficiary of his saving activity. Encouraging readers to become disciples in this sense is one of the major goals of the author as he goes about telling the story.

2. The Pattern of Discipleship in Matthew's Telling

Essential to any narrative is the establishment of a normative point of view — that is, the need to provide a set of values concerning the good, the true, and the desirable by means of which the characters and their actions can be evaluated. This is accomplished in a variety of ways: (1) through the mediation of a reliable narrator, one who has sufficient knowledge and insight into the story so as to be able to take the readers anywhere they need to go to experience the story; (2) through explicit commentary, which has to do with direct statements concerning the significance of a person or event; and (3) through various less explicit forms of comment, such as the identification of reliable characters, or certain value-laden descriptions, symbolism, irony, and the like. In the case of Matthew's Gospel, our interest is in the way that the evangelist, by means of the story he tells about Jesus and his disciples, guides his readers to an understanding of what it means to be a disciple of Jesus. Space and time do not allow a full study of Matthew's telling. Some salient points, however, should be noted.

41

In telling the story about Jesus, Matthew is often an intrusive narrator. Frequently he breaks into the story to make explicit comments about the significance of various events — especially, of course, in the form of Old Testament fulfillment quotations. In telling the story about the disciples, however, he is more reticent, being content to show rather than to tell. Discipleship norms are communicated in Matthew's Gospel primarily by means of depicting the disciples' relationship with Jesus (Jesus having been established as the eminently reliable character from the beginning).

Despite their initial identification as Jesus' helpers and agents, the disciples appear in Matthew's Gospel, for the most part, as companions of Jesus and observers of his activity. Occasionally they go off to carry out some task and then return (21:1-7; 26:17-19). But only rarely do we encounter events where the disciples engage in an activity apart from Jesus. And it is not without significance that in most of these cases the disciples get into difficulties — as, for example, their crossing of the Sea of Galilee (14:24), their attempt to heal an epileptic boy (17:14-18), their falling asleep at Gethsemane (26:36-46), and Peter's denial (26:69-75).

It is in Jesus' interaction with his disciples, then, that the discipleship ideal is communicated by Matthew in his Gospel. In what follows, we will look first at the means by which this communication takes place (the "how" of the communication), and then turn our attention to the substance of the discipleship ideal itself (the "what").

The Means of the Telling

In telling the story, Matthew uses a variety of means to guide his readers to a correct understanding of discipleship. The most obvious of these is direct teaching, especially in the five great discourses (chs. 5:3–7:27; 10:5-42; 13:3-52; 18:1-35; 23:2–25:46), each of which is addressed to the disciples (in several cases, also to the crowds). Since Matthew eventually makes it clear that he wants his readers to become disciples and recipients of Jesus' teaching as well, readers — at least on repeat readings — become aware of an invitation to join the original disciples as they are taught by their teacher and lord. In addition, Matthew includes a number of statements — some in the discourses and some elsewhere — where Jesus speaks directly about the nature of discipleship. For example, he speaks of disciples as salt, light, and a mountaintop city

(5:13-16); of disciples as called to be like their master (10:24-25), especially in taking up their cross (16:24); and of disciples, inasmuch as they "do the will of my Father in heaven," as Jesus' true family (12:46-50).

Discipleship lessons also emerge frequently in the narratives, as events unfold in such a way as to bring some aspect of discipleship into focus. Several patterns can be discerned. In some cases, Jesus himself maneuvers the disciples into learning situations, as when he tells them to provide food for the crowd (14:16) or puzzles them with an enigmatic comment about the "yeast of the Pharisees and Sadducees" (16:6; also 15:32; 16:13-14; 19:23-24; 24:2). On other occasions, outsiders object to the behavior of the disciples, giving Jesus an opportunity to defend and explain the significance of their actions — as, for example, not fasting (9:14-17) or plucking grain on the sabbath (12:1-2; cf. 15:2).

Sometimes the learning situations are precipitated by the disciples themselves. For example, at times they ask questions of Jesus (cf. 17:10; 18:1, 21), react adversely to something he has said or done (cf. 19:10), raise objections against what he has said or done (cf. 13:10; 15:12; 16:22; 21:20; 26:8-9), or attempt to keep the needy away from him (cf. 14:15; 15:23; 19:13-15).

A number of Matthew's narratives contain explicit statements to the effect that the disciples did eventually come to understand what Jesus was teaching them (13:16-17, 51; 16:12; 17:13). Since Matthew stands in sharp contrast to Mark on this point, some commentators have drawn exaggerated conclusions about the understanding of the disciples in Matthew's Gospel (e.g., Barth, "Matthew's Understanding" 105-12). But as Luz has pointed out ("Disciples" 101-3), these passages function primarily to demonstrate Jesus' role as an effective teacher, and so highlight learning as the hallmark of a true disciple.

Furthermore, the profile of true discipleship in Matthew is sharpened by means of contrasts drawn with other groups. For as the recipients of special revelation, the disciples are differentiated from the crowds (especially in 13:11-17; also 5:1; 8:18, 23). In their way of life (6:32) and patterns of leadership (20:25) they are to be distinct from the Gentiles. They are even differentiated from other believers in Jesus — like those who say "Lord, Lord," but do not do God's will (7:21-23) or those who fall away through lack of love (24:9-13). And it goes without saying that they are contrasted with the Jewish leaders. Indeed, in chapter 23 the scribes and Pharisees are held up to the disciples and crowds as explicit examples of what not to do.

43

Out of all of this, a discipleship vocabulary emerges — terms that, once they are introduced and identified, function as further guides for the readers. Many of these terms are verbs (e.g., "follow," "worship," "believe," "doubt," "understand," "come to"); others are nouns (e.g., "faith," "righteousness," "lawlessness") or adjectives (e.g., "little faith," "righteous"); some, even, are prepositions (e.g., "with," 1:23; 9:15; 12:30; 28:20). While full documentation is not necessary for our purposes here (a few minutes with a concordance would turn up the relevant material), a surprising number of these terms are used in the closing climactic verses of the Gospel, that is, in 28:16-20. So by means of these various devices, Matthew attempts, in his own way, to make disciples of his readers (cf. 28:19).

The Substance of the Telling

But what is the substance of discipleship in Matthew's Gospel, as the evangelist himself sees it? The answer is multifaceted. A whole array of actions, attributes, and qualities come to be associated in his narration with the discipleship ideal. There is, in fact, no real indication in the Gospel of any system by which these actions, attributes, or qualities are to be classified or ranked. Perhaps they cohere in the maxim of 10:25 that disciples are to be like their master, though in its Matthean context this is not a generalized statement. Perhaps they could be grouped under the two activities associated with disciple-making in 28:19-20 — that is, personal attachment to Jesus (as indicated by baptism) and a lifestyle shaped by his commands. For the sake of convenience, however, we will group them here under three categories, as determined by the disciples' relationship (1) to Jesus and God, (2) to other disciples, and (3) to the wider world. In each case, the positive aspects of the ideal are often given further definition by means of some corresponding negative.

A number of recurring attributes of discipleship have to do with *the disciples' relationship to Jesus and God*. As is evident from the call of Jesus' first disciples (4:18-22), disciples are those who follow Jesus, which is a relationship that involves both commitment and cost (cf. Kingsbury, "The Verb AKOLOUTHEIN"). Disciples have to be prepared to expect hardship (8:20), to leave houses and family (10:37; 19:27-30), and to deny themselves, take up their cross, and even lose their lives for Christ's sake (10:38-39; 16:24-26). Set over against such true disciples are those

44

who love family more (10:37), who try to save their lives (10:39; 16:25-26), and who cling to riches and so turn away (19:22-24).

Closely related to all these attributes is the response of faith. Interestingly, however, the kind of faith that meets Jesus' approval in Matthew's portrayal is typically exhibited not by the disciples, but by supplicants (8:10; 9:2; 15:28). For the tendency is for the disciples to be rebuked for their lack of faith (6:30; 8:26; 14:31; 16:8). And since doubts occur even in the presence of the risen Jesus (28:17), unwavering faith is to be seen more as a goal of discipleship than as a prerequisite.

For a prerequisite, we need to look instead at keeping Jesus' commands and doing the will of the Father. In 28:19, observing Jesus' commands is one of the explicit features of discipleship. Its appearance here at the end of Matthew's Gospel, however, simply recapitulates a theme found throughout his Gospel. For those who do the will of the Father are Jesus' true family (12:50); those who do not, even if they acclaim Jesus as "Lord," will hear the fateful words "I never knew you" (7:21-23) — they are the people who work lawlessness (7:23; cf. 13:41; 24:12), but the people who enter the kingdom are those who seek righteousness (5:6, 20; 13:49). Those who hear and act on Jesus' words inhabit a sturdy house built on rock; those who do not will see their house collapse in the first storm (7:24-27).

But in order to hear and act on Jesus' words, understanding is necessary. The disciples do not have understanding as a natural ability. Any understanding they have has been granted by the Father (11:25-27; 13:16-18). Furthermore, statements about their understanding usually come only after they have displayed their lack of it and then have been instructed by Jesus (13:51; 16:12; 17:13). Nor is their understanding total. On at least one occasion disciples are rebuked for their lack of understanding without any counterbalancing indication that understanding was finally achieved (15:16). Yet the Matthean disciples have been granted sufficient understanding of who Jesus is (16:16-17) and of what his message is about (13:11-17, 51-52) for them to serve as models for Matthew's readers.

Discipleship in Matthew's Gospel, however, is characterized not only by a relationship to Jesus and God, but also by *the disciples' relationship to other disciples* in community. This is set out in programmatic fashion near the beginning of the Sermon on the Mount, where the disciples (addressed directly as "you") are called the salt of the earth, the light of the world, a city set on a mountain — that is, a community living a righteous life of such visibility that others will be led to give glory to God (5:13-16). We will consider the outward dimensions of this call in a moment. For the present we need note the corporate emphasis in Matthew. For here, in the only Gospel that refers to the church (16:18; 18:17), discipleship takes place in the context of a distinct, discipled community.

Of the various characteristics of this community of disciples, several, in particular, may be noted. The first is that of love. For Jesus sums up the whole law in the twofold command of love: love for God and love for one's neighbor (22:34-40; cf. 7:12). Furthermore, while love for neighbor is mentioned again (19:19), the love exhibited by Jesus' community of disciples is to include even enemies among its objects (5:43-46). And while the connection is not made explicitly, the concern for love probably underlies the fact that Matthew sees the church as existing as a *corpus mixtum* until the final judgment (e.g., 13:24-30, 36-43; 22:11-14). Thus love forbids any premature attempt to uproot weeds from the field. And when Matthew's Jesus looks ahead to dark days for the church, these are described in terms of hate, betrayal, and lack of love (24:10, 12).

Closely related to love are two other characteristics of the community of disciples. One is forgiveness. Forgiveness is the only feature of the Lord's Prayer to receive an elaborative comment (6:14-15), and it forms the subject of a significant portion of the community discourse in chapter 18 (esp. vv 21-35). The other characteristic, which comes to expression earlier in that same discourse, is care for the "little ones" who belong to the community of disciples (18:1-14, esp. v 6; cf. 10:42).

This leads, in turn, to the final characteristic to be mentioned here: servant leadership. To be part of Jesus' community, it is necessary to become like children (18:1-5). Hierarchical (23:8-10) and tyrannical (20:25) patterns of leadership are to be guarded against. Rather, greatness in the community of Jesus' disciples is to be measured in terms of humble service to all (20:26-28; 23:11-12).

But the actions, attributes, and qualities of discipleship are also categorized in Matthew's Gospel by *the disciples' relationship to the wider world*. Positively, this relationship is one of mission. The community is called to make disciples of all nations. This task is to be carried out both centripetally, as others are attracted by the community's life of "good works" (5:16), and centrifugally, as disciples go out in active mission to others (so the commission of 28:18-20, which reaffirms and expands on the instructions in ch. 10). Negatively, this relationship involves persecution. The disciples' message will not be received everywhere, and steadfastness under persecution will be called for (cf. 5:10-12; 10:16-36; 23:34-36; 24:9-14). But this is, of course, just part of the cost of discipleship, bringing us back to the theme with which this section began.

3. The Challenge for Contemporary Disciples in Reading Matthew's Gospel

After consideration of the story and its telling, we come finally to the reading. Without a reader, a story remains inert and its narrator ineffectual. The possibility of meaning emerges only when there is a reader to read — that is, when there is one who will enter into the world of the narrative under the guidance of the narrator, and so encounter the characters, experience the plot as it unfolds, form opinions, anticipate events, revise opinions and expectations in the light of subsequent events, and thereby eventually grasp the story as a whole.

But what reader? Narrative theory is populated with a wide array of readers. Some are imaginary constructs, others real flesh and blood; some first-time readers, others repeaters; some compliant, others resistive; some constrained, others autonomous; some past, others present. This opens up an equally wide array of fascinating studies. For example, it would be interesting to trace the responses of ideal first-time readers as they come to the realization, first, that Jesus is of ultimate and universal significance, and, second, that the appropriate way to respond to him is to become a disciple. Even here, however, it would be necessary to differentiate between the experience of a Jewish reader who becomes a Christian and that of a Gentile reader who becomes a Christian. For though by the end of the Gospel they have arrived at the same point, their routes have been significantly different.

But space is limited, and so we must move quickly to the situation of contemporary readers of the Gospel, especially to that of the intended readership of this chapter ("intelligent laypeople, theological students, and ministers"). What of significance for contemporary Christian discipleship might emerge from a reading of Matthew's Gospel? We will presume neither to speak for this group, nor to prescribe in advance the results of its reading. Nonetheless, a few concluding observations need to be made about our own reading of Matthew's Gospel vis-à-vis the subject of Christian discipleship.

At some points, to speak quite personally, I must admit that I am a somewhat resistive reader. I wish, for example, that Matthew had been more prepared to use the term "disciple" of the female followers of Jesus, many of whom displayed the characteristics of a true disciple more faithfully than did their male counterparts (e.g., 27:55-56, 61; 28:1-10, esp. v 9, where worship is not mingled with doubt, *contra* v 17). Also, I wish that the harsh and uncompromising depiction of the community's Jewish opponents had been more tempered by the injunction about love of one's enemies in 5:43-48 — though at the same time I observe that the disciples are never encouraged to engage in denunciation, judgment being left to Christ.

But if I were to single out one aspect of Matthew's depiction of discipleship that is of crucial importance for the church today, it would be the vision of the church as a visible community of salt and light. For increasingly the church finds itself today in a post-Christian environment. It is a situation no longer conducive to the making of disciples. Yet it is a situation where, if there are to be Christian disciples in the future, they will need to be made, not simply born (cf. Hauerwas and Willimon, *Resident Aliens*). The church, in fact, needs to see itself as Matthew saw it: as a distinct and appealing counterculture; a city set on a hill, making visible the reality of God's reign in the midst of the old order; a community concerned not so much to root out the weeds in its midst as to cultivate wheat of such quality that others will see it "and give glory to your Father in heaven" (cf. 5:16). For contemporary readers, the narrator's injunction of 24:15 — "let the reader take note" — can just as profitably be applied to this vision of the community of Jesus' disciples.

Selected Bibliography

Barth, G. "Matthew's Understanding of the Law," in G. Bornkamm, G. Barth, and H. J. Held, *Tradition and Interpretation in Matthew*. London: SCM, 1963, 58-164, esp. 105-25.

Deutsch, C. *Hidden Wisdom and the Easy Yoke: Wisdom, Torah and Discipleship in Matthew 11.25-30*. Sheffield: Sheffield Academic Press, 1987.

Donaldson, T. L. "The Mockers and the Son of God: Two Characters in

Matthew's Story of Jesus," *Journal for the Study of the New Testament* 41 (1991) 3-18.

Edwards, R. A. "Uncertain Faith: Matthew's Portrait of the Disciples," in *Discipleship in the New Testament*, ed. F. F. Segovia. Philadelphia: Fortress, 1985, 47-61.

Hauerwas, S., and W. H. Willimon. *Resident Aliens*. Nashville: Abingdon, 1989.

Kingsbury, J. D. *Matthew as Story*. Philadelphia: Fortress, 1986.

————. "On Following Jesus: The 'Eager' Scribe and the 'Reluctant' Disciple (Matt. 8:18-22)," *New Testament Studies* 34 (1988) 45-59.

————. "The Verb AKOLOUTHEIN ('to follow') as an Index of Matthew's View of His Community," *Journal of Biblical Literature* 97 (1978) 56-73.

Luz, U. "The Disciples in the Gospel of Matthew," in *The Interpretation of Matthew*, ed. G. Stanton. Philadelphia: Fortress, 1983, 98-128.

Minear, P. "The Disciples and the Crowds in the Gospel of Matthew," *Anglican Theological Review*, suppl. series 3 (1974) 28-44.

Patte, D. *What Is Structural Exegesis?* Philadelphia: Fortress, 1976.

Powell, M. A. "The Plot and Subplots of Matthew's Gospel," *New Testament Studies* 38 (1992) 187-204.

————. *What is Narrative Criticism?* Minneapolis: Fortress, 1990.

Rengstorf, K. H. "*manthanō, ktl.*," in *TDNT* 4.390-461.

Sheridan, M. "Disciples and Discipleship in Matthew and Luke," *Biblical Theology Bulletin* 3 (1973) 235-55.

Wilkins, M. J. *The Concept of Disciple in Matthew's Gospel*. Leiden: Brill, 1988.

Taking Up the Cross Daily: Discipleship in Luke-Acts

RICHARD N. LONGENECKER

Luke's use of the term "disciple" *(mathētēs)* is less frequent and less nuanced than that of the other canonical evangelists (see the Introduction above). But his treatment of the theme of discipleship is more extensively developed, more radically expressed, and more consistently sustained. As one of the so-called Synoptic Gospels, Luke's Gospel may be presumed to have many points in common with Mark's Gospel and Matthew's Gospel. It also has features in common with some of the material of John's Gospel, particularly the Johannine Passion narrative. Yet Luke's treatment of discipleship is unique, with a number of distinctive features — not only in his Gospel but also in his Acts, which together comprise about thirty percent of the New Testament.

We are, of course, quickly alerted to the distinctiveness of Luke's treatment by the fact that he alone among the New Testament writers has given his readers not only an account of Jesus' ministry but also a narrative sequel to that account, which sets out the ministries of Peter and Paul in roughly comparable fashion. More important, however, is the redactional "spin" that Luke gives to the materials he has derived from his sources. For in analyzing how he treats his sources, we are often confronted with data that indicate quite clearly not only how Luke wanted his readers to respond to the question "Who is Jesus?" but also how he wanted them to answer the question "What does it mean to be a follower of Jesus?"

Therefore, we will first set out here the basic lines of the structure of Luke's two volumes, suggesting what this structure signals for the topic of discipleship (section 1). Second, we will survey how the disciples of Jesus are portrayed in Luke's Gospel, comparing the Lukan portrait with that of the other Synoptic Gospels and giving attention to the disciples' didactic function as models of Christian discipleship (section 2). Following that, we will highlight a number of distinctive features in Luke's use of his sources in the writing of his Gospel, with those features selected because of what they tell us about the evangelist's understanding of discipleship (sections 3-6). Then we will do likewise for certain distinctive features in Luke's Acts (section 7). And finally, we will identify some ten lessons that Luke seems to have wanted to teach his readers regarding the nature of Christian discipleship today, whether that "today" be taken as only Luke's day or also ours (section 8). Throughout our depiction of discipleship in Luke-Acts there will appear something of a crescendo in the explicitness, development, and intensity of the data dealt with. That is not a pedagogical ploy on our part. Rather, that is how, it seems, Luke himself treated the subject, being somewhat more restrained — though frequently quite suggestive — when more controlled by his sources, but more expansive when feeling free to go beyond them.

Our method will be largely redaction-critical in nature, assuming, in the process, that Luke used a number of literary sources in his writing. In the preface to his two volumes he says that he knew of such sources (Luke 1:1-4), implying, as well, that he had studied them and used them in his own account — at least for the writing of his Gospel, but probably also in Acts. Presumably, as seems most critically supportable, the major sources for the writing of his Gospel were Mark's Gospel and a Sayings collection, which has commonly been designated "Q" (from the German *Quelle,* or "source"). From Mark, evidently, he derived the account of Jesus' ministry in Galilee and the basic narrative for Jesus' final week and passion in Jerusalem; from Q, he received sayings of Jesus that were not included in Mark but are shared by Matthew — with those sayings constituting about one sixth of both Matthew's Gospel and Luke's Gospel. Possibly Luke also used a "parable-travel" source for the writing of his travel narrative (9:51–19:27), or perhaps materials drawn from such a source or sources. It also appears that he used other source materials in addition to Mark's Gospel in his passion narrative (22:1–23:56), and these materials seem also to have been used in the composition of the Fourth Gospel.

51

As for his writing of Acts, we will proceed on the assumption that source materials drawn from the early Jewish Christian mission were at his disposal for Acts 1–12, however he may have come to have such materials. Also, reminiscences from various participants in the Pauline mission and his own travel notes served as the bases for Acts 13–28 (cf. the "we" sections in 16:10-17; 20:5-15; 21:1-18; and 27:1–28:16).

1. The Structure of Luke-Acts vis-à-vis Discipleship

What immediately strikes the reader of Luke-Acts is the basic architectural structure of the work. For not only are the two volumes almost equal in size (the Gospel being the longest of our New Testament writings, with Acts only about one-tenth shorter) and almost identical in chronological coverage (about thirty-three years for both), they also, more importantly, exhibit, as Charles Talbert puts it, "a remarkable series of correspondences between what Jesus does and says in Luke's Gospel and what the disciples [i.e., mainly Peter and Paul] do and say in the Acts" ("Discipleship in Luke-Acts" 63). Talbert has set out in quite detailed fashion a large number of parallels of event and expression — even of sequence — that can be found in Luke's two volumes: (1) parallels between Jesus' Galilean ministry (Luke 4:14–9:50) and Jesus' Perean-Judean ministry in the travel narrative (9:51–19:27) in his first volume; (2) parallels between the church's mission to the Jewish world (Acts 2:42–12:24) and the church's mission to the Gentile world (12:25–28:31) in his second volume; and (3) parallels between the two volumes themselves (cf. *Literary Patterns* 1-65). Talbert has also argued that the literary genre of Luke-Acts "is similar to the biographies of certain founders of philosophical schools, that contained within themselves not only the life of the founder but also a list or brief narrative of his successors and selected other disciples" ("Discipleship in Luke-Acts" 63; cf. *idem, Literary Patterns* 125-40; *idem, What Is a Gospel? The Genre of the Canonical Gospels* [Philadelphia: Fortress, 1977]; *idem,* "The Gospel and the Gospels," in *Interpreting the Gospels,* ed. J. L. Mays [Philadelphia: Fortress, 1981] 14-26; building on a suggestion of H. von Soden, *Geschichte der christlichen Kirche,* I: *Die Entstehung der christlichen Kirche* [Leipzig: Teubner, 1919] 73).

Talbert has been criticized, of course, for overdrawing the redactional parallels that can be found both within and between Luke's Gospel and his Acts and for identifying too precisely the literary genre of Luke's two-volume work. But his main points have certainly been established: (1) that the architectural structure of Luke-Acts requires that the two volumes be read together, the first interpreted by the second and the second by the first, and (2) that the ministry of the early church, as depicted in Luke's second volume, must be seen as shaped by the Jesus tradition, as portrayed in his first. Indeed, in setting out numerous parallels between Jesus' mission and the church's mission, Luke must be seen as actually proposing the thesis that Jesus' ministry and the church's mission *together* constitute the fullness of God's redemptive activity on behalf of humanity. For though Jesus' mission and the church's mission are not to be taken as identical, they are, nonetheless, comparable and inseparable — that of Jesus being the announcement and effecting of redemption, that of the church being the proclamation, extension, and application of what Jesus effected.

Just how Luke first came to think of relating the mission of the church to the ministry of Jesus, juxtaposing the two as comparable and inseparable entities, will always remain a mystery. Perhaps it was by association with the apostle Paul, from whom he might have heard such things as: "We are children and heirs — heirs of God and co-heirs with Christ — if, indeed, we share in his sufferings, in order that we may also share in his glory" (as in Rom 8:17), "I want to know Christ and the power of his resurrection and the fellowship of sharing in his sufferings, becoming like him in his death, and so, somehow, to attain to the resurrection of the dead" (as in Phil 3:10-11), or "I rejoice in what was suffered for you [understanding the Greek phrase *en tois pathēmasin hyper hymōn* as referring to Christ's sufferings, which were highlighted in vv 20b and 22a], and I fill up in my flesh what is still lacking in regard to Christ's afflictions, for the sake of his body, which is the church" (Col 1:24). But however it came about in Luke's mind, once formed, such a conception would have had explosive consequences for an understanding of Christian discipleship. For now the thesis could be made that what was foundational in Jesus' ministry — being, often, only somewhat embryonically present there — was (and is) to be explicated and more fully expressed in the church's mission.

It is, in fact, just such an idea that Luke expresses over and over again, both explicitly and implicitly, throughout the length and breadth of his two volumes, showing that what was basic in Jesus' ministry has been and should continue to be the pattern for all of the church's life

53

and ministry. The major topics that he treats in this fashion are: (1) the Spirit's presence and power, (2) the inauguration of a prophetic ministry, (3) the universality of the gospel, (4) the importance of the apostles and their witness, (5) the necessity of dependence on God, and therefore of prayer, and (6) concern for the poor, the imprisoned, the blind, and the oppressed (whom sociologically we would call "the disenfranchised") — all of which need be explicated more fully in what follows.

2. The Twelve in Luke-Acts vis-à-vis Discipleship

Our canonical Gospels were written to tell the story of Jesus. Yet that story also includes the story of Jesus' disciples, who are repeatedly designated "the Twelve" by Mark and Luke (e.g., Mark 4:10; 6:7; 9:35; 10:32; 11:11; 14:10, 17, 20; Luke 8:1; 9:12; 18:31; 22:3, 47; cf. Acts 6:2; 1 Cor 15:5) — and less frequently by Matthew and John (Matt 26:14, 20, 47; John 6:67, 70, 71; 20:24). There is no doubt that all four evangelists meant their readers to identify, in one way or another, with the Twelve, and so to learn from them what it means to follow Jesus.

Each of the evangelists, however, portrays the Twelve somewhat differently. In Mark's Gospel, after being initially called (cf. 1:16-20; 2:14) and appointed to be with Jesus (3:13-19), the Twelve are depicted, for the most part, quite negatively. Indeed, after those first positive portrayals, the picture of the disciples in Mark becomes rather dark — concluding, as it does, with the accounts of Judas' betrayal (14:43-45), the disciples' desertion (14:50-52), and Peter's threefold denial (14:66-72).

In Matthew's Gospel the portrait is not quite as bleak. For while Matthew takes over from Mark many passages that present Jesus' disciples rather negatively (e.g., Matt 8:23-27; 14:15; 15:16-17; 16:5-12; 17:16, 19; 19:13; 20:20-24; 26:36-46, 56), he also portrays them elsewhere in his Gospel in a somewhat more favorable light — both by deleting some of Mark's negative comments and by saying things about them of a more positive nature. So, for example, Matthew omits Mark's reference to the disciples being unable to understand (13:18; cf. Mark 4:13). Likewise, he omits Mark's derogatory statements about their hearts being "hardened" (14:32; 16:9; cf. Mark 6:52; 8:17). And while he continues to speak in some places of the disciples being slow to understand (e.g., 15:16-17; 16:8-9), he also reports that, at times, they did understand what Jesus was teaching them (e.g., 13:51; 16:12; 17:13). Moreover, more clearly than in Mark's Gospel, Matthew points to the significant role that the disciples will play in the postresurrection era (cf. 17:9; 18:18-20; 19:28; 24:14; 27:64; 28:16-20). The portrait of the disciples presented by Matthew, therefore, is somewhat brighter than that given by Mark — though, admittedly, not much brighter.

In Luke's Gospel, however, the Twelve are portrayed much more positively. True, Luke retains some of Mark's negativism. For example, Luke also reports that the disciples were unable to cast out an evil spirit (Luke 9:40; cf. Mark 9:18) — though Luke omits Mark's later reference to the disciples asking Jesus why they could not cast it out (cf. Mark 14:28). Furthermore, following Jesus' second passion prediction, Luke says of the disciples: "They did not understand what this meant. It was hidden from them, so that they did not grasp it, and they were afraid to ask him about it" (9:45; cf. Mark 9:32). Similarly, Luke reproduces Mark's story about the disciples rebuking those who brought children to Jesus for his blessing (18:15-17; cf. Mark 10:13-16). And he retains Mark's account of their dispute over who would be the greatest (22:24-27; cf. Mark 10:35-45), though he abbreviates it and relocates it.

On the other hand, Luke omits much of Mark's harsh treatment of the disciples. For example, he omits (1) Mark's statement about them being unable to understand Jesus' parables (Luke 8:11; cf. Mark 4:13), (2) Mark's references to their "hardened hearts" (Mark 6:52; 8:17), and (3) Mark's account of Peter's rebuke of Jesus (Mark 8:32-33). He also tones down the failure of three of their number to stay awake and pray with Jesus in Gethsemane, reporting only once that they fell asleep — and then excusing them with the comment that they slept because they were "exhausted from sorrow" (22:45-46). More significant, however, are (1) Luke's omission of Jesus' prediction: "You will all fall away; for it is written, 'I will strike the shepherd, and the sheep will be scattered'" (Mark 14:27, quoting Zech 13:7), and (2) Luke's depiction of the Twelve (minus, of course, Judas) as actually remaining faithful to Jesus in his hour of trial (*contra* Mark 14:50). In fact, Jesus in Luke's Gospel declares to the Eleven at the Last Supper: "You are those who have stood by me in my trials" (22:28). And the disciples are probably thought of in Luke's account as present at Jesus' crucifixion, for the evangelist states: "All those who knew him [Jesus], . . . stood at a distance, watching these things" (23:49).

55

The portrayal of the Twelve in John's Gospel is rather unique. Never does the author of the Fourth Gospel give a list of the disciples, as can be found in all three Synoptic Gospels. Only six of the disciples, in fact, are referred to by John (in various settings) by name: Andrew, Peter, Philip, Nathanael, Judas, and Thomas. And only in four verses does John speak of them as "the Twelve" (6:67, 70, 71; 20:24). Rather, in John's Gospel (as also in Matthew's Gospel) the disciples are, for the most part, a unified group, who are distinguished from the followers of John the Baptist, from "the Jews," from "the world," and from some "secret believers" such as Nicodemus (3:1-15; 7:50-51; 19:39), Joseph of Arimathea (19:38-40) and "others" (12:42-43). But "disciples" also designates a larger group than the Twelve in the Fourth Gospel (as also in Matthew's Gospel), as is evident from the comment: "From this time on, many of his disciples turned back and no longer followed him" (6:66). This ambiguity seems to suit the evangelist's purpose, for the term can thus have a more direct application to members of the Johannine community as well. One disciple in particular, the "Beloved Disciple," is depicted in John's Gospel as the ideal or model disciple, for he followed Jesus in a close, believing relationship (cf. 13:23; 19:26-27; 21:7, 20).

In Luke's depiction of the disciples, however, the Twelve are several times referred to as "apostles" (cf. Luke 6:13; 9:10; 17:5; 22:14; 24:10; see also 11:49). This feature, together with his more positive treatment of the Twelve in both his Gospel and his Acts (cf. Acts 6:2), is probably to be explained by the fact that Luke sees the Twelve — minus Judas, but later augmented by Matthias — as being prepared (in his Gospel) for their roles as leaders of the church (in Acts). It is also important to note that Luke, like Matthew and John, does not limit "disciple" to the Twelve (cf. 6:17; 19:37; see also 24:9, 33), as is more or less true of Mark. For Luke, evidently, viewed discipleship in somewhat broader categories — such as would include Matthias later as Judas's replacement (Acts 1:26), but also believers in Jesus generally (cf. his twenty-eight masculine uses and one feminine use of the term in Acts).

Despite, therefore, the differing portrayals of the Twelve in our four canonical Gospels, each evangelist, it seems, meant for his readers to identify with the disciples and to learn from them — both in their failures and in their successes — what it means to be a follower of Jesus. Admittedly, Luke's portrait of the Twelve is less detailed and less developed than those of Mark or Matthew; likewise, less than John's treatment of the "Beloved Disciple," whoever he was. But it is certainly far more positive than the portrait given by Mark, who seems to have been Luke's main narrative source — and even than that of Matthew, who follows in the same literary tradition. For Luke views the disciples as modeling the essential characteristics of Christian discipleship. It is not their failures that he highlights. Rather, what he emphasizes are the new commitments, orientation, and lifestyle that they reflected in their lives by association with Jesus their Master. And so, as Luke reports it, Jesus' statement about discipleship applies not only to his immediate disciples but also to all succeeding believers who identify with them: "Disciples are not above their teachers, but all those who are fully trained will be like their teachers" (6:40; cf. Matt 10:24-25).

3. Luke's Use of Mark vis-à-vis Discipleship

Luke's use of Mark vis-à-vis the theme of discipleship can be seen at the very beginning of the Synoptic Gospels' common narrative, that is, in his portrayal of the ministry of John the Baptist in 3:1-6 (cf. Mark 1:2-6). For while Luke knows that believers in Jesus originally called themselves "Those of the Way" (cf. Acts 9:2; 19:9, 23; 22:4; 24:14, 22), he seems not to put any emphasis on the word "way" *(hodos)* here — even though it appears twice in Mark's quotations of Mal 3:1 and Isa 40:3, being what linguistically ties these two testimony passages together. Rather, Luke's stress in 3:1-6 is on (1) the proclamation of "the word of God" and (2) the universality of the gospel. The proclamation of "the word of God" is depicted as meaning for John the preaching of "a baptism of repentance for the forgiveness of sins" (vv 2-3). Elsewhere in Luke's volumes, however, it has to do with proclaiming the "kingdom of God" as focused in Jesus (as is prominent in the Gospel, but also in Acts) and/or proclaiming God's "salvation" as focused in Jesus (as is prominent in Acts, but also in the Gospel). The second emphasis in 3:1-6, that of the universality of the gospel, is seen in Luke's extension of Mark's quotation of Isa 40:3 to include verses 4 and 5 of the prophecy (though without the glory motif of v 5a), which concludes with the ringing affirmation: "And all flesh shall see the salvation of God" (Luke 3:4-6).

These two themes, of course, are only somewhat embryonically set out in Luke 3:1-6, for the evangelist's purpose, it seems, is only to lay the basis for them at this point in his presentation and then to develop them more fully later. Nonetheless, they serve here to inaugurate two very important features in Luke's overall profile of Christian discipleship: (1) involvement in the proclamation of "the word of God," which focuses on the work and person of Jesus, and (2) possession of a universal view, not a parochial perspective, regarding the outreach and application of the Christian gospel.

After going on to present the ministry of John the Baptist in further detail (3:7-20), the baptism of Jesus by John (3:21-22), the genealogy of Jesus (3:23-28), and the temptation of Jesus by the devil in the wilderness (4:1-13) — with each of these presentations evidencing a number of redactional features of importance for all sorts of other issues — Luke then focuses on the Nazareth pericope in 4:14-30. It is important to note here not only that Luke has moved this passage up from where he found it in Mark's Gospel (cf. Mark 6:1-6a), but also that he has (1) set it in a distinctive context, (2) expanded it to include the central features of Jesus' preaching, and (3) used it as the introductory episode or frontispiece for all that he wants to portray throughout his two volumes concerning the ministries of both Jesus and the church.

The Lukan context for the Nazareth pericope focuses on the presence and power of the Spirit: "Jesus returned in the power of the Spirit into Galilee" (v 14a). This context is unique, since Mark (cf. also Matthew) has only "Jesus came [or "withdrew"] into Galilee." The important features highlighted in Luke's account of Jesus' reading of Isa 61:1-2a in the Nazareth synagogue, which only Luke presents, are (1) the presence of "the Spirit of the Lord" on God's servants (v 18a) and (2) the good news of the new epoch of redemption to be proclaimed to the poor, the captives, the blind, and the oppressed, with release and blessing for them (vv 18b-19). Also highlighted in Luke's portrayal of Jesus' preaching at Nazareth — which is considerably expanded in Luke's account — are the themes of (1) the universality of God's grace, particularly by references to God's acceptance of a Gentile widow and a Syrian general (vv 25-27), and (2) rejection of Jesus by his own people, mainly because they saw that a universality of divine grace included an acceptance of Gentiles (vv 23-24, 28-30).

It is 4:14-30, with its distinctive context and themes, that Luke uses as the introduction to all that he desires to present regarding the ministry of Jesus (in his Gospel) and the ministry of the church (in his Acts). Moreover, it is these themes that he highlights throughout his two volumes as being vitally important for Christian discipleship:

58

(1) the presence and power of the Spirit; (2) release and blessing for the poor, the captives, the blind, and the oppressed; (3) the universality of God's grace (with that universality, of course, expressed preeminently in the Christian gospel); and (4) rejection experienced by Jesus (with that rejection extended also to followers of Jesus).

It also needs to be noted that there is a greater emphasis in Luke's Gospel on Jesus' disciples being "apostles" *(apostoloi)* than can be found in Mark (or Matthew or John) — with, then, that emphasis being unfolded in Luke's Acts in terms of apostolic teaching and authority, and so the apostolic tradition. According to Luke 6:13 the twelve disciples were identified as "apostles" by Jesus himself. Probably this appearance of "apostle" for the disciples is Luke's own addition to his Markan source. For though the external textual tradition (esp. codices Vaticanus and Sinaiticus) largely supports the reading "whom he also named apostles" in Mark 3:14, which is the passage that Luke evidently had before him when he wrote, the wording of that Markan passage is less cumbersome without the seemingly intrusive "whom he also named apostles" between "he appointed twelve" and "in order that they might be with him." So most scholars, for internal reasons, have viewed the reference to "apostles" in Mark 3:14 as a scribal harmonization under the influence of Luke 6:13 (as well, perhaps, an attempt to parallel the word for "sent out," *apostellein*, in v 14b), with the result that most have taken "whom he also named apostles" in Luke 6:13 as a Lukan addition.

The term "apostle" appears six times in Luke's Gospel (here at 6:13; also 9:10; 11:49; 17:5; 22:14; and 24:10) and twenty-nine or thirty times in Acts. It is, however, used only once by each of the other evangelists (assuming its absence at Mark 3:14): Mark 6:30; Matt 10:2; and John 13:16. We may take it, therefore, that apostleship was a major theme in Luke's mind. It is signaled here in 6:13 only by Luke's comment "whom he also named apostles." But it becomes developed, principally in Acts, with a stress on the apostles' teaching and authority, and thus on the apostolic tradition. For Luke, the church is only faithful to its calling as it perseveres in the teaching and tradition of the apostles, who constitute the human link with Jesus. And Christian discipleship is only authentic as it does likewise.

Much more could be derived from a study of how Luke redacted Mark for an understanding of his treatment of discipleship. We have only highlighted some of the differences — whether of arrangement, addition, emphasis, or omission. But before leaving this section, two observations need to be made. The first is that, while we have highlighted differences, the agreements between Luke and Mark are also significant. For by including Markan materials in his account, Luke makes many of Mark's points on discipleship his own as well. The second is that where Luke effects changes of Mark, often those changes are more subtle than overt, often more suggestive than definitive, with adroit hints given of what might be expected in the narration of developments later. But this phenomenon is in line with what seems to be Luke's general policy and approach: that in his Gospel — particularly where he is using Mark as his source — the foundations of the gospel proclamation are set out, with the inclusion of various suggestive hints and embryonic statements that will lay the basis for further developments; whereas in Acts are portrayed the explications, applications, and extensions of what was effected by Jesus in his teaching, death, resurrection, and ascension.

4. Luke's Use of Q vis-à-vis Discipleship

Luke's other main source for the writing of his Gospel, it seems, was a collection of the sayings of Jesus that was either written or retained in the church's collective memory and that has been dubbed "Q." Matthew seems to have used this source as well. So by comparing the non-Markan sayings in Luke's Gospel with the non-Markan sayings in Matthew's Gospel — which make up about one sixth of what each evangelist presents — we are able to arrive at some approximation of what was contained in the original, postulated Q used by both Matthew and Luke (whether they worked from closely similar copies of Q or from somewhat different recensions).

The Q sayings evidently included teachings of Jesus regarding discipleship. In a study of Luke's treatment of the theme of discipleship, therefore, it is necessary to note how he used Q, just as it was necessary to observe how he used Mark. For by comparing Luke and Matthew in their respective uses of Q, it is possible to identify certain of his emphases in the editing of this material. Three Q passages in Luke's Gospel are particularly significant for such a study: (1) "the beatitudes" in 6:20b-26 (cf. Matt 5:3-12), (2) the "conditions for following Jesus" in 9:57-62 (cf. Matt 8:18-22), and (3) "the cost of discipleship" in 14:25-33 (cf. Matt 10:37-38).

The differences between Matt 5:3-12 and Luke 6:20b-26 are well known. The most important are (1) that Matthew speaks of those who are blessed by God as being "the poor in spirit," "those who hunger and thirst for righteousness," and "the pure in heart," thereby stressing more spiritual qualities, whereas Luke has "the poor" and "the hungry" as blessed by God and "the rich" and "the full" as under God's curse, thereby emphasizing more economic and social conditions; and (2) that Matthew has a list of nine situations that deserve the appellative "blessed" *(makarioi)*, whereas Luke sets out four conditions that are designated "blessed" and four that call for the prophetic "woe" *(ouai)*.

It may be debated as to which evangelist most closely reproduced the actual words found in Q — whether Matthew with his emphasis on spiritual qualities or Luke with his focus on economic and social conditions. Most have concluded that Luke is closest, since here Jesus' words, both in form and in content, closely parallel Jewish ethical teaching as found in Jer 22:13-17; Sirach 11:18-19; and *1 Enoch* 94:8-10; 96:4-8; and 97:8-10. And with that opinion I agree, and so view Matthew's portrayal as having been reworked for Matthew's own purposes. But even when we judge Luke's Beatitudes to be closest to the actual words recorded in Q, it is important to remember that all of what Luke has taken over from his source or sources was incorporated by him into his Gospel because it fit his own interests and purposes.

Luke has a definite interest in the poor, in captives, in those who are afflicted and oppressed, and in the disenfranchised, as witness his inclusion of the words of Isa 61:1-2a in the Nazareth pericope of 4:14-30 and his emphases at many places throughout his two volumes (which we will refer to later). And Luke also has a number of things to say about the rich, those of the establishment, and the well-off, constantly setting them in a bad light and calling on them to repent. The infancy narrative in 1:5–2:52 provides us with quite a few illustrations of his attitude on these matters. For there, in material that is certainly Luke's own, (1) women — even a widow — have a significant part in God's redemptive program, (2) the pious poor are lauded, and (3) the rich are condemned. The Magnificat (1:46-55) epitomizes such attitudes, particularly in the statements: "he has been mindful of the humble state of his servant"; "he has brought down rulers from their thrones, but lifted up the humble"; and "he has filled the hungry with good things, but sent the rich away empty" (1:48a, 52-53). Likewise, John the Baptist's responses to questions asked him by "the crowds," the "tax collectors," and "some soldiers" in 3:10-14 — a passage found only in Luke's Gospel — are all framed in terms of one's attitude toward money and material goods. And elsewhere throughout Luke's two volumes (as we will see later), such attitudes come repeatedly to the fore.

While the Lukan Beatitudes can be paralleled in both form and content with some of the material found in *1 Enoch* 94–104/105 (the so-called "Epistle of Enoch," which is very old material), Jesus' teachings on poverty and riches as they appear elsewhere in Luke's Gospel and the teachings of the church on these matters found in Acts differ in a number of respects. Most prominently, while the sage of *1 Enoch* 94–104/105 only condemns the rich and their riches, Jesus and the church call on believers to have a new attitude toward possessions and their use — that is, not just to dispense with possessions, but to repent of selfishness and to use their riches for the benefit of others (cf., e.g., Acts 2:45; 4:32-37; 5:1-11). Or as Joseph Fitzmyer says with regard to Jesus' warning about riches in Luke 18:24-25, which uses the metaphor of a camel going through the eye of a needle: "The reason why it is hard for the rich to get through the eye of the needle (18:25) is not because of amassing in itself, but because of the iniquitous seduction that invariably comes with it, distracting that person from the consideration of what life is all about" — which Fitzmyer admits "may sound like bourgeois piety," but which he insists "is part of the message of the Lucan Jesus" (*Luke* 2.972).

In Luke's version of the Beatitudes, therefore, concerns for the poor and the hungry are highlighted, with corresponding denunciations of the rich and the well-off. Luke shares with Matthew interests in the spiritual disposition and religious persecution of believers (so the third and fourth sets of his blessings and woes). But he differs from Matthew in that he expressly presents Jesus as being vitally concerned about the economic and social conditions of people — in fact, he brings these concerns right to the fore in Jesus' teaching (so the first and second sets of his blessings and woes). In so doing, of course, he carries on themes already emphasized in the Nazareth pericope, particularly those set out in Jesus' quotation of Isa 61:1-2a. And in so doing, he points up issues regarding poverty and riches that he sees as important for anyone who would be a follower of Jesus.

There are, however, two other major Q passages in Luke's Gospel where Jesus speaks directly regarding Christian discipleship. The first is 9:57-62 (cf. Matt 8:18-22), where "conditions for following Jesus" are enumerated; the second, 14:25-33 (cf. Matt 10:37-38), where "the cost of discipleship" is detailed. Both of these passages are in Luke's travel narrative, and so could be reserved for a later discussion. But both are from Q and so can rightfully be treated here. More importantly, both evidence distinctive Lukan redactional interests.

In the pericope on "conditions for following Jesus" (Matt 8:18-22; Luke 9:57-62), Matthew and Luke set out in fairly comparable fashion two sayings of Jesus. The contexts for the sayings, of course, differ, with each evangelist introducing what is said in terms of the narrative development of his own Gospel — that is, Matthew speaks of "great crowds," of going over to the other side of the Sea of Galilee, of a "scribe," of another "disciple," and of Jesus being addressed as "teacher"; whereas Luke speaks of "a certain person" *(tis)* and "another" *(heteros)* who spoke to Jesus as he and his disciples were "going along the road" (or "on the way"). But the words addressed to Jesus in the two Gospels are identical: "I will follow you wherever you go" and "Lord, let me first go and bury my father." More significantly, the two sayings of Jesus in response are also identical: "Foxes have holes, and birds of the air have nests; but the Son of man has nowhere to lay his head" and "Follow me. Leave the dead to bury their own dead." So in portraying what Jesus said in these two responses, Matthew and Luke agree: Christian discipleship has as its conditions (1) willingness to live an unsettled and insecure lifestyle for Jesus' sake and (2) being unencumbered by other allegiances.

But Luke adds more to his portrayal of Jesus' words on discipleship, attaching an addendum to the second saying and going on to present a third saying. The addendum gives a positive spin to the subject of discipleship, for not only are Jesus' followers not to be encumbered by other allegiances but they are also to "go and proclaim the kingdom of God" (9:60b). The third saying, however, which is absent from Matthew's account, heightens the radicalism of what it means to be unencumbered by other allegiances in following Jesus. For it speaks not just of letting others bury a deceased father but also of not being detained by farewells to one's own family at home — using the aphorism "No one who takes hold of the plow and looks back is fit for the kingdom of God" (9:61-62).

And as though this were not enough, Luke intensifies this note of radicalism in his treatment of "the cost of discipleship" (Matt 10:37-38; Luke 14:25-33). For whereas Matthew presents Jesus as speaking of loving Jesus more than one loves one's own father and mother and taking up one's cross and following Jesus, Luke has it: "If anyone comes to me and does not hate father and mother, wife and children, brothers and sisters — yes, even life itself — such a person cannot be my disciple. Those who do not carry their cross and follow me cannot be my disciples" (vv 26-27). And then, as though to reinforce that radicalism, Luke adds a further saying of Jesus about builders needing to consider carefully the cost of building before beginning construction and kings needing to consider carefully the cost of warfare before going to war, with the application for discipleship being: "So, therefore, those of you who do not give up everything you have cannot be my disciples" (vv 28-33).

It may never be conclusively determined whether, when Matthew and Luke differ in their selection of Q materials, the one added or the other deleted certain sayings — or, when they differ in wording or emphasis, which is closest to Q. Nonetheless, analyzing Luke's use of Q vis-à-vis the theme of discipleship, it is clear that Luke wants his readers to know that being a follower of Jesus requires (1) new attitudes toward wealth, poverty, and the use of riches for the benefit of others and (2) a radical new type of lifestyle that puts following Jesus before every other allegiance — so radical, in fact, that every other allegiance, of whatever nature, can be characterized as "hate" by comparison.

5. Luke's Travel Narrative vis-à-vis Discipleship

The so-called travel narrative in Luke's Gospel, that is, 9:51–19:27, is a lengthy section with numerous references to Jesus and his disciples traveling from Galilee to Jerusalem (9:51, 52-56, 57; 10:1, 38; 11:53; 13:22, 33; 17:11; 18:31, 35; 19:1, 11). Some have seen it as ending at 18:30 or 19:10; others, at 19:44. But the wording of 19:28 — "After Jesus had said these things [understanding the Greek demonstrative pronoun *tauta* as referring to the parabolic teachings of the travel narrative], he went on ahead, going up to Jerusalem" — seems to function as a hinge between "travel to Jerusalem" and "ministry in Jerusalem," with the travel narrative, therefore, ending at 19:27. Luke had earlier, of course, portrayed Jesus as traveling (e.g., 4:42; 8:1). Now, however, Jerusalem comes into view as the goal of Jesus' travels.

Up through 9:50 (minus the infancy narrative and the genealogy), Luke's Gospel had been largely dependent on Mark for its narrative and on Q for its (non-Markan) sayings. From 9:51 through 19:27, however, most of the evangelist's material appears to have been drawn from other sources, with only a limited use of Mark (i.e., some use of Mark 10:1-52) and Q (i.e., Luke 9:57-62/Matt 8:18-22 and Luke 14:25-33/Matt 10:37-38, as treated above). Debate has been extensive over whether Luke's source material for the travel narrative was one connected "parable" or "travel" source, either written or oral, or various sources that contained both parables of Jesus and further information about his ministry in Transjordan. Yet whatever the source or sources of this section, most of what Luke presents here must be considered unique to the evangelist, for it appears neither in any of the other Gospels nor in what can be postulated about Q. And as distinctive to Luke, it must be seen as incorporating the evangelist's own understanding of how Jesus' ministry progressed and how his teaching should be understood — particularly, for our purposes, of what Jesus taught about discipleship.

The narrative in 9:51–19:27 is fragmentary and only loosely joined together. It seems to skip about somewhat, in almost a haphazard manner (e.g., first in Samaria, 9:52-56; then at Bethany, outside of Jerusalem, 10:38-42; then "passing along between Samaria and Galilee," 17:11; and finally at Jericho before entering Jerusalem, 18:35; 19:1). Numerous parallels are set up between Jesus' ministry in Galilee and his ministry in Perea and Judah (e.g., a leper healed in 5:12-16 and ten lepers healed in 17:11-19; controversies with the Pharisees in 5:17–6:11 and in 11:14-54; the "Sermon on the Plain" in 6:17-49 and other sermonic materials in 17:1-10 and *passim;* sending out the Twelve in 9:1-11 and sending out the Seventy in 10:1-24; and two passion predictions in 9:22-27, 43-45 and a third in 18:35-43). But the main content of the travel narrative is made up of fifteen or sixteen parables, sometimes two or three just strung together, though usually the parables are framed by the rather loose travel narrative.

Some of the parables in the travel narrative are addressed to the crowd and some to opponents, but most are told by Jesus to his disciples. Mark, of course, after recounting Jesus' seed parables (i.e., the sower and the seed, the growing seed, and the mustard seed in 4:1-32), concludes by saying: "With many such parables Jesus spoke the word to them, as much as they could understand. He did not say anything to them without using a parable. But when he was alone with his own disciples, he explained everything" (4:33-34). So having Mark's Gospel before him, Luke well knew — if not, of course, also from Christian tradition generally — that Jesus often used parables in his teaching, even though Mark himself records only the three seed parables (4:1-32) and the parable of the wicked tenants (12:1-12). Luke, in fact, uses three of the Markan parables, distributing them throughout his Gospel: the sower and the seed in his section on Jesus' Galilean ministry (8:4-15; cf. Mark 4:1-20), the mustard seed in his travel narrative (13:18-19; cf. Mark 4:30-32), and the wicked tenants in his section on the ministry of Jesus in Jerusalem (20:9-19; cf. Mark 12:1-12). But Luke obviously knew of a number of other parables of Jesus — as did also Matthew, though Matthew included fewer additional parables in his Gospel than did Luke.

What Luke seems to have intended in setting out the parables of his travel narrative was to give his readers something of a collage — or, a number of multifaceted pictorial representations — of what Jesus taught his disciples about following him, with not too veiled applications about how the readers, as well, should conduct their lives as Christians. Matthew's Gospel presents Jesus as telling parables mostly about (1) the nature of the kingdom (the sower, the mustard seed, the weeds and the grain, the yeast/leaven, the hidden treasure, and the net in 13:1-50; also, perhaps, the unmerciful servant in 18:21-35), (2) Israel's rejection (the wedding banquet in 22:1-14 and the two sons in 21:28-32; and, of course, the wicked tenants in 21:33-46), and (3) future eschatological judgment (the ten virgins, the talents, and the sheep and goats in 25:1-46). But Luke's parables in his travel narrative are instructional for how believers should live their lives here and now — and so function as parables of the Christian life.

The parables of Luke's travel narrative have often been used for devotional and homiletical purposes. That is not only because of their multivalent imagery, but also because they have been tailored by Luke — as well as, it may be presumed, by Jesus — for easy application to living as a follower of Jesus. It is impossible in short compass to deal with all that is taught in these parables. Suffice it here merely to set out their major topics:

1. loving and helping others (the good Samaritan, 10:25-37),
2. prayer (the persistent friend, 11:5-13; the persistent widow, 18:1-8),
3. possessions and true riches (the rich fool, 12:13-34; the rich man and Lazarus, 16:19-31),

4. service to God (the unproductive fig tree, 13:1-9; proper attitude in serving God, 17:7-10; the ten minas/pounds, 19:11-27 [cf. Matt 25:14-30]),
5. the importance of response to God (the great supper, 14:15-24 [cf. Matt 22:1-14]; the rich man and Lazarus, 16:19-31 [see also 3 above]),
6. God's love for the lost (the lost sheep, 15:1-7 [cf. Matt 18:12-14]; the lost coin, 15:8-10; the prodigal son, 15:11-32),
7. humility (the Pharisee and the tax collector, 18:9-14; also the "parable" in 14:7-14, which is without imagery), and
8. shrewdness in one's affairs (the shrewd manager, 16:1-12).

Almost all of these parables are multivalent in their imagery and application. But their main point or points are usually readily understandable — though admittedly the parable of the shrewd manager is somewhat perplexing. All of them, however, were evidently intended by Luke to teach regarding what it means to follow Jesus and so to provide pictorial patterns for Christian discipleship.

6. Luke's Passion Narrative vis-à-vis Discipleship

The greatest degree of agreement among the four Gospels is found in their passion narratives (Mark 14:1–15:47; Matt 26:1–27:66; Luke 22:1–23:56; and, probably, John 18:1–19:42). This might not be too surprising for the Synoptic Gospels. For they seem to represent, in the main, a single tradition regarding the events of Jesus' passion — one that, evidently, Mark used as the basis for his Gospel, which then both Matthew and Luke essentially followed. It is, however, somewhat surprising for John's Gospel. For while the Fourth Gospel is quite different from the Synoptic Gospels in its portrayal of the ministry of Jesus, its account of Jesus' passion is remarkably similar — in fact, of the six percent of material in John's Gospel that may be said to be comparable to that of the Synoptics, almost all of it is to be found in John's passion narrative.

Such a commonality suggests that the events of Jesus' passion, more than any other events of the Jesus story, were relatively fixed in the proclamation and traditions of the early church. That does not mean, however, that the passion narratives of the four Gospels should be assumed to be identical. Certainly the Fourth Gospel, while comparable in its overall presentation, is different from the others in its selection, arrangement, and wording of material; and the Synoptic Gospels differ among themselves, to some extent, on such matters as well. Nor should it be assumed that the four evangelists interpreted the events of Jesus' passion in exactly the same way.

At least two major traditions regarding the telling of the passion story seem evident in our Gospels: (1) that incorporated by Mark, which was basically followed by Matthew and Luke, and (2) that incorporated by John, with some features of this tradition appearing also in Luke. Moreover, each evangelist appears to have included some data that only he, for one reason or another, seems to have been interested in — for example, Mark's story of the flight of the naked young man at Jesus' arrest (14:51-52) and Luke's report of Jesus being sent to Herod by Pilate (23:6-12). Of even more importance in reading the passion narratives of the four Gospels, however, is the recognition that each of the evangelists has given his own redactional "spin" to the data presented, following out his own interests and speaking to the concerns of his addressees. So it is necessary when studying any particular passion narrative to ask: (1) What tradition seems to be represented? (2) What additional data are presented? and (3) How has the evangelist portrayed the data he incorporates?

Luke's passion narrative has much in common with Mark's, as well as that of Matthew. Its narrative follows, in the main, the order and structure of Mark's narrative, omitting only four episodes recorded by Mark: the anointing of Jesus at Bethany (Mark 14:3-9), Jesus' prediction of the desertion of his disciples (Mark 14:27-28), the flight of the naked young man (Mark 14:51-52), and the soldiers' mocking (Mark 15:16-20) — with each omission probably explainable in terms of Luke's own interest (or lack of interest), as can be seen elsewhere in his two volumes. Luke adds only the four sets of statements at the end of the Last Supper (22:21-23, 24-30, 31-34, 35-38) and the two reports of Jesus being sent to Herod (23:6-12) and then again to Pilate (23:13-16). Yet at some places in their respective narratives, Luke and John share details not found in Mark (or Matthew). Furthermore, the percentage of Markan words in Luke's passion narrative is far less (about twenty-seven percent) than in Luke's portrayal of Jesus' Galilean ministry (about fifty percent).

Some have surmised from these data that Luke knew and used John's Gospel in the writing of his own passion narrative. Others have concluded that he used, in addition to Mark's account, another connected account of Jesus' passion — one used by John as well — and still others that he knew and used "an early form" or "earlier forms" of material about Jesus' passion that had not as yet been organized into a connected account — though later it might have been — and so used in the composition of John's Gospel. That Luke's narrative depends on John seems highly debatable; that it is based on Mark and another account also used by John is possible. More likely, however, is the hypothesis that Luke's passion narrative is based mainly on Mark, with supplementary data added from other developing traditions within the church and one Q saying (i.e., 22:28-30).

More significant for our purposes, however, is to note how Luke portrays Jesus in his passion narrative. For in Luke's Gospel, Jesus' passion and the cross are not depicted in terms of vicarious suffering, human redemption, or the expiation of sins as much as they are in Mark's account (or Matthew's). Rather, they are presented primarily in exemplary fashion as the culmination of Jesus' unconditional obedience to God and so as patterns for the lives of his followers. Luke has already hinted at such an understanding in 9:23 by the addition of the adverbial expression "daily" *(kath' hēmeran)* to Jesus' words from Mark 8:34: "Those who would come after me must deny themselves and take up their cross *daily* and follow me." And he has also suggested such an understanding by his inclusion of Q material in 14:27: "Those who do not carry their cross and follow me cannot be my disciples." It may be thought, of course, that the addition of only one small expression to a saying found in Mark is a very minor matter and that the repetition of a saying reported also by Matthew is of little consequence. In reality, however, 9:23 and 14:27 — which, it may be observed, are balanced nicely in the two parts of Luke's Gospel — provide the reader with two rather deft touches in Luke's use of his sources that signal what the evangelist wanted to emphasize later in his writings, especially here in his passion narrative (and also, as we will note, throughout his Acts).

This is not to say that suffering, sacrifice, or soteriology are absent in Luke's portrayal of Jesus' passion. The evangelist has spoken earlier in 9:31 about Jesus going to Jerusalem in order to fulfill his "departure" — or, more literally, his "exodus" *(exodos)*, which is a term that would certainly have evoked ideas about the redemptive significance of Jesus' passion to anyone knowing the Old Testament. And here in his passion narrative Luke explicitly refers to the Last Supper as a Passover meal (22:7, 8, 11, 13, 15) and repeats Jesus' words of institution at that meal: "This is my body given for you; . . . This cup is the new covenant in my blood, which is poured out for you" (22:19-20). But in his omission in 22:24-30 of the Markan ransom saying "to give his life a ransom for many" (Mark 10:45b; cf. also Matt 20:28b), Luke indicates that what he wanted his readers to think about when they thought of Jesus' passion, of his service for others, and of their service for God was not just a soteriological theory. And throughout Luke's passion narrative the theme of Jesus' passion and cross as exemplary for Christian living and service is to the fore.

The theme of exemplary service is highlighted in the distinctly Lukan portrayal in 22:27, where, at the Last Supper, Jesus resolves a conflict among his disciples by saying: "Who is greater, the one who is at the table or the one who serves? But I am among you as one who serves." Admittedly, Jesus does not refer explicitly here to his suffering on the cross as exemplary for discipleship. But his approaching passion provides the setting for what is said. Likewise, Luke's depiction of Jesus praying on the Mount of Olives in 22:39-46 (cf. Mark 14:32-42; Matt 26:36-46) is set out in distinctly exemplary fashion. For though verses 43 and 44 ("an angel from heaven appeared to him and strengthened him"; "his sweat was like drops of blood falling to the ground") may be textually in doubt (being omitted by the early third-century papyrus 𝔭75, the fourth-century codex Vaticanus, and the fifth-century codex Alexandrinus), the twice-repeated exhortation to his disciples to "pray so that you will not fall into temptation" is certainly authentic. Here, in fact, is a clear echo of the Lord's Prayer in its request "Lead us not into temptation" (Luke 11:4; Matt 6:13). And here Jesus exhorts his disciples to take on in their lives an important feature of his ministry: that of prayer, particularly at the crisis points of life.

More directly associated with the cross, however, is Luke's rather cryptic reference to Simon of Cyrene (23:26), who was made to bear the cross of Jesus (cf. Mark 15:21; Matt 27:32). For Luke adds to the Markan reference the observation that Simon carried the cross "behind" (opisthen) Jesus. It seems, therefore, that what the evangelist saw in Simon's carrying of Jesus' cross and following after him was a concrete example of Jesus' teaching that Luke incorporated earlier in 9:23: "Those who would come after (opisō) me must deny themselves and take up their cross daily and follow me." For Luke, Simon of Cyrene, it appears, symbolized the attitude of the Christian disciple, carrying the symbol of Jesus' suffering — which, as Luke's addition to Jesus' instruction in 9:23 highlights, must be an attitude and action that takes place "daily."

7. Luke's Acts vis-à-vis Discipleship

At the end of Luke's Gospel, Jesus tells "the Eleven and those with them" (24:33): "You are witnesses of these things. I am going to send you 'the promise of my Father' [*tēn epangelian tou patros mou*]; but stay in the city until you have been clothed with power from on high" (24:48-49). At the beginning of Luke's Acts, "the promise of the Father, which you heard me speak about" is first explained as baptism "with the Holy Spirit" (1:4-5) and then spoken of as a filling "with the Holy Spirit" (2:4). And with the coming of God's Spirit to believers on the day of Pentecost, the gift of prophecy is given and believers in Jesus begin to proclaim the word of God about Jesus of Nazareth — who was accredited by God throughout his ministry, who was crucified, but whom God raised from the dead — as being both Lord and Christ (cf. Peter's sermon in 2:14-40).

So as Acts begins, the two basic themes of Luke's Nazareth pericope (Luke 4:14-30), themes that he carried on throughout his Gospel, are again highlighted: (1) the presence of God's Spirit on his servants and (2) the proclamation of the good news of God's redemptive activity. The joining of these two themes is, in fact, claimed to be rooted in Old Testament prophecy. For Peter is presented in Acts 2 as quoting Joel 2:28-32 (3:1-5 in the Hebrew text) to the effect that it is precisely these two features that are to characterize "the last days" inaugurated by Jesus: "'In the last days [Hebrew "afterward"],' God says, 'I will pour out my Spirit on all people. Your sons and daughters will prophesy, your young men will see visions, and your old men will dream dreams. Even on my servants, both men and women, I will pour out my Spirit in those days'" (vv 17-18a) — with, then, Peter breaking into the quotation, evidently for emphasis and to highlight what was at that time taking place in his preaching, with the added words: "and they will prophesy" (v 18b). In addition, it needs to be noted that the quotation from Joel ends with a statement regarding the universality of God's grace as expressed in the gospel: "And everyone who calls on the name of the Lord will be saved" (v 18b) — which is, of course, a further important theme of the Nazareth Pericope (cf. Luke 4:25-27).

Each of these themes — the Spirit's presence, the proclamation of God's redemptive activity, and the universality of God's grace — is not only an important feature of Luke's writing, but also is presented in both his Gospel and his Acts as factors that are to characterize the

71

self-consciousness of a follower of Jesus, and so to be accepted and worked out in Christian discipleship. In addition, all of the other major themes of discipleship that appear in Luke's Gospel recur, with greater explication, in his Acts. In particular: being rooted in and shaped by the apostolic tradition (cf. 2:42, *passim*); being dependent on God in prayer (cf. 1:14, 24-25; 2:42; 6:4; 12:5); being committed to a lifestyle that allows no allegiance to take the place of allegiance to Jesus *(passim);* and being concerned for the poor, the imprisoned, the blind, and the oppressed (cf. 2:44-46; 4:32–5:11).

But in Acts Luke never refers to the twelve disciples (Judas having been replaced by Matthias) with the term "disciple" *(mathētēs).* He calls them that less frequently than the other evangelists in his Gospel, and he never does so in Acts. Nor in the early part of Acts does he call believers "disciples" *(mathētai).* Rather, in 1:16 he refers to believers as "brothers" *(adelphoi,* or "brothers and sisters," inclusively understood). It is, in fact, only in Acts 6:1-7, when portraying problems that arose with the influx of Hellenistic Jewish believers, that Luke first uses "disciples" of believers in Jesus. And it is in that passage that he first brings all these designations together in describing the constituency of the early church: "In those days when the number of *the disciples* was increasing, . . . *the Twelve* gathered all *the disciples* together and said: . . . *Brothers and sisters,* . . . So the word of God spread, and the number of *the disciples* in Jerusalem increased rapidly." Thereafter, Luke uses "disciple/disciples" and "brothers and sisters" interchangeably for believers in Jesus ("disciple/disciples" some twenty-nine times; "brothers and sisters" thirty-two times). He also reports that the apostles addressed Jewish audiences as "men and brothers," "men, brothers, and fathers," or simply "brothers" (e.g., 2:29; 3:17; 7:2; 13:26, 38; 22:1; 23:1, 6; 28:17) and that Jews referred to one another as "brothers" (e.g., 2:37; 13:15; 28:21; cf. Luke 6:41-42).

Just what to make of (1) Luke's nonuse of "disciple/disciples" for the Twelve in Acts, whereas they were so designated in his Gospel, and (2) his interchangeable use of "disciples" and "brothers and sisters" for believers in Jesus, with the latter seeming to be his preference, may be debated. Perhaps it was because "disciple," though common among the various philosophical schools of the day, had only recently become acceptable in religious associations. On such an understanding, one could argue that being more controlled in the writing of his Gospel by his sources, which reflected the rising use of "disciple" in the religious parlance of Palestine, Luke continued to use that language in his Gospel; but being freer in the writing of Acts, and knowing that "disciple" was not a common designation for a follower of a religious figure in the Hellenistic world, he may have wanted to tone down that term somewhat in favor of the expression "brother." And that is certainly a possible and plausible explanation.

Just as likely, however, is the explanation that Luke himself — for both theological and egalitarian reasons — felt some reticence in the postresurrection period about continuing to use "disciple/disciples" for the Twelve and for other believers in Jesus. For the term "disciple," while carrying many important nuances, also suggested ideas about subordination and inequality, whereas "brother" carried more the nuances of familial oneness and equality. On such a rationale, it could be argued that Luke saw no problem in describing relations between Jesus and his followers during his earthly ministry in "master-disciple" or "teacher-pupil" language, but that in describing relations within the church he preferred to speak of believers as "brothers and sisters" — while continuing, as well, to refer to them as "disciples," evidently trusting that his interchangeable use of the terms would be self-defining and so aid his readers' understanding. In all likelihood, it may be further proposed, both explanations should be seen as being in some manner complimentary rather than mutually exclusive.

Of more importance for our consideration here, however, is that with Luke's preference for designating believers in Jesus as "brothers and sisters" — though, again, without refusing to call them "disciples" — two somewhat inchoate features of discipleship in Luke's Gospel take on greater significance in his Acts. The first is that of Luke's exemplary emphasis, which is worked out in his Gospel in terms of following Jesus and in Acts in terms of patterning one's life by the example of the apostles, particularly Paul. In the Gospel Luke has highlighted Jesus' exemplary life of service (cf. 22:27; also 6:40), his exemplary praying (cf. 22:39-46), and his exemplary cross-bearing (cf. 23:26; also 9:23). But without denying the importance of Jesus in the evangelist's thought, Paul was, in reality, Luke's great hero. And so in the portrayals of Paul's strenuous exertions in carrying out his missions, his magnanimous attitudes toward his colleagues, his staunch defenses against opposition, and his magnificent missionary sermons (especially in Acts 13–14) and trial speeches (chs. 22–26) — all of which are lauded by Luke, though probably more than they were by Paul himself and certainly more than they were by some of his converts (especially at Corinth) — the example is set before believers of the one who "turned the world upside down" (17:6, freely translated).

A second feature of discipleship that Luke expresses more fully in his Acts is that of a developing life of relationship with Christ and of service to others. Development is a theme that Luke hinted at in his Gospel, particularly in closing off his infancy narrative with "The child grew and became strong; he was filled with wisdom, and the grace of God was upon him" (2:20) and "Jesus grew in wisdom and stature, and in favor with God and people" (2:52). But it underlies all of Acts as Luke seeks to show how "the word of God" progressed from its earliest Jewish Christian roots to its full expression in Paul's ministry to Gentiles, with finally "the kingdom of God" being preached in Rome itself "boldly and without hindrance" (Acts 28:31). And implicit in all these depictions of progress and development is the exemplary exhortation for believers also to progress and develop in their lives of faith and service.

8. Patterns of Discipleship for Today

Luke has frequently been accused of shifting the focus of early Christian thought from the *eschaton*, the eschatological future, to the *sēmeron*, the present, "today." Many, in fact, have seen him perverting the original gospel by a shift from an imminent coming of Christ to the everyday life of Christian living, from the charismatic to the ecclesiastical, from following Jesus (i.e., orthopraxis) to preaching about and believing in Jesus (i.e., orthodoxy), and from worship to mission. To some extent, of course, much of this is true. We may acknowledge the truthfulness of many of these observations without also acceding to the accusations that they imply. For Luke has not set aside eschatological expectations (cf. Luke 17:22-37; 21:5-36; Acts 11), nor has he minimized in any way the work of the Spirit, following Jesus, or the worship of God by his people. Nonetheless, it is quite true that Luke's major interest in the writing of his two volumes seems to have been the everyday matter of Christian discipleship — that is, in setting out for his readers the self-consciousness that one should have and the manner in which one should live as a follower of Christ.

Luke makes no catalogue of the qualities, characteristics, attitudes, or actions involved in Christian discipleship. What he presents are por-

trayals of the ministry of Jesus and of the missions of the early church
— particularly, the missions of his hero Paul. But those portrayals evidence from beginning to end their author's distinctive redactional "spin" in their telling. And from those redacted portrayals one can infer that Luke meant to teach his readers, whether of his day or ours, at least the following things about Christian discipleship:

1. Discipleship is based on what Christ has effected for the redemption of humanity.
2. Discipleship must always be rooted in and shaped by the apostolic tradition.
3. Discipleship needs always to be dependent on God and submissive to his will, hence the importance of prayer.
4. Discipleship must always recognize the presence and power of the Holy Spirit.
5. Discipleship is to be involved in prophetic proclamation, with that proclamation focused on the work of Jesus.
6. Discipleship is to cherish, both in thought and in action, the understanding of God's grace and the gospel as being universal.
7. Discipleship is to be committed to a lifestyle that allows no allegiance to take the place of allegiance to Jesus.
8. Discipleship is to be concerned for the poor, the imprisoned, the blind, and the oppressed.
9. Discipleship is to follow the examples of Jesus and the apostles, particularly Paul, in matters of service, prayer, and cross-bearing.
10. Discipleship is to be a life of development in both one's faith and one's practice.

Selected Bibliography

Beck, B. E. " 'Imitatio Christi' and the Lucan Passion Narrative," in *Suffering and Martyrdom in the New Testament: Studies Presented to G. M. Styler,* ed. W. Horbury and B. McNeil. Cambridge: Cambridge University Press, 1981, 28-47.

Cassidy, R. J., and Scharper, P. J., ed. *Political Issues in Luke-Acts.* Maryknoll: Orbis, 1983.

Fleddermann, H. T. "The Demands of Discipleship: Matt 8,19-22, Par. Luke 9,57-62," in *The Four Gospels 1992: Festschrift Frans Neirynck,* 3 vols., ed. F. van Segbroeck, C. M. Tuckett, G. van Belle, J. Verheyden. Leuven: University Press, 1992, 1.541-61.

Fitzmyer, J. A. "Discipleship in the Lucan Writings," *Luke the Theologian: Aspects of his Teaching.* New York/Toronto: Paulist, 1989, 117-45.

————. *The Gospel According to Luke.* 2 vols., Anchor Bible, New York: Doubleday, 1985.

Hengel, M. *The Charismatic Leader and His Followers,* tr. J. Greig. Edinburgh: T. & T. Clark/New York: Crossroad, 1981.

Johnson, L. T. *The Literary Function of Possessions in Luke-Acts.* Missoula: Scholars, 1977.

Longenecker, R. N. "The Acts of the Apostles," in *The Expositor's Bible Commentary,* 12 vols., ed. F. E. Gaebelein. Grand Rapids: Zondervan, 1981, 9.205-573.

Marshall, I. H. *The Gospel of Luke: A Commentary on the Greek Text.* New International Greek Testament Commentary, Grand Rapids: Eerdmans, 1978.

Martin, R. P. "Salvation and Discipleship in Luke's Gospel," *Interpretation* 30 (1976) 366-80.

Nickelsburg, G. W. E., "Riches, the Rich and God's Judgment in 1 Enoch 92–105 and the Gospel according to Luke," *New Testament Studies* 25 (1979) 324-44.

Rengstorf, K. H. *"manthanō, ktl.,"* in *Theological Dictionary of the New Testament,* 10 vols., ed. G. Kittel and G. Friedrich, tr. G. W. Bromiley. Grand Rapids: Eerdmans, 1964-76, 4.390-461.

Schweizer, E. *Lordship and Discipleship.* London: SCM, 1960.

————. *Luke: A Challenge to Present Theology.* Atlanta: John Knox, 1982.

Talbert, C. H. "Discipleship in Luke-Acts," in *Discipleship in the New Testament,* ed. F. F. Segovia. Philadelphia: Fortress, 1985, 62-75.

————. *Literary Patterns, Theological Themes, and the Genre of Luke-Acts.* Missoula: Scholars, 1974.

They Believed in Him:
Discipleship in the Johannine Tradition

MELVYN R. HILLMER

The confession made by Thomas in the Fourth Gospel's postresurrection story represents a climax to that Gospel's narrative. For Thomas affirms the risen Christ in the words "My Lord and my God" (20:28) — thereby confessing by his use of the first person pronoun that he belongs to Jesus as his willing subject. Thomas is identified as "one of the twelve" (20:24) and he speaks on behalf of all of the disciples. More than that, however, his confession is the proper response of every Christian disciple — of all believers in Jesus and of the church at all times — to the revelation in Christ.

Thomas came to this recognition through the visible presence of Jesus after his crucifixion and resurrection, a privilege not possible for later generations. But it is a greater act of faith to believe and to make this christological confession without the immediacy of the physical presence of Christ. So a blessing is pronounced on "those who have not seen and yet have come to believe" (20:29). And thus this same confession is appropriate for anyone who would be Jesus' follower today, for everyone who would be Jesus' disciple must confess him as "My Lord and my God" in personal allegiance.

Before entering directly into the theme of discipleship in the Johannine tradition, two introductory issues need to be treated — even though, of necessity, only in a rather general manner. The first concerns the nature of the material, particularly in the Fourth Gospel. For though

77

the narrative of the Fourth Gospel is the story of the ministry of Jesus in association with his followers, interpretation of that Gospel is complicated by the fact that the story has been presented in such a fashion that it can be read on two levels at the same time: (1) as portraying the story of Jesus and his immediate disciples and (2) as reflecting issues and concerns within the community in which that written Gospel came to birth. On the one hand, then, John's Gospel is the story of the historical Jesus and of events taking place in his time; on the other, however, it speaks to the concerns of the community out of which it came.

The second introductory matter to which the reader needs to be alerted concerns authorship and provenance. For it is generally agreed today that the Fourth Gospel and the Johannine letters are products of a particular group of Christians who based themselves on the witness and ministry of the apostle John, but whose writings evidence various levels of editing within their particular Christian community. The community out of which these writings came has been described by a number of different terms: a church or group of churches, a school, a circle, a conventicle on the fringes of the church, or simply a community (cf. Brown, *Community*, who provides the most thorough study of the history of the group, and whose term "community" will be used most often in what follows). It evidences characteristics belonging to each of these descriptions. What seems to have been the case, however, is that it was a relatively small community of early Christians who were deeply concerned about life as a group of believers in the corporate body of the church, about the church's theological formulations, and about the church's mission in the world.

1. The Identity of the Disciples

The disciples in John's Gospel are at one and the same time those who responded to Jesus during his earthly life and those who were believers in Jesus when the Gospel was written. Some texts must clearly be interpreted in the context of the life of the community at the latter time because they reflect language appropriate to the concerns of such a later setting (e.g., 9:22; cf. Martyn, *History and Theology*). Thus, for the most part, "disciples" in the Fourth Gospel are those who were with Jesus during his earthly ministry *and* those who made up the Johannine group of believers in Jesus. At the same time, however, the same understanding of discipleship characterizes all true believers in every period of history.

Many times in John's Gospel it is difficult to know exactly what is meant by references to Jesus' disciples who were with him during his ministry, whether a small group of followers or a much larger number. Their identity is worked out largely in terms of contrasts with other elements in the church and society. Thus the disciples of Jesus are portrayed as standing over against the followers of John the Baptist, "the Jews," society at large referred to as "the world," certain crypto-believers, and some other Christians, perhaps of the apostolic churches.

The first disciples of Jesus came from among the ranks of the followers of John the Baptist (1:36-51). John is portrayed as the first to bear witness to Jesus, identifying him as "the Lamb of God who takes away the sin of the world" (1:29, 35). Two of the disciples of John, at his urging, immediately follow Jesus, remaining with him in anticipation of a more complete following later. They address him as Rabbi, translated "teacher," which was the usual way for a disciple to address his master. Andrew is identified as one of the two who left John to follow Jesus, while the other is never named. Andrew finds his brother Simon (Peter) and announces to him: "We have found the Messiah." It is noteworthy that Peter is not the first of the disciples in chronological terms, nor, as we shall note later, was he first in rank. Then Philip and Nathanael are called, completing the list at this point.

One of the distinctive features in the Johannine account of the calling of the disciples is the certainty that exists from the outset that Jesus is the Messiah. Most of the christological titles in John's Gospel, in fact, occur at this point. There is no hint that the disciples only slowly became aware of who Jesus was, as in the Synoptic Gospels.

The Fourth Gospel never provides a complete list of the disciples. In addition to the four identified at their call, only Thomas (10:4; 16:5; 20:24-29), the sons of Zebedee (21:2), and Judas (12:4; 13:30; 18:2) are specifically named. The evangelist shows little interest in "the Twelve" as a group, and he never refers to them as "apostles" in a technical sense. The usual designation is simply "the disciples," with considerable ambiguity as to whether it is the Twelve who are in mind or a larger (or perhaps smaller) number.

Ernst Haenchen, commenting on references to "his disciples" in the story of the encounter between Jesus and the woman at the well in Samaria (4:31, 33), says that here and throughout the Gospel the disciples appear to be a unified group without individualization (*John* 224). Bruce Malina, on the other hand, holds that John presents a range of individual types of people in his story, including the frequent naming of the disciples as they play a part in narrative or dialogue (*Sociolinguistic Perspective* 9) — which observation, among other arguments, leads him to place the Johannine community in the weak group/low grid quadrant in social-scientific terms. What seems clear in all of this, however, is that the author of the Fourth Gospel was concerned to identify specific followers or to refer to "the disciples" generally, but not to give an important place to "the Twelve" as such.

While the first disciples of Jesus came from among the followers of John the Baptist, not all of John's disciples changed their allegiance. A group of disciples of the Baptist continued to exist in the time of the early church (cf. Acts 19:1-7). According to the Fourth Gospel, John continued to preach and baptize during the ministry of Jesus (3:22-30; 4:1). And in each instance where the Baptist appears in John's Gospel, there is a negative statement made either by him or about him. John is portrayed as saying emphatically: "I am not the Messiah" (1:20; 3:28); "I am not worthy to untie" Jesus' sandals (1:27); and "He must increase but I must decrease" (3:30). This emphatic affirmation that Jesus is the Messiah, not John, and the sharpness of the denials suggest that there was a tension between the Johannine community and the followers of the Baptist when the Gospel was being written. Robert Kysar argues, alternatively, that such put-downs of the Baptist may be in the Gospel because of charges by Jewish leaders that Jesus was nothing more than a prophet similar to John (*Maverick Gospel* 34). The evidence, however, seems more in keeping with the former suggestion, that the Fourth Gospel asserts firmly that Jesus, not John, is the Messiah, and so to be followed.

The disciples also stand over against "the Jews," a term frequently used in the Gospel to designate those who reject Jesus. Relatively little distinction is made among the various sects of Judaism. Instead, opponents of Jesus are simply identified as "the Jews" (seventy occurrences in John, compared with five or six in each of the Synoptic Gospels). The term is in John's Gospel almost a technical title for the religious authorities, particularly those in Jerusalem, who were hostile to Jesus (cf. Brown, *John* lxxi).

Not only, however, was the hostility of the Jewish authorities to the historical Jesus in mind in John's references to "the Jews," but also the situation of conflict between the Jewish synagogue and the Johannine church. At the heart of the conflict was the Christian affirmation that Jesus is the Messiah and the firm refusal of the Jewish leaders to accept this claim. The conflict became so sharp, in fact, that anyone making the Christian confession was put out of the synagogue.

On three occasions John's Gospel refers to the removal of believers in Jesus from the synagogue: in 9:22; 12:42; and 16:2, with the language in each case being that of a formal decision and formal dismissal. In the discussion following the healing of the blind man by Jesus in chapter 9, for example, the man's parents avoid questioning because they feared the Jews — for, as the evangelist comments, "The Jews had already agreed that anyone who confessed Jesus to be the Messiah would be put out of the synagogue" (9:22). The language is technical and the verb "agree" means to reach a formal decision or make a decree. Literally, a person so dealt with would become an "excommunicant" *(aposynagōgos)* from the synagogue, would be completely dismissed. We are dealing here not with spontaneous acts or a temporary removal, but with a definite agreement reached by some authoritative Jewish group. The conflict between Johannine Christians and the Jews had reached a level of intense hostility, with, undoubtedly, some believers in Jesus having been excluded from the synagogue.

This is the situation that came about around A.D. 90 (cf. Brown, *John* lxxv; Martyn, *History and Theology* 56ff.), with John's Gospel reflecting that situation. It is questionable, however, whether it is possible to locate such a decision firmly in the Jewish councils of that period. It may have been made somewhat earlier. But whenever it was made, this Jewish decision to excommunicate believers in Jesus from the synagogue must have had a traumatic effect on the Johannine community. For now to confess Jesus to be the Messiah not only marked the believer in Jesus as a disciple of Jesus, but also served to excommunicate that believer from the Jewish synagogue.

A further definition of discipleship is to be seen in separation from "the world," which is another term with negative connotations, for the most part, in the Fourth Gospel. At times, "the world" means the whole world of humanity, as, for example, in the statement "God so loved the world that he gave his only Son" (3:16). More often, however, it designates those who reject Jesus. In this sense, "the world" is almost identical with "the Jews."

Jesus is an alien in this world; he is the one who came down from heaven (e.g., 6:38) and is "not of this world" (17:14-16; cf. 8:23). The motif of the descent and ascent of Jesus, particularly as the Son of Man, is a central christological theme in John's Gospel, which depicts him as the one who came from heaven and returns to the place from which he came (cf. Meeks, "Man from Heaven"). But this was offensive — even scandalous — to the Jews (cf. 6:60-70). A similar interpretation of this high christology is elaborated by Jerome Neyrey in the formulation "equal to God but not of this world" (*Ideology of Revolt* 94). Both Meeks and Neyrey have offered helpful insights into the social and cultural situation of the Johannine community, which was a group apart from the world of its time and so suffered social alienation and even persecution.

The disciples, like Jesus, do not belong to this world. The criteria for authentic membership in the group of disciples or in the community are seen in the discussion with Nicodemus in 3:1-21. Nicodemus is a Pharisee, a member of the Jewish ruling council, and hence stands for the Jewish people. Jesus speaks to him of the necessity of rebirth (vv 3, 5), but Nicodemus fails to understand what this means. The technique of misunderstanding is found frequently in John, and it provides Jesus with the occasion to elaborate and clarify whatever is the point at issue. Opponents and disciples alike understand the words of Jesus only on a superficial level, or even incorrectly. In the episode with Nicodemus, Jesus speaks of a birth from above, a birth from the Spirit, in contrast to physical birth of the flesh. The disciple who experiences this rebirth is related to the world above, the world of spirit, to which Jesus belongs and from which he has come. In contrast, the Jews are part of the world and belong to the realm of the flesh: "You are from below; I am from above. You are of this world; I am not of this world" (8:23). The disciples, however, do not belong to this world: "You are not of the world, just as I am not of the world" (17:14).

Followers of Jesus experience separation from the disciples of John the Baptist, from the Jews, and from the world. The language of the Fourth Gospel in presenting this separation has been described as "antilanguage" (cf. Malina, *Sociolinguistic Perspective*, based largely on linguistic studies by M. Halliday). Antilanguage is used by an antisocietal collectivity. It creates and expresses a reality that is an alternate reality, constructed to function as an alternative to society at large. John's Gospel in its clear contrasts between Jesus and his disciples, on the one hand, and the world, on the other, has been described also as the language of revolt against the world (cf. Neyrey, *Ideology of Revolt* 106). The perspective is first a christological one: "Equal to God." But Jesus' followers were also alienated from the world: "Not of this world." Thus discipleship in John's Gospel means (1) to be born from above, (2) to be related to the realm of the Spirit, and (3) to be not of this world — even as Jesus was and was not!

To some degree, the understanding of discipleship in the Fourth Gospel reflects the situation of the Johannine community and has to do with believers of any historical period. The distinction between the larger group of followers and the Twelve is set out in John 6 as focused in their response to Jesus as the bread that came from heaven, the Son of Man, who also ascends to where he was before. This was a hard teaching, which led some to leave: "From this time many of his disciples turned back and no longer followed him" (v 66). They left because they were not really believers and because the Father had not enabled them to come.

In contrast to those who have an inadequate faith, the Twelve are those who not only believe but are also chosen by Jesus himself. Peter is the one who speaks for the group, expressing the true confession in response to Jesus' question as to whether they, too, want to leave like the others, when he says: "Lord, to whom shall we go? You have the words of eternal life. We believe and know that you are the Holy One of God" (vv 68-69). True disciples are those who break through the offense of the One from Heaven and make the proper christological confession. So from chapter 12 through to the end of the farewell discourses in chapters 14–17, the disciples are in focus — though it is not clear whether reference to the disciples is intended to mean only the Twelve, or whether others are included as well.

The affirmation of faith expressed by Peter compares closely with the words of Martha that speak of Jesus as the resurrection and the life: "I believe that you are the Christ, the Son of God, who was to come into the world" (11:27). Martha also calls Jesus "Teacher" and addresses him as "Lord" (11:27, 28), which are the same designations used by the disciples (13:13). Are Martha and Mary, therefore, to be included among the disciples of Jesus? Other women were present at Jesus' crucifixion, along with "the Beloved Disciple." But none of the other disciples was there. Mary Magdalene is also presented as the first to witness the removal of the stone from the tomb and the one who had the first encounter with the risen Lord. Yet women are never explicitly called disciples in John's Gospel — even though in their recognition of Jesus as Master, in Martha's affirmation of faith, in their attendance at the cross, and in the presence of Mary at the tomb, women evidenced the characteristics of discipleship, and that in a more faithful fashion than their male counterparts.

One further matter in the identification of the disciples in John deserves brief mention: the references to certain secret or crypto-disciples who were evidently afraid to be open in their response to Jesus (cf. Brown, *Community*). Nicodemus, a ruler of the Jews, who came to Jesus at night and continued to be a part of the Jewish ruling council, was one of these (cf. 3:1-21; 7:50-52). Joseph of Arimathea "was a disciple of Jesus, but secretly because he feared the Jews" (19:38). Others also were afraid to make open confession of their allegiance to Jesus, because of the Pharisees and for fear that they would be put out of the synagogue (12:42). The true disciple, however, the one who has real faith, must be open in acknowledging Jesus, whereas secrecy only shows that the crypto-disciple does not truly believe.

2. Discipleship as Relational

Discipleship in the Fourth Gospel is presented in terms of relationship with Jesus and as action, with a whole series of verbs used to express both aspects. There are close connections between relationship and action, but for our present purposes of analysis it is helpful to make a distinction between them.

The first of Jesus' signs was done at Cana of Galilee as he changed water to wine at a wedding feast. At the end of the story the evangelist writes, "He thus revealed his glory, and his disciples believed in him" (2:11). The statement of purpose at the end of John's Gospel also indicates that the proper response to Jesus is to believe that he is "the Christ, the Son of God" (20:31). The verb "believe" characterizes the true disciple throughout. It is used about one hundred times in this Gospel, which is an obvious indication of the tremendous importance that the evangelist placed on it. The same kind of statistic is true of the verb "know," which occurs with almost equal frequency and almost equivalent meaning. But while "believe" and "know" are used in John's Gospel with central significance, their cognate nouns "faith" and "knowledge" are totally absent — undoubtedly because of connotations associated with these nouns in a developing Gnosticism.

The objects of the verbs "believe" and "know" are virtually the same throughout the Fourth Gospel. The disciple is the one who believes in Jesus and through Jesus believes in the Father who sent him (e.g., 3:16, 36; 5:24; 6:29; 12:44). A variety of terms express the author's understanding of believing. It is to believe in Jesus (3:16), to believe in the Son (3:36), to believe that he is the Messiah, the Son of God (11:27; 20:31), to believe his works (10:38), and to believe in the One who sent him (12:44). But while several expressions are used, the meaning of all of them is virtually identical: they emphasize the necessity of believing in Christ in order to have eternal life. For it is in believing that relationship with Jesus is established and maintained. The statement of purpose for writing the Gospel is expressed in the same terms: "These [signs] are written that you may believe [or "continue to believe"] that Jesus is the Christ, the Son of God, and that believing you may have life in his name" (20:31).

In an almost identical fashion the verb "know" involves the same themes, as in Peter's words of confession in 6:69: "We have come to believe and know that you are the Holy One of God" (cf. 11:27). The content of knowing is Jesus, to know that he has been sent by the Father, that he is the Messiah, and — as with believing — that all this is related to eternal life: "This is eternal life, that they may know you, the only true God, and Jesus Christ whom you have sent" (17:3).

Discipleship, therefore, is dependent on believing in Jesus. The faith of the disciples is highlighted throughout John's Gospel — even though they consistently fail to understand what is happening, often revealing a remarkable lack of insight (cf. 4:33; 13:1-11, 37; 14:1-7; 16:18). But true understanding was not possible until after the resurrection (cf. 20:9), when the Holy Spirit came. For it is the Holy Spirit who will "teach you everything, and remind you of all that I have said to you" (14:26). The whole story of Jesus, in fact, is written from a post-Easter perspective, and therefore could not have been understood until after the events of crucifixion and resurrection. It is the role of the Paraclete, the Holy Spirit, who was promised to the disciples and who came after the resurrection, to provide the interpretation of the words and actions of Jesus (cf. 16:12-15).

The Johannine community claimed that its interpretations and teachings were developed under the guidance of the Spirit. But the disciples during Jesus' earthly ministry could have had only a partial grasp of the meaning of Jesus. Yet it is important to note that, even though the disciples did not understand all that was happening, they still believed in Jesus. And it is this primary mark of discipleship — that of believing in Jesus — that is highlighted throughout John's Gospel.

This relational feature of discipleship is made closely personal in John 10 by means of the image of the good shepherd and his flock. For the good shepherd takes a personal interest in his flock: he calls his own sheep by name, and the sheep follow him because they know his voice (vv 3, 4). The good shepherd knows his sheep and his sheep know him (v 14), which is a relationship comparable to that of Jesus and his Father (v 15). The expression "follow" signifies to follow in faith, and to "know his voice" means to know the revelation (cf. Schnackenburg, *John* 283).

The image of the true vine and the branches in 15:1-17 emphasizes most fully the intimacy of the relationship between Jesus and his disciples. This is the last of the "I am" sayings in the Fourth Gospel, all of which present Jesus as the fulfillment of the religious hopes and aspirations of the Jewish people. The imagery of the "I am" sayings is drawn from the Old Testament and Jewish tradition. The predicates present Jesus as living water, the bread of life, the door, the good shepherd, the way, the truth, the life, and the resurrection. He is also the "I am" in the absolute sense (cf. 8:58). Thus used absolutely, "I am" identifies Jesus with God, who in Exod 3:14 speaks of himself in the same absolute manner. And as Jerome Neyrey notes, the confession of Christ in terms of the Johannine "I am" expressions is a criterion of authentic discipleship, linking those who make such a confession with the world above (Neyrey, *Ideology of Revolt* 106).

In the saying "I am the true vine," it is the image of Jesus as the vine that is foremost, although the Father as the vinedresser stands in the background. The relationship of the believer with Christ is patterned on that of the Son with the Father. For as Jesus says, "as the Father has loved me, so have I loved you (v 9). Both the Father and the Son are involved in the redemptive action. The background for the imagery is the Old Testament, where Israel is often depicted as a vine or vineyard, although the nation never fulfilled its calling to be fruitful for God (cf. Beasley-Murray, *John* 273, for an extensive discussion). In contrast, Jesus is the true vine who now brings fulfillment to reality.

The focus in John 15, however, is on Jesus as the vine and his disciples as the branches. They are called to abide or remain in him, just as the branches remain in the vine, the source of life and sustenance. To fail to remain in him is to be unfruitful and to face judgment. It is to remain alone. To remain in Jesus is to respond in faith to him and his revelation. It is to accept him as the Messiah, the Son of God, the one sent by the Father. It is to be in union with him in a close, personal relationship.

To remain in Jesus is further expressed as remaining in his love (15:9, 10). This is a development of what it means to remain in him, now understood in parallel with the recognition that throughout his life Jesus remained in his Father's love. The disciple who remains in Jesus' love demonstrates this in relationships with others (which will be discussed further below).

The relational aspect of discipleship is seen also in Jesus' use of the term "friends" for his followers: "I no longer call you servants. . . . I have called you friends" (v 14). This is directly related to the love Jesus shows and is distinguished from servanthood. For to be a friend is to share a personal union and to be made aware of the plans and purposes of the other. Thus just as Jesus learned from the Father, so now he makes known his purposes to his disciples. It may be sufficient to look to the Old Testament for examples of those who are friends of God, including Abraham (cf. 2 Chron 20:7; Isa 41:8) and Moses (cf. Exod 33:11). It is also to be noted, however, that friendship was important in the tradition of the Greek philosophical schools — as can be seen, for example, in the Pythagorean maxim "Friends have all things in common" (cf. Culpepper, *Johannine School* 250-51).

Finally in connection with discipleship as relational, some mention must be made of that puzzling figure in the Fourth Gospel usually referred to as "the Beloved Disciple." This disciple is presented as the one who had the closest relationship with Jesus during his ministry. But his appearance in the story of Jesus also raises some difficult questions.

The first appearance of the Beloved Disciple in John's Gospel is in the account of Jesus washing his disciples' feet in 13:1-30 — unless, of course, the unnamed disciple among the first followers is the same person (cf. 1:35ff.), which is possible but unlikely. In the setting of the meal of Jesus with his disciples in chapter 13, one is identified simply as "the one whom Jesus loved" (v 23). He is said to have reclined on the bosom of Jesus (NRSV translates "reclining next to him"), using identical terminology as used to express Jesus' relation to God as being "in the bosom of the Father" (1:18). This disciple, who was in closest physical proximity to Jesus at the supper, is singled out as the one specially loved by Jesus. References to "the other disciple" refer to the same figure, for the two terms are used together in the statement "the other disciple whom Jesus loved" (20:2).

This disciple appears at the trial of Jesus, where he was known to the High Priest (18:15), and at the cross, where he was the only one of the disciples present — the only one of them who was a witness to Jesus' death (19:26). To him was given the care of Jesus' mother. He was also the first to arrive at the empty tomb and the first to believe in the risen Lord (20:3, 8). And in the epilogue, he is the one who gave testimony to the things written in the Fourth Gospel, and so, clearly, had an important place in the Johannine tradition (21:24; cf. also 19:35).

The Beloved Disciple is regarded in John's Gospel as the ideal disciple of Jesus. He is the one loved by Jesus, the only one to witness the crucifixion, the first to see and believe at the empty tomb, an eye-witness, and the one who gives testimony. Some have asked whether he should be considered a historical person or an idealized figure. The way in which he is presented in the Fourth Gospel makes it appear that he was a historical person who stood particularly close to Jesus. He is also, however, presented as representative of the true disciple, evidencing in his loving relationship and faithfulness what authentic discipleship is (cf. Nicodemus as representative of believing Jews and the woman at the well as representative of believing Samaritans).

But difficulties arise when one attempts to determine the identity of the Beloved Disciple. Tradition, of course, has held that he is John, the Son of Zebedee, who was also the author of the Fourth Gospel. Interpreters today, however, often come to a different conclusion. Alan Culpepper notes that both Raymond Brown and Rudolf Schnackenburg once held that John was the Beloved Disciple, but have more recently come to believe that, while an eyewitness of the ministry of Jesus, he was not one of the Twelve. Culpepper himself agrees with this position (*John, Son of Zebedee* 73), as does George Beasley-Murray (*John* lxxi). And such a view should probably be accepted, albeit somewhat cautiously, as there is no clear evidence in the Gospel itself to enable us to reach a firm conclusion regarding this disciple's identity.

It seems evident, however, that the Beloved Disciple played a central role in the Johannine community as an eyewitness of the events recorded in the Fourth Gospel and as the one who testified to and interpreted those events. He therefore had a formative role in the teaching and development of the tradition on which the community was based. He was not himself the author of the Gospel, but the one who testified to what was written in a trustworthy and authoritative manner.

Furthermore, with respect to relations between the Beloved Disciple and Peter, it needs to be noted that at each point in the Fourth Gospel where the two appear together the Beloved Disciple is portrayed as superior to Peter (cf. 18:15-16; 20:3-10, 21). There does not seem to be any polemic against Peter, but his secondary position suggests that in the Johannine community he was not regarded as the first of the disciples, as he was in other churches. The disciple Jesus loved seems to have had the central and authoritative place in the Johannine community.

Whoever the Beloved Disciple was, and whatever his role was among the disciples and in his community, he represents in John's Gospel the ideal of Christian discipleship. His relationship with Jesus was one of loving intimacy. And in that relationship, discipleship as relational is seen most clearly — for a disciple of Jesus not only believes in Jesus but also remains in his love.

3. Discipleship as Action

In addition to discipleship involving a relationship with Jesus, the Fourth Gospel also speaks of what the disciple is to do. Foremost among the verbs that the evangelist uses in speaking of discipleship as action is "follow" *(akolouthein),* which both brackets and dominates all of the material of his Gospel. For at the beginning of his Gospel (1:35-51) and in the epilogue (21:20-23) it is made clear that to be a disciple of Jesus is to follow him, and throughout the Gospel this theme of following Jesus constantly reappears.

In some cases "follow" is used in a neutral sense of mere physical following, of simply going about with Jesus (e.g., 6:6; 18:15). In most instances, however, the verb has the more particular meaning of following as a disciple, as at the call of the first disciples who leave John the Baptist to follow Jesus (1:37-43). To be a disciple of Jesus, therefore, is to accept him as the Messiah, to live in accordance with his teachings, and to pattern one's life after him.

The call to follow Jesus also has a clearly spiritual sense in the recognition that he is the light of the world, as he says, "Whoever follows me will never walk in darkness but will have the light of life" (8:12). The setting for this statement is the Feast of Tabernacles with its use of lights. And the reference to light would have recalled for the Jewish

89

people the pillar of fire in the wilderness and the story of how Israel followed it to the promised land. To follow Jesus as the light of the world, therefore, is to have life and eschatological deliverance.

Furthermore, John's Gospel also speaks of "following" Jesus into death. The early sections of the farewell discourses (chs. 14–17) are dominated by the theme of going away and coming again, which are variously understood as going into death to come again in resurrection, leaving this world so that the Spirit may come, or going in ascension to come again in the parousia. In the introduction to the farewell discourses (13:31-38) it is clear that the first of these is in mind, that Jesus is going away into death and that the disciples cannot follow. "Where I am going," Jesus said, "you cannot follow now" (v 36). They cannot follow because this going into death is the eschatological salvation and is his alone to accomplish. Peter understands, partially, that Jesus' death is involved, and Jesus tells him that he cannot participate in that now — but also that he will follow later in the sense of martyrdom.

To follow Jesus, then, is more than simply to go around with him as the crowds do. It is to follow in the way that is life, to follow his teachings and his example.

Several other verbs of action are used in 15:1-17, the passage that depicts Jesus as the vine and the disciples as the branches. These verbs are intertwined with the relational features highlighted by the use of the vine-branches metaphor. The central purpose of the branches, of course, is to bear fruit, which is a possibility only so long as a branch remains in the vine — receiving life, strength, and nourishment from it. Separated from the vine, the branch is unfruitful and subject to judgment: "Apart from me you can do nothing" (v 5).

But chapter 15 gives no definition of what it is to bear fruit. It undoubtedly includes love, which is a demonstration of the vitality of faith in Christ, with a call to reciprocal love being presented in the following verses. It also includes involvement in mission, bringing men and women to the same kind of faith and love. For those who believe through the preaching of the followers of Jesus are the fruit of the vine (cf. Beasley-Murray, *John* 273), and in fulfilling this mission of bearing fruit the followers of Jesus show that they are indeed his disciples. The original readers of the Fourth Gospel would have interpreted this to mean working for that which strengthens and expands the community.

Disciples of Jesus are also instructed to obey his commandments. Only one commandment of Jesus is given in John's Gospel, and that is to love each other (15:12). This is directly related to the love that Christ has for his own, which in turn is based on the love of God, as in the assertion that "God so loved the world that he gave his only Son" (3:16). God gave his Son in order to bring eternal life to those who believe; that giving is thus the supreme expression of God's love for humanity. In like manner, the whole event of Jesus, especially his crucifixion, is understood in John's Gospel as an act of love, for "no one has greater love than this: to lay down one's life for one's friends" (15:13). The love of God, the love of Christ, and the love of the disciples, therefore, together constitute one profound whole.

The love commandment in John's Gospel is developed most extensively in the farewell discourses in chapters 13–17 (cf. Brown, *John* 573-603, for a helpful discussion of the literary genre of these discourses). The theme is introduced in a dialogue with Peter in chapter 13. Here Jesus says, "I give you a new commandment: that you love one another" (v 34). The act of service in washing the disciples' feet is an act of love, and they are called to follow the example thus set by the Lord. In a sense, of course, this is not a new commandment, for others have called on their followers to love. But it is new in that the mission of Jesus was a decisively new situation in the affairs of humanity, and the commandment to love is grounded "in the new reality of God's love manifest in the Son" (Furnish, *Love Command* 138). Those who keep this commandment demonstrate to the world that they are disciples of Jesus. And keeping this commandment, says Jesus, is the basic requirement for true discipleship.

Following Jesus and showing love for one another are directly related to service, as is dramatically portrayed in the episode of Jesus washing his disciples' feet. The relationship of the disciples with Jesus is one in which he calls them his friends. But this does not negate his call to service. Rather, it heightens it. The disciples call him Teacher and Lord, and correctly so (13:13). It is in these roles that he washes their feet and in this context of service that he calls them friends.

Service is also the focus of the epilogue to the Gospel in chapter 21, and here again service is closely related to love. Three times Peter is asked by the risen Christ if he loves Jesus and three times his response is affirmative — intentionally, it seems, recalling the scene of the trial of Jesus, where three times Peter denied even knowing Jesus. A central purpose of the epilogue is the reinstatement of Peter as a disciple and as one called to a role in the mission of the church. For each time Peter confesses his love for Jesus he is called to service: "Feed my lambs"

(21:15), "Tend my sheep" (v 16), and "Feed my sheep" (v 17). Love for Jesus and service to the community, therefore, are interwoven.

After these statements of love and service, Jesus calls Peter to follow him. The first occasion is in relation to Peter's death, with Jesus speaking of Peter following him in martyrdom. Earlier Peter could not follow Jesus into death because it was God's decisive act of salvation that was being accomplished in the crucifixion of Christ (13:36, 37). Now, however, Jesus says simply "Follow me" (21:19), and that means to follow him in death. The other instance of a command to follow is in a discussion of the place of the Beloved Disciple. It is not clear whether this disciple had died when this was written, but the words of Jesus in 21:23 had evidently caused confusion in the community (cf. Beasley-Murray, *John* 412). What is clear, however, is that Peter's concern about the Beloved Disciple evidences that their respective discipleships were to follow different courses. And what is important for Peter is that he is to follow Jesus even to the extent of martyrdom (21:22).

One further verb of action needs to be noted in relation to discipleship in the Fourth Gospel: "keep" *(tērein)*. Discipleship involves keeping the word or words of Jesus and keeping his commandments. And keeping his words and his commandments is also directly connected with one's love for Jesus. For as Jesus says, "If you love me you will keep my commandments" (14:15); and again, "Those who love me will keep my word" (v 23); and in negative form, "Whoever does not love me does not keep my words" (v 24).

Discipleship, therefore, includes a whole complex of terms, all of which mean much the same thing: keeping Jesus' word, obeying his commandments, and thereby remaining in his love, just as Jesus also has kept the commandments of the Father and remains in his love (15:10).

The vocabulary used with regard to discipleship in John's Gospel — both as relational and as action — is tremendously varied, with considerable interweaving of themes. To be in relationship with Jesus is to believe in him, to know him, to remain in him and in his love, and to be called his friend. Discipleship as action is directly related to relationship with Jesus. It is to follow Jesus, to bear fruit, to obey his commandments, to keep his words, to serve, and above all to love one another. The tendency throughout the Fourth Gospel is to use many words and phrases to cover the same area of concern. This phenomenon has been called "overlexicalization" and is a feature of the antilanguage of the Johannine community. It is language that reflects the "in group" or social identity of the Johannine community in its divergence from society at large and its distinctiveness from the wider church (cf. Malina, "Maverick Christian Group" 173-74).

4. Conclusions regarding Discipleship in the Fourth Gospel

Our study of discipleship in the Fourth Gospel has led to an examination of a wide variety of terms — some relational in nature, others words of action. There is a sense in which all of this is summed up in the confession of Thomas, who recognized the risen Jesus as "My Lord and my God" (21:28). This is the affirmation of faith of all who believe in Christ, for Thomas speaks for the entire group of disciples of that day and for all followers of Jesus throughout the subsequent history of the church.

In speaking of Jesus as "Lord" and "God," Thomas's confession reflects a high christology that includes an understanding of the risen Jesus as "equal to God," as "not of this world," and as given both the creative and judging powers of God (Neyrey, *Ideology of Revolt* 25ff.). It is the confession that represents the true response of an authentic disciple to the revelation presented in Christ through his life and ministry, his crucifixion and resurrection.

The immediate followers of Jesus believed in him and were called blessed. Those who come later and believe are even more blessed because they do not have the possibility of response to Jesus through immediate association (21:29). They come to believe on the basis of the church's preaching — including that of the Johannine community at the time that John's Gospel was being written — and are urged to "continue to believe that Jesus is the Christ, the Son of God" (21:31). So it is for all who come to believe at all times and in all places, with people called to respond in like faith. To be a disciple of Jesus, therefore, is to make this confession of faith in Jesus, to live in intimate relationship with Jesus, and to do what Jesus calls his followers to do.

5. Discipleship in the Johannine Letters

Discipleship in the Johannine letters is depicted in essentially the same terms as in the Fourth Gospel, although there are some shifts of emphasis. These differences can be accounted for by recognizing that the letters were written at a later period in the history of the Johannine community and addressed to specific concerns of that time. They were, evidently, not written by the author of the Fourth Gospel, but by one who had a special position of leadership within the group and who stood firmly within the same theology, teaching, and tradition. The letters give no attention to the immediate followers of Jesus. Rather, attention is drawn to the responsibilities of the members of the community, to their theology and their behavior. Internal tensions had led to some rather bitter conflicts within the community — even to divisions — and it is to these conflicts that 1 John especially is directed (cf. Brown, *Community*, for a plausible account of the history of the group). So it is important to note both the continuities of the Johannine letters with the Fourth Gospel and also their divergences from it.

One of the central themes of 1 John is that of the responsibility of Christians to love one another. As in the Fourth Gospel, love for each other arises out of God's love, particularly in his sending of his Son into the world. The author writes, "Whoever does not love does not know God, for God is love. God's love was revealed among us in this way: God sent his only Son into the world so that we might live through him" (4:8-9). Also thoroughly consistent with John's Gospel is the theological affirmation that the crucifixion of Jesus was a demonstration of his love: "We know his love by this, that he laid down his life for us — and we ought to lay down our lives for one another" (3:16). And while it is love for one another or for the "brother" — that is, love within the community — that is spoken of in 1 John, we can surely expand this to include love of all other human beings (so Furnish, *Love Command* 154).

Believers are called to obey the commandment of love, which is a new commandment and at the same time an old one (2:7). The language is clearly reminiscent of the Fourth Gospel: "This is his commandment, that we should believe in the name of his Son Jesus Christ and love one another as he commanded us" (1 John 3:23). The same exhortation to express the commandment of love is found in 2 John (v 5), which suggests a firmly fixed theology existing throughout the history of the Johannine community.

In contrast to this focus on love for one another, the author of 1 John elaborates in negative terms on the subject of hate, love's opposite. The hatred of the world toward believers in Jesus was to be expected. It was the experience of both Jesus and his disciples (cf. John 15:18), and was also

94

that of the community. The difficulty now facing the community, however, is that hatred is being expressed within the community, with a resultant sharp conflict. A rift has developed among the members; some have left primarily on theological grounds and feelings are running high.

The writer has little patience with those who have gone. As he says, "They went out from us, but they did not belong to us; for if they had belonged to us, they would have remained with us" (1 John 2:19). Strong words are said repeatedly in this letter about those who show hatred. To hate one's brother is to be in darkness, rather than in the light (2:6); the one who hates his brother cannot have eternal life (3:15); those who claim to live in God must walk as Jesus did (2:6). So while the commandment of love is expressed in terms closely similar to those of the Fourth Gospel, 1 John's application to a specific situation in terms of hate, love's opposite, has led to very pointed formulations.

Accompanying these personal struggles is a theological conflict that has precipitated a crisis in the Johannine community. In the Fourth Gospel, to believe in Jesus — that is, to believe that he is the Christ, the Son of God — is central to discipleship. The Johannine letters reflect the same theology, but now that theology is expressed polemically. There are some who deny that Jesus is the Christ; they do not know the truth, but are liars; they are antichrists (2:21-23). They do not confess that Jesus Christ has come in the flesh, or simply do not confess Jesus (4:2-3, some early manuscripts read "abolish Jesus"). The polemic is directed against those who deny the reality of the physical Jesus or the identification of Jesus as the Christ, reflecting some form of docetic christology in which Christ only appeared to be human. True theology, however, acknowledges that Jesus Christ has come in the flesh, and this form of teaching is of God. Those who departed from the community were expressing a docetic interpretation and moving in the direction of a developing Gnosticism.

The mark of authentic discipleship in 1 John now comes to be "to know the truth" (2:21), which is a theological criterion. It is the Spirit who testifies to the truth, for he is the "Spirit of truth" (4:6). And the test of the Spirit is acknowledgment that Jesus Christ has come in the flesh (4:2). Spiritual inspiration is not adequate. It must now be tested by theology.

This same concern for truth and for walking in the truth, with the same emphases on Christ as having come in the flesh and on the importance of this teaching, are major features of the brief letter known as 2 John — together, of course, with a concern for the new commandment: to love one another. And the readers of 3 John are also commended for walking in the truth (cf. vv 3 and 4).

In the Johannine letters, followers of Christ are always addressed as "children," and members of the community are also referred to as "brothers" (or, inclusively, "brothers and sisters"). The concern is to affirm a theology and establish a manner of life within the community that is in close accord with the teachings of the Fourth Gospel. The community was torn apart by conflict and division, with the departure of some dissident members. Speaking to such a situation, two main criteria of discipleship are stated: love for one another and acknowledgment of Jesus as the Christ, the Son of God.

The word "disciple" is absent from the Johannine letters, and there is no reference to the Twelve or the apostles. The writer assumes a pastoral and teaching role, having an obvious position of authority and leadership. The author of 2 John and 3 John is identified as the elder who addresses the church, but again without any acknowledgment of hierarchy or apostolate.

The doxology in 3 John aptly sums up the concern of the writer: "Grace, mercy, and peace will be with us from God the Father and from Jesus Christ, the Father's Son, in truth and love" (v 3).

6. Postscript

Discipleship is an important theme in the Johannine tradition. In the Fourth Gospel the disciples are at one and the same time the immediate followers of Jesus and the members of the Johannine community. To be a disciple is to remain in a relationship with Jesus, believing in him and living in his love. It is also to do what he calls his own to do: to follow him and to obey his commandment to love one another. In the Johannine letters these same concerns are expressed, but now in relation only to the community. Its members are to believe that Jesus is the Christ and are to love one another. These are the true criteria for authentic discipleship in the Johannine tradition — whether that of the first followers of Jesus, of the Johannine community in a post-Easter setting, or of authentic discipleship in our time.

Selected Bibliography

Beasley-Murray, G. R. *John.* Word Biblical Commentary, Dallas: Word, 1987.

Brown, R. E. *The Community of the Beloved Disciple.* New York: Paulist, 1979.

———. *The Gospel According to John,* 2 vols. Anchor Bible, Garden City: Doubleday, 1966.

Culpepper, R. A. *The Johannine School.* Missoula: Scholars, 1975.

———. *John, the Son of Zebedee.* Columbia: University of South Carolina Press, 1994.

Furnish, V. P. *The Love Command in the New Testament.* Nashville: Abingdon, 1975.

Haenchen, E. *John,* 2 vols. Hermeneia, Philadelphia: Fortress, 1984.

de Jonge, M. "The Fourth Gospel: The Book of the Disciples," in *Jesus: Stranger from Heaven and Son of God: Jesus Christ and the Christians in Johannine Perspective,* ed. and tr. J. Steely. Missoula: Scholars, 1977.

Kysar, R. *John, the Maverick Gospel.* Atlanta: John Knox, 1976.

Malina, B. *The Gospel of John in Sociolinguistic Perspective.* Berkeley: Center for Hermeneutical Studies, 1985.

———. "John's: The Maverick Christian Group: The Evidence of Sociolinguistics," *Biblical Theology Bulletin* 24 (1994) 167-82.

Martyn, J. L. *History and Theology in the Fourth Gospel.* Nashville: Abingdon, 1979.

Meeks, W. A. "The Man from Heaven in Johannine Sectarianism," *Journal of Biblical Literature* 91 (1972) 44-72.

Neyrey, J. H. *An Ideology of Revolt: John's Christology in Social-Science Perspective.* Philadelphia: Fortress, 1988.

Schnackenburg, R. *The Gospel According to Saint John,* 3 vols. Montreal: Palm/New York: Crossroad, 1968-82.

Segovia, F. F. *Love Relationships in the Johannine Tradition.* Chico: Scholars, 1982.

———. " 'Peace I Leave with You; My Peace I Give to You': Discipleship in the Fourth Gospel," in *Discipleship in the New Testament,* ed. F. F. Segovia. Philadelphia: Fortress, 1985, 76-102.

"How You Must Walk to Please God": Holiness and Discipleship in 1 Thessalonians

JEFFREY A. D. WEIMA

For a writer who never once uses the term "disciple," Paul certainly has many pointed things to say about what it means to be a follower of Jesus Christ — that is, about Christian discipleship. In 1 Thessalonians it is the theme of holiness that is prominent when the apostle speaks about how one ought to live as a disciple of Christ. The frequent occurrences of the noun "holiness" (*hagiōsynē* or *hagiasmos*), the adjective "holy" (*hagios*), and the verb "make holy" (*hagiazein*) — together with the repeated use of a number of other words and expressions that have to do with ethical purity (e.g., "righteous," "blameless," "to walk worthy of God") — suggest that holiness is the most important theme of 1 Thessalonians. And this concern for holiness comes to the fore most clearly in 4:1-12, where Paul deals with two specific problems that were apparently threatening the Thessalonian church: sexual immorality and idleness.

Before turning to the specific issues of 4:1-12, however, it is necessary, first, to survey the theme of holiness in 1 Thessalonians as a whole. In so doing, we hope to highlight the importance of holy living in the overall framework of Paul's teaching in 1 Thessalonians and the theological perspective from which the apostle issues his exhortations to his readers. Then we will turn our attention to the two problems addressed in 4:1-12, examining each in terms of its historical and social context and its treatment by Paul. Throughout we will attempt to demonstrate (1) that

98

Paul's exhortations in 4:1-12 are grounded in his conviction that the predominantly Gentile believers at Thessalonica, as part of the renewed Israel or the eschatological people of God, already possess the gift of holiness, which was one of the anticipated blessings of the "new" or "everlasting" covenant in the Messianic Age, and (2) that in 1 Thessalonians Paul teaches that the distinguishing sign or boundary marker of authentic Christian existence, what separates believers in Christ from those of the world, is holiness — whether it be holiness in the specific areas of sex or work, or, indeed, in all the activities of life. Consequently, Christian discipleship in 1 Thessalonians must be seen as being fundamentally a positive response to the gospel's call to holiness.

1. Holiness in the Letter as a Whole

Although the theme of holiness comes most clearly to expression in the second half of 1 Thessalonians (i.e., 4:1–5:28), this concern is foreshadowed in the first half of the letter as well (i.e., 1:1–3:13). The thanksgiving section in 1:2-10 — which is the epistolary unit that anticipates the key topics to be developed in the rest of the letter — opens by commending the Thessalonians for their "work of faith and labor of love" (v 3), that is, for the outward and visible signs of a holy life that testify to their salvation in Jesus Christ. In fact, their "faith in God" (v 8), which was evident in their holy living, has served as a powerful example to all the believers in Macedonia and Achaia (vv 7-9).

The opening thanksgiving leads into an extended discussion in 2:1–3:13 of Paul's ministry at Thessalonica. In this section Paul defends his apostolic work among his converts by appealing to the "holy, righteous, and blameless" lives of both himself and his missionary companions (especially 2:10; cf. his earlier statement in 1:5b). This holiness that was exemplified in the apostles' ministry becomes, in turn, the ground on which Paul challenges the Thessalonians "to walk worthy of God" (2:12). And this concern for holiness also comes out in the prayer that climaxes the first half of the letter: "May the Lord . . . establish your hearts unblamable in holiness *(en hagiōsynē)* before God our Father at the coming of our Lord Jesus with all his holy ones *(hagioi)*" (3:13).

The second half of 1 Thessalonians, with its parenetic focus, highlights to an even greater degree the theme of holiness. The Thessalonians are called to conduct themselves in a manner that is pleasing to God (4:1). This manner of conduct is explicitly identified as "your holiness *(ho hagiasmos hymōn)*" (4:3). Believers must abstain from sexual immorality and know how to control their sexual organs "in holiness *(en hagiasmǭ)* and honor" (4:4). The motivation for such sexual purity is that "God has not called us to uncleanness but in holiness *(en hagiasmǭ)*" (4:7) — and it is for the purpose of holiness that God "gives" or places "his Spirit, which is holy *(hagios)*, into us" (4:8). Holy lives are further characterized by mutual love within the family of God, by quiet living, by nonmeddling behavior, and by self-sufficient work — all of which are important features in "walking honorably" before non-Christians (4:9-12).

The importance of the theme of holiness in 1 Thessalonians is also evident in the fact that this concern even comes to the fore in the midst of the lengthy discussion of the return of Christ in 4:13–5:11. For in this section Paul reminds his converts that, though the day of the Lord is a day of judgment that will come like a thief in the night, they need not fear that day nor be caught unaware — for they are "children of the light and children of the day," in contrast to those who "belong to the night or to the darkness" (5:5; see also vv 4, 7, 8). The metaphors of light and day versus night and darkness, which are common to the literature of the Old Testament and Second Temple Judaism, are used here, as in Paul's others letters (especially Rom 13:11-13; also Rom 1:21; 2:19; 1 Cor 4:5; 2 Cor 4:6; 6:14; Eph 4:18; 5:8-11; 6:12; Col 1:13), to refer to holy living among believers. Thus the return of Christ, which is also a key theme in the letter, is intimately connected with Paul's preoccupation with holiness throughout 1 Thessalonians.

Paul's concern with holiness is likewise evident in the final exhortations (5:12-22) and in the closing peace benediction (5:23-24). For in the exhortations he directs the Thessalonian believers to respect their leaders (vv 12-13a), to be at peace with one another (v 13b), to encourage the fainthearted (v 14b), to help the weak (v 14c), to express patience to all (v 14d), to pursue what is good (v 15), and so on. But what needs to be noted here is that all these exhortations are rooted in Paul's desire that holiness characterize *all* aspects of his readers' lives. And this is also evident in the extended use of "all" *(pas)* in the closing exhortations in verses 14, 15 (twice), 16, 18, 21, and 22, which stress the comprehensive nature of living a holy life.

It also needs to be noted that Paul closes 1 Thessalonians not with his typical peace benediction, but with a greatly expanded peace benediction that echoes, among other things, his concern for holiness. For instead of ending the letter with the simple and expected formula "May the God of peace be with you" (cf. Rom 15:33; 2 Cor 13:11; Phil 4:9b), Paul writes in 5:23: "May the God of peace himself sanctify you wholly; and may your spirit, soul, and body be kept whole and blameless at the coming of our Lord Jesus Christ." The importance of living a life of holiness is expressed in this peace benediction by means of two optative verbal constructions that express Paul's great desire for his converts: "May he sanctify you (or "make you holy," *hagiasai*)," and "may your spirit, soul, and body be kept blameless *(amemptōs tērētheiē)*." And that this holiness involves the entire life of a person is stressed by two adverbs, which in Greek form an alliteration: "wholly" *(holoteleis)* and "complete (or whole)" *(holoklēron)* — as well as by the threefold reference to "spirit, soul, and body."

Paul's seemingly deliberate adaptation and expansion of the expected form of the peace benediction, therefore, results in a closing epistolary formula that summarizes well the call to holy living that has been developed throughout the letter (cf. Weima, *Neglected Endings* 176-79). It also further confirms that holiness is, indeed, the key theme of discipleship in 1 Thessalonians.

This pervasive emphasis on holiness in 1 Thessalonians reveals an important truth about the theological perspective from which Paul views the Thessalonian believers and issues his exhortations to them. For holiness was the defining characteristic and desired purpose for Israel, God's covenant people. It was the attribute by which the people of God were to be distinguished from all other nations. This is explicitly stated by God when he constitutes the nation of Israel at Mount Sinai as his chosen covenant people: "And now if you indeed obey my voice and keep my covenant, you will be to me a distinctive people out of all the nations. For the whole earth is mine. You will be to me a kingdom of priests and a holy *(hagios)* nation" (Exod 19:5-6 LXX).

This divine command for Israel to let holiness be the distinguishing feature of its existence is repeated in the renewal of the Sinai covenant: "And the Lord has chosen you today that you may be to him a distinctive people, as he promised, that you may keep his commandments, and that you may be above all the nations, as he has made you renowned and a boast and glorious, in order that you may be a holy *(hagios)* people to the Lord your God, as he promised" (Deut 26:18-19 LXX).

Likewise, the book of Leviticus repeatedly calls on Israel to imitate the holiness of their God: "You shall be sanctified *(hagiasthēsesthe)* and you shall be holy *(hagios)*, because I, the Lord your God, am holy *(hagios)*" (Lev 11:44 LXX; cf. also 11:45; 19:2; 20:7; 22:32).

The basic concept associated with this call to holiness is that of "separation" — that is, of the need for Israel to "come out" and be "distinct" from the surrounding peoples (cf. N. H. Snaith, *The Distinctive Ideas of the Old Testament* [New York: Schocken, 1944] 24-32). Thus holiness is the boundary marker that separates God's people from all other nations: "And do not follow the practices of the nations whom I am driving out before you. . . . I am the Lord your God who has *separated you from all the nations*. You shall therefore make a distinction between clean and unclean. . . . And you will be holy *(hagioi)* to me, because I, the Lord your God, am holy *(hagios)*, the one who *separated you from all the nations* to be mine" (Lev 20:23-26 LXX).

Any first-century Jew would have been familiar with all of this. For Leviticus 17–26 (the so-called "Holiness Code"), where God's call to holiness is clearly set forth, was well known among Jews in both Palestine and the Diaspora (cf. Hodgson, "1 Thess 4:1-12 and the Holiness Tradition"). Certainly Paul was familiar with the material in Leviticus 17–26. For he had been an active member of the Pharisees — that group within Judaism whose name, "the separated ones" (Greek *Pharisaioi* comes from the Aramaic and Hebrew verb *paresh*, which means "separate, make distinct"), reflected their desire to distance themselves from other Jews who did not share their passion for following the Torah's call to holiness. It is not at all surprising, therefore, that Paul viewed holiness as God's desired purpose for and defining characteristic of Israel, his covenant people.

What is surprising, however, even astonishing, is that Paul applies this standard of holiness to predominantly Gentile believers in Jesus at Thessalonica. The holiness that previously has been the exclusive privilege and calling of Israel has now also become God's purpose for Gentiles at Thessalonica who have "turned from idols to serve the true and living God" (1:9). The holiness that has previously been the characteristic that distinguished Israel from the Gentile nations has now also become the boundary marker that separates the Thessalonian Gentile believers from "the Gentiles who do not know God" (4:5), those who are "outside" God's holy people (v 12).

Paul, it seems clear, viewed his Gentile converts at Thessalonica as the renewed Israel — as those who, together with Jewish Christians, were now full members of God's covenant people. And on the basis of their privileged new position, he exhorts them to exhibit the holiness that God's people have always been called to possess. Paul's moral exhortations in 1 Thessalonians, particularly those in 4:1-12, are not to be seen as rooted in dependence on the moral traditions of the Greco-Roman philosophers, as some have argued (e.g., R. F. Hock, *The Social Context of Paul's Ministry: Tentmaking and Apostleship* [Philadelphia: Fortress, 1980] 44-47). Rather, Paul's exhortations to holiness originated from his own Jewish background and from his conviction that Gentile Christians at Thessalonica constituted a part of renewed Israel — a vital portion of the covenant people of God — and as such had come into the realm of both the blessings and the challenges of that new status.

2. Holiness in Sexual Conduct (4:3-8)

After opening the parenetic section of 1 Thessalonians with an appeal to increase in holy living (4:1-2), the first topic that Paul takes up is the problem of sexual immorality (4:3-8). Martin Dibelius's thesis was that the hortatory sections of the New Testament are made up of rather stock ethical maxims or "topoi" drawn from the moralistic teachings of the Greco-Roman world and were used in only a general fashion without any direct application to matters being discussed (cf. *A Fresh Approach to the New Testament and Early Christian Literature,* 1936, *passim*). A number of commentators have followed this thesis in claiming that Paul's exhortations here are only of a general nature and do not reflect actual problems in the Thessalonian church (e.g., H. Koester, "1 Thessalonians — Experiment in Christian Writing," in *Continuity and Discontinuity in Church History: Essays Presented to George Hunston Williams on the Occasion of his 65th Birthday,* ed. F. F. Church and T. George [Leiden: Brill, 1979] 38-40; U. Schnelle, "Die Ethik des 1. Thessalonicherbriefes," in *The Thessalonian Correspondence,* ed. R. Collins [Leuven: Leuven University Press, 1990] 295-305).

The specificity of Paul's exhortations in 4:3-8, however, coupled with their strategic location at the beginning of the parenetic section, the threatening tone of vv 6-8, and the widespread nature of sexual immorality *(porneia)* among Gentile Christians in the early church, all strongly suggest that Paul is, in fact, addressing here a real situation among the Thessalonian believers, one that he has learned about from Timothy (3:6). And although the apostle was generally pleased with the progress of his converts at Thessalonica and so encouraged them to go on in their Christian lives "more and more" (4:1, 10), he nevertheless was also concerned about the very real danger of them reverting to previous pagan practices (so, e.g., the commentaries by Frame 14-15, 145; Best 160; and Wanamaker 146, 158-59).

Historical and Social Context

To illuminate what Paul is exhorting in 4:3-8, it will be helpful to give some attention to questions of sexual conduct and morality in the Greco-Roman world of the first century. One must, of course, when examining the sexual attitudes and practices of the ancient world, guard against oversimplifying a complex topic that involves a host of larger issues. Nevertheless, it can be confidently stated that there existed in the Greco-Roman world of Paul's day a very tolerant attitude toward sexual conduct, particularly sexual activity outside marriage.

Marriages in Greco-Roman society were not usually love matches, but family arrangements. Typically, men in their middle twenties were paired with young women barely in their teens whom they usually had never met. So it was expected that married men would have sexual relations with other women, such as prostitutes, female slaves, or mistresses from lower social classes. This explains why Demosthenes (384-322 B.C.), probably the greatest of the Greek orators and a respected citizen of Athens, could state matter-of-factly: "Mistresses we keep for our pleasure, concubines for our day-to-day physical well-being, and wives in order to bear us legitimate children and to serve as trustworthy guardians over our households" (*Orations* 59.122). That attitudes had not changed at all some three centuries later is evident from the words of the Stoic philosopher and moralist Cato (95-46 B.C.), who praised those men who satisfied their sexual desires with a prostitute rather than with another man's wife (so his contemporary Horace, *Satire* 1.2.31-35). Similarly, Plutarch (ca. A.D. 46-120), the Platonist philosopher, advised prospective brides that it was better to close their eyes to the philandering activities of their husbands than to complain and so jeopardize good relations with them (*Moralia* 104B, 144F).

A very tolerant view toward adultery and other sexual practices can also be demonstrated from a variety of other sources. For example, funerary inscriptions evidence that concubinage was common. Prostitution was a business like any other, and profit from prostitutes working at brothels was an important source of revenue for many respectable citizens. In addition, innkeepers and owners of cookshops frequently kept slave girls for the sexual entertainment of their customers. Adulterous activity was, in fact, so widespread that the emperor Augustus (63 B.C.–A.D. 14) established a new code of laws having to do with adultery and marriage — the "Julian Laws" (since he assumed the name Julius and the title Caesar, adding them to his own name) — in a failed attempt to reform sexual practices. Within such a social context, it is not at all surprising that the Jewish Christian leaders of the Jerusalem church felt the need to include in their letter to Gentile Christians in Syria and Cilicia — the so-called "Apostolic Decree" — a warning "to abstain from sexual immorality" (Acts 15:20, 29; 21:25).

Sexual activity was frequently an important part of pagan religious practice. As a result, temples often had a reputation for immorality (cf. Ovid, *Art of Love* 1.77-78; Juvenal, *Satires* 6.486-89, 526-41; 9.22-26; Josephus, *Antiquities* 18.3-4 [65-80]). Especially significant for our study of 1 Thess 4:3-8 is the evidence that a number of religious cults in Thessalonica incorporated sexual activity as part of their worship practices (for the following discussion, see C. Edson, "Cults of Thessalonica," *Harvard Theological Review* 41 [1948] 153-204; Donfried, "Cults" 336-56; R. Jewett, *The Thessalonian Correspondence: Pauline Rhetoric and Millenarian Piety* [Philadelphia: Fortress, 1986] 126-33; R. E. Witt, "The Kabeiroi in Ancient Macedonia," in *Ancient Macedonia*, 2 vols., ed. B. Laouras and C. Makaronas [Thessaloniki: Institute for Balkan Studies, 1977] 2.67-80).

The most popular cult at Thessalonica in the time of Paul was the Cabirus cult. Although many of the ritual practices associated with this cult remain a mystery, the available sources indicate that they had a strong phallic and sexual character. Rex Witt is typical of a number of scholars who are struck by the "grotesquely phallic" scenes in Cabiric art. He concludes that "the core of the mystery was a phallic ritual" and that "the stress during the initiation ceremony fell . . . on sex" ("The Kabeiroi in Ancient Macedonia" 72, 73).

The second most popular cult at Thessalonica seems to have been that of Dionysus. Karl Donfried, after noting the sexual symbols and erotic activity associated with Dionysiac worship, highlights the possible link between this cult and the situation addressed in our passage: "Already in an anticipatory way we might ask whether this emphasis on the phallus and sensuality offers a possible background for the exhortations in 1 Thess 4.3-8" ("Cults" 337). The cults of Isis and Aphrodite at Thessalonica have also been connected with sexual activity. So while sexual immortality *(porneia)* may not necessarily have been an everyday occurrence in the pagan temples of the city, such activity at Thessalonica was by no means rare or unexpected.

In light of the general sexual laxity and promiscuity practiced throughout the ancient Greco-Roman world — as well as the sexual component in a number of the pagan religions of the day, particularly in the most popular cults of Thessalonica — we can better appreciate Paul's concern in 1 Thess 4:3-8 that his Gentile converts not revert to their former pagan practices. In fact, there is evidence in the letter that the believers of Thessalonica were not merely being tempted to revert to their previous lifestyle, but were being strongly pressured by their fellow citizens to do so. For the many references in 1 Thessalonians to the suffering being experienced by the church (1:6b; 2:2, 14-15; 3:1-5; cf. 2 Thess 1:4-7; 2 Cor 8:1-2; Acts 17:5-7, 13) are best understood as referring not primarily to physical persecution but to social harassment for the Christians' refusal to take part in their former cultic activities.

There is virtually no evidence that Christians anywhere in the Roman empire during the 50s suffered any form of organized physical persecution. But many sources suggest that social harassment was an all too common experience. John Barclay has rightly observed ("Conflict" 514-15):

> From our cultural and historical distance we easily underestimate the social dislocation involved in turning, as Paul puts it, from "idols" to the "true and living God" (1:9) and we barely appreciate the offense, even disgust, which such a change could evoke. . . . Many sources, both within and without the NT, portray the surprise and resentment felt by non-Christian friends when Christian converts declined to take part in normal social and cultic activities.

Exegetical Analysis

Knowing full well the temptations and pressures faced by his young converts at Thessalonica, Paul recognized the very real danger that they would revert to their previous pagan practices — practices that included, among other things, many that were sexually immoral. So he exhorts the Thessalonian believers to let their sexual conduct be characterized by holiness.

His exhortations regarding sexual conduct are set out in a clear tripartite structure: First, in 4:3a he opens with a thesis-like statement that God's will for the lives of his readers has to do with holiness. Second, in vv 3b-6 he issues three commands (vv 3b, 4-5, 6a) that spell out in concrete terms how holiness ought to control their sexual behavior. Third, in vv 6b-8 he concludes by giving three reasons (vv 6b, 7, 8) that they should be holy in this area of their lives.

That holiness captures, for Paul, the essence of a life of Christian discipleship is indicated by his equating it with the will of God: "For this is the will of God — your holiness" (v 3a). Although the following verses deal with the specific topic of sexual purity, this opening thesis-like statement shows that Paul considered holiness in *all* areas of life to be the primary goal of Christians, in keeping with the broader will of God for their lives.

The first of the three exhortations that focus on holiness in sexual behavior is rather brief and general: "Keep away from sexual immorality" (v 3b). The Greek term used is *porneia* — a word that literally means sexual relations with a prostitute *(pornē)*. Here, however, as in all Jewish and Christian writings, the word refers to sexual activity that takes place outside marriage. This restriction of sex to the marriage relationship certainly would have sounded strange to the Greco-Roman world of Paul's day, for, as we have seen, it tolerated and even encouraged, at least in the case of men, various forms of extramarital sexual activity. Christians, however, were to follow a different standard of behavior, that of holiness. And this standard of holiness requires that they "keep away from sexual immorality."

The verb "keep away from" *(apechesthai)* used in verse 3b is a strong one that expresses not mere moderation but absolute abstinence. Like the noun "holiness," which it explains (v 3a), this verb conveys the notion of separation — separation from the moral standards of the contemporary culture. Paul has in effect made holiness in the area of sexual conduct the boundary marker that separates the Thessalonian believers from the pagan community to which they previously belonged.

The second of the three exhortations, in verses 4-5, has generated a great deal of debate since the earliest days of the church. The controversy centers on the intended meaning of two words, the noun *skeuos*, which literally means "vessel" or "household utensil," and the verb *ktasthai*, which normally means "gain" or "acquire." One common interpretation takes *skeuos* as a metaphorical reference to "woman" or "wife," so that Paul here is exhorting each of his readers "to take a wife for himself in holiness and honor" (so, e.g., RSV, NAB, and the commentaries by Frame 149-50; Best 161-63; and Stott 83-84).

The alternative interpretation also adopts a metaphorical understanding of *skeuos*, but understands it as referring not to "woman" but to one's own "body." This interpretation also rejects the normal meaning of the verb *ktasthai*, "gain," and understands it as meaning here "gain mastery over" or "take control of." The resulting translation has Paul exhorting each of his readers to "take control over his own body in holiness and honor" (so, e.g., NEB, JB, NIV, NRSV, and the commentaries by Rigaux 504-6; Morris 121; Bruce 83; Marshall 107-10; and Williams 72-73). Although neither interpretation is completely free from criticism, the majority of recent commentators have found the second to be more convincing.

Within this second interpretation, some have seen the noun *skeuos* as a euphemistic reference to the male sex organ (so, e.g., Marxsen, *Der erste Brief* 60-61; James M. Reese, *1 and 2 Thessalonians* [Wilmington: Michael Glazier, 1979] 44; Wanamaker, *Thessalonians* 152). In secular Greek *skeuos* clearly had such a euphemistic use. This meaning is also supported by the strongly phallic character of the Cabirus and Dionysian cults, which were popular at Thessalonica. But whether Paul is referring to the body in general or the male genital organ in particular, the sense of the second exhortation is clear: Christians must control their sexual urges and activities, conducting themselves according to the standard of "holiness and honor." And this moral standard of holiness that is to control the sexual behavior of Christians is sharply contrasted with the standard that controls the sexual behavior of non-Christians: "not in the passion of lust like the Gentiles who do not know God" (v 5).

Here in verse 5 we have, in fact, additional support for the two principal claims that we made earlier. First, it shows that Paul views the Gentile converts at Thessalonica as members of the renewed Israel, the covenant people of God. For his placing of the Thessalonian Christians, who were themselves Gentiles, in sharp antithesis to "the Gentiles who do not know God" is incomprehensible apart from an understanding of believers in Jesus as full members of God's covenant people. As T. J.

Deidun notes, the phrase "the Gentiles who do not know God" immediately places this verse in a covenant context, for "to know God" is a technical reference in the Old Testament to the covenant relationship (*New Covenant Morality* 19, n 61). Second, verses 4 and 5 illustrate once again that Paul viewed holiness — here specifically holiness in sexual behavior — as the distinguishing sign or boundary marker of believers in Jesus that sharply separates them from the world, from "those who do not know God."

The last of the three exhortations, which explains more concretely how holiness impacts sexual behavior, is given in verse 6a: "No one should wrong a brother in this matter." This command, like the previous one, has also led to a great deal of debate among interpreters. For since the verb *pleonektein* can have the sense of "defraud" or "cheat," some view Paul as here no longer talking about sexual behavior but about business matters. According to this understanding, this third command should be translated: "No one should wrong his brother in matters of business" (so, e.g., marginal note in RSV; R. Beauvery, "*Pleonektein* in I Thess. 4.6a," *Verbum Domini* 33 [1955] 78-85; Traugott Holtz, *Der erste Brief an die Thessalonicher* [Zurich: Benziger, 1986] 161-62; Marxsen, *Der erste Brief* 62).

There are, however, a number of reasons to view this understanding as mistaken. For one thing, there is no transitional epistolary formula here to mark the beginning of a new topic, as can be found in 4:1, which begins with an appeal formula ("We appeal to you . . ."); 4:9, which begins with a *peri de* formula ("Now about . . ."); and 4:13, which begins with a disclosure formula ("We do not want you not to know . . ."). Secondly, the use of the word "uncleanness" in verse 7 suggests that Paul is still concerned with the topic of sexual behavior. And, thirdly, the fact that verses 3-6 constitute a single sentence in the Greek text, with the first two infinitive clauses plainly dealing with sexual conduct, makes it unlikely that Paul shifts in the third clause to a new topic dealing with conduct in business practices. For these and other reasons, most scholars rightly understand the third exhortation to be also dealing with the issue of sexual purity.

Paul in verse 6a, therefore, should be understood as warning against the kind of adulterous sexual activity that would result in a "brother" — that is, a Christian man, the husband or father of the woman involved — being wronged. In our contemporary gender-sensitive culture, some may very well take offense that it is a "brother"

and not a "sister" that might be wronged. But Paul is completely understandable, given the patriarchal model of family and household
structures of his day. More important, and more significant for our
purposes here, is that Paul's concern in this exhortation, as in his two
previous exhortations in verses 3b and 4-5, is that the Thessalonian
Christians not be guilty of any kind of sexual impropriety, so that their
holy conduct will distinguish them from their Gentile neighbors.

The three exhortations to holiness in sexual conduct in verses 3-6a
are followed in verses 6b-8 by three reasons that Paul's converts are to
be holy in this area of their lives. This triple motivation for holy living
involves each person of the Trinity. The first reason is the future judgment of Christ: "Because the Lord is an avenger about all these things,
as we told you beforehand and testified" (v 6b). The second is the past
call of God: "For God has not called us for uncleanness but in holiness"
(v 7). And the third involves the present gift of the Holy Spirit: "Therefore, whoever disregards this disregards not human authority but God,
who gives his Spirit, which is holy, into you" (v 8). It is, however, the
third reason — the present gift of the Holy Spirit — that is most significant for understanding the theological perspective from which Paul
views his Thessalonian converts and issues to them his call to holiness.
For here Paul picks up the language of the Old Testament prophets
about the blessed presence of God's Spirit in the messianic age — language associated with the "new" or "everlasting" covenant — and applies
it to the Thessalonian believers (cf. Deidun, *New Covenant Morality* 19,
53-56; F. Thielman, *Paul and the Law* [Downers Grove: InterVarsity,
1994] 76-77).

Jews of the first century were painfully aware that their nation, both
in its past and in its present, was not living according to the standard of
holiness that God had called for when he first established his covenant
with them. But most Jews also believed, on the basis of his promise given
through the prophets, that God would not abandon his people, but would
restore their holiness by pouring out his Spirit on them as part of the
covenant blessings to be enjoyed in the messianic era. This eschatological
hope for holiness, which is made possible through the presence of God's
Spirit, is most clearly seen in Ezek 36:25-27 (LXX): "I will sprinkle clean
water on you, and you will be purged from all your uncleanness and from
all your idols, and I will cleanse you. And I will give you a new heart, and
will put a new spirit in you *(pneuma kainon dōsō en hymin)*; and I will take
away the heart of stone out of your flesh, and will give you a heart of flesh.

110

And I will put my Spirit in you *(to pneuma mou dōsō en hymin)* and will cause you to walk in my commands and to keep my judgments and do them" (cf. also Ezek 11:19).

The gift of God's Spirit as a key blessing of the eschatological age is also stressed in Ezek 37:6 and 14, where it is twice stated: "I will put my Spirit into you" *(dōsō pneuma mou eis hymas)*." And while other prophets like Jeremiah and Isaiah do not highlight the gift of God's Spirit quite as explicitly as Ezekiel does (but see Isa 59:21), they do hold out the future hope of a "new" or "everlasting" covenant in which God will live in and among his people in such an intimate way that they will be able to obey his commands and live holy lives (cf., e.g., Jer 31[LXX 38]:31-34; 32:40; 50:5; Isa 55:3; 59:21).

Paul takes this new covenant language, which articulates the eschatological hope of the Jewish people, and applies it to Gentile Christians at Thessalonica. The parallels with Ezek 36:25-27 are especially striking. For as Ezekiel prophesied ("You will be purged from all your uncleanness . . . and I will cleanse you," 36:25), God has cleansed the Thessalonian believers from their "uncleanness" (4:7) so that their sexual conduct now is to be controlled by "holiness" (4:3, 4, 7). And as Ezekiel prophesied (". . . and from your idols," 36:25), God has cleansed Paul's converts at Thessalonica from their idolatry, with the result that they "have turned from idols to serve the living and true God" (1:9). Likewise, as Ezekiel prophesied ("I will cause you to walk in my commands, and to keep my judgments and do them," 36:27), God has now enabled Gentile Christians to "walk" *(peripatein)* according to his commands (4:1 [twice] and 10). But most significantly, as Ezekiel prophesied ("I will put my Spirit in you," 36:27; also 37:6, 14), Paul can now say to Gentile believers in Jesus that God "is giving his Holy Spirit into you" (4:8).

That Paul did, in fact, quite consciously have in mind the eschatological age envisioned by Ezekiel can be seen in his description of God giving his Holy Spirit "into you" *(eis hymas)*, an expression that, though somewhat awkward in English, echoes exactly the words of the prophet (cf. Ezek 37:6, 14 LXX; see also 36:27). But while the gift of God's Spirit was for Ezekiel and others in Judaism only a future hope ("I *will* give my Spirit," *dōsō to pneuma mou)*, for Paul it had become a present and ongoing reality (for the significance of the present participle *didonta,* "who gives," see G. D. Fee, *God's Empowering Presence* [Peabody: Hendrickson, 1994] 52-53).

Paul's exhortations in 4:3-8, therefore, indicate that he viewed the conversion of Gentiles at Thessalonica as a fulfillment of the eschatological promises made to Israel. The Thessalonian believers were no longer simply "Gentiles who do not know God," but now were members of the renewed Israel, the covenant people of God. This privileged status meant that they were to observe the boundaries of holiness that the new covenant marked out for them, whether in the area of sexual conduct or any other human activity. And the key to living such lives of holiness is the present and ongoing presence of God's Spirit. So here, as elsewhere in Paul's letters, the Holy Spirit is the power that enables believers to live holy lives.

3. Holiness in Work (4:9-12)

In 1 Thess 4:9-12, Paul moves from the need for holiness in sexual conduct to the need for holiness in work. He continues to address the whole church, for the problem of idleness had consequences for how all the members of the congregation were to conduct themselves. Paul's primary concern in verses 9-12, however, is with a specific group in the church, whom he exhorts to "work with your own hands as we commanded you, so that you may walk honorably before those who are outside and may have need of no one" (vv 11-12). This group is later identified in 5:14 as "the obstinate/rebellious" or "the idle/lazy" *(ataktoi)*. They evidently posed such a serious threat to the well-being of the church that Paul had to deal with them a second time at greater length in 2 Thess 3:6-13.

Historical and Social Context

In order to understand more adequately Paul's exhortations in 4:9-12, the historical and social context of his words needs to be investigated. Two questions, in particular, are important for an understanding of the issues that Paul addresses. First, what precisely was the wrong of which these troublesome members were guilty? Second, what was the cause of their problematic behavior?

The first question involves translating properly the Greek root *atakt-*, which Paul uses four times in his two letters to describe this group (the adjective *ataktoi* in 1 Thess 4:11; the adverb *ataktōs* in 2 Thess 3:6, 11; the verb *ataktein* in 2 Thess 3:7). This root has two possible meanings, either of which may be appropriate to the Thessalonian situation. One is derived from its use in military contexts to depict soldiers who would not keep step or follow commands — that is, those who were "obstinate" or "rebellious." The other stems from its use in the papyri of the Hellenistic period to describe students or workers who failed to do their work — that is, those who were "idle" or "lazy." The first meaning, "obstinate" or "rebellious," nicely captures the resistance of the *ataktoi* to their leaders (1 Thess 5:12-14a) and to Paul's exhortations. The second meaning, "idle" or "lazy," is supported by Paul's explicit commands to work (4:11-12) and his lengthy rebuke in 2 Thess 3:6-13. Both possible meanings of *ataktoi*, therefore, seem to come together in the issue addressed by Paul in 4:9-12: an obstinate and rebellious refusal of some within the Thessalonian church to submit to their leaders and to Paul's authority, and idleness and laziness on the part of the same people, which occasioned Paul's command, "work with your own hands" (v 11a).

The second question, why this group was not willing to work, is by no means easy to answer. The traditional explanation is that their idleness was rooted in their eschatological excitement over the imminent return of Christ (so, e.g., the commentaries by Best 175-76; Bruce 90-91; Frame 159-60; Morris 131; Rigaux 519-21). In other words, the belief that Christ would return soon led some in the church to abandon ordinary earthly pursuits, such as working for a living, so that they could give full attention to spiritual preparation, eschatological discussion, and (perhaps) preaching. This group, following out such an explanation, must have reasoned to themselves: "Since the end is near, work is a waste of time."

Although Paul nowhere in the two Thessalonian letters explicitly makes a direct connection between eschatological excitement and the problem of idleness, there are at least three factors that support such a link. First, the problem of idleness, which is raised twice in 1 Thessalonians (4:11-12; 5:14), frames the extended discussion of matters concerning Christ's return (4:13–5:11) — suggesting, thereby, that the two topics are related. And this juxtaposition of topics occurs also in 2 Thessalonians, where the treatment of idleness (3:6-13) appears only shortly after a lengthy discussion of the Day of the Lord (2:1-12). Second, the frequent and lengthy references in both letters to the parousia, that is, the expected return of Christ, far more than in any of Paul's other letters, suggest that the Thessalonian church possessed a heightened expectancy regarding Christ's return.

113

Third, the frequency with which eschatological excitement has led to idleness in a variety of religious groups over the centuries testifies to how easily this problem could have occurred at Thessalonica. One recent and well-known example is that of the Dami Mission Church in Korea, whose members, in the belief that Christ was going to return on Reformation Day 1992, sold their homes, emptied their bank accounts, and quit their jobs.

Not all scholars, however, have found the "eschatological argument" convincing. They stress that Paul never explicitly links the problem of idleness with a belief in the imminent return of Christ. They also point out that Paul needed to command his Thessalonian converts to work from the very beginning of his ministry among them (cf. 4:11; also 2 Thess 3:6, 10), which suggests that idleness was already a problem prior to their conversion. Thus instead of an eschatological cause for the unwillingness of some in the Thessalonian church to work, these scholars argue for a sociological origin of the problem.

Some have appealed to the general disdain toward physical labor that was prevalent in the Greco-Roman world (so, e.g., W. Bienert, *Die Arbeit nach der Lehre der Bibel. Eine Grundlegung evangelischer Social-ethik* [Stuttgart: Evangelisches Verlagswerk, 1954] 270-72; Marshall, *Thessalonians* 116, 223). This negative attitude toward work, however, was a viewpoint that only the wealthy upper class could afford to have. Laborers and artisans, who probably made up the majority of Thessalonian believers, would not have had the luxury of such an outlook.

Others in the sociological camp of interpreters have tried to explain this problem of idleness at Thessalonica in terms of the patron-client relationship that was popular in that day (so, e.g., R. Russell, "The Idle in 2 Thess 3:6-12: An Eschatological or a Social Problem?" *New Testament Studies* 34 [1988] 105-19; B. Winter, "'If a Man Does Not Wish to Work...': A Cultural and Historical Setting for 2 Thessalonians 3:6-16," *Tyndale Bulletin* 40 [1989] 303-15; Williams, *Thessalonians* 150). In this relationship, members of the lower class would attach themselves to benefactors from among the upper class, from whom they would then receive sustenance and help in various matters in exchange for the obligation to reciprocate with expressions of gratitude and support. It is argued that Paul's converts included those of the urban poor who had formed client relationships with wealthy members in the Thessalonian church, but who exploited the generosity of their new Christian patrons.

114

But while patron-client relationships may well have existed in the Thessalonian church, this relationship in and of itself does not appear to be the specific cause for the idle behavior of some Christians of the city. For the obligations that clients typically had to fulfill for wealthy patrons (e.g., greet them each morning with the *salutatio* or "morning salute," appear with them in public, work in their political campaigns) involved sufficient activity that clients would not likely be accused of idleness.

There does not appear to be enough evidence available to determine with any high degree of certainty why some in the Thessalonian church were guilty of idleness. Still, the eschatological argument seems to provide a more convincing explanation than any of the sociological arguments for this state of affairs at Thessalonica. That Paul warned against idleness from the very beginning of his ministry at Thessalonica in no way negates such a conclusion. For his ministry there lasted long enough for the problem of eschatological enthusiasm to manifest itself in the church.

Exegetical Analysis

Paul's exhortations in 4:9-12 fall into two distinct units of material: verses 9-10a deal with the exercise of mutual love (*philadelphia*, "brotherly love") within the church, and verses 10b-12 deal with the problem of the idlers. This structure reflects Paul's desire to deal with the specific problem of idleness within the broader context of the church's call for its members to interact with each other in love.

The text of the first unit reads: "But now concerning mutual [or "brotherly"] love, you have no need that anyone should write to you, for you yourselves have been taught by God to love one another. For indeed you do love all the brothers and sisters throughout Macedonia." The emphasis here on the proper exercise of mutual love serves as a corrective to the improper behavior of idleness, which is taken up in the second unit. For the refusal of some in the church to work, and so to take advantage of the generosity of other believers, is a clear violation of the command to live in love with one another.

The key to changing this unholy behavior of the idlers, so that they — along with the whole church — may genuinely live in mutual love, lies in the presence and work of the Holy Spirit. For though Paul makes no explicit reference to the Spirit in this passage, he does, once again, use language that refers to the new covenant blessing of being taught directly by God — a blessing that the prophets attribute to the presence of God's Spirit. This new covenant language is found in verse 9 in the unique expression "God-taught" *(theodidaktoi)*. Paul here seems to be alluding to Isaiah's description of the messianic age as a time when God will live so intimately in and among his people through his Spirit that they will no longer have to be taught by human intermediaries, but will be "taught of God" *(didaktous theou,* Isa 54:13; cf. also John 6:45, where Jesus quotes the same verse to show that "all will be taught by God" [*didaktoi theou*] in the messianic age).

Paul likely also had in mind Jeremiah's portrait of the new covenant as a period when God's people will not need others to teach them the law but will know it innately, for God will write it on their hearts (Jer 31[LXX 38]:33-34). But since Paul's use of the term *theodidaktoi* occurs so close to his clear allusion in the previous verse to Ezekiel's description of the gift of God's Spirit in the messianic age, it seems reasonable to argue that the apostle had in mind here, specifically, the Holy Spirit's role in teaching and empowering believers to live the kind of holy life that is characterized by "mutual love" (so Marshall, *Thessalonians* 115; Williams, *Thessalonians* 96). And this double use of new covenant language in both verse 8b and verse 9a further supports one of the central claims of the present chapter — namely, that Paul's exhortations to holiness in 4:1-12 are rooted in his conviction that the Gentile Christians at Thessalonica are included in the renewed Israel, the eschatological people of God who enjoy both the blessings and the challenges of that privileged relationship.

After reminding the Thessalonian Christians in the first unit, verses 9-10a, that they, as the new covenant people of God who are taught by his Spirit, must let mutual love characterize all of their relationships within the church, Paul in the second unit, verses 10b-12, addresses the specific problem of idleness. The first of the four imperatival clauses that make up this second unit, however, looks back to the first unit and shows how closely the two sections are connected. For Paul's first exhortation, "to increase more," refers to increasing in the expression of that mutual love of which he has just been speaking. Paul does not want the idlers to exploit the generosity of other believers. But he also does not want the church to decrease its commitment to showing love to all its members.

The second exhortation, "make it your ambition to lead a quiet life," has a somewhat oxymoronic character that is better captured by this translation: "Make it your ambition to have no ambition!" This exhortation suggests that the idleness of some at Thessalonica allowed them the time and opportunity to be involved in the kind of meddling and busybody activity that offended others. As Paul would later write in his second letter, these Christians were "not busy" doing their work, but, instead, had become "busybodies" (2 Thess 3:10). Paul therefore exhorts such believers in his third exhortation "to mind your own affairs." The fourth and final exhortation involves a straightforward challenge for the Thessalonian believers "to work with your own hands" — which is the same challenge that he had given them orally during his ministry at Thessalonica.

The purpose of Paul's fourfold appeal to live loving, quiet, non-meddling, and hard-working lives is given in verse 12: "in order that you may walk honorably before those outside and be dependent on no one." Although the preceding four exhortations address a variety of practices that are to characterize a life of holiness, the fourth and final exhortation "to work with your own hands" seems to have been the most prominent in Paul's mind. For it is the problem of idleness that he chooses to take up once again in this purpose clause, expressing his desire that the Thessalonian believers "be dependent on no one."

Paul does not mean, of course, that those who could not work, whether through lack of opportunity or infirmity, should not turn to the church for support (cf. Eph 4:28; 1 Tim 5:3-8). Rather, he is addressing here the specific problem at Thessalonica of those who were unwilling to work, content to live instead as parasites on the Christian community. Not only is such slothful behavior incompatible with genuine mutual love within the church, it also fails to meet the goal of "walking honorably before those outside." As a people divinely called to be separate from "those outside," the Thessalonian church must ensure that the holy character of its community and its God is not brought into disrepute by the idle and meddling conduct of some of its members.

The identification of non-Christians as "those outside" is significant. For as in the preceding section, verses 3-8, where Paul saw holiness in sexual conduct as a distinguishing sign of the Thessalonian church that separates it from "those who do not know God" (v 5), here in verses

117

9-12 he similarly sees holiness in work as a boundary marker that sets the church apart from "those outside." As full members of God's covenant people, Gentile believers at Thessalonica are and must continue to be a holy community whose conduct in all aspects of life distinguishes it from the surrounding world.

4. Holiness in the Church Today

The two problems that Paul takes up in 1 Thess 4:1-12 — sexual immorality and idleness — pose just as great a threat to the church today as they did to the Thessalonian church of the apostle's day. For though both sex and work are good creation gifts that have been instituted by God prior to the Fall, these gifts continue to be distorted and abused in our sin-tainted world. Modern society, in fact, is even more adept than that of the ancient Greco-Roman world in tolerating, encouraging, and justifying all sorts of illicit sexual conduct. And some today are unwilling to work, content rather to exploit the support provided by government welfare programs. At the same time, others, who are willing to work, view their labor only as a means to an end — that is, as the price they must pay in order to obtain the pleasures of material wealth or weekend revelry.

In such a social context, it is necessary for Christians to remember that they are the eschatological people of God — that they are members of the new covenant, to whom has been given the blessing of holiness made possible through the ongoing presence and power of the Holy Spirit. This privileged new status carries with it, however, the concomitant challenge to holy living. In sexual conduct and in work, as in all human activity, the distinguishing sign or boundary marker of the church, that which separates it from the world, is holiness. "Alien and archaic as the idea may seem," as Chuck Colson has reminded us, "the task of the church is not to make men and women happy; it is to make them holy" (*The Body: Being Light in Darkness* [Dallas: Word, 1992] 46).

Selected Bibliography

Barclay, J. "Conflict in Thessalonica," *Catholic Biblical Quarterly* 55 (1993) 512-30.

Best, E. *A Commentary on the First and Second Epistles to the Thessalonians.* Black's/Harper's New Testament Commentaries, London: Black/New York: Harper and Row, 1972.

Bruce, F. F. *1 and 2 Thessalonians.* Word Biblical Commentary, Waco: Word, 1982.

Deidun, T. J. *New Covenant Morality.* Rome: Biblical Institute Press, 1981.

Donfried, K. P. "The Cults of Thessalonica and the Thessalonian Correspondence," *New Testament Studies* 31 (1985) 336-56.

Frame, J. E. *A Critical and Exegetical Commentary on the Epistles of St. Paul to the Thessalonians.* International Critical Commentary, Edinburgh: T. & T. Clark, 1912.

Hodgson, R., Jr. "1 Thess 4:1-12 and the Holiness Tradition (HT)," in *Society of Biblical Literature Seminar Papers 21,* ed. K. H. Richards. Chico: Scholars, 1982, 199-215.

Kieffer, O. *Sexual Life in Ancient Rome.* New York: Dutton, 1935.

Marshall, I. Howard. *1 and 2 Thessalonians.* New Century Bible Commentary, Grand Rapids: Eerdmans, 1983.

Marxsen, W. *Der erste Brief an die Thessalonicher.* Zurcher Bibelkommentare, Zürich: Theologischer Verlag, 1979.

Morris, L. *The First and Second Epistles to the Thessalonians.* New International Commentary on the New Testament, Grand Rapids: Eerdmans, 1959, rev. 1991.

Rigaux, B. *Saint Paul. Les Épitres aux Thessaloniciens.* Paris: Gabalda, 1956.

Stott, J. *The Gospel and the End of Time: The Message of 1 and 2 Thessalonians.* Downers Grove: InterVarsity, 1991.

Wanamaker, C. *Commentary on 1 and 2 Thessalonians.* New International Greek Testament Commentary, Grand Rapids: Eerdmans, 1990.

Weima, J. A. D. *Neglected Endings: The Significance of the Pauline Letter Closings.* Sheffield: Sheffield Academic Press, 1994.

Williams, D. J. *1 and 2 Thessalonians.* New International Biblical Commentary, Peabody: Hendrikson, 1992.

"Imitate Me, Just as I Imitate Christ": Discipleship in the Corinthian Correspondence

LINDA L. BELLEVILLE

The language of discipleship is scarce in Paul's letters. The noun *mathētēs* ("disciple," "follower") and the verb *mathēteuein* ("make a disciple of," "be a disciple"), which abound in the Gospels and Acts, do not appear at all in Paul's writings. Even rough equivalents like *mimētēs* ("imitator"), *mimeomai* ("imitate," "follow another's example"), *typos* ("pattern," "example"), *hypotypōsis* ("pattern," "example"), and *akolouthein* ("follow") are quite rare. This makes the task of explicating discipleship in Paul a difficult one.

Yet while the language is scarce, the idea of discipleship is very much present. In virtually every letter, Paul devotes a major segment to spelling out for his readers what it means to live a life worthy of the gospel. He also presents Jesus, himself, and other colleagues — even other churches — as models of discipleship. So the task of tracing out this theme in the Pauline corpus is, in fact, a rather large one.

The theme of discipleship comes to expression in the Corinthian correspondence in many ways. Most obviously, it comes to the fore in Paul's calls to imitate himself and Christ in 1 Corinthians. It can also be seen in the examples of discipleship that are set out in 2 Corinthians, which receive repeated emphasis even though they are somewhat more subtly presented. The *imitatio* theme of 1 Corinthians and the examples that are highlighted as models of the Christian life and ministry throughout 2 Corinthians make an important contribution to our un-

120

derstanding of discipleship in Paul's thought. Both will be treated in what follows, beginning with the data of 1 Corinthians and moving on to 2 Corinthians.

1. Calls to Imitation in 1 Corinthians

Paul exhorts his converts to a life of imitation twice in 1 Corinthians. Once he invites them to imitate him (4:16); another time, he asks them to imitate Christ (somewhat indirectly) through imitating him (11:1). In so doing, he calls them to a life of discipleship that has as its exemplars himself immediately and Christ ultimately.

Imitating Paul (4:16)

In 4:16 Paul exhorts his converts: "Imitate me" *(mimētai mou ginesthe)*. The noun "imitator" *(mimētēs)* and verb "imitate" *(mimeomai)*, except for Heb 6:12; 13:7 and 3 John 11, are found in the New Testament exclusively in Paul's writings. Five times he exhorts a church to "imitate" him (1 Cor 4:16; 11:1; Phil 3:17; 2 Thess 3:7, 9; cf. Gal 4:12; Phil 4:9), twice he applauds successful imitation (1 Thess 1:6-7; 2:13-15), and once he urges the imitation of God (Eph 5:1). Interestingly, Paul calls only those churches he has personally founded to imitate him — that is, the churches of Galatia, Philippi, Thessalonica, and Corinth. Where he had modeled the life of discipleship, there he could expect imitation.

Paul's request was by no means unique in the ancient world. Nor can it be called presumptuous on his part. Imitating some sort of moral exemplar was quite common in antiquity (cf. Fowl, "Imitation" 430; E. Best, *Paul and His Converts* [Edinburgh: T. & T. Clark, 1988] 60-63). In Greco-Roman society, fathers in particular were expected to model appropriate ethical behavior, thereby educating their children in the way of a virtuous life (e.g., Isocrates, *To Demonicus* 4.11: "Regard your father's conduct as your law and strive to imitate and emulate your father's virtue"). In Judaism, the father's role was to exhort, encourage, and exemplify the life that is "worthy of God" (so, e.g., 1 Thess 2:11-12; cf. D. M. Williams, "Imitation of Christ" 50-54).

This, undoubtedly, is why Paul appeals to the Corinthians as their "father," not as their apostle (1 Cor 4:15; cf. DeBoer, *Imitation of Paul*

146). He "gave" them "birth through the gospel," thereby forging a familial union with them that no other itinerant preacher or pastor could claim. Paul was their father. All the rest were mere "nannies" *(paidagōgoi)*, numerous though they might be. So it fell to Paul to provide his spiritual children with a model worthy of emulation. This evidently occurred during his founding visit, which explains why he does not stop at this point in the letter to spell out in more detail the life of discipleship. All the Corinthians needed was a reminder to imitate what they had previously observed — although Paul does take the occasion to send another "child," who had successfully reproduced the ways of the father, to jog their memory (v 17: "I am sending Timothy my beloved child . . . who will remind you of my ways in Christ").

What exactly was involved in imitating Paul? Some argue that it entailed following a general pattern of behavior (e.g., H. Lietzmann and W. G. Kümmel, *An die Korinther I–II* [Tübingen: Mohr, 1949]; H.-D. Wendland, *Die Briefe an die Korinther* [Göttingen: Vandenhoeck und Ruprecht, 1962]) or manner of living (e.g., W. Bauder, "Imitate," *New International Dictionary of New Testament Theology* 1.491) rather than a set of particular instructions. But as William Orr rightly notes, the plural "my ways" *(tas hodous mou)* points to something more particular than general (*1 Corinthians* [New York: Doubleday, 1976] 179). Others maintain that "imitate me" is equivalent to "obey my commands." It is not so much a matter of following a personal standard as it is of heeding objective precepts (e.g., W. Michaelis, *"mimeomai," Theological Dictionary of the New Testament* 4.668-69; Orr, *1 Corinthians* 182). There is merit in this latter interpretation. Parental authority, to be sure, laid on children an obligation to observe what was said. Paul himself states that his "ways in Christ" were something that he "taught" *(didaskein)* — and not just at Corinth but "in all the churches everywhere" *(pantachou en pasē ekklēsia,* v 17) — so that his instructions regarding ethical conduct had obligatory and normative value.

Yet one must not dismiss the idea of a personal exemplar too quickly. The injunctions in 4:16-17 are unquestionably familiar: "Imitate *me*" *(mimētai mou ginesthe);* "he will remind of *my* ways" *(anamnēsei tas hodous mou).* It is, therefore, reasonable to think that Paul had in mind moral standards that he himself observed in his own life and enjoined in a normative fashion in his teaching (cf. C. K. Barrett, *A Commentary on the First Epistle to the Corinthians* [New York: Harper and Row, 1968] 117; F. F. Bruce, *I and II Corinthians* [Grand Rapids: Eerdmans, 1980] 51).

Can the *imitatio* be pinned down more specifically? Some say yes and locate it (1) in the cultivation of personal virtues such as humility and self-sacrifice (e.g., A. Robertson and A. Plummer, *A Critical and Exegetical Commentary on the First Epistle of Paul to the Corinthians* [New York: Scribners, 1911] 90; DeBoer, *Imitation of Paul* 146; Tinsley, *Imitation of God* 139), or (2) in the relational qualities of peace, harmony, and unity (e.g., Sanders, "Imitating Paul" 361-63; Castelli, *Imitating Paul* 110-11), or (3) in a life of suffering (e.g., Furnish, *Theology and Ethics* 223; G. D. Fee, *The First Epistle to the Corinthians* [Grand Rapids: Eerdmans, 1987] 186; Fowl, "Imitation" 428). The first of these proposals finds some support in Paul's mention of the humble lot of an apostle in verse 11: "we go without adequate food, drink, clothing, and shelter." The second, a call to harmony and unity, certainly fits the broader context of chapters 1–4, where Paul responds to news of congregational divisions over which itinerant preacher possessed the superior oratorical and rhetorical skills that would justify personal loyalty. The third, conformity to a life of hardship and suffering, figures, to be sure, in the immediately preceding block of verses (vv 9-13) and is set in contrast to the paradigm of superspirituality that the Corinthian believers were opting for — that is, the self-identification as a spiritual people on whom the fullness, riches, and power of the end of the age had come (cf. v 8).

It is doubtful, however, for epistolary reasons, that verses 14-17 are to be linked that closely with the concrete concerns of the preceding chapters. The epistolary formula "I am writing these things" *(graphō tauta)* in verse 14 signals a transition to the body closing section of the earlier chapters. Paul shifts from a litany of apostolic woes in verses 9-13 to his purpose in writing the letter (v 14: "*I* am not writing these things to shame you"), a fatherly plea to imitate the pattern of Christian living that he teaches in all his churches (vv 15-16), and news of the forthcoming visit of an emissary to insure that such imitation occurs (v 17). This would suggest that the Pauline exemplar is to be found in a common core of ethical teachings and norms of Christian practice that were routinely passed along to new congregations.

Paul mentions universal norms of teaching and practice three other times in 1 Corinthians. Such norms included retaining the place in life that one has been assigned ("This is the rule I lay down in all the churches," 7:17), appropriate head covering for women functioning in liturgical roles ("We have no other practice, nor do the churches of

God," 11:16), and carrying out worship in a fitting and orderly fashion ("As in all the congregations of the saints," 14:33; cf. v 36). These few passages indicate that discipleship was fleshed out in very concrete ways in the Pauline churches. Such a practical dimension arose, in part, out of a need to avoid whatever might prove to be an obstacle to faith and witness (cf. 9:12: "We put up with anything rather than hinder the gospel of Christ"; also 14:23). This is especially evident from passages in which Paul reprimands the church for not living in accordance with society's minimum standards — for sexual immorality of a kind that does not occur even among pagans (5:1), a woman not covering her head while functioning in a leadership capacity, which is a social "disgrace" (11:6, 13), and uncontrolled use of tongues in public worship, which will elicit the comment "you are out of your mind" from a visitor (14:23). Discipleship, therefore, involves an evangelistic sensitivity to the mores and ethical norms of one's own society.

Imitating Christ (11:1)

In 11:1 Paul issues a second call to imitation: "Imitate me, just as I imitate Christ" (mimētai mou ginesthe kathōs kagō Christou). It is noteworthy that Paul does not command direct imitation of Christ, but, instead, asks for an act of imitation that mirrors his own conformity to Christ. This points up the authoritative role that Paul's imitatio played in the formation of those he evangelized. Whatever his converts learned, received, heard, and saw in him, they, in turn, were expected to do (cf. Phil 4:9). It also suggests that discipleship was not something that occurred after evangelization, but was part and parcel of it. Paul shared with his converts not only the gospel but his very self (1 Thess 2:8). And it further explains why Paul set forth his conduct not simply as something worthy of following but with every expectation that it would be followed; for it was the formation of Christ in him, and not merely a human exemplar, that his converts were expected to imitate. This has far-reaching implications for a society like ours that is afloat in a sea of ethical relativism. In Paul's example believers have not only helpful guidelines but an authoritative norm for conduct, irrespective of time and place.

The normative character of the imitatio accounts for why Paul went to such lengths to defend himself whenever his conduct was called into question. He viewed his life as so bound up with the gospel that to call into question his conduct was to call into question the very message he preached. 2 Corinthians is a case in point. In virtually every chapter Paul is concerned to underline his personal integrity: "frankness and honesty" mark his conduct (1:12); "sincerity" distinguishes his preaching (2:17); "openness" characterizes his dealings (4:2); his ministry is available to the scrutiny of all (5:11); meticulous care is taken to avoid anything that would discredit his ministry (6:3; 8:20-21); and "purity," "insightfulness," "patience," "kindness," and "sincere love" typify his life (6:6-7).

All of this might sound somewhat exaggerated and presumptuous to our ears today. We do well, however, to keep in mind that Paul was up against intruders at Corinth who claimed to be authentic transmitters of Christian tradition but whose behavior belied their claim. They, like some today, peddled the word of God for profit (2 Cor 2:17, "like so much cheap merchandise," GNB), used deceptive practices (4:2), and tampered with God's word to make it more palatable for the listeners and more lucrative for themselves (4:2). They also sought to dominate and intimidate the Corinthians by bullying them, consuming their finances, taking advantage of them, putting on airs, and engaging in verbal put-downs (11:20). In such circumstances, authentic witness to the *imitatio Christi* becomes imperative.

What, then, is the *imitatio Christi?* Some think what is to be imitated is to be found in the preexistent Christ's voluntary curtailment of his divine prerogatives to assume the role of a servant (e.g., Lietzmann and Kümmel, *An die Korinther* 53; Bruce, *I and II Corinthians* 102) or in the incarnate Christ's willing sacrifice, which extended even to death (e.g., H. Conzelmann, *1 Corinthians* [Philadelphia: Fortress, 1975] 180; Fee, *1 Corinthians* 490). Others identify the *imitatio* with behavior consistent with the lordship of the exalted Christ (e.g., Bauder, "Imitate," 491). Most, however, look to the historical Jesus and locate the *imitatio* in his humility (e.g., Kurz, "Kenotic Imitation," 106), his mission to seek and save the lost (e.g., Orr, *1 Corinthians* 251), his self-giving for the salvation of the world (e.g., DeBoer, *Imitation of Paul* 158; Williams, "Imitation of Christ" 351-54), or his setting the well-being of others above his own (e.g., Robertson and Plummer, *I Corinthians* 225-26; Fowl, "Imitation" 429).

Fortunately, the immediate context of 1 Cor 11:1 provides some help. For unlike the *imitatio* appeal of 4:16, this one in 11:1 is closely tied

125

to the preceding verses. In fact, 11:1 functions as Paul's concluding statement to a rather lengthy discussion of the nature and limits of Christian freedom. In that discussion, the question is raised: Are Christians free to engage their culture — even to the point of eating meat that has been tainted by idolatrous associations? Paul's response is "Yes," provided that commitment to Christ is not compromised (10:1-22) and that one does not cause another brother or sister to stumble in such a way that their ability to distinguish right from wrong is impaired (8:12: "wound their weak conscience"). These are, however, rather significant qualifications. Indeed, Paul goes on to say that his aim in all that he does is to "please everyone in every way" (10:33a) — which would imply that in practice the Christian is not free at all. Paul's further statement that he does not seek his "own good but the good of the many that they might be saved" (10:33b) provides additional confirmation of such a limitation.

All this suggests that conformity to the example of Christ is to be found in setting aside personal rights and privileges for the good of others. The identical thought appears in Rom 15:2-3, but phrased in the form of a command: "Each of us should please our neighbor for the good purpose of building up the neighbor, for even Christ did not please himself." Instead, Christ made himself the servant of all (cf. Mark 10:45; Luke 22:27). Servanthood, then, was something that Jesus exemplified, something that Paul, in turn, modeled, and something that we, as well, are called to emulate. Because the goal is not only the good of others but also their salvation, setting aside one's rights to serve others becomes not merely desirable but required of the disciple. In a society like ours that prides itself on personal rights and freedoms — first and foremost being "life, liberty, and the pursuit of happiness" — this exemplar is much needed.

2. Examples of Discipleship in 2 Corinthians

The task of determining the form that discipleship takes in 2 Corinthians is somewhat more challenging. Discipleship language is nonexistent in 2 Corinthians. Moreover, there is no discrete section that sets out norms for Christian living, as one finds in Paul's other letters. To be sure, there is the periodic injunction and occasional listing of ethical dos and don'ts. The Corinthians, for instance, are enjoined about halfway through the letter not to be unequally yoked with unbelievers (6:14) and to purify themselves from everything that contaminates body and spirit (7:1). They are also commanded toward the close of the letter to examine themselves to see whether they are in the faith (13:5) and charged to mend their ways, exhort one another, be of one mind, and pursue peace (13:11).

But apart from these few-and-far-between injunctions, the life of discipleship is something that is implicitly urged rather than explicitly commanded in the letter. At no point in 2 Corinthians does Paul call on the congregation to imitate him, as he does in 1 Corinthians. Instead, he lays before his readers carefully chosen examples of what the Christian life entails, drawn from the life of Christ, his own life and ministry, and the congregational life of the Macedonian churches. Each example urges the same course of action: If anyone would follow after Christ it is necessary to deny self and to take up one's cross. This is, of course, not Paul's phraseology, but a teaching of Jesus found in the Synoptic tradition. Yet 2 Corinthians reads very much like a commentary on this early church tradition.

The Example of Jesus

The primary examples for Christian discipleship in 2 Corinthians are drawn from Jesus' life. They are models that have generally been overlooked because of a common scholarly perception that Paul was largely unfamiliar with and showed little interest in the earthly life of Christ. In 2 Corinthians, however, Paul evidences a clear knowledge of the common core of Jesus traditions. Traditional materials are introduced in a matter-of-fact way that suggests that author and readers alike were familiar with Jesus' life and ministry: Jesus was gentle and forbearing (10:1); his earthly life was marked by poverty (8:9); his ministry was characterized by such hardships and distress that it could be called "the dying of Jesus" (4:10); and, in the end, he died like every human being because he was frail and mortal (13:4). Yet he was made sin for us (5:21), died for the sake of all humanity (5:14), and was raised from the dead by God's power (13:4; cf. Belleville, "Gospel and Kerygma" 140-42).

The Grace of Christ (8:9)

The Jesus traditions in 2 Corinthians focus on Christ's incarnation, crucifixion, earthly demeanor, and ministerial hardships. In each case the traditional materials are cited for their paradigmatic value. The first of these traditions appears in a text that is quoted in the typical Christian worship service just prior to the receiving of the tithes and offerings: "For you know the grace of our Lord Jesus Christ, that, though he was rich, for your sakes he became poor so that we through his poverty might become rich" (8:9). Paul turns to the example of Christ at this juncture in 2 Corinthians in an effort to stimulate the Corinthians to follow through on a charitable pledge made the year before. To this end he cites a tradition that they were quite familiar with, as the introductory phrase "for you know" *(ginōskete gar)* and the full christological title "our Lord Jesus Christ" *(tou kyriou hēmōn Iēsou Christou)* make plain.

As the final appeal in a lengthy argument, Paul asks the Corinthian congregation to gauge the sincerity of their commitment to the larger body of believers by "the grace of our Lord Jesus Christ" *(tēn charin tou kyriou hēmōn Iēsou Christou).* Paul's choice of terms is instructive. "The grace" *(hē charis)* denotes unmerited favor, with the definite article pointing to a decisive moment in history when such favor was concretely demonstrated. This decisive moment happened, according to Paul, when Christ set aside his riches and became poor. By "rich" *(plousios)* Paul is probably thinking of the riches of heavenly existence — in particular, Christ's preexistent majesty and power — as the emphatic "our Lord Jesus Christ" would indicate. By "he became poor" *(eptōcheusen)* he undoubtedly has in mind the incarnation, when Christ gave up the riches of heavenly existence to assume an earthly state of poverty. The aorist verb *eptōcheusen* is likely ingressive: "he entered into a state of poverty." The voice is active rather than passive and so suggests that Christ's state of poverty was voluntarily assumed and not imposed on him from without or due to circumstances beyond his control.

What this state of poverty entailed is debated. Perhaps Paul was thinking of Jesus' birth into a poor family and his association with prostitutes, tax collectors, and the like (e.g., J. Héring, *The Second Epistle of Saint Paul to the Corinthians,* tr. A. W. Heathcote and P. J. Allcock [London: Epworth, 1967] 60; D. Macdonald, "The Price of Poverty," *Review for Religious* 45 [1986] 5). Alternatively, his association with those who are "poor in spirit" could be in view (so, e.g., J. D. G. Dunn). Another possibility is the condescension involved in Christ becoming a human being (so, e.g., Bruce, *I and II Corinthians* 222; Furnish, *2 Corinthians* 417; R. P. Martin, *2 Corinthians* [Waco: Word, 1986] 263).

Or, perhaps it is his identification with the human condition as such (e.g., Robertson and Plummer, *First Corinthians* 241; F. B. Craddock, "The Poverty of Christ: An Investigation of 2 Corinthians 8:9," *Interpretation* 22 [1968] 166) — which, on balance, offers the best point of contrast to a forfeiture of heavenly riches.

In any event, the exemplar that Paul places before his Corinthian converts in 8:9 is clear. The one to whom honor and service was due freely took the form of one from whom obedience and service was expected. In Christ's case, that which was due him was incalculable: equality with God, with all its attendant privileges and honors (cf. Phil 2:6). And the form of servanthood that Christ assumed was unimaginable: the one who knew no sin was made sin for us (cf. 2 Cor 5:21). The incarnation, therefore, exemplified a generosity that goes far beyond human conception, which Paul quite rightly calls "God's indescribable gift" (9:15).

What, then, is being asked of Paul's addressees at Corinth — and, by extension, of all those who seek to follow Christ? The intent of Christ's self-imposed poverty was that we "through his poverty might become rich" (8:9). Simply put, he laid aside the wealth that was rightfully his so that others might have riches that were not rightfully theirs. So is Paul asking his readers — both then and now — to give up their material wealth so that others can become rich? This very misunderstanding is forestalled in verse 13: "Our desire," Paul states, "is not that others might be relieved while you are hard pressed." What, then, is his desire for the church? It is important to observe that it is "the *grace* of our Lord Jesus Christ" — a denial of self to serve others, not the forfeiture of riches *per se* — that Paul holds up for emulation. Moreover, it is an unmerited denial of self that is in view — a denial of self to serve not merely those who merit our service but also those who do not merit it. What Paul is asking the Corinthians to do, then, is to don the mantle of servanthood, a servanthood that is not merely a reflex of the pocketbook but a habit of the heart. "Ordinary charity," says James Denney, "is but the crumbs from the rich man's table; but if we catch Christ's spirit, it will carry us far beyond that" (*The Second Epistle to the Corinthians,* second ed. [New York: Armstrong, 1900] 268). This is Paul's hope for the Corinthians as well as for us as a church today.

It might, at first glance, seem somewhat strange that Paul looked to the preexistent Christ rather than to the historical Jesus as his exemplar for service. That is not because he was unfamiliar with the life of Christ. Rather, it is because the full extent of Christ's sacrifice can only be grasped from the perspective of his preexistence and incarnation. No more powerful example of putting aside one's rights to seek the advantage of another exists — what Ralph Martin appropriately calls "the highest illustration of love-in-action" (*2 Corinthians* 262).

The Love of Christ (5:14)

Another feature of the Jesus tradition that profoundly shaped Paul's concept of discipleship was that of Christ's crucifixion. And here, it is not Christ's obedience even to death, as might be expected, but his self-effacing love that is the formative idea: "the love of Christ compels us" (5:14). While the genitive construction "of Christ" could be objective: "our love for Christ" (so, e.g., Héring, *Second Corinthians* 42), Paul's subsequent reference to the death of one for all points to a subjective genitive interpretation: "Christ's love for us."

Exactly what role did Christ's love play in Paul's understanding of Christian discipleship? That it exercised a profound influence on him is beyond doubt. But Paul's choice of the verb *synechein* suggests that something more specific is in view. The verb's basic sense is "hold together," with related meanings of "restrain," "maintain," "compel," "hem in," and "control." The exact contextual nuance is more difficult to ascertain. That Christ's love "restrains" us from all self-seeking is surely one aspect of the larger picture, for Paul goes on in verse 15 to give as an implication of Christ's death that we no longer live for self but for Christ, who died for us and was raised (cf. Robertson and Plummer, *Second Corinthians* 173; M. Thrall, *The Second Epistle of St Paul to the Corinthians* [Edinburgh: T. & T. Clark, 1994] 408). That it "urges" us on to service accords with the idea in verse 13 of being prepared to follow whatever course of action advances the cause of the gospel ("If we are out of our mind, it is for God; if we are in our right mind, it is for you"). Yet that it "compels" us to follow Christ provides the best connection with what follows: "Christ's love compels us," Paul states, "because we have concluded that one died for all." In short, Paul was a driven person. The love of Christ had him in its grasp, and he had no choice but to follow its lead (cf. Denney, *Second Epistle* 193).

Why this should be so is summed up in the credal formula "one died for all." This text is a notorious crux. How encompassing is "all"?

Does "for" denote substitution ("Christ died in the place of all") or representation ("Christ died on behalf of all")? To focus only on such exegetical issues, however, is to miss Paul's point. It was a personal conviction about Christ's death ("we are convinced that") and not just a consciousness of his apostolic responsibility that compelled Paul to carry out his ministry. The verb *krinein* ("convince") was commonly used in Paul's day of a conclusion drawn after thoroughly evaluating the facts. Here in 5:14 it emphasizes a carefully considered judgment, as opposed to a casual acceptance of something at face value. Paul has assessed the evidence and come to the conclusion that, far from dying for something he himself had done, Christ died for what we have done. The cross, then, becomes the supreme demonstration of God's love for us — a love that compels us to follow Christ. George Matheson summed this up well up when he penned the words: "O love that wilt not let me go, I rest my weary soul in Thee. I give Thee back the life I owe, that in Thine ocean depths its flow may richer, fuller be."

The Gentleness and Forbearance of Christ (10:1)

A further feature of the Jesus tradition that had a formative influence on Paul's concept of discipleship was Christ's earthly demeanor. There is, of course, no laudatory Christ hymn in 2 Corinthians comparable to Phil 2:6-11. Yet Paul does highlight virtues worthy of emulation. In 10:1 he writes: "I myself, I Paul, appeal to you Corinthians through the gentleness and forbearance of Christ." The genitive is likely subjective: Paul appeals to the church "by the gentleness and forbearance that characterized Christ's dealings with us."

The combination "gentleness" *(praÿtēs)* and "forbearance" *(epieikeia)* is predicated of Christ nowhere else in the New Testament. The adjective "gentle" *(praÿs)* is used twice of Jesus in Matthew's Gospel. In Matt 11:29 the would-be disciple is instructed to bear Jesus' yoke and learn from him, since Jesus is "gentle and humble in heart," and in 21:5 the manner of Jesus' entry into Jerusalem is understood as being in fulfillment of the prophecy that Israel's king would come "gentle and riding on a donkey" (Zech 9:9 LXX). Although *praÿtēs* here in 2 Cor 10:1 is often rendered "meekness" (KJV, NASB, NKJV, GNB, RSV, NIV, NRSV), this is not the most felicitous translation since meekness is commonly used today of someone deficient in spirit and courage. "Gentleness" (Phillips, NEB, REB, JB, LB) is the better option. It accords with extrabiblical usage of the term to denote a mild and friendly disposition, as opposed to a harsh and severe one (cf. F. Hauck, "*praÿs, praÿtēs*," *TDNT* 6.645-46; C. Spicq, *Theological Lexicon of the New Testament*, 3 vols. [Peabody: Hendrickson, 1994] 3.161-63).

Paul alone of the New Testament writers attributes the virtue of "forbearance" to Christ. *Epieikeia* ("forbearance"), which is a close synonym of *praÿtēs* ("gentleness"), denotes the yielding and tolerant disposition of those in positions of power — for example, a judge who is fair and lenient in judgment or a king who is kind in his rule. In the LXX, *epieikeia* is that quality of justice and government that treats people with mercy and clemency (cf. Ps 86:5; Dan 3:42; 2 Maccabees 2:22; 10:4; Wisdom of Solomon 12:18; Baruch 2:27). The REB's "magnanimity" catches the sense (cf. Héring, *Second Corinthians* 69).

So Paul saw in the gentleness and forbearance of Christ's earthly dealings a model to emulate. Is it a model appropriate only for the exercise of apostolic authority? Not at all! Gentleness and forbearance are critical dispositions for all who lead God's people. This is evident from the fact that these same virtues appear in New Testament lists of qualifications for church leaders (1 Tim 3:3; 6:11; 2 Tim 2:25). Both virtues presuppose a servanthood attitude that is at odds with the "top down" hierarchical style of leadership so prevalent in our churches today. The disciple who follows the model of Jesus will seek to persuade rather than command, to speak kindly rather than domineer. These two virtues also presuppose a self-mastery of temper and tongue that translates into a friendly word and a soft voice (cf. Spicq, *Theological Lexicon* 3.165). Do they preclude a rod? By no means — but they do not require it to lead (cf. 1 Cor 4:21).

Why does Paul single out these two particular virtues? Jesus was also compassionate, patient, forgiving, kind, generous, and considerate. Why are none of these virtues also highlighted? The context of this verse helps us out. Paul had been accused of trying to frighten the Corinthians with his letters (v 9). So he takes pains to reassure them that he carries out his commission as the apostle to the Gentiles in exactly the same manner that Christ carried out his earthly ministry — with gentleness and forbearance.

But Christ's example is something of a two-edged sword. For while some had been frightened by Paul's letters, others were jeering that he was all words and no action — someone who talked big at a safe distance but would turn tail in a face-to-face encounter (cf. 10:1). Paul's opponents most likely were recalling his last visit to Corinth, when he (or perhaps his representative) was publicly challenged (cf. 13:3) but chose to deal with the insult in a letter of rebuke rather than by personal confrontation (cf. 1:23–2:4). They evidently mistook a demeanor of gentleness for cowardice and mildness for passivity, thereby forgetting that "gentleness" and "forbearance" are dispositions of one who has the authority to command obedience and punish disobedience. Here, too, Jesus is the model. While his earthly demeanor was usually one of gentleness and forbearance, there were times when he wielded a whip instead of a kind word (e.g., Matt 21:12-17; 23:1-39).

The Ministerial Hardships of Christ

A final feature of the Jesus tradition that shaped Paul's understanding of discipleship was the ministerial suffering that Christ endured. Ministerial suffering is acknowledged by virtually everyone to be the central theme of 2 Corinthians, and rightfully so. It surfaces in almost every chapter of the letter: "The sufferings of Christ overflow to us" (1:5); "we always carry around the dying of Jesus" (4:10); "we groan, longing to be clothed with our heavenly dwelling" (5:2); "as servants of God we commend ourselves through great endurance in troubles, hardships, and distresses" (6:4); "when we came into Macedonia . . . we were harassed at every turn" (7:5); "I have known hunger and thirst . . . I have been cold and naked" (11:27); "I delight in weakness, insults, hardships, persecutions, and difficulties" (12:10); and "we are weak in him" (13:4) — to highlight just a few references.

It is sometimes claimed that Paul's sufferings were unique to his commission as the apostle to the Gentiles and that he did not intend this aspect of his ministry to be a point of imitation for his converts (so, e.g., S. Hafemann, "The Comfort and Power of the Gospel: The Argument of 2 Corinthians 1–3," *Review and Expositor* 86 [1989] 327-28). Yet already in chapter 1 Paul is quite explicit about God's intent to produce in the Corinthians "patient endurance of the same sufferings we suffer" (1:6). Moreover, suffering is presented as something not incidental, or even accidental, but basic to the Christian life (1:7, "as you share in our sufferings"). Why this should be so is not difficult to ascertain. If the call to be a disciple includes a call to service, then this service will expose the disciple to the same dangers to which Christ was exposed. As Dietrich Müller aptly states: "Jesus went before them in suffering; the disciple can expect no less" ("Disciple," *NIDNTT* 1.488-89).

What kind of suffering does Paul have in mind? Is it the routine trials of daily life in an imperfect world? Or is it the hardships and persecutions that come our way as a result of bearing the name of Christ — and so to be seen as ministerial suffering? Paul's references in 1:5; 4:10; and 13:4 to Jesus' trials during his earthly ministry suggest the latter, and it is to these passages we need now turn.

The Sufferings of Christ (1:5). "The sufferings of Christ," Paul asserts in 1:5, "overflow to us." Some argue that the phrase "the sufferings of Christ" is equivalent to "the sufferings endured for Christ's sake." But the second part of 1:5, which reads "so also through Christ comes the encouragement," seems to be against such a construal of the genitive. A likelier possibility is that the genitive is possessive: "the sufferings that Christ endured" — which accords with Paul's references elsewhere to "the dying of Jesus" (4:10) and "Christ's sufferings" (Phil 3:10; cf. Col 1:24).

What is the nature of these sufferings? It is unlikely that Paul is referring to the sufferings that the glorified Christ currently experiences through union with his church (so, e.g., R. Bultmann, *The Second Letter to the Corinthians,* tr. R. A. Harrisville [Minneapolis: Augsburg, 1985] 24; Tinsley, *Imitation of God* 145; Ahern, "Fellowship of His Sufferings" 21, 31-32; Proudfoot, "Imitation or Realistic Participation" 147). The progression of Christ's sufferings in verse 5a to apostolic sufferings in verse 5b to church sufferings in verse 7 is contrary to such an understanding. Nor is it probable that Paul is reflecting the rabbinic notion of the woes of the Messiah that will usher in the age to come (so, e.g., C. K. Barrett, *A Commentary on the Second Epistle to the Corinthians* [New York: Harper and Row, 1973] 62; Martin, *2 Corinthians* 9), since these woes are destined for God's people and not for the coming Messiah himself. The most plausible option is a reference to the earthly sufferings of Christ that issued in his death, along the lines of Phil 3:10, where Paul writes that sharing in Christ's sufferings leads to becoming like him in his death.

But in what way do Christ's earthly sufferings "overflow to us" (*perisseuei eis hēmas*) — a turn of phrase that occurs only here in Paul's letters? Some say that they do so through our intentional imitation of

Christ's life (e.g., H. Windisch, *Der zweite Korintherbrief* [Göttingen: Vandenhoeck und Ruprecht, 1924] 40; E.-B. Allo, *Seconde Épitre aux Corinthiens* [Paris: Gabalda, 1956] 9). But while imitation is an active idea in Paul's writings (e.g., "imitate me," 1 Cor 4:16; 11:1), identification with Christ's sufferings is distinctly passive. Paul's converts became imitators of Christ by virtue of their passive endurance of affliction, not their active pursuit of the same (cf. 1 Thess 1:6).

Possibly, then, Christ's sufferings overflow as a result of the sufferer's union with Christ. It is sometimes argued that Paul understands the unity between Christ and Christians to be so close that what happened to Christ on the cross becomes part of the church's own experience (e.g., Furnish, *2 Corinthians* 120). Identification with Christ is certainly a theme that Paul develops elsewhere in his writings. For example, in Rom 6:5 to be united with Christ in his death is to be united with him in his resurrection. But it is not a theme that surfaces in 2 Corinthians.

More probably, then, Christ's sufferings become our sufferings because we continue the mission of Christ (e.g., R. V. G. Tasker, *The Second Epistle of Paul to the Corinthians* [Grand Rapids: Eerdmans, 1958] 41). Jesus told his disciples: "If they persecuted me, they will persecute you" (John 15:20; cf. Matt 20:23). Since the theme of ministerial suffering figures so prominently in 2 Corinthians, this seems the most plausible interpretation here in 1:5.

The Dying of Jesus (4:10). Paul's second reference to Jesus' earthly trials appears in 4:10: "always carrying around the dying of Jesus *(tēn nekrōsin tou Iēsou)* in our body." The Greek is sometimes rendered "the death of Jesus," but "the dying of Jesus" is more accurate because *nekrōsis* denotes a process or state rather than the event of death itself (cf. J. Lambrecht, "The *Nekrosis* of Jesus: Ministry and Suffering in 2 Cor 4,7-15," in *L'Apôtre Paul. Personnalité, style, et conception du ministère,* ed. A. Vanhoye [Leuven: University Press, 1986] 120). The simple name "Jesus" *(Iēsous)* without qualification associates this process with the earthly Christ. So while we might instinctively connect "the dying of Jesus" with the cross, it is the whole of Jesus' ministry that is in view here.

In what way, though, can Jesus' ministry be described as a "dying"? The metaphor of the clay pot three verses earlier evokes images of frailty, vulnerability, and mortality. But Paul is not thinking merely of physical sufferings and hardships, as is clear from the phrase "*always* carrying

135

around in our body." It is more likely that he has in mind the toll that ministry exacts on the human frame. In Jesus' case, pressures, frustrations, and hardships come to mind — not to mention loneliness, disappointment, exhaustion, constant harassment by opponents, and the continuous demands of the crowd.

The impact of Jesus' ministry on Paul is that Paul "always carries around the dying of Jesus" in his "body" (v 10) and "is always being given over to death for Jesus' sake" (v 11). The expression "carrying around in the body" could refer simply to the aging process or to the normal trials of human existence. But the phrase "for Jesus' sake" places this experience in the context of Christian ministry. While Paul is undoubtedly thinking of the exhaustion and hardships that typify the life of an itinerant preacher (cf. 11:23-29), carrying around the dying of Jesus applies to anyone actively engaged in proclaiming the good news. The present tenses are to be noted: "continually carries around" Jesus' dying and "is constantly being surrendered into" the hands of death (NEB). What this meant in practical terms for Paul can be gauged from the specifics of his tribulation lists in 6:4-5 and 11:23-27. What it means for us today may not match Paul's list point for point, but to "spend and be spent" in Christ's service is certainly one aspect of the larger picture (12:15).

The Weakness of Christ (13:4). Paul's third and final reference to Jesus' earthly trials is in 13:4: "He was crucified out of weakness." The meaning of Paul's statement is debated. He could be speaking of an erroneous human perception, similar to that spoken of in 5:16: "Though we once regarded Christ from a worldly standpoint, we do so no longer." By the world's standards, Jesus' ministry was a failure. He claimed to be the Messiah and asserted that he would usher in the kingdom of God. But in the end he succumbed to weakness and died a criminal's death.

Yet this reading of the text overlooks the aorist tense of the verb *estaurōthē.* Christ "*was* crucified" in weakness, not just seemed to be or was regarded as such. The opening particles "for indeed" *(kai gar)* confirm this. This makes it probable that the term "weakness" *(astheneia)* denotes human frailty and powerlessness. Thus whether the preposition *ex* with the noun *astheneias* specifies the reason ("by reason of human frailty") or the underlying principle ("because of human frailty"), the point is the same: The crucifixion demonstrated Jesus' essential humanity and therefore his mortality.

Suffering and Imitation. To stop here, however, is to miss the real point of Paul's references to the earthly sufferings of Jesus. It is not suffering *per se* that conforms us to Christ. Paul nowhere calls his converts to imitate the sufferings of either Christ or himself. He asks them to pray for his deliverance from affliction (2 Cor 1:11; cf. Phil 1:19; Col 4:3). He also acknowledges that parallels exist among Christ's sufferings, his own sufferings, and the church's experience of suffering (2 Cor 1:5-7). But he nowhere urges the Corinthians to suffer in order to realize the *imitatio Christi,* because the *imitatio* lies elsewhere.

Still, suffering does play a role in Paul's thought in producing the *imitatio.* For one, it develops Christlikeness. Suffering, Paul holds, produces patient endurance, and through patient endurance comes divine encouragement (1:6-7). Furthermore, suffering is the training ground for ministry. "God encourages us in all our troubles," Paul states, "so that we can, in turn, encourage those in any trouble with the encouragement that we ourselves have received from God" (1:4). In short, suffering equips us to better serve God's people.

Finally, suffering is the occasion for serving Christ, since it is through weakness and suffering that God's power can be seen and appropriated. In fact, Paul claims that the reason we carry around the dying of Jesus is so that the life of Jesus may be revealed in our human frailty (4:10-12). As Calvin Roetzel observes, "the incarnation of life comes from the incarnation of death" ("As Dying" 13). This was true for Paul. It is also true for all who serve Christ and his church today. While death is at work in us, life is at work in the lives of those we are called to serve (4:12).

The Example of Paul (1:24; 4:5)

A second model of discipleship that Paul placed before his readers was himself — a model of servanthood. As an apostle of Christ, he could have merely said the word and commanded the Corinthians' obedience. To lead by force of will was, to be sure, the prevailing style of leadership in that day. But domination was not Paul's style. His style of leadership was synergetic — that is, working alongside his converts *(synergoi)* — not autocratic — that is, ruling over them (1:24).

Moreover, instead of extolling himself in his preaching, Paul preached "Jesus Christ as Lord" (4:5). Others flaunted their credentials

(3:1-3), their heritage (11:21-22), their eloquence (10:10), their knowledge (11:6), and their spirituality ("visions and revelations," 12:1; "signs, wonders, and miracles," 12:12). And the world applauded them for it. They also proclaimed themselves as "lord." In an intriguing statement in 11:20 Paul states that the Corinthians embraced traveling preachers who "enslaved" and "exploited" their hearers, "pushed themselves forward," and "slapped" the church "in the face." Domination was not, however, the way of Paul, who defines his role as that of a "servant" (NIV) — or, perhaps better translated, "slave" (NRSV; *doulos*) — not that of a lord (4:5).

In 1 Corinthians Paul reminded his converts that on his founding visit he did not use eloquence, superior wisdom, or persuasive words. This was so that the Corinthians might know nothing while he was with them except Jesus Christ — and Christ crucified (1 Cor 2:1-4). Now that they have become believers in Jesus, he is concerned that they know not only the crucified Christ but also Jesus as "Lord" — that is, Jesus as the master of their congregational life. This is an important reminder for those of us in leadership positions today. If Christ is to be truly Lord of the church, we must be content with the role of servant. This idea is reinforced by the prepositional phrase *dia Iēsoun,* which is commonly translated "for Jesus' sake" (so KJV, Phillips, JB, GNB, REB, NIV, NRSV), but the more likely rendering is "because of Jesus." Paul counted himself a servant of the church because of him who first took on the form of a servant (Phil 2:7) and exhorted his disciples to do the same (cf. John 13:14-17).

Paul's denial of self to serve the Corinthians was played out in many ways. It could be seen in his refusal to use the common manipulative techniques of the day to get the crowd's attention (4:2), in his plying a trade so as not to be a financial burden on the church (11:7-9), and in his expending himself over and over again for the congregation (11:28-29; 12:15). Yet because he did not fit the first-century model of an impressive leader, he was belittled for his timidity (10:1), his unimpressive appearance (10:10), and his contemptible oratory (10:10). In fact, the term Paul's opponents used of him was "contemptible" *(exouthenēmenos).*

It is not much different in our day, where equal if not greater value is placed on a speaker's imposing personality and oratorical abilities. Yet if Christ is to be given his rightful place as Lord of the church, we must take the role of servant and not give in to the world's standards of successful leadership. Paul resisted this kind of pressure — even to the point of ridicule. And so must we.

The Example of the Macedonian Churches (8:1-5)

A final model of discipleship that Paul set before his readers was the example of the Macedonian churches. Sadly, it is often those having the least, rather than the most, who model discipleship the best. The Macedonian churches are a case in point. For though they were experiencing severe persecution, which left them in a state of extreme poverty, they overflowed in liberal giving (v 2). No details are provided about the nature of the persecution that they weathered except that it resulted in, quite literally, "down to the depth poverty" *(hē kata bathous ptōcheia)* — or, as P. E. Hughes translates, "rock-bottom poverty" *(Paul's Second Epistle to the Corinthians* [Grand Rapids: Eerdmans, 1962] 288).

The Macedonian churches are a rare testimony that it is possible not merely to experience joy in the midst of difficult circumstances, but also to be generous as well. Indeed, Paul states that their poverty "overflowed in a wealth of liberality" (v 2). It is, of course, fairly easy to see how affluence can well up in generous giving. But how is it possible for extreme poverty to overflow in a wealth of liberality? In the case of the Macedonian churches, this was due to three things. First, they gave not merely what they could afford but beyond (v 3). How much beyond Paul does not say. But there is no hint that this was a reckless action on their part. The sense is that they determined what they could comfortably contribute and then went beyond that figure. Second, what they gave, they gave "willingly" (v 3). They were not pressured into making a contribution. Rather, they asked urgently and repeatedly to be involved (v 4). This was because they considered involvement in the relief effort a "privilege" *(tēn charin)* and a "sharing" *(tēn koinōnian)*. Finally, the Macedonian generosity was possible because they committed themselves to the Lord first and only then to Paul (v 5). So great was their desire to serve Christ that they would not allow their economic situation to hinder them. Just as Christ set aside his rights and privileges to serve others, so the Macedonian churches gave no thought to themselves in their desire to follow Christ.

3. Conclusions

What can be said by way of conclusions to our study of discipleship in the Corinthian correspondence? First, discipleship has an objective content. It was something that was taught "everywhere in every church" (1 Cor 4:17) and included a common core of ethical teachings and norms of practice that were faithfully transmitted as part of Christian tradition. As such, it is something that we, in turn, are obliged to observe, teach, and call the church at large to heed.

Second, discipleship necessitates obedience. Belief is not sufficient. Genuine profession of the gospel of Christ must issue in a life of obedience (2 Cor 9:13). Consequently, making disciples, for Paul, meant bringing every thought into submission to Christ (10:5). It should mean no less for us.

Third, discipleship entails imitation of a personal exemplar. Paul called his churches to imitate his "ways in Christ." He could do this because his life was a concrete expression of what it meant to follow Christ. The task is no less ours. We, too, are called to live the kind of exemplary life that calls forth imitation.

Fourth, discipleship requires conformity to Christ. Although Paul does not command direct imitation of Christ, he does set forth Jesus' life and ministry as worthy of emulation. Christ's gentleness and forbearance are a paradigm of good leadership; his self-effacing love compels imitation; his setting aside of rights for the good of others evokes service; his earthly hardships elicit self-sacrifice.

Fifth, discipleship has a corporate dimension. The corporate life of the Macedonian churches had a recognizable shape that other churches could take as their exemplar.

Sixth, while the call to follow Christ is not a call to imitate his sufferings, suffering is a natural result. Paul, in fact, treats the sufferings of Christ as a given in the life of those who would follow Christ. This is because denial of self to serve others is not the way of the world. Personal ambition, self-interest, and self-sufficiency are what society deems admirable virtues. Self-denial, on the other hand, is "foolish" and "weak" (1 Cor 4:10) — something to ridicule and even to persecute.

One final observation. It is easier to locate the *imitatio Christi* in a life of economic hardship and physical suffering. Suffering can be an ego-building process and hardship can elicit public sympathy. It is harder to live out an ethic of self-denial in the service of others in a society like ours that is so wholly given over to a materialistic ideology and a survival-of-the-fittest mentality. Yet this is exactly what the followers of Christ are called to do — that is, to imitate the self-effacing love of Christ, not calling attention to ourselves but to Christ. How do we do this? We do well to consider the words of John the Baptist that stand at the very beginning of the early Christian tradition: "I must decrease, so that he can increase" (John 3:30).

Selected Bibliography

Ahern, B. M. "The Fellowship of His Sufferings, Phil. 3.10: A Study of St. Paul's Doctrine of Christian Suffering," *Catholic Biblical Quarterly* 22 (1960) 1-32.

Belleville, L. L. "Gospel and Kerygma in 2 Corinthians," in *Gospel in Paul: Studies on Corinthians, Galatians and Romans for Richard N. Longenecker,* ed. L. A. Jervis and P. Richardson. Sheffield: Sheffield Academic Press, 1994, 134-64.

————. *2 Corinthians.* IVP New Testament Commentary, Downers Grove: InterVarsity, 1996.

Castelli, E. A. *Imitating Paul: A Discourse of Power.* Louisville: Westminster, 1991.

DeBoer, W. P. *The Imitation of Paul.* Kampen: Kok, 1962.

Fowl, S. E. "Imitation," in *Dictionary of Paul and His Letters,* ed. G. F. Hawthorne, R. P. Martin, and D. G. Reid. Downers Grove: InterVarsity, 1993, 428-31.

Furnish, V. P. *2 Corinthians.* Anchor Bible, New York: Doubleday, 1984.

————. *Theology and Ethics in Paul.* Nashville: Abingdon, 1968.

Kurz, W. S. "Kenotic Imitation of Paul and of Christ in Philippians 2 and 3," in *Discipleship in the New Testament,* ed. F. F. Segovia. Philadelphia: Fortress, 1985, 103-26.

Proudfoot, C. M. "Imitation or Realistic Participation? A Study of 'Suffering with Christ,'" *Interpretation* 17 (1963) 140-60.

Roetzel, C. J. "'As Dying and Behold We Live': Death and Resurrection in Paul's Theology," *Interpretation* 46 (1992) 5-18.

Sanders, B. "Imitating Paul: 1 Cor 4:16," *Harvard Theological Review* 74 (1981) 353-63.

Schelkle, K. H. *Discipleship and Priesthood,* tr. J. Disselhorst. New York: Herder and Herder, 1965.

Stanley, D. M. "Become Imitators of Me: The Pauline Conception of Apostolic Tradition," *Biblica* 40 (1958) 859-77.

Tinsley, E. J. *The Imitation of God in Christ.* Philadelphia: Westminster, 1960.

Williams, D. M. "Imitation of Christ in Paul, With Special Reference to Paul as Teacher." Columbia University Ph.D. dissertation, 1967.

Becoming like God through Christ:
Discipleship in Romans

L. ANN JERVIS

It may seem curious to study discipleship in Romans when neither the noun "disciple" *(mathētēs)* nor the verb "follow" *(akolouthein)* appears in Romans — or, for that matter, in any of Paul's letters — and when neither in Romans nor in any of his other writings does Paul describe believers in Jesus Christ in ways analogous to the use of the term "disciple" in the Gospels. For whereas the Gospels speak of disciples as those who follow Jesus (e.g., Mark 1:17) and often lack faith (especially in Mark and Matthew), Paul never refers to believers in Jesus Christ as either disciples or followers of Jesus — and his primary characterization of them is as those who have faith! In Romans Paul refers to believers in Christ not as disciples but as "holy," "beloved," "called," "elect," "justified," "belonging to Jesus Christ," "those who have been baptized into Christ's death," "those who are under grace," "slaves of God," "those free from sin and death," "sons and daughters of God," "children of God," "brothers and sisters of Christ," "heirs of God," "heirs with Christ," "in Christ," "in the Spirit," "those who are saved," etc. Furthermore, he does not speak of believers as learners, nor are his churches directly analogous to the ancient philosophical schools (cf. Meeks, *First Urban Christians* 84).

That Paul does not speak of discipleship either in the Gospels' sense or in the sense that it would have had in the philosophical schools, however, does not prevent us from investigating discipleship in Romans.

143

It means, rather, that we must do so using a paradigm of discipleship that fits both the evidence of Romans and the ancient world's understanding of the goal of discipleship. With regard to the latter, we distinguish between discipleship as a social phenomenon in the ancient world — that is, association with a particular philosophical school — and the broad purpose of discipleship.

It is the broad purpose of discipleship in the ancient world that provides a useful comparative context for studying discipleship in Romans. Consequently, this chapter will proceed not by attempting to import the definition of discipleship that appears in the New Testament Gospels, which were written later than Paul's letters. Nor will it seek to understand Paul and his churches by reference to the ancient philosophical schools. Rather, it will attempt to explicate Paul's understanding of the purpose of discipleship by studying his reflections, explanations, and descriptions of the significance of faith in Jesus Christ against the backdrop of the ancient world's understanding.

The ancient world, I will argue, considered that the purpose of discipleship was to achieve likeness to God. It will also be contended that Paul's presentation of the significance of faith in the death and resurrection of Jesus Christ reflects an awareness of and response to just such an understanding, which pervaded the world of his day.

Investigating the topic of discipleship in Romans using the paradigm of discipleship's goal as becoming like God has several advantages. First, it locates Paul in a historical context. Given that the ancient world understood the goal of discipleship to be godlikeness, as we will attempt to demonstrate, such a paradigm enables one to see how Paul, in his particular historical circumstances, may have used this aspiration for the purpose of communicating or clarifying his gospel. For since this aspiration was shared by both Jews and Gentiles, it provided a natural bridge between the essential Jewishness of Paul's proclamation and his Gentile audience, as well as between Jewish believers in Jesus and Gentile Christians. Second, given that both Paul's "mystical" language and his "juridical" language fit into this broad category of discipleship as godlikeness, as we will also attempt to demonstrate, such an approach enables one to resolve the scholarly dilemma of how these two types of language related to one another in Paul's thought.

1. Discipleship in the Ancient World: Seeking to Achieve Likeness to God

A common theme running through the religious reflections and moral deliberations of antiquity was the desire to achieve likeness to God. This is true of the philosophical and religious thought of the Greco-Roman world as well as that of Judaism.

Greek Thought

Aristotle (384-322 B.C.), for example, recommended study or contemplation as the superior form of human activity because that is the kind of activity in which the gods are perpetually engaged. God's function, essence, or *telos* ("end," "purpose") is study, as should also be ours. Contemplation, therefore, is an end in itself — it is, in fact, "the only activity that is loved for its own sake; it produces no result beyond the actual act of contemplation" (*Nicomachean Ethics* 1177b1). In the *Metaphysics*, Aristotle writes, "if then, God is always in that good condition [i.e, studying], in which we sometimes are, this compels our wonder" (xii.1072b25-26). So Aristotle counsels in Book 10 of the *Nicomachean Ethics*: "The activity of God, which is transcendent in blessedness, is the activity of contemplation; and therefore among human activities that which is most akin to the divine activity of contemplation will be the greatest source of happiness" (1178b20-23). Human beings ought to realize that the most important thing they can do is study, for "the activity of the intellect . . . constitutes complete human happiness. . . . If . . . the intellect is something divine in comparison with man, so is the life of the intellect divine in comparison with human life . . . we ought so far as possible to achieve immortality" (117b19-33).

The Cynics, a school of philosophy that probably began with Antisthenes of Athens (born ca. 444 B.C.) and sought to develop the ethical teachings of Socrates (Antisthenes' teacher), pursued a life characterized by freedom, self-sufficiency, and self-control. The goal of life was to live according to nature — which was, coincidentally, a life of freedom. According to the Cynics, one of the most practical ways to be free was to be poor, for this meant freedom from the claims of others. Such was the way of the gods: "And often when I reflect on

145

why God is happy and blessed, I perceive that he far surpasses us in that he needs nothing. For that is a characteristic of a most splendid nature, that by not requiring much it is always ready to have enjoyment" (*Epistle of Socrates* 6.4; cf. Malherbe, *Cynic Epistles* 235). And the goal of the Cynic was to imitate the lifestyle of the gods: "It is indeed reasonable that he is wise who copies himself after the wisest, and he is happiest who assimilates himself as much as possible to one who is happy" (*ibid.*).

The Stoics, who were based on the teachings of the early fourth-century philosopher Zeno, regarded the goal of discipleship as achieving a "smooth flow of life" or "living consistently." This ideal was to be achieved as humans perfected their rational nature. Both humans and gods share a rational nature. As the Stoic philosopher Cleanthes (331-232 B.C.), who studied under Zeno and succeeded him as head of the Stoic school, says in his *Hymn to Zeus,* "we are God's offspring" and so "bear a likeness to god" (*Stoicorum Veterum Fragmenta* 1.537). The difference between the gods and humans is that the gods' rational nature is perfected, living in absolute harmony with the whole of nature. According to Chrysippus (ca. 280-207 B.C.), who succeeded him as head of the Stoic academy, the divine power resides in reason and in the intellect of universal nature. God is the world/nature itself and so is the universal pervasiveness of its mind.

The goal of the Stoic disciple was to live as the gods live. Chrysippus described the goal of life as "living according to our own nature and that of the universe" (*Diogenes Laertius* 7.88). As Brad Inwood observes, for the early Stoics "in a rational and therefore consistent Universe, consistency with one's own life will be a necessary condition for consistency with the whole of which one is a part. This consistency with oneself will also be a corollary of consistence with Nature as a whole" (*Ethics and Human Action in Early Stoicism* [Oxford: Clarendon, 1985] 106).

Disciples in the Epicurean school, which was founded by Epicurus (c. 342-271 B.C.), tried to achieve the same sort of life as the gods. Epicurus and his followers considered that the gods were in a state of deepest peace since they were separated from all concerns. The gods feared nothing. And so Epicurus sought to help his followers also fear nothing — neither pain nor loss, and not even death. In this way they, too, could live like the gods. Epicurus even suggested that Epicureans should worship each other. In a letter to the philosopher-sculptor

Colotes, who produced the great statue of Zeus at Olympia and the table on which rested the victors' crowns there, he wrote:

> You revered what we were saying on that occasion and were seized with an unscientific desire to embrace us by the knees, laying hold of us in the full extent of the contact that has become established in revering and supplicating certain beings. So you caused us to worship and revere you in return. . . . To me you are imperishable — walking around, and thinking of us as imperishable, too (quoted by Plutarch, *Against Colotes* 1117bc).

Plutarch, speaking sarcastically about the Epicurean claims, alludes to this particular self-understanding: "What great pleasure these men have, what bliss they enjoy, when they rejoice in suffering no evil, no distress, and no pain! Don't they deserve to be proud of that and say what they say, when they call themselves 'imperishable' and 'equal to the gods'" (*A Pleasant Life* 1091bc).

The Platonist Plutarch (ca. A.D. 46-120) also taught that what human beings really desire is to be as God is — that is, incorruptible, all powerful, and, most importantly, completely virtuous. Plutarch writes: "Divinity, to which such men are eager to adapt and conform themselves, is believed to have three elements of superiority — incorruption, power, and virtue; and the most revered, the divinest of these, is virtue" (*Aristides* 6.2-3). And again: "Consider first that God, as Plato says, offers himself to all as a pattern of every excellence, thus rendering human virtue, which is in some sort of assimilation to himself, accessible to all who 'follow God' . . . For man is fitted to become settled in virtue through copying and aspiring to the beauty and the goodness that are his" (*De Sera* 550D).

Not only the philosophical schools, but also the mystery religions of the ancient world considered that the goal of life was to achieve likeness to God. In fact, for the mystery religions, the goal was to achieve not just likeness but union with God. As Wilhelm Bousset wrote, the goal of "Greek mystery piety" was "a mystical identity with the deity" (*Kyrios Christos* [Nashville: Abingdon, 1970] 164). There were a variety of conceptions about how and when this union might take place — whether in the body or after death with the separation of soul and body. Nevertheless, the common goal was to become like God. In the *Liturgy of Mithras* the god Hermes says to Tat, "Do you not know that you have become god, and the son of god, just like me?" (Wikenhauser, *Pauline Mysticism* 201).

147

Hellenistic Jewish Thought

The goal of becoming like God also runs through the Hellenistic Jewish writings of Second Temple Judaism (ca. 200 B.C.–A.D. 100). The chief distinction between the two worlds of thought is that the Greek philosophical schools viewed likeness to God as achieved through self-mastery, whereas the Jewish world saw it as involving obedience to God's law and a divine gift of grace.

For Philo (ca. 30 B.C.–A.D. 45), discipleship's goal is to be able, through the perfection of the mind, to enter the intelligible world, the world of the forms — that is, to see God (cf. S. Sandmel, *Philo of Alexandria: An Introduction* [New York/Oxford: Oxford University Press, 1979] 101). This is achieved partly through self-striving, but ultimately it is a gift of God (e.g., *De Somniis* 1.60). The Patriarchs achieved such a goal, as Philo writes of Abraham: "God marveling at Abraham's faith in Him repaid him with faithfulness by confirming with an oath the gifts which He had promised, and here He no longer talked with him as God with man but as a friend with a familiar" (*De Abrahamo* 273). Moses' ascent of Mount Sinai, in fact, was viewed by Philo as an ascent into the realm of God. So Philo writes that Moses entered

> into the darkness where God was, that is into the formless, invisible, incorporeal, and archetypal essence of existing things. Thus he beheld what is hidden from the sight of mortal nature, and, in himself and his life displayed for all to see, he has set before us . . . a piece of work beautiful and godlike, a model for those who are willing to copy it. Happy are they who imprint, or strive to imprint, that image in their souls (*De Vita Mosis* 1.158).

So Moses, "the most perfect of men," was a partner of God and even "named god and king of the whole nation" (*De Ebrietate* 94).

A passion for godlikeness is evident also in the Jewish apocalyptic writings of the Second Temple period. Both the authors and the addressees of the Jewish apocalyptic writings viewed themselves as the righteous and elect of God, so that they alone were capable of reflecting God's being. Thus, just as God is holy and righteous, so are the elect. In the coming judgment, sinners will "not be able to behold the faces of the holy ones, for the light of the Lord of the Spirits is seen upon the face of the holy, the righteous, and the elect" (*1 Enoch* 38:4, the literal translation in J. H. Charlesworth, *Old Testament Pseudepigrapha* [New York: Doubleday, 1983] 1.30). At present, however, "the righteous" need to hold on until the end, at which time they will be vindicated and "shine like the lights of heaven" (*1 Enoch* 104:2).

The texts from Qumran reveal a similar aspiration to godlikeness. The goal of the Qumran covenanters was to "love all that [God] has chosen and hate all that [God] has rejected" (1QS [*Manual of Discipline*] 1; cf. CD [*Cairo Damascus Covenant*] 2; tr. from G. Vermes, *The Dead Sea Scrolls in English* [London: Penguin, 1987] 62). This great goal is to be accomplished through strict observance of God's law and complete dependence on God's grace. While by definition human beings are sinful — that is, not righteous ("righteousness, I know, is not of man, nor is perfection the way of the son of man: to the Most High God belong all righteous deeds," 1QH [*Psalms of Thanksgiving*] 4, tr. Vermes) — the goal of the Qumranites was, on the basis of God's grace, forgiveness and revelation to live like God: "I lean on Thy grace and on the multitude of Thy mercies, for Thou wilt pardon iniquity, and through Thy righteousness [Thou wilt purify man] of his sin" (1QH 4, tr. Vermes).

The Qumranites, as also the authors of the Jewish apocalyptic writings, viewed humanity as divided into two kinds of people: the righteous and the wicked. They considered themselves the elect, since they knew the truth about God and had been cleansed from sin through God's righteousness: "through his righteousness he will cleanse me of the uncleanness of man and of the sins of the children of men" (1QS 11, tr. Vermes). While the elect still battle sin, they are, nonetheless, capable of purity through repentance and God's cleansing: "As for me, if I stumble, the mercies of God shall be my salvation always" (1QS 11:11-12, tr. from F. C. Martinez, *The Dead Sea Scrolls Translated: The Qumran Texts in English* [Leiden: Brill, 1994]). The elect of the Qumran community, therefore, are sinners who are made righteous by God: "By Thy goodness alone is man righteous" (1QH 12, tr. Vermes). As a consequence, they have attained a resemblance to God: "For your glory, you have purified man from sin, so that he can make himself holy for you . . . so that he can take his place in your presence" (1QH 19:10-11, tr. Martinez).

The Jewish milieu of the Second Temple period, then, as much as that of the broader ancient Mediterranean world, aspired through discipleship to achieve godlikeness. Josephus (A.D. 37–95/100) wrote about

Judaism for the Gentile world: "Our legislator [Moses], . . . having shown that God possesses the very perfection of virtue, thought that men should strive to participate in it" (*Antiquities* 1.23). "That sage [Moses] deemed it above all necessity for one who would order his own life aright and also legislate for others, first to study the nature of God, and then, having contemplated his works with the eye of reason, to imitate as far as possible that best of all models and endeavour to follow it" (*Antiquities* 1.19).

Given such evidence for a common recognition in the ancient world that the task of discipleship was to achieve resemblance to God's character, it is likely that Paul appealed to and reflected this understanding of discipleship in his role as evangelist and pastor — particularly when writing to Christians at Rome. For in Romans, Paul must bridge the gap between the Jewish and Gentile religious mind-sets, communicating with Gentile believers who have been converted by Jewish Christians (cf. Fitzmyer, *Romans* 33) without either losing the essential Jewishness of his gospel or discounting the Gentileness of his hearers. For one of Paul's chief concerns in Romans is to convince his hearers of the equality of Jew and Gentile in the church (cf. J. C. Beker, *Paul the Apostle: The Triumph of God in Life and Thought* [Philadelphia: Fortress, 1980] 74).

We will proceed, therefore, to discuss discipleship in Romans on the basis that the goal of discipleship is to attain godlikeness. It will be argued that in Romans Paul's major descriptions of the result of faith in Jesus Christ speak to this motivation for discipleship.

2. Discipleship in Romans

In Romans Paul focuses the attention of believers on Christ's death and resurrection. There is no reference to following the pattern of Jesus' earthly life. Even 15:2-3, where Paul exhorts his addressees to please their neighbors for their good, to build them up, "for even Christ did not please himself," refers not to Christ's life but to his death. The death and resurrection of Jesus Christ, in fact, comprise the central core of Paul's gospel, and references to Christ's death and resurrection — whether singly or in tandem — are interwoven at various levels in Paul's letter to the Romans. Morna Hooker correctly notes, "it is clear from Paul's letters that the death and resurrection of Jesus are absolutely basic to his faith" (*Not Ashamed of the Gospel* 25).

At times in Romans, Jesus' death and resurrection are explicitly stated as facts to which the faithful agree (e.g., 1:4; 4:24), while at other times they are alluded to almost in passing as the basis for ethical behavior (e.g., 14:15). Throughout Romans, these events form the crux of Paul's gospel. As Richard Hays has demonstrated, Paul's message rests on a narrative substructure that focuses on Jesus' obedient death (*Faith of Jesus Christ* 247-48 and *passim*). The repeated theme of Jesus as crucified and risen is the *continuo* underlying all the settings and variations of Paul's message. Paul's gospel is not about Jesus as a good teacher or a great example. Rather, his gospel focuses on Jesus as "the son of God," "the Christ," whose death and resurrection have defeated sin and death and so provide salvation.

Paul interprets Jesus' death and resurrection as the means by which one becomes like God, and this in two ways: by conformity to Christ and by the manifestation of the "righteousness of God" received by faith. Our task will be to elucidate these two interpretations. In the process we will suggest that both address the ancient world's longing to attain godlikeness.

Conformity to Christ

Romans makes reference to being "in Christ," to being "crucified with Christ," to "dying with Christ," to "living with Christ," etc. These themes have often been understood, particularly by the comparative religions school, to have originated in the mystery religions of the Greek world. Subsequent scholarship, however, has demonstrated the inadequacy of this explanation (cf., e.g., Wedderburn, "Soteriology of the Mysteries"). These themes have also often been classed under the category of "mysticism," albeit of Paul's own brand of mysticism (e.g., A. Schweitzer, *The Mysticism of Paul the Apostle*, tr. W. Montgomery [London: Black, 1931]; Wikenhauser, *Pauline Mysticism*). But such an understanding also has its difficulties. For whereas "mysticism" — which scholars understand to mean "the entry of man into the Divinity and the entry of the Divinity into man" (so R. Reitzenstein, as quoted by Wikenhauser, *Pauline Mysticism* 19) — connotes an ontological union of God and humans, Paul speaks rather of participation in God's son. So to categorize the "in

Christ" and "with Christ" themes as "mystical" suggests that Paul envisioned believers becoming united with the being of God, when, in fact, in the letter to the Romans he speaks of believers being united with Christ in his death and in his resurrection life.

This unique claim of participation in God's son is found also in those passages in Paul's letters where Paul combines "dying with Christ" with "being made righteous." In Rom 8:1, for example, he writes: "there is therefore now no condemnation for those who are in Christ Jesus"; and in 2 Cor 5:21: "for our sake he made him to be sin who knew no sin, so that in him we might become the righteousness of God." These verses have often been taken as problematic when Paul's thought is categorized as either "mystical" or "juridical." Yet the fact that Paul could so intimately combine the ideas of believers being "in Christ" and believers being made righteous suggests that — while scholars may compartmentalize his thought — Paul did not see a hard-and-fast distinction between a mystical and a juridical interpretation of Christ's death.

Furthermore, in describing Paul's language as purely "mystical," it is sometimes easy to miss the fact that Paul considered the whole being of believers, including their "mortal bodies," as vitally affected by their faith in Christ's death and resurrection. Paul writes: "If the Spirit of him who raised Jesus from the dead dwells in you, he who raised Christ Jesus from the dead will give life to your mortal bodies also through his Spirit, which dwells in you" (Rom 8:11). Mystical understandings of antiquity often regarded the body as a grave for the soul and looked forward to the separation of body and soul, since only then could one achieve union with the incorporeal, intelligible God. But such was not Paul's hope (cf. 2 Cor 5:2-4)!

Paul's language of being "in Christ," of "dying with Christ," and the like is most aptly described as different expressions of the one "conformity to Christ" theme. In Romans this theme is evidenced in several ways. For example, in chapter 6 believers are spoken of as conforming to Jesus' death (vv 3, 4, 8), as being crucified with Jesus (v 6), as dying with Jesus (v 8), and as united with Jesus in a death like his (v 5). This last verse reads quite literally "we have been united with the likeness of his death" (cf. Engberg-Pedersen, *Hellenistic Context* 115). Yet one should not understand "united with the likeness of his death" as indicating a union that is distinct from death. Robert Tannehill's observation is proper: Rom 6:5 "rather speaks of a direct union [of believers] with Christ's death" (*Dying and Rising with Christ* 35). And this understanding fits well with other statements of Paul in Romans, such as those in 6:8, "died with Christ," and 8:17, "suffer with him."

The concept of conformity to Jesus' death is related in chapter 8 to the theme of Christ in us. For Christ and the Spirit of God dwell in the believer, with the event of Christ's death and resurrection (vv 10-11) being the effective cause of both Christ's and the Spirit's indwelling. And consequently, from the fact of both Christ's and the Spirit's indwelling, righteousness and not sin, life and not death, are now the defining characteristics of the believer's existence.

"In Christ" language is part of the theme of conformity to Christ, as 6:8-11 demonstrates, where the phrase incorporates references to the death of Jesus Christ. Paul's statement in chapter 3 that believers are made righteous through the redemption that is *in* Christ Jesus (v 24) is immediately followed by a reference to Christ's death (v 25; cf. 5:9: "much more, then, now that we have been justified by his blood"). Rom 8:1-4 is another passage where Paul uses "in Christ" in connection with Christ's death, indicating again that "in Christ" directly alludes to Christ's death.

Moreover, Paul interprets Christ's death as defeating sin (5:19), which is why there is a polar distinction between being in sin and being in Christ (6:2, 11). The two are mutually exclusive. Those in Christ Jesus do not receive condemnation (8:1), for they are no longer living as sinners, but rather have been liberated from sin and death through being in Christ Jesus. Believers do not live in a divine remote being, but in one who is the historical crucified Jesus and the risen Christ. As Rudolf Schnackenberg writes: "the statements about dying etc. with Christ are not derived from the eschatological formula of 'life with Christ,' but rest on the historical Christ event" (*Baptism in the Thought of St. Paul*, tr. G. R. Beasley-Murray [New York: Herder and Herder, 1964] 176). Believers live in Christ Jesus and so in the love of God (8:39) — a love demonstrated by God giving his son for us (8:32).

That Paul stresses the corporate nature, and so the ethical features, of the "in Christ" theme indicates again the foundational role that the death of Christ plays in his thinking. Christ's death was for all. Paul writes that Christ died for the ungodly (5:6), which, as he has demonstrated in the previous chapters, means every human being. Since Christ died for all, conformity to Christ — that is, being "in Christ" and so sharing in his death — means living a life for others and a life with others who are also conformed to his death. The life of believers in

Christ, therefore, is a corporate life (12:5). Believers' new existence as those who are conformed not to the world but to Christ (12:2) means that their life in Christ is a life with others who are in Christ.

Furthermore, this new corporate life of believers is a life blessed by God's gifts for the building of their corporate spiritual existence — gifts such as prophecy, service, and teaching (12:6-8). It is a life together that, at its best, should be lived with each believer attuned to the same mind, the mind of Christ (15:5). Paul's greetings at the end of Romans demonstrate the high value he places on cooperation between believers (16:3, 9).

Life in Christ is also, of course, life of a certain character, for it is a life that reflects Christ's character. This is why the behavior of believers can be spoken of as being "in the Lord" (16:2). In fact, Paul sums up his exhortations concerning believers' communal life by saying "put on the Lord Jesus Christ" (13:14). Thus conformity to Christ's death means that, just as Christ defeated sin, so also believers in Christ are those over whom sin has no dominion (6:14).

The image of "putting on virtue" was common in the ancient world. Philo, for example, wrote: "The wise must be adorned with prudence . . . he must put on the unadorned robe of truth which nothing mortal shall touch" (*De Ebrietate* 86.5). For Paul, however, it is by "putting on *Christ*" that believers live apart from "the flesh." And by "putting on Christ" believers are not only conformed to Jesus' death, and so freed from sin (6:11), they also live in hope of participating in his risen life (6:5; 5:17) — a life that is eternal (6:23; 5:21).

The language of "conformity to Christ" in Romans, then, addresses a concern to be like God. What Paul declares is that believers are privileged both to share in Jesus' death and to hope for participation in Jesus' resurrection, and so a godlike (eternal) life. Paul addresses the ancient world's motivation for discipleship by claiming that faith in Jesus' death and resurrection means that one can become like God through conformity to God's son. And so Paul writes:

> All who are led by the Spirit of God are children of God. For you did not receive the spirit of slavery to fall back into fear, but you have received the spirit of adoption. When we cry, "Abba! Father!" it is the Spirit himself bearing witness with our spirit that we are children of God, and if children, then heirs, heirs of God and fellow heirs with Christ, provided we suffer with him in order that we may also be glorified with him (8:14-17).

Conformity to Christ means that believers are "children of God," which is a designation not to be taken lightly. And being conformed to the image of God's son (8:29) — whom Paul speaks of in his other letters as the one who "knew no sin" (2 Cor 5:21) and was equal with God (Phil 2:6) — brings believers themselves into a new relationship with God.

Paul's interpretation of the significance of faith in the death and resurrection of Christ, therefore, directly addresses the ancient world's desire to achieve likeness to God. For Paul, faith in Christ means that believers attain conformity to Christ, and so through Christ come into a new relationship with God.

The Righteousness of God Revealed

In addition to a "conformity to Christ" theme, Paul also describes his gospel as that in which "the righteousness of God is revealed" (1:17). The first chapters of Romans stress that sin is the problem for all human beings. Paul, like those of the Qumran community, believed, of course, that God is righteous, but that human beings are sinful (3:21-26). The distinction between God and humans, therefore, focuses on the difference between having and not having righteousness (3:5), with the gulf between God and humans bridgeable only through divine initiative. The law could reveal that gulf, but could not bridge it. It was, therefore, apart from the law that God revealed his righteousness (3:21) — the righteousness that is now revealed in the death of Christ (vv 24-25). And so the gift to those who believe is that the righteousness of God becomes their own (v 26). That is, God's character, which is righteousness, is given to those who believe in God's revelation in the death and resurrection of Jesus Christ.

The phrase "righteousness of God" *(dikaiosynē theou)* is rare both within and outside the New Testament. Elsewhere in the New Testament (outside Paul's letters) it appears only in Jas 1:20 and 2 Pet 1:1 (cf. also Matt 6:33: *tēn dikaiosynēn autou*). In Paul's letters it occurs in Rom 1:17; 3:5, 21, 22, 25, 26; 10:3; and 2 Cor 5:21. A quotation of Ps 112:9 containing this phrase is found in 2 Cor 9:9, while in Phil 3:9 "the righteousness from God" *(tēn ek theou dikaiosynēn)* occurs. There has been a tendency to treat the phrase "righteousness of God" as a formula or as shorthand for a set of theological conceptions. Ernst Käsemann, for instance, understands it as a formula that originated in such Jewish writings as the *Testament of Daniel* and the Qumran *Manual of Discipline* and thought that Paul took it over to indicate "the redemptive activity of God, which manifests itself in the gift without being absorbed in it" ("God's Righteousness" 103). Yet as Mark Seifrid has demonstrated, there is really no evidence for a formulaic use of the phrase "righteousness of God" in Second Temple Judaism, or indeed throughout the New Testament (*Justification by Faith* 99-108, 213-14). In light of Seifrid's work, this phrase should be understood in its literary contexts rather than as a signal for a certain implicit set of theological ideas.

The first decision to be made when attempting to understand the phrase "righteousness of God" is grammatical: What type of genitive construction is represented here? Three answers have been given. If "of God" is an objective genitive, then the phrase indicates, as Luther argued, that divine righteousness is given to those who have faith. "The righteousness of God," then, refers not to an attribute of God, but rather to a gift from God to human recipients (cf. H. N. Ridderbos, *Paul: An Outline of His Theology,* tr. J. R. De Witt [Grand Rapids: Eerdmans, 1975] 159-81, esp. 163-66). The weakness of this view is that it divorces the gift of righteousness from the character of the giver.

A second option is that "of God" is a subjective genitive, a construction almost indistinguishable from a possessive genitive, and so the phrase "righteousness of God" means God's own righteousness (e.g., G. Schrenk, *"dikē, ktl.," TDNT* 2.203, 205). Usually when the phrase is construed in this manner it is interpreted to indicate not a static attribute of God, but rather God's activity. Käsemann, for instance, defines God's righteousness as "a noun of action" that speaks of God's saving power ("God's Righteousness" 104). And Joseph Fitzmyer believes that the construction is a possessive or subjective genitive "descriptive of God's upright being and of his upright activity" (*Romans* 257).

Yet Paul continually stresses that the salvific activity of God in this world is focused in a very specific event — the death and resurrection of Jesus Christ. For Paul, in fact, it is in the gospel itself, which has to do with the death and resurrection of Jesus Christ, that God's saving power is demonstrated (1:16). As Sam Williams rightly points out, "it is not 'righteousness of God' which [Paul] describes as God's power; rather the *gospel* is God's *dynamic* for salvation *because* the 'righteousness of God' is being revealed through it" ("Righteousness of God" 238, emphases his). God's actions, of course, will always be righteous, but we should neither limit nor make diffuse our understanding of the phrase "righteousness of God" by taking it to mean simply divine activity.

A third way to interpret "of God" is as a genitive of origin, and so to read the phrase "righteousness of God" as meaning that God confers on believers the status of righteousness. Righteousness originates with God and proceeds to humanity, thereby bestowing on humanity what is typically referred to as "righteous status" (e.g., C. E. B. Cranfield, *A Critical and Exegetical Commentary on the Epistle to the Romans* (Edinburgh: T. & T. Clark, 1975] 97). According to Rudolf Bultmann, the phrase refers to "the righteousness from God which is conferred upon [humanity] as a gift by God's grace alone" (*Theology of the New Testament* [New York: Scribner, 1951] 1.285).

The strength of this third position is that it most closely fits the grammatical construction. Both the objective and subjective genitive options prove problematic in that they require the noun "righteousness" to carry a verbal sense — comparable, for example, to the expression "the love of God" *(agapē theou)*. But "righteousness of God" does not contain any verbal idea necessarily. By taking "righteousness" to mean "righteous status," this third interpretive option respects the fact that the phrase "righteousness of God" contains two nouns. The difficulty with this option, however, corresponds with that of the first option: it is an anthropocentric interpretation, for it lays emphasis on the believer's "righteous status" and not also on righteousness as an attribute of God.

Another way of understanding "righteousness of God" — which, admittedly, has not usually been entertained — is to view the genitive as an appositive genitive, similar to what one finds in the expressions "obedience of faith" *(hypakoēn pisteōs)* in 1:5 and "sign of circumcision" *(sēmeion peritomēs)* in 4:11. The sense of the phrase, on this reading, would then be: "righteousness, that is, God." This option respects the fact that the phrase contains two nouns, taking them as being in apposition. It is recognized that the first noun does not contain a verbal idea, and so we are not led immediately to speak of God's righteousness as an activity. Regarding the construction as an appositive genitive makes sense of its occurrence in 3:21, where it is the subject of the verb "reveal" *(phanerein)*. The righteousness of God that is revealed would not then be an activity of God, but rather the nature of God. That is, the focus is on God and not on what he has done to benefit people. And this

157

reading also makes good sense of 3:26, where God's righteousness (God's character) is distinct from God's action of making humans righteous (God's activity).

Understood in this way, the phrase "righteousness of God" functions to indicate that God's character, which is righteousness, is now available to those who believe in Jesus Christ. Those who put their faith in Christ's death and resurrection can be like God — that is, righteous. God's character is not, of course, entirely described by the category "righteous" or "righteousness." At various places in his letters Paul describes God in other ways as well, for example, as "God of hope" (Rom 15:13), as "God of peace" (1 Cor 14:33), and as faithful (1 Cor 1:9). While these descriptions of God's character and of its relationship to believers are not grammatically equivalent to "righteousness of God," they are semantically analogous. In all these cases, faith and the activity of the Spirit allow these divine characteristics to become those of believers (cf. Rom 15:13).

In Romans Paul chooses to characterize God's character primarily as "righteous" or "righteousness." The reason for this may be rooted in the historical dynamics of Paul's address to the Roman Christians. For Paul wrote to a group of predominantly Gentile believers who, as suggested above, had been converted to faith in Jesus Christ through Jewish Christians and were in the process of reassimilating Jewish believers in Christ back into their churches after Claudius's edict banning Jews from Rome had become either disregarded or revoked. Since their understanding of the significance of faith in Christ was informed by a Jewish Christian interpretation, Paul uses extensively the language and Scriptures of Judaism when writing to them.

Elsewhere in the New Testament, as noted earlier, the phrase "righteousness of God" is confined to explicitly Jewish Christian writings, being found outside Paul's letters only in Jas 1:20; 2 Pet 1:1; and (in cognate form) Matt 6:33. Paul may well have focused on the expression because his readers had already been doing so and because one of his purposes in writing to the Roman Christians was to reshape their understanding of the significance of the "righteousness of God" theme for their own self-definition and behavior as Christians.

Understanding the phrase "righteousness of God" in this way gives it a flavor that explodes beyond the juridical context in which interpreters usually contain it, thereby making sense of the fact that the construction also occurs in nonjuridical contexts (e.g., 1:17; 10:3).

"Righteousness of God" describes God's character — a character that is now revealed (1:17) or manifested (3:21). God's righteousness should be understood as revealed not so much in the context of judging as of giving.

While the wrath (1:18) and judgment (2:16) of God are closely related to the idea of God's righteousness, they are nevertheless separate from it. God's righteousness functions in relationship to humanity not in a forensic context but in a much broader context — that of grace. That is why it must be that God's righteousness is manifest apart from the law (3:21). For God shares his character with those who have faith in the death and resurrection of Jesus Christ. "Made righteous" is not so much a juridical term (God declaring righteous) as it is a term of creativity (God making righteous). Contrary to what commentators often do in pairing "righteousness" with "status," we need to disassociate the two terms — not only because the word "status" does not appear in Paul, but also because such a pairing suggests a complex of ideas that is absent from Paul's discussions. For Paul usually uses the verb "justify" in the context of speaking of God's creativity rather than of God's judgment or of ranking humans. So, for example, in Romans 4 Abraham's righteousness is a gift not from a judge but from the one who creates *(tithēmi)* and who "gives life to the dead and calls into existence things that do not exist" (4:17).

Faith in Christ's death and resurrection is, of course, also faith that God's rightful judgment of humanity's sin no longer applies to the believer. Yet God's righteousness and human faith do not function in the arena of judgment. So when Paul speaks of God making humans righteous, God is described not as one who judges but as one who loves (cf. 5:8-9). The faithful are saved from the wrath of God because they now share the character of God (5:9) and because God is willing to forego judgment (3:25). Although interpreters have frequently found a juridical context for the phrase "righteousness of God" in 3:21-26, the phrase in this passage is better explained as describing the righteous character of God in opposition to the sinful character of humanity.

Viewed in such a light, 3:21-26 should be understood to mean that the righteousness of God, which before the coming of Christ was revealed in the law, is now revealed through faith in Jesus Christ — that is, that before Christ God revealed his character through the law, but now he does so through faith in Jesus Christ. That God revealed his character as that of righteousness both in the law and now through faith in Jesus Christ means that God has always desired — and continues to desire — humanity to recognize, respond to, and reflect his character.

The goal of the law is righteousness. The commandment or requirement *(dikaiōma)* of the law is that humans become like God — that is, righteous and not sinners. Yet none of this is attainable through the law. For while the law was meant to help Jews attain righteousness (i.e., the character of God), it merely revealed human beings as the sinners that they are (7:7). Likeness to God (i.e., righteousness) could not be achieved through following the law, since the law was no match for sin because of human weakness. Sin, which plagues every human being, cannot be overcome through human effort. Only God through Jesus Christ could deal with sin (7:25). Thus God's son "condemned" sin in humanity so that what the law required might come to fruition in believers. God's son, in fact, defeated sin, since he was sinless and therefore incapable of himself being defeated by sin. And so the law's good intention is realized only in Christ (10:4), and it is now only through faith in Christ's death and resurrection that "the gift of righteousness" is received (5:17).

The ethical component of righteousness fits with the understanding of "righteousness of God" just delineated. Brendan Byrne rightly describes Paul's ethics as based on a life "in Christ," "in which the righteousness lived out by Christians is seen as the righteousness of Christ, the continuing offer to the world of the righteousness of God" ("Living Out the Righteousness of God" 581). In God there is no sin, only righteousness. Believers are now to act as if they are free from sin and capable of living from a character of righteousness (6:13). This new self-understanding will result in holiness (6:19) — that is, in being as God is. The central role of the Spirit in Christian ethical living indicates again that Paul considers that believers are those who resemble God. The Spirit is, as Gordon Fee contends, "the personal presence of God" (*God's Empowering Presence* 6). The Christian life is a Spirit-filled and Spirit-led life that reflects the character of God.

The gospel, for Paul, is the manifestation of the "righteousness of God," that is, the manifestation of God's own character. God's revelation of his own character in the gospel (1:17) is an invitation and opportunity for human beings to become as God is. This is not possible through human endeavor, for righteousness is not a property of humanity but of God. Humans may become righteous only by recognizing that righteousness is not a property of humanity, but only of God, and submitting to the "righteousness of God" (10:3).

3. Conclusion

In his letter to the Roman Christians, Paul presents his gospel in terms of both conformity to Christ and the manifestation of the "righteousness of God," thereby reflecting and responding to the ancient world's aspiration to become like God. The religious and moral aspiration to become like God was shared by both Gentiles and Jews and so could serve as a basis of conversation between these two groups. Paul appeals to this aspiration in writing to believers at Rome in order that his readers might recognize both the incredible gift their faith in Christ has given them and its social consequences (15:5-6).

Paul's interpretations of the death and resurrection of Jesus in terms of both conformity to Christ and the manifestation of the righteousness of God cohere within the category of discipleship when the disciple's goal is defined as attaining godlikeness. Consequently, there is no need to see a tension between Paul's "mystical" and "juridical" language. For, as we have seen, what have usually been distinguished as either his mystical or his juridical interpretations of Christ both fit into a paradigm in which the goal of discipleship is becoming like God.

Christian discipleship as Paul describes it is challenging and disturbing. For to be like God is to be like the God who revealed himself in Jesus Christ. This God is neither the contemplative God of Aristotle, nor the incorporeal, intelligible God of Philo and Plutarch, nor the detached God of Epicurus, nor the demanding but forgiving God of Qumran. Rather, the Christian disciple will resemble the involved God revealed in Jesus Christ. Likeness to God for the Christian disciple in Paul's thought world entails continual participation in the death of Jesus Christ. It means being, in an unrighteous world, righteous as God is.

Paul claims that likeness to God comes through faith in the death and resurrection of Jesus Christ. This does not make for a detached or a serene life, since God's character as revealed in the gospel is one of love and involvement (cf. 8:32). In a world of "tribulation, distress, persecution, famine, nakedness, and peril" (8:17), reflecting such a character means suffering. Yet the conviction and hope of Christian disciples is that if we suffer with Christ "we will also be glorified with him" (8:17).

Selected Bibliography

Byrne, B. "Living Out the Righteousness of God: The Contribution of Rom 6:1–8:13 to an Understanding of Paul's Ethical Presuppositions," *Catholic Biblical Quarterly* 43 (1981) 557-81.

Engberg-Pedersen, T., ed. *Paul in His Hellenistic Context.* Minneapolis: Fortress, 1995.

Fee, G. D. *God's Empowering Presence: The Holy Spirit in the Letters of Paul.* Peabody: Hendrickson, 1994.

Fitzmyer, J. A. *Romans.* Anchor Bible, New York: Doubleday, 1993.

Hays, R. B. *The Faith of Jesus Christ: An Investigation of the Narrative Substructure of Galatians 3:1–4:11.* Chico: Scholars, 1983.

Hock, R. F. "Cynics," *Anchor Bible Dictionary.* New York: Doubleday, 1992, 1:1221-26.

Hooker, M. D. *Not Ashamed of the Gospel: New Testament Interpretations of the Death of Christ.* Grand Rapids: Eerdmans, 1994.

Käsemann, E. "God's Righteousness in Paul," *Journal for Theology and Church* 1 (1965) 100-110.

Malherbe, A. *The Cynic Epistles.* Atlanta: Scholars, 1977.

Meeks, W. A. *The First Urban Christians: The Social World of the Apostle Paul.* New Haven: Yale University Press, 1983.

Seifrid, M. *Justification by Faith: The Origin and Development of a Central Pauline Theme.* Leiden: Brill, 1992.

Tannehill, R. C. *Dying and Rising with Christ: A Study in Pauline Theology.* Berlin: Töpelmann, 1966.

Wedderburn, A. J. M. "The Soteriology of the Mysteries and Pauline Baptismal Theology," *Novum Testamentum* 29 (1987) 53-72.

Wikenhauser, A. *Pauline Mysticism: Christ in the Mystical Teaching of St. Paul.* Freiburg: Herder, 1960.

Williams, S. K. "The 'Righteousness of God' in Romans," *Journal of Biblical Literature* 99 (1980) 241-90.

Ziesler, J. A. *The Meaning of Righteousness in Paul: A Linguistic and Theological Inquiry.* Cambridge: Cambridge University Press, 1972.

The Imitation of Christ: Discipleship in Philippians

GERALD F. HAWTHORNE

"Disciple" *(mathētēs)* is a very old word derived from the Greek verb "learn" *(manthanō)*. So a disciple was a learner, a person actively engaged in the process of acquiring a practical skill or theoretical knowledge. The acquisition of such skills and knowledge in antiquity, however, was gained primarily (perhaps exclusively) not from books or scrolls but rather from teachers — that is, from people who were recognized and respected for the ability they possessed as artisans or for the attractiveness of their persons and the power of the ideas that they promulgated. There is thus no disciple without a teacher (cf. K. H. Rengstorf, *TDNT* 4.416). Socrates (ca. 470-399 B.C.) is perhaps the classic example in pre-Christian times of a charismatic teacher to whom would-be learners flocked to be with him and hear what he had to say. Physical proximity of student to teacher was, therefore, almost necessarily implied in the use of the word "disciple" — although there are instances when the meaning of discipleship was extended to include pupils separated from their masters even by centuries (cf. John 9:28; Dio Chrysostom 38[55].3-5).

Greek philosophers had their disciples, people who voluntarily attached themselves to these teachers and who committed themselves to them and willingly paid whatever fee was demanded for permission to attend their lectures (cf. Plato, *Apology* 33e; Diogenes Laertius 10.12

[6], 7 [3]) The Rabbis, under the influence of Hellenism, had their disciples who also came to them of their own initiative, joined themselves to them, listened to them, carefully memorized what they said, and passed on their teachings with precision to the next generation of scholars — disciples like Eliezer b. Hyrcanus, who was described as "a plastered cistern which loseth not a drop" (Mishnah *Pirke Aboth* 2.10). John the Baptist, the forerunner of Jesus, in the same fashion, had his disciples, his loyal followers, people who came to him to be with him, learn from him, care for him, and carry on his mission when he was put to death (cf. Matt 9:14; 11:2 par.; Mark 2:18 par.; 6:29; Luke 11:1; John 3:22-26; Acts 19:1-5). Similarly the Pharisees had their disciples (cf. Matt 22:16; Mark 2:18). In each instance there was something overwhelmingly attractive about these individuals, the causes they espoused, or the teachings they proclaimed that drew people to them to become their devoted adherents, their followers, those who pledged themselves to learn from them.

The earthly Jesus, an itinerant rabbi, also had his disciples, both men and women (cf. Mark 14:40-41). They gathered around him and loyally followed him on his journeys, ministered to his needs (cf. Luke 8:1-3), heard him teach (cf. Matthew 5–7), adopted what he had to say, and embodied his message by living out in their lives the things they had seen in him and heard from him (cf. Matt 7:24-27). It is about this Jesus, crucified, dead, raised from the dead, and now exalted to the right hand of God that all of this book — more particularly, this chapter — concerns itself. What does it mean today in the concrete experiences of everyday life to be a disciple of this risen Jesus, this exalted Christ?

The letter to the Philippians is almost universally accepted as a genuine letter of Paul. Here it will be considered to be originally an integrated whole. The structure and vocabulary of the prologue (1:1-11), the epilogue (4:10-23), and the two main sections between (1:12–2:30; 3:1–4:20) argue against any claim that this letter is a compilation of several separate letters or letter fragments woven together into one document (cf. P. Rolland, "La structure littéraire et l'unité de l'Épître aux Philippiens," *RSR* 64 [1990] 213-16; Hawthorne, *Philippians* xxix-xxxi; O'Brien, *Philippians* 10-18; Silva, *Philippians* 14-16). It is perhaps the best New Testament writing to correct erroneous views of discipleship by clearly showing, not in words but in life, what it truly means to be a disciple of Jesus today — and, in the process, to suggest a replacement word for the more elusive term "disciple."

1. The Inadequacy and Replacement of Discipleship Words

The Gospel writers portray Jesus "in the days of his flesh" (Heb 5:7) as one who possessed an extraordinary personal magnetism, so that when he called people to become his disciples — and it is perhaps this that set Jesus' true disciples off from all other disciples of all other charismatic leaders, namely that *he* took the initiative and issued the invitation for them to join him (cf. Luke 9:57-58, 60-62; Mark 5:18-20, unlike Mishnah *Pirke Aboth* 1.6, cf. 1.16) — they immediately and without question or hesitation left what they were doing and identified themselves wholly with him (cf. Matt 4:19; 1:17; 2:14 par.; John 1:43-44). During Jesus' earthly ministry, in order to be his disciple one had to be with him, in close proximity to him, within hearing distance of his voice, so as to learn from him. This, of course, necessitated that his disciples leave their businesses (Matt 4:18-20; Mark 2:14 par.), their friends (Matt 4:21), their homes, and their families (Mark 1:19-20; Luke 14:26) — in a word, everything (Mark 10:28). For as an itinerant rabbi, Jesus was sometimes in Judea, sometimes in Galilee, sometimes in the city, sometimes in villages, sometimes in the mountains, sometimes along the seacoast. Wherever he went, his disciples had to follow him, since they had committed themselves to him and his cause, even though this meant a wandering, itinerant life for them, marked by hardship, deprivation of normal comforts, poverty, a lack of privacy, and the possibility of death (cf. Luke 14:26-27).

Discipleship, then, when Jesus was on earth, required precisely this: the total abandonment of a previous way of life for those who were called by him to be his disciples, and a ready willingness on their part to go wherever he chose to go. It is not surprising, therefore, to find that the term "disciple" *(mathētēs)* never appears in the New Testament outside the Gospels and Acts, where the life and teachings of Jesus are the primary focus of attention, or that the verb "follow" *(akolouthein)*, while used frequently in the Gospels to describe what Jesus' disciples did in relation to him, is used only twice outside the Gospels for any kind of personal relationship between Jesus and his followers (cf. Rev 14:4; 19:14).

This suggests, then, following the lead of the writers of the New Testament letters, that the words "disciple" and "discipleship" and the expression "making disciples" might better be abandoned in our modern Christian vocabulary and replaced with a more appropriate word or words. These discipleship terms are too easily misunderstood or misinterpreted, or their original requirements misapplied, unless great care is taken to explain precisely what is meant by them (cf. Hengel, *Charismatic Leader*; Schweizer, *Lordship and Discipleship*; also the more popular study by M. J. Wilkins, *Following the Master: A Biblical Theology of Discipleship* [Grand Rapids: Zondervan, 1991]). Paul for one, therefore, seems ready to alert his readers to the fact that to be a disciple of Jesus in the post-resurrection era does not necessarily mean that one must leave home and employment and go to a distant land with the gospel, as some have preached. Neither does it entail rigid adherence to an established set of rules and regulations, as others have taught. Nor does it mean that one must comply unquestioningly to a certain codified belief system, as still others have urged. The pattern of discipleship, at least as it is outlined in Philippians, is less a matter of belief than of practice, less a matter of orthodoxy than of orthopraxis, less a matter of what one thinks than how one lives. It is, in fact, imitating the model of life exemplified by Jesus himself — that is, cutting the cloth of one's life according to the pattern for authentic living that has been given by Jesus Christ and so following his example with respect to one's attitudes and actions.

2. Christ, the Supreme Model to Be Imitated

In none of his other letters, and certainly not in Philippians, does Paul ever use the term "disciple" to describe his relationship with the risen, exalted Lord. Never does he introduce himself to his audience as "Paul, the disciple of Jesus Christ." Rather, he refers to himself as one who imitates Christ (cf. 1 Cor 11:1); and in his letter to the Philippian church he calls on his converts there, whom he addresses as "saints in Christ Jesus" (not "disciples of Christ Jesus"), to do precisely the same thing. It seems clear that he urges them to become disciples of Jesus Christ, not by making use of this word, but rather by pleading with them to become Christ's followers by imitating his thoughts and actions. So he writes in Phil 2:5: "Let the same mind be in you that was in Christ Jesus" (NRSV) — or as Moisés Silva has paraphrased the difficult Greek of this text, "Adopt [then] this frame of mind in your community — which indeed [is proper for those who are] in Christ Jesus" (*Philippians* 107). For just as the ancient moral teachers urged their students to pattern their lives after extraordinary people who were models of virtue and goodness, and as they themselves learned from them and imitated them (cf., e.g., Seneca, *Letters* 6.5-6; 11.9-10; Pliny, *Letters* 8.13; Plutarch, *Moralia* 40B; Marcus Aurelius, *Meditations* 1.9) — and as Jewish writers held up the character and conduct of virtuous people of their own history as examples for their readers to emulate (cf., e.g., 4 Maccabees 1:7-8; 13:9; *Testament of Benjamin* 4:1-4; Sirach 44–50) — so the apostle Paul calls on Christian believers to focus their whole attention on Jesus Christ and to make him the supreme model for both their overall attitude toward life and their conduct in day-to-day living. Phil 2:5-11, thus, is the strongest possible appeal of the apostle to his readers to shape their lives as Christians (i.e., those "in Christ Jesus") according to the pattern left behind for them by Christ Jesus himself.

3. Objections and Response to the *Imitatio Christi* Interpretation of 2:5-11

Not everyone, however, agrees that Phil 2:5-11 is a call to imitate Christ. Many scholars cannot imagine that Paul could be interpreting this hymnic portion in terms of the imitation of Christ. Wilhelm Michaelis, for one, argued unequivocally that the plea "for an *imitatio Christi* finds no support in the statements of Paul" (*TDNT* 4.672). Ernst Käsemann also rejected any ethical interpretation of this section, that is, any view that Christ is presented here as a pattern for the behavior of his followers (cf. his "Critical Analysis"). Ralph Martin, in his important 1967 monograph *Carmen Christi*, argued that it was not Paul's intent in recounting the story of Jesus in 2:6-11 to set before the church an example of humility and obedience. "The Apostolic summons," he wrote, "is not: Follow Jesus by doing as He did — an impossible feat in any case, for who can be a 'second Christ' who quits His heavenly glory and dies in shame and is taken up into the throne of the universe" (*Carmen Christi* 290). And in the 1983 edition of that same work Martin reaffirmed this position (pp. xi-xii). More recently, W. Bauder, too, has proposed that when Paul makes reference to imitating Christ, "he is not thinking of specific occasions in the earthly life of Jesus, but rather of the authority of the Exalted One present in his word and his Holy Spirit and of the kind of behaviour that would be consistent with existence in the sphere of the Lordship of Christ" ("Disciple" 491-92).

Perhaps the fundamental reason for objecting to the claim that Phil 2:5-11 constitutes a plea for Christians to imitate Christ, or that it portrays Christ as a pattern for Christian behavior, is that for many devout scholars Christ is a far too exalted figure for any person even to dream of emulating — that is, it is just too incredible for any mere human to consider the possibility of becoming like Christ "who quits His heavenly glory" (so Martin, *Carmen Christi* 290). In arguing in this way, they seem to be reflecting the thinking of writers like the first-century Roman rhetorician Quintilian, who taught that while emulation of the best promotes progress in the more advanced learners, beginners who are still of tender years make greater progress by imitating their comrades than their masters (*Institutio Oratoria* 1.1.26).

Morna Hooker, however, has aptly noted with respect to such a position: "It is only the dogma that the Jesus of History and the Christ of faith belong in separate compartments that leads to the belief that the appeal to a Christian character appropriate to those who are in Christ is not linked to the pattern as seen in Jesus himself" ("Philippians 2:6-11" 154). And Larry Hurtado, in arguing for Jesus' actions in the Christ-hymn being a pattern for the Philippian Christians to define their own behavior, points out: though it may be the action of the preexistent, heavenly one that is referred to in 2:6-7, "this action is directly linked with the action of the earthly Jesus in 2:8. . . . That is, the unseen and ineffable action of heaven is described after the fashion of the observed, historical action" ("Jesus as Lordly Example" 121). If the book of Acts is to be believed, then most certainly the Jesus of history and the Christ of faith are, indeed, one and the same person (cf. Acts 2:22, 36). Therefore, one should not think of the Christ only as a divine being so far above human reach that his attitude and actions can and must be dismissed as examples to follow.

A number of questions regarding the composition and original setting of the Christ-hymn of 2:6-11, of course, merit thorough discussion, and have been extensively treated (cf., e.g., O'Brien, *Philippians* 188-203 and bibliography there). But these matters are not immediately pertinent for our purposes here. For whether the original composer was Paul or someone other than Paul, the fact is that Paul chose to make use of the hymn. And whether it originally was composed as a free-standing hymn or for a different context than what we find it in, the fact is that Paul placed it precisely here. Hence, it is within its present setting in Paul's letter to the Philippians that the hymn must be first explained.

When one looks, therefore, at the immediate context in which the Christ-hymn is placed, it seems rather clear that the point Paul is making is not that Christians should attempt to become second Christs, who quit their heavenly glory, but that they should strive to emulate the attitude and actions of servanthood that marked the character and conduct of the preexistent Christ, who was also the Jesus of history. The appeal here is identical with the appeal Paul makes when he urges his Corinthian converts to be lavish in their giving to the poor: "For you know the generous act of our Lord Jesus Christ, that though he was rich, yet for your sakes he became poor, so that by his poverty you might become rich" (2 Cor 8:9).

Nor is it Paul's point to urge the Philippian believers to pattern their lives after Christ for personal gain, to receive a heavenly accolade, or to be exalted. Rather, he cites the hymn in its entirety, including the latter portion, which deals with the exaltation of Christ, to remind his readers that God's estimate of the ideal life is very different from their own. Whereas the Philippians have been acting in a spirit of selfish ambition — thinking themselves better than others, believing that they are above serving, studying how they might promote themselves and get ahead of their neighbors, assuming that the surest way "up" is to climb up at the expense of others — Paul holds before them the example of Christ to show the wrongheadedness of such a way of thinking and acting. There is in this hymn, which sings the praises of the divine who became human, a grand transvaluation of values. For the attitude and actions of Christ outlined here clearly show God's ideal pattern for discipleship — indeed, the ideal pattern for human existence in general. And it is the direct opposite of the behavior of the Philippians.

The life of Christ shows that the way up is by stepping down, that the way to gain for oneself is by giving up oneself, that the way to life is by death, and that the way to win the praise of God is by steadfastly serving others. The teaching of Jesus during his years on earth was articulated not only by the words he spoke but by the life he lived. In fact, tradition has it that his emphasis was on doing before teaching — that is, that one must do the law before one has the right to teach the law (cf. Matt 5:19b). In his humility, Jesus did what he asked others to do (cf. Matt 23:12; Luke 14:11; 18:14). And it was his great act of humility that was sung about by the church as its members met together to worship and praise him who is now exalted to the highest station in heaven. Placing the Christ-hymn precisely in this place in his letter, Paul simply wants to say, "Follow his example, pattern your life after his life." Imitation of Christ, then, is *the* pattern of discipleship in Philippians.

The presence of the *imitatio Christi* theme in Phil 2:6-11 becomes yet more clear when one considers that these verses may have constituted one of the earliest of the Christian hymns sung by believers at worship and that the source of the idea for its composition may have stemmed from the life and teaching of Jesus himself as recorded in the early Gospel tradition (cf. Matt 16:25-26; 18:4; 23:12; Luke 14:11; 18:4). More particularly, it may have stemmed from a single incident recorded in that tradition coupled with deep and reverent meditation on that incident by its composer. For it has been cogently argued that not only the existence of the hymn but even the shape it originally was given may have flowed from the church's recollection of Jesus washing his disciples' feet, which was later recorded in John 13:3-17.

A number of parallels between Phil 2:6-11 and John 13:3-17 have been observed and can be briefly highlighted here. The opening section of the hymn, for example, where it is said that Jesus existed in the "form of God" (v 6) — which is a statement that calls attention to his preexistence — parallels the wording of John 13:3, where Jesus is described as knowing that the Father had given all things into his hands, that he had come from God, and that he was going back to God (cf. also John 17:5; Heb 1:3). Furthermore, as the hymn proceeds to state that Jesus, in spite of his exalted position ("in the form of God," "equal with God"), laid all this aside and "emptied himself" (v 7), one is reminded of what the evangelist in the Fourth Gospel said happened immediately upon and in spite of Jesus' awareness of his high and exalted origin — namely, that he got up from the table where he and his disciples were dining and laid aside his outer garments (John 13:7).

The hymn then continues by saying that he who existed in the form of God took the form of a slave. That is to say, he who was truly equal with God became truly human, a person who voluntarily humbled himself in order to serve others (vv 7-8). Such words echo exactly the action of the Jesus in the Gospel tradition. For he who knew he had come into this world from God and was returning to God took a towel, wrapped it around himself, put water in a basin, and washed his disciples' feet. Thus he became a servant to his followers, himself doing the humble task that was usually assigned to slaves (John 13:5; cf. 1 Sam 25:41).

As a consequence, continues the hymn, God exalted Jesus to the highest place and gave him "the name that is above every name" (v 9), which may be the hymn's way of saying that Jesus returned once again to the exalted place from which he had come. Just so in the Gospel narrative. For when Jesus finishes serving his disciples, he once again puts on his outer garments and returns to the place from which he got up (John 13:12).

Finally, the hymn concludes with the words: God exalted him to the highest place, so that "every tongue should confess that Jesus Christ is Lord [*kyrios*]" (v 11). This statement recalls Jesus' own words to his disciples: "You call me . . . Lord [*kyrios*], and rightly so, for that is what I am" (John 13:13).

It is this hymn, which so closely parallels the Gospel tradition of Jesus taking on himself the servant's role and humbly washing his disciples' feet, that Paul places immediately after his plea to the Philippian Christians to forego their own personal ambition and arrogance and selfishness — and, on the contrary, to follow the example of their Lord and in humility begin to regard others better than themselves. He holds up before these Christians the attitude and actions of Jesus Christ as *the* pattern for the attitudes and actions of all those who claim to be "in Christ," and so followers of Christ.

When seen, therefore, in the light of its context, this understanding appears to be the most reasonable interpretation of Phil 2:5-11. Whether or not one agrees that what Jesus did at the Last Supper, as recorded later in John 13, was the incident that prompted the composition of this Christ-hymn, it is nevertheless striking and instructive to note, first, that John closes this account with the words of Jesus, "If I, your Lord and Teacher, have washed your feet, you also ought to wash one another's feet. For I have set you *an example* that you should do as I have done to you" (13:14-15), and, second, that when one compares John 13:3-17 with Phil 2:6-11 it becomes clear that the purpose of both is the same. As we have noted elsewhere: "The Johannine account is an acted parable to summarize the essence of Jesus' teaching: 'Whoever wants to be great among you must be everybody's slave' (Mark 10:43-44), while the Philippian text is a hymn to illustrate powerfully Paul's teaching, which at this point is identical with that of Jesus: humble, self-sacrificing service to one another done in love is a must for a Christian disciple who would live as a Christian disciple should (Phil 2:3-4)" (Hawthorne, *Philippians* 79; see also 77-79). John 13 not only summarizes Jesus' teaching, but, more importantly, it describes in graphic detail the very essence of the way he lived (cf. Mark 10:45; Matt 20:28). In the same fashion, all the ideas and expressions in Phil 2:6-11, especially those in verses 6-7b, are to be interpreted in light of Paul's fundamental identification of Christ as the "slave" and "servant" *(doulos* and *diakonos)* par excellence. He who was in the form of God, as the hymn of 2:6-11 expresses it, took on the form of a slave so that as a human being he might live out the ideal way for humans to live — that is, not as people to be served but as people whose purpose is to serve and to give, even to the point of giving up one's life for others.

4. The Imitation of Christ Illustrated: The Life of Paul

In antiquity, the way great teachers lived — their lifestyle — was equally as important in the education of their followers as what they taught. So the first-century Stoic philosopher Seneca (ca. 4 B.C.–A.D. 65) observed regarding the relationship of Zeno (335-263 B.C.), the founder of the school of Stoic philosophy, and Cleanthes (331-232 B.C.), his first successor: "Cleanthes would never have been the image of Zeno if he had merely heard him lecture; he lived with him, studied his private life, watched him to see if he lived in accordance with his own principle" (*Letters* 6.5; cf. also 11.9-10; 95.72). Paul, like any of the ancients, was as much influenced — perhaps more — by the life of his teacher and model, Christ, as he was by his words. One can safely infer that Paul would have been less inclined to pattern his own life so closely after that of Jesus, with all of the hardships it entailed, including death, had he not first had a radical, life-changing personal encounter with this Jesus (cf. Acts 9:1-5; 1 Cor 9:1; 15:8), not researched carefully the traditions about Jesus — for he did not know Jesus from his years on earth (cf. 1 Cor 11:23-26; 15:1, 3-4, *passim*), not observed Jesus' private life through the eyes of one of his biographers (cf. Acts 1:1-8; 16:10-17; 20:5-15; 21:1-18; 27:1–28:16 with 2 Tim 4:11), and not investigated to see if Jesus' life matched his words through various conversations he had with one of the disciples who had followed Jesus from the beginning of his ministry to his death — that is, by speaking with Peter, a disciple who had lived with Jesus, ate with him, slept with him, and observed his every action (cf. Gal 1:18; 2:11-15; see also Acts 15:7-11; 2 Pet 3:14-16). In any case, Paul unself-consciously presents his own life to the Philippians as a life copied from the life of Jesus.

It is not surprising, therefore, to note that Paul begins his letter to the Philippians by laying aside any authoritative title he might have rightfully used to introduce himself, such as "apostle," and salutes his readers as a "slave" (1:1). He chooses for himself the very same word, *doulos*, that is used of Christ in the hymn (2:6-7). Thus, just as the preexistent Christ took the form of a slave, so here Paul deliberately refuses any term descriptive of position or privilege and, wishing now to imitate his master, chooses a term that describes his mission in life as one of humble service.

Early in his letter to the Philippians Paul reminds his converts that he is a prisoner for no other reason than that he is a follower of Christ (i.e., *en Chrisṭǫ*; cf. 1:7, 13, 14), and so his deprivations, hardships, and sufferings are for Christ's sake (cf. 1:17; 29-30). There is no record in the gospel tradition, of course, of Jesus ever having been imprisoned, and there is no reason to surmise that he ever was. So in such a literal sense Paul cannot be claiming to be imitating him. But the preexistent Christ had humbled himself by becoming obedient to the point of death (2:8), and Paul was glad to follow the lead of his model by experiencing the humiliation of imprisonment (1:17-18; cf. Epictetus 2.6.27) — with the possibility of that imprisonment also eventuating in his death (2:17-18). The letter to the Philippians, therefore, appears to be something of what might be called a "pathfinder writing," one that sets out a new understanding of Christian discipleship. For in it, Paul, who was himself a prisoner for Christ, writes from his cell with the added moral authority that imprisonment gives him to encourage others to imitate the life of Christ in fearless fashion, regardless of the consequences (cf. 1:14).

The autobiographical section of the letter, 3:4-11, is striking, not only for its content but for the fact, often overlooked, that it parallels the structure of the Christ-hymn. In so doing, it reinforces the thesis that Paul looks to Jesus Christ as *the* model for his own thinking and acting.

Just as the hymn of 2:6-11 begins with the preexistent Christ — who existed in the form of God, was equal with God, and was thus a person of the highest rank and stature — so Paul begins his self-story by describing himself, without arrogance, as one who was heir to extraordinary privileges and whose life was marked by extraordinary personal accomplishments: "circumcised on the eighth day, a member of the people of Israel, of the tribe of Benjamin, a Hebrew born of Hebrews; as to the law, a Pharisee; as to zeal, a persecutor of the church; as to righteousness under the law, blameless" (3:5-6, NRSV). The description of the exalted state of Christ is immediately followed by an account of his voluntary self-emptying and self-humiliation (2:6-7): he did not consider *(hēgēsato)* his being equal with God something to be used to his own advantage, but rather he deprived himself of all previous advantages and took the form of a slave. And Paul gives the telling of his own story precisely the same sequence when he continues with essentially these words (3:7-8): "In spite of all the privileges and achievements that were mine, those things that I once thought of as having supreme worth I now have come to consider and continue to consider [*hēgēmai . . . hēgoumai:* note this verbal link with 2:6] them all as loss. I have voluntarily given them all up. I have emptied myself of them all."

Furthermore, just as the Christ-hymn does not end on a note of self-emptying, humiliation, and death, but, rather, because of this self-abnegation, it concludes on a note of exaltation (2:9-11), so Paul's autobiography does not end on a note of self-renunciation and loss, but on a note of exaltation as well. Although Paul had renounced an impeccable pedigree and sterling accomplishments, he received back far more than he surrendered. For he received Christ and life in Christ, and on top of that the supreme pattern for behavior and the hope of resurrection. Everything that he had once considered gain in his life he had come to recognize, when compared with Christ, as in reality loss: "I regard everything as loss because of the surpassing value of knowing Christ Jesus my Lord. For his sake I have suffered the loss of all things, and I regard them as rubbish [literally, "excrement"], in order that I may gain Christ and be found in him, not having a righteousness of my own that comes from the law, but one that comes through faith in Christ. . . . I want to know Christ and the power of his resurrection and the sharing of his sufferings by becoming like him in his death, if somehow I may attain the resurrection from the dead" (3:8-11, NRSV). These words stress once more the eager desire of the apostle to conform his life to that of Christ — that is, to imitate him even in his suffering and death, with the prospect of sharing in his resurrection and exaltation.

5. The Imitation of Christ Illustrated: Timothy and Epaphroditus

Between the hymn of 2:6-11, which sets out the example of Christ's attitude and conduct and shows how a follower of Christ should think and act, and the autobiographical section of 3:4-11, which demonstrates that this pattern for living can indeed be traced out in the everyday experiences of human existence, appear two brief biographical sketches:

first of Timothy, then of Epaphroditus. These two biographical segments further underscore the thesis that it is possible to pattern one's life according to the model of Christ's life.

In the first segment, in 2:19-24, Paul reminds the Philippians of Timothy. According to 1 Tim 4:12, Timothy was a young man who illustrated the fact that youth is no impediment to imitating Jesus. Because his lifestyle was known to the Philippians, Paul points to him as a person who has lived his life according to the pattern exemplified by Christ Jesus. He calls on his readers to remember that Timothy is a person of high repute, who carries with him the best of recommendations (cf. v 20: "I have no one like him"). He is genuinely concerned for the welfare of others — being more concerned, in fact, about Christ's interests and the interests of others than he is about his own affairs. He is also a person who has made himself a "slave" in the sense that he served with Paul in the spread of the gospel (vv 19-22). Quite decidedly, therefore, the model of Christ set out in the hymn of 2:6-11 was being worked out in the life of Timothy, both in the way he lived and in the way he served.

In the second biographical segment, in 2:25-30, Paul calls attention to Epaphroditus, one of the Philippians' own people. Epaphroditus, as well as Timothy, is used by Paul to demonstrate to his readers that the example of Christ is not so exalted that it cannot be imitated. Paul reminds them that, like Christ, Epaphroditus left the safety and security and stability of home, traveled on a mission — perhaps a very great distance from home — to help someone in need. He reminds them, too, that Epaphroditus descended into illness and nearly into death because of this mission, thereby risking his own life in order to serve. But now he returns to Philippi with the highest of laudatory commendations from the apostle: "my brother and co-worker and fellow soldier, your messenger and minister to my need" (v 25, NRSV), a person worthy to be welcomed home with joy and honor (cf. v 29). Here, once again, are echoes of significant motifs from the life of Christ as set out in the hymn in 2:6-11. And so Epaphroditus, too, is a disciple of Christ in that he is an imitator of Christ.

6. The Case of Euodia and Syntyche

In addition to these two men, later in 4:2-3 Paul singles out two women named Euodia and Syntyche for both blame and praise. Nothing is known about these women other than what is said here. But from Paul's few remarks, certain things may be inferred, namely that Euodia and Syntyche were prominent in the church at Philippi and exercised some influence — perhaps holding positions of leadership in the Christian community, but certainly women who were looked up to and whose opinions were respected.

These women, however, had serious differences of opinion between them. And because of the strength of their personalities, their differences could have had serious consequences for the church at Philippi, fracturing the fellowship *(koinōnia)* and so putting an end to the necessary Christ-centered unity that makes it possible for any church to move forward in faith (cf. 1:5, 7; 2:1; 3:10; 4:13, 15). Though their differences seem to have been considerable, what may have troubled Paul most was the way in which these differences were expressed — a way that seems to have been precisely the opposite of the way of Christ as portrayed in the hymn of 2:6-11. For the word that Paul uses in exhorting these women to agree with one another, the verb *phronein* in 4:2, carries not only the idea of thinking (i.e., "be of the same mind") but also the nuance of feeling that involves one's emotions, attitudes, and will — suggesting, perhaps, that emotions were running rather high in the expression of their differences. And if so, then in this respect Euodia and Syntyche were neither illustrations of the model of Christ nor examples themselves to be imitated.

Yet more important than their differences was the fact that these women had been extensively involved in the ministry of the gospel. They had "struggled beside" Paul in his missionary endeavors. They were his coworkers, giving of themselves for others. In this respect, they had imitated the life of Christ and were to be commended. Their differences, although serious, must not be allowed to overshadow the fact that they imitated the life of Christ in pouring themselves out for the apostle and for all who needed their help or needed to hear the gospel. Nonetheless, judging both their strengths and their weaknesses, it must be said that their imitation of Christ was less than ideal.

7. Imitating Christ by Imitating Christ's Imitators

Having placed so much emphasis on Christ as *the* person to imitate and on Christ's own attitude and actions as those that all believers in Christ should emulate, it may seem somewhat strange that Paul should suddenly exhort his Philippian friends: "Brothers and sisters, join in imitating me, and observe those who live according to the example you have in us" (3:17, NRSV) — with the "us" referring not only to Paul but also to Timothy and Epaphroditus (cf. 2 Thess 3:9; 1 Tim 4:12; Titus 2:7). Here, indeed, Paul calls on his Philippian "brothers and sisters" to emulate in their lives what they had seen in his own life and in the lives of Timothy and Epaphroditus — that is, in their self-denying, their self-giving actions, their willingness to suffer in order to help, and their risking all for the sake of Christ and others.

The strangeness of this sudden shift from the supreme model to lesser examples, however, disappears when one realizes that Paul was urging the Philippians to join in imitating him and the lives of other worthy examples, not because he considered that he and they were such great and important people, better than anyone else — and certainly not because he believed that they had already reached perfection (note his own disclaimer of this in 3:12) — but only because he knew that they had been continually patterning their lives after Christ, the example par excellence (cf. 1 Cor 11:1; 1 Thess 1:6; 2 Thess 3:7). Only for this reason, and only insofar as they continued to imitate Christ, could they be considered people worthy of being imitated. And it is in this light that his final appeal to the Philippians should be viewed: "Keep on doing the things that you have learned [note that the Greek word here is *emathete*, from the verb *manthanein*, "to learn," which is the closest that Paul ever comes to using the term *mathētēs*, "disciple"] and received and heard and *seen in me*" (4:9) — with the emphasis by its position in the Greek sentence being on these last words, "seen in me."

8. Concluding Remarks

What, then, can be said about the pattern of discipleship as set forth in Paul's letter to the Philippians? In a word, it has to do with imitating Christ, who himself is the model or pattern of authentic living. Believers in Christ are to conduct their lives in conformity to the attitude and actions of Christ as depicted in the Christ-hymn of 2:6-11: Precisely because he existed in the form of God and was equal with God, Christ did not consider this exalted position a status to be held onto or a platform for his own interests. Rather, in an act of open-handed

177

giving, he purposefully and voluntarily relinquished all this, set it aside, emptied himself, and poured himself out for others. In so doing, he humbled himself, chose the role of a slave, chose to put his life at risk in the service of others, and chose to be obedient to the will of his Father, even to the point of death — and that death by crucifixion (vv 6-8). For this reason — because the whole of Christ's life, including his death, was a life and death spent for the benefit of others — God exalted him to the highest place and gave him the name above all names (vv 9-11).

The grand climax of this hymn must not be read or understood in such a way as to mean that Christ humbled himself in order to be exalted. If that were the case, as Peter O'Brien points out, "the humbling would have been no true humiliation at all, and as such would have been self-regarding, not self-denying" (*Philippians* 234). Rather, it must be read and understood to mean that the humiliation-exaltation theme of the hymn characterizes the way that God planned the universe to operate and for human life to function, and that Christ expresses in his attitudes and actions the true model for authentic Christian living. In the divine economy of things one receives by giving, one is served by serving, one finds life by losing one's life, one is exalted by taking the lowly place. The one follows the other as day follows night — but always in the order of self-sacrifice and then exaltation (cf. Matt 23:12; Luke 14:11; 18:14; see Hawthorne, *Philippians* 90, 95-96).

One final word, however, needs to be offered. For it is necessary to recognize that the urging of Paul to the Philippians to allow the thinking and actions of Christ to shape their lives — that they imitate him both in their thoughts and their actions — is not an appeal to do this wholly on their own or by dint of their own determination. There is within the difficult wording of 2:5 a hint as to the source of the power by which one can achieve this high goal of imitation. And that hint is to be found at the end of the verse in the expression "in Christ Jesus" (cf. M. Silva's translation: "Adopt [then] this frame of mind in your community — which indeed [is proper for those who are] in Christ Jesus" [*Philippians* 107]). Thus the call to imitate Christ Jesus is made possible by the power of the living, exalted Christ, who is present and at work within the lives of believers through the work of his Holy Spirit (cf. 1:11, 19; 2:12b-13).

Selected Bibliography

Bauder, W. "Disciple," *NIDNTT* 1.491-92.

Culpepper, R. A. "Co-Workers in Suffering: Philippians 2.19-30," *Review and Expositor* 77 (1980) 349-58.

De Boer, W. P. *The Imitation of Paul.* Kampen: Kok, 1962.

Hawthorne, G. F. *Philippians.* Word Biblical Commentary, Waco: Word, 1983.

Hengel, M. *The Charismatic Leader and His Followers,* tr. J. Greig. Edinburgh: T. & T. Clark/New York: Crossroad, 1981.

Hooker, M. "Philippians 2:6-11," in *Jesus und Paulus* (*Festschrift* for W. G. Kümmel), ed. E. E. Ellis and E. Grässer. Tübingen: Mohr-Siebeck, 1975.

Hurtado, L. W. "Jesus as Lordly Example in Philippians 2:5-11," in *From Jesus to Paul* (*Festschrift* for F. W. Beare), ed. G. P. Richardson and J. C. Hurd. Waterloo: Wilfred Laurier University Press, 1984, 113-26.

Käsemann, E. "A Critical Analysis of Philippians 2:5-11," in *God and Christ: Existence and Province,* ed. R. W. Funk. New York/Tübingen: 1968, 45-88 (originally "Kritische Analyse von Phil. 2, 5-11," *Zeitschrift für Theologie und Kirche* 47 [1950] 313-60).

Kurz, W. S. "Kenotic Imitation of Paul and of Christ in Philippians 2 and 3," in *Discipleship in the New Testament,* ed. F. F. Segovia. Philadelphia: Fortress, 1985, 103-26.

Martin, R. P. *Carmen Christi: Philippians ii.5-11 in Recent Interpretation and in the Setting of Early Christian Worship.* Cambridge: Cambridge University Press, 1967; republished with a new introduction, Grand Rapids: Eerdmans, 1983.

Michaelis, W. *"mimeomai, ktl.,"* *TDNT* 4.659-74.

O'Brien, P. T. *Philippians.* New International Greek Testament Commentary, Grand Rapids: Eerdmans, 1991.

Rengstorf, K. H. *"manthanō, ktl.,"* *TDNT* 4.390-461.

Schweizer, E. *Lordship and Discipleship.* London: SCM, 1960.

Silva, M. *Philippians.* Baker Exegetical Commentary on the New Testament, Grand Rapids: Baker, 1992.

Stanley, D. M. "'Become Imitators of Me': The Pauline Conception of Apostolic Tradition," *Biblica* 40 (1959) 859-77.

"Christ in You, the Hope of Glory": Discipleship in Colossians

MICHAEL P. KNOWLES

It is widely observed that the christology and theological anthropology of Colossians are more exalted, more oriented to the transcendent, than in any other New Testament writing apart from the Johannine Apocalypse. For scholars who hold to Pauline authorship, Colossians represents in these areas the apostle's theology at its most developed. For others, these same developments appear to carry the letter beyond the ambit of the genuine Pauline corpus. Whichever position one adopts — and here we accept Pauline authorship as a working premise — it remains clear that this letter translates an exalted theological vision of Christ into practical considerations of personal and corporate conduct. Both aspects, the theological and the practical alike, come together in Colossians under the rubric of what can be called "discipleship."

In theological terms, discipleship in this letter demands a choice between competing visions of the cosmos — that is, between competing visions of reality itself. Paul argues vigorously for a radically christocentric vision of the entire created order, wherein Christ is the ontological, epistemological, and soteriological focus of all human thought and experience. Christ is the foundation of reality itself, he will argue, for "all things have been created through him and for him . . . and in him all things cohere" (1:16-17). In terms of how we perceive and understand what is real, says the apostle, in Christ "are hidden all the treasures of wisdom and knowledge" (2:3). And as to the means of human salvation, "through him God was pleased to reconcile all things to himself, whether on earth or in heaven" (1:20). Accordingly, it is the central purpose of the letter to the Colossians to refute a number of competing theological visions and perspectives within the Colossian community that threaten to encroach on a proper Christian understanding of life generally and a faithful Christian discipleship in particular.

In practical terms, the primary axiom of discipleship in Colossians is that neither heavenly visions that promise mystical access into the divine realm nor "otherworldly" longings for eschatological fulfillment are sufficient justification for the asceticism and escapism that seem to have captured the Colossian church. Rather, being presently "in Christ" and eagerly awaiting God's final consummation of all things through Christ should lead believers in just the opposite direction — into practical and concrete expressions of their faith that are demonstrated in their individual lives, in relationships within their Christian community, and within the wider society in which they live.

1. The Relational Dimensions of Discipleship: The Thanksgiving Section (1:3-14)

The letter to the Colossians succinctly states its vision of Christian discipleship in its opening thanksgiving section in 1:3-14. For after the salutation of 1:1-2, and conforming to the standard conventions of ancient letters generally, the thanksgiving section of Colossians provides its readers with an agenda, or a kind of "table of contents," that sets out in brief the main matters to be discussed in the body of the letter that follows. Here one may note a number of salient features that will recur throughout the letter, each of which has a significant bearing on the question of discipleship.

In verses 3-6 Paul begins the thanksgiving section by stating his personal interest in the lives of his addressees and telling them that their situation is the subject of his ongoing prayers and thanksgivings before God:

> In our prayers for you, we always thank God, the Father of our Lord Jesus Christ, for we have heard of your faith in Christ Jesus and of the love that you have for all the saints, because of the hope laid up for you in heaven. You have heard of this hope before in the word of

the truth, the gospel that has come to you. Just as it is bearing fruit and growing in the whole world, so it has been bearing fruit among yourselves from the day you heard it and truly comprehended the grace of God.

Paul did not found the Colossian church (cf. vv 7-10). Yet he feels responsible for the believers' growth in their life of faith, obedience, and good works. He will expand on his own role in furthering their discipleship later on in 1:24–2:7.

The dual focus of this thanksgiving is on "God, the Father of our Lord Jesus Christ" (v 3) — or, in other words, on the character of God ("God, the Father") and the identity of Jesus of Nazareth ("our Lord Jesus Christ"). The description of God as the "Father of . . . Jesus" echoes the blessing in the previous verse, "Grace to you and peace from God *our* Father" (v 2). This simple juxtaposition suggests that the dynamic of faith in Jesus, who called God his Father, brings disciples of Jesus into a relationship with God that is at least analogous to, if not the same as, that which Jesus himself enjoyed.

But this relationship with God through Jesus is not merely a matter of intellectual assent or mystical identification. Faith in Jesus carries with it an obligation of obedience and moral conformity to Jesus, and so Paul speaks of Jesus as "our *Lord.*" It is this common allegiance on the part of the apostle and believers in Jesus at Colosse ("*our* Lord") that forms the basis for both Paul's interest in them and his expectation that they will receive his instructions. Such a theological interpretation of Jesus' identity is firmly tied to issues of historical specificity, and so Paul retains for Jesus the distinctly Jewish title of "Christ" — or "Messiah," that is, "Anointed One."

In verses 4 and 5 Paul states what he has heard about the Colossian church in terms of his favorite triad of "faith, hope, and love" (e.g., Rom 5:1-5; 1 Cor 13:13; Gal 5:5-6; Eph 1:15-18; 1 Thess 1:3; cf. O'Brien, *Colossians* 10-11). In these verses, certain basic features of Christian discipleship come to the fore: (1) discipleship is based on "faith in Christ Jesus"; (2) discipleship is inextricably tied to the nature and person of Jesus, in whom the believer exercises religious trust; (3) the believer has entered into a kind of fiduciary relationship with God, which involves God holding all that pertains to the believer's future in trust; and (4) this relationship is not to be viewed in an individualistic — certainly not a self-centered — fashion, for "love for all the saints" is a critical component. Indeed, we must not overlook the fact that this letter is not directed to individual believers at all, but to the community as a whole, with its address to the church consistently in the plural.

If discipleship, then, involves significant relationships both with Christ and with other believers, its expression also includes temporal as well as transcendent dimensions. For Paul speaks of discipleship as entailing "hope," a term that carries with it connotations of waiting in expectation of fulfillment, of the fuller expression of something only partly experienced at present. Yet that future-oriented hope is also described, paradoxically, as having been "laid up for you in heaven" — that is, as possessing a temporally immediate, transcendent dimension (cf. Lohse, *Colossians* 17-18). This tension between temporal anticipation and transcendent immediacy constitutes a key feature of discipleship in the letter to the Colossians.

A further feature to note in the first part of Paul's thanksgiving is the tension between future hope and present spiritual reality, which comes to practical expression in the idea of the gospel "bearing fruit" among the believers (vv 6, 10). Paul does not credit his addressees with themselves "bearing fruit" (contrast the exhortations of John the Baptist and Jesus to their hearers to "bear fruit" in Matt 3:8-10; 7:16-20, etc.). Rather, he says that the gospel is itself "bearing fruit and growing in the whole world." In other words, a spiritual reality whose full manifestation is still future nonetheless emerges into the present to the degree that the lives of believers manifest spiritual "fruit." In the same way, the transcendent reality of "the heavenlies" (v 5) becomes visible on the human plane.

Moreover, such a realization of the future and reification of the transcendent in the lives of the Colossian believers comprise but a microcosm of a much greater process already at work in the world as a whole (v 6). Thus the Colossians' own experience is understood to exemplify God's work in the world, just as, on an even greater scale, God's work in the world constitutes the inbreaking of the eternal and ultimate into the here and now.

The specific content of spiritual "fruitfulness," however, becomes clearer in Paul's prayer for his readers in the latter part of the thanksgiving section, in 1:9-14. For in verses 9-10a he prays that they will be filled with the knowledge of God's will and lead lives [literally "walk"] worthy of the Lord. Conduct worthy of the Lord is then explained in verses 10b-12 in four adverbial participle clauses as consisting of: bearing fruit by means of good works, increasing in the knowledge of God's will, being strengthened by the power of God, and joyfully giving thanks to God for salvation — with reasons for such thanksgiving given in verses 13-14.

The tension between the "already" and the "not yet" of Christian discipleship again comes to expression in the prayer "may you be prepared to endure everything with patience" (v 11b). For the strength and encouragement that flow from a believer's convictions about and participation in divinely ordered reality do not obviate struggle, endurance, and simple waiting, particularly in the midst of a world that is far from submissive to the Lordship of Christ (cf. Caird, *Letters from Prison* 171). Rather, however paradoxical it may seem, joyful thanksgiving and spiritual strength, on the one hand, and the need for patience and endurance in the face of suffering, on the other, all coexist in Christian experience (cf. Paul's own testimony in 1:24).

In this prayer, therefore, it is evident that Paul was vitally concerned with both the theological content and the practical expression of the Colossian believers' lives of discipleship. So he seeks to ground their Christian living in a truer theological understanding and, in the process, to articulate principles and patterns of conduct that will reflect the dynamic of the divine activity in their midst.

One further matter, however, must be noted here regarding Paul's statements in the Colossian thanksgiving section: that the emphasis on divine initiative articulated throughout this section is not meant to obviate either the responsibility of believers to take appropriate moral action or Paul's own responsibilities toward the communities in his care. The former concern will occupy the final two and a half chapters of the letter. The latter finds expression in 1:23-29, where the apostle speaks about the divine commission given him "to make the word of God fully known" or "to bring the word of God to fulfillment" (v 25). Paul sees himself as having a critical role in assisting his addressees in their lives of discipleship. And to that end, he says, he must toil and struggle, "warning everyone and teaching everyone in all wisdom, so that we may present everyone mature in Christ" (v 28).

To summarize, the thanksgiving section sets out the relational dimensions of discipleship: faith toward Christ and love toward the saints. It likewise sets out the temporal and transcendent dimensions of discipleship, whereby the full reality of God remains in one sense distant, whether in the future or transcendent realms, while in another sense it comes even now to expression and experience in the lives of the believers.

2. The Christological Foundations of Discipleship: The Confessional Section (1:15-20)

Col 1:15-20 has been variously understood: as an early hymn (whether of Gnostic or early Christian origin), as a *homologia* or confessional statement of the early church, or as a free composition originating with the apostle. But whatever its origin — whether Paul composed it himself or simply reworked preexisting material — the passage as it presently stands reflects Paul's own theological understanding and coheres with the broader purposes of the letter. Accordingly, our own analysis of this confessional portion must focus on its relevance for the subject of discipleship.

The starting point for Christian discipleship and the focus of a Christian's theological vision is the assertion that God has been made fully known through the man Jesus: "He is the image *(eikōn)* of the invisible God" (v 15; cf. 2 Cor 4:4). Notwithstanding a primary interest in Wisdom christology (e.g., Lohse, *Colossians* 47-48; Sappington, *Revelation and Redemption* 172-74; Wright, "Poetry and Theology" 451-55), Paul almost certainly has here in mind Gen 1:26-27 (cf. Col 3:10), which speaks of humans being created "according to the image of God" (LXX: *kat' eikona theou*). The implication is that Jesus not only represents divine Wisdom but also is the perfect expression of human identity as God intended it from the beginning (cf. 1 Cor 11:7; see Moule, *Colossians* 62-63; O'Brien, *Colossians* 43; Lincoln and Wedderburn, *Later Pauline Letters* 24, 40-41).

But anthropological considerations should not obscure the main purpose of verse 15, which is to highlight the revelatory nature of Christ's character vis-à-vis the otherwise "invisible God." By way of comparison, it may be noted that Philo makes similar affirmations regarding the character of the divine Logos (e.g., *De Opificio Mundi* 8; *De Confusione Linguarum* 20, 97, 147; *De Profugis* 19), of heavenly Wisdom (cf. *Legum Allegoriae* 1.43; see also Wisdom of Solomon 7:26) and of human beings generally (cf. *De Vita Mosis* 2.65) as representing the "image" of God. So while the notion of God's self-revelation in these terms was not unknown in the world of Hellenized Judaism, the assertion that Christ is God's "image" is altogether striking. For according to the exposition that follows, Christ is not simply one such revelation among many, but rather represents the full and true revelation of the divine nature (so v 19; see also 2 Cor 4:4; cf. Caird, *Letters from Prison* 180-81).

The remainder of the confessional portion spells out the theological foundations for the centrality of Christ in the life of a believer, describing Christ in parallel phrases, first as the "firstborn of all creation" (v 15b), then as the "firstborn from among the dead" (v 18). The first situates Jesus in relation to the entire creation. For not only have "all things been created through him and for him," but he serves, as well, a role analogous to that of the Johannine Logos — that is, as the coherent principle of material and spiritual existence in whom "all things hold together" (v 17; cf. Lohse, *Colossians* 52; Lincoln and Wedderburn, *Later Pauline Letters* 18-19). The second phrase situates Jesus in relation to the church, the "body" of which he is the "head" (v 18). And this is so by virtue of Christ's redemptive work, for "through him God was pleased to reconcile to himself all things, whether on earth or in heaven, by making peace through the blood of his cross" (v 20).

The juxtaposition of Christ's role in creation and his role in redemption reveals not only the theological magnitude of his work but also the theological magnitude of Christian discipleship as based on his work. For Paul claims nothing less than that redemption in Christ orients believers to the true nature and purpose of the universe. The corollary of this is that the church, the body of those who collectively confess Christ's headship and supremacy, represents God's intentions for the entire created order. Or to state matters somewhat differently, the choice to become a follower of Jesus involves more than simply a different lifestyle, attitude, or understanding. Far more profoundly, choosing to follow Jesus involves a choice between different visions of the cosmos and its purpose — that is, between different visions of reality itself. Furthermore, as the data of this letter indicate, the difficulty of discipleship consists in the fact that the alternatives to a Christ-centered cosmos still exercise considerable power over even the most faithful follower. And this difficulty, as pointed out earlier, is due in no small measure to the fact that the full experience of redemption lies yet in the future, the object of hope and longing.

The implication of the christological and soteriological affirmations of 1:15-20 is that followers of Jesus become conformed not only to Christ himself, but also to the God whom Christ reveals (cf. v 10). If humanity is created in the image of God and if Christ is the "image" of God in all its fullness, then redemption through Christ restores believers to their true identity, which is itself a reflection of the divine identity. This reflection of the divine identity, then, is the true goal of

Christian discipleship, which Paul takes pains to articulate in detail before he moves on to deal with various problems in the Colossian church.

3. Competing Visions of Discipleship: The Concerns of 2:8-19

The practical implications of these christological and cosmological underpinnings begin to emerge as Paul deals with competing visions of discipleship in 2:8-19. The vision of discipleship that, much to the apostle's dismay, had come to prevail at Colosse amounts in his view to submission to false powers and authorities as well as to false practices. Paul, by contrast, strives to reassert a vision of discipleship that is rooted in the transcendent identity, authority, and power of the risen Christ.

This passage bristles with theological, grammatical, and therefore hermeneutical difficulties. So that we are not sidetracked from our main task, the present treatment will attempt to build on the main outlines of the argument while acknowledging areas of detail where consensus is more difficult to obtain. For, notwithstanding the volume of scholarly discussion concerning the nature of the heresy that Paul confronted, the issues at stake in what he has written here concern not just theology or ideology, but also praxis and discipleship.

Col 2:8 spells out two opposing visions of discipleship. One is predicated on what Paul characterizes as mere philosophy, empty deceit, and human tradition, all "according to the elemental spirits of the universe" *(kata ta stoicheia tou kosmou)*, whereas the other is predicated "on Christ" *(kata Christon)*. Although, like much else in this passage, the precise nature and origin of the heresy that Paul counters is a matter of considerable debate, the context indicates that it involved "matters of food and drink [and] of observing festivals, new moons, and Sabbaths" (1:16), "self-abasement" and "the worship of angels" (2:18, whether understood as a subjective or an objective genitive), and, in particular, prohibitions regarding what one may rightfully handle, taste, and touch (2:20-22). All of these, according to 2:23, promote "self-imposed piety, humility, and severe treatment of the body."

The emphases on calendrical observance (especially "Sabbaths") and asceticism favors an interpretation of "elemental spirits" (*stoicheia*, literally "elements") as referring not only to cosmic powers or spirits in general (perhaps represented by the "angels" of 2:18), but also to elemental principles or teachings of Judaism in particular, which were understood to have been delivered by mediatory angels on Mount Sinai (cf. Gal 3:19b). If this is the case, the situation at Colossae would seem to bear some degree of resemblance to what we see in the letter to the Galatians. For in both instances, Paul stands opposed to features of Jewish origin that would seek to establish (or perhaps reestablish) Torah-centered piety and the Jewish halakhic tradition as the basis for a life of Christian discipleship (see especially Gal. 4:3, 9-10; cf. further Caird, *Principalities and Powers* 46-51; Moule, *Colossians* 90-92; Lohse, *Colossians* 96-98; O'Brien, *Colossians* xxxiii, 129-32; Lincoln and Wedderburn, *Later Pauline Letters* 10-11). This is not to minimize, however, the significant differences in the respective situations at Galatia and Colossae to which such premises or principles are applied, as the remainder of our discussion will indicate.

The question that concerns Paul here is the basis on which a life of faith is established and discipleship rightfully proceeds. For in his view allegiance to the principles — and the principalities — at work in the church at Colossae amounts to a rejection of Christ, a failure to adhere to the true source of spiritual nourishment and growth. Accordingly, Paul is at pains to explain the nature of a proper relationship to Christ. And key to his explanation is the statement in 2:9-10: "For in him the whole fullness [*plērōma*] of deity dwells bodily, and you have come to fullness [*peplērōmenoi*] in him." The language of "fullness" (cf. 1:9, 19, 25, on which see Moule, *Colossians* 164-69; Lohse, *Colossians* 57-58; Lincoln and Wedderburn, *Later Pauline Letters* 31-34) emphasizes both the completeness of salvation in Christ and the fact that such salvation entails, once again, an experience of God similar to that which Jesus himself embodied. So what Paul is here proclaiming is that only through following Christ, becoming conformed to him, is the "full" reality and experience of God to be encountered.

The four ensuing examples of circumcision, baptism, legal victory, and triumphal procession in 2:11-15 are intended to explain how this conformation to Christ takes place. In each case, the purpose of the metaphor or illustration is to indicate the true means of mystical union with Christ. First, just as Christ's death was a kind of spiritual "circumcision," a shedding of the flesh, so also the believer is said to "put off" human flesh by identifying with Christ in his bodily death. Second, just as Christ "descended" to death and was "raised" to life again, so the physical descent into the cleansing waters of baptism and subsequent reemergence represent a mystical and moral union with Christ's death and resurrection. Third, just as Christ was literally nailed to the cross, the legal force of that sacrifice is such that those who identify with it have their own moral debts nailed to the cross and eradicated (cf. Rom 7:6). And finally, to return to the question of "principalities and powers," Christ's victory was such that even those spiritual authorities to whom the Colossians had wrongly submitted are themselves now displayed as the vanquished spoils of Christ's triumphal procession.

What Paul steadfastly opposes is a vision of discipleship that places primary emphasis on the faithful observance of certain rites, rituals, and religious practices, whether the goal of such observance is merely pietistic or, as will subsequently appear, mystical as well. These, he says, are "simply human commands and teachings" (2:22), principles of human religious endeavor that proceed (at best) from an understanding of the covenant that has now been superseded. They are "only a shadow of what is to come," the reality of which is Christ (2:17).

On the most obvious level, the passage seeks to defend a crucial principle of divine initiative, which accounts for the repetition of the passive voice throughout ("you have been brought to fullness," 2:10; "you were circumcised," 2:11; "you were buried . . . you were raised," 2:12). More subtly — even paradoxically — it asserts that it is not the prerogative of the believer to seek to imitate Christ, "following in his footsteps" in the sense of undertaking spiritually efficacious endeavors (cf. Moule, *Colossians* 8-9). Rather, spiritual benefit will be found only in "following" Jesus (whether metaphorically or by mystical union) to the place of his death and resurrection, becoming identified with him by submitting to the unconstrained divine initiative that these events represent. The Colossian Christians' emphasis on strict observance and self-denial seems to suggest (at the very least) a pragmatic, behavioristic attempt to rectify or avert religious misconduct. What Paul insists, however, is that the cross has already swept away the moral bondage of sin.

The letter to the Colossians thus affirms that the true foundation of discipleship is not strict observance and pious endeavor, but rather identification with the accomplishment of Christ. It is not the role of the disciple to "crucify" the flesh through the rigors of asceticism, for Christ has already been crucified, and the disciple with him.

189

4. Discipleship as Death and Rebirth with Christ: The Exposition in 2:20–3:17

It is with both practical and metaphysical dimensions in mind that Paul sets out in Colossians two parallel sections of expositional material, each of which spells out the proper implications to be drawn from the fact of a believer's identification with the death and resurrection of Christ. The structures of these two sections are readily discernible in the wording of the English text:

Section A: 2:20–3:4
1. Death   "If with Christ you died. . . ."   (2:20-23)
2. Resurrection "So if you have been raised
                  with Christ. . . ."   (3:1-4)

Section B: 3:5-17
1. Death   "Put to death . . . whatever
                  in you is earthly. . . ."   (3:5-11)
2. Resurrection "As God's chosen ones . . .
                  clothe yourselves. . . ."   (3:12-17)

The first section deals primarily with death and resurrection from the perspective of spiritual dominion, or the metaphysical dimension of discipleship: "dying" to "elemental spirits" and union with the new life of Christ. The second section then places greater emphasis on the concrete and practical outworking of this union: "death" to immoral conduct and the appropriation of a new, Christlike set of behavior patterns.

Section A.1: Death (2:20-23)

First, then, to matters of spiritual principle: "If with Christ you died [i.e., through identification with his death] to the elemental spirits of the world, why do you acquiesce as though still living in their world?" (2:20). In Greek, this question and that of 3:1 are both phrased as first class conditional sentences (that is, they use the form "if . . . then. . . ."), which assume in the first part of each sentence (i.e., the protasis) the likelihood or truthfulness of what is being affirmed. Specifically, their purpose is first to describe situations that likely or actually exist, then

190

to set forth certain corollaries or consequences that follow. Although the wording of these sentences in Greek is considerably more subtle, we might here "overtranslate." 2:20 as "*Since* you died with Christ . . ." and 3:1 as "*Since* you have been raised. . . ."

The implication of these statements is that whereas, not unlike Paul's converts of Galatia, the Colossians first began their life of faith on the right basis, their subsequent practice of Chrstian discipleship had somehow gone astray (cf. Gal 1:6; 3:3; 5:7). Paul's strategy throughout this letter, in fact, is to recall the community to the theological foundations on which it was first established: "for we have heard of your faith in Christ Jesus" (Col 1:4); "the gospel that has come to you" (1:5-6); "provided that you persevere, grounded and secure in the faith" (1:23); "as you have received Christ Jesus the Lord, continue to walk in him, rooted and built up in him, . . . just as you were taught" (2:6-7). It is not the case, therefore, that the Colossian believers had no understanding of faith in Christ. On the contrary, Paul builds on the community's earlier theological foundations, which he affirms as valid and true. And on the basis of those foundations he insists that his addressees cannot claim faith in and identification with Christ for entry into the Christian life and then proceed to live out their lives of discipleship based (even unwittingly) on some other principle.

According to 2:20, the Colossian believers had mistakenly "acquiesced" or "submitted to regulations" *(dogmatizein)* that were characteristic of "the elemental powers of the universe" (*ta stoicheia tou kosmou;* cf. 2:8, 15), from which their identification with the death of Christ ought to have freed them. The meaning of this difficult passage can be clarified by comparison with Romans 6, where the apostle insists that since sin and death no longer "exercise lordship over" Christ (*kyrieuein,* v 9), no longer must sin enslave (*douleuein;* v 6) or reign over (*basileuein,* v 12; *kyrieuein,* v 14) those who have been united with Christ. In both letters, what might appear as nothing more than a matter of moral conduct actually entails significant spiritual allegiances. In Romans, "sin" operates as a spiritual power, while in Colossians cosmic powers and principalities are said to exercise dominion over the believers' behavior.

Ironically, the Colossians' concern with ascetic and mystical spiritual devotion places them, in fact, more firmly in the power of the very bondage they wish to escape. So Paul responds emphatically that in matters of spiritual cosmology, Christ's authority is supreme. And just as he reminds Christians at Rome that Christ's death sets them free from the dominion of sin (Romans 6), so here he insists that union with Christ in his death liberates believers at Colossae from bondage to religious asceticism and self-denial. Neither the conduct itself nor its metaphysical underpinnings ought to hold sway over followers of Jesus.

Section A.2: Resurrection (3:1-4)

Just as believers are included in Christ's death, so also, according to 3:1, they are included in his resurrection. This passage expands on the idea of "the hope laid up for you in heaven" (1:5), to which extended reference has already been made. Here, too, there is a careful balance between the transcendent and the future dimensions of Christian experience. For, with regard to the transcendent dimension, followers of the risen Jesus are exhorted to keep before them a vision of their exalted Lord, to "seek the things that are above, where Christ is seated at God's right hand." Furthermore, with regard to the future dimension, they are to do so because they have been identified with Christ in his death and resurrection and so included in what God has in store for Christians in the future: "for you have died, and your life is hidden with Christ in God" (3:3).

But how literally did Paul expect his exhortation, "Seek the things that are above, where Christ is seated at God's right hand" (3:1), to be understood? Certainly visionary experience was, if not normative, then at least highly significant for Paul's own Christian life, as he indirectly confesses in 2 Cor 12:2-4: "I know a person in Christ who fourteen years ago was caught up to the third heaven . . . into Paradise, and heard things that are not to be told." Whether on the basis of a mystical experience, or merely an imaginative situation, this passage suggests that for the recipients of the Colossian letter, faithful discipleship in a post-resurrection context will involve "following" Jesus not only through to the cross and the resurrection — but even beyond into the realm of his heavenly enthronement.

It is significant for our present purposes to note that the pursuit of heavenly visions, which had at their core the assurance of God's effective reign, was a common theme among the Jewish apocalyptic writers of the Second Temple period (ca. 200 B.C.–A.D. 100). While the letter to the Colossians is not, strictly speaking, an apocalyptic writing, it shares with such writings the conviction that insight into the heavenly realm reveals the true meaning of history. In the face of discouragement occasioned by historical events that seemed to deny God's providential control, the apocalyptic visionary reassured the faithful that God remains seated on his throne and continues to unfold his purposes for them (e.g., Dan 7:9-10; *1 Enoch* 14:18–16:3; 4 Ezra 8:20-23; 13:1-50; Rev 4:2-11; *Apocalypse of Abraham* 18–29; cf. Collins, *Apocalyptic Imagination* 42, 80, 181-182, 212-213; and, more fully, Sappington, *Revelation and Redemption* 89-111).

Since, therefore, the Colossian believers have been "raised with Christ" (2:12, 3:1), they are to adopt the perspective of such an exalted position, complete with its own depiction of Christ enthroned at God's right hand. This is itself an eschatological vision, the significance of which is even greater if the essence of the Colossian error was their pursuit of revelatory experiences — that is, visions of heaven and of God enthroned in heaven — on the basis, not of Christ's victory, but of rigorous ascetic observances (cf. F. O. Francis, "Humility and Angelic Worship in Col 2:18" and "The Background of *Embateuein* [Col 2:18] in Legal Papyri and Oracle Inscriptions," in Francis and Meeks, *Conflict at Colossae* 163-95 and 197-207; especially 168-71, 173-76; O'Brien, *Colossians* 142-45; Rowland, "Apocalyptic Visions"; Sappington, *Revelation and Redemption* 150-70). Remarkably, Paul argues that a normative feature of Christian discipleship is inclusion not only in the salvific accomplishment of Christ, but — more boldly still — in the identity, the reality, even the transcendent *location* of God: "for your life is hidden with Christ in God" (3:3; cf. Phil 1:23; 1 Thess 4:17).

Paul and the Colossian errorist, whoever he was (the Greek indefinite pronoun *tis* in 2:8, meaning "anyone" or "someone," suggests a single person), apparently agreed that insight into the heavenly plane provides believers with the key to God's purposes and the meaning of human history. Where they differed, however, was in Paul's insistence on an ethical and eschatological understanding of salvation, rather than an understanding of salvation based on a dualistic cosmology or metaphysics, and on Christ as the only one who could bring believers into an experiential knowledge of "the things that are above." So Paul rejected the errorist's call for some kind of ascetic-mystical piety and devotional discipline, not so much because the errorist's spiritual aims were mistaken, but because such an ascetic-mystical piety is incapable of accomplishing what it promises (2:23). But even more than that, Paul rejected such a call because Christ had already accomplished as much and more (3:1-3) — and, therefore, to revert to such "elemental teachings of the world" would be to renounce Christ and what he had accomplished already.

Excursus: The "with Christ" and "in Christ" Language of Colossians

At this point it will be helpful to digress briefly in order to explore a related theme that is not only central to Colossians, but also to Pauline thought generally. For in 3:3 Paul speaks of the lives of believers being "hidden with Christ in God" *(kekryptai syn tǭ Christǭ en tǭ theǭ).* It is the phrase "with Christ in God" that requires further explanation.

The concept of participation "with Christ" is characteristic of Colossians (cf. 2:12, 13, 20; 3:1, 3). Its meaning is virtually equivalent to that of Paul's "in Christ" language (so Lohse, *Colossians* 105; contra O'Brien, *Colossians* 170). Although the idea of believers being "in God" appears only rarely in the wider Pauline corpus (cf. Eph 3:9), the phrase "in Christ" and its cognates (i.e., "in Christ Jesus," "in Jesus Christ," "in the Lord," "in him," and "in whom") are used some 163 times by Paul to express the fact that those who place their trust in the Christ are mystically joined to him, and, through him, to one another in a common "body" (cf. Best, *One Body in Christ,* 1-33, for a full discussion and historical survey).

The function of the "in Christ" terminology in Paul's letters ranges from (1) designating the soteriological accomplishments of Christ himself to (2) describing that which obtains in the life of believers by virtue of association with Christ to (3) explaining the consequent basis for moral action on the part of believers. So, as examples of the first usage: in Christ "all things were created" and "in him all things hold together" (1:16-17); in him "are hidden all the treasures of wisdom and knowledge" (2:3), and "in Christ all the fullness of deity dwells in bodily form" (1:19; 2:9). By the same token, as examples of the second usage: those who are identified with Christ "have come to fullness in him," and "in him [they] were also circumcised . . . in the circumcision of Christ" (2:10-11), "in whom [they] have redemption, the forgiveness of sins" (1:14). The apostle describes the goal of his own ministry as that of presenting believers "mature in Christ" (1:28), even as he is able to speak of another disciple, Archippus, as having received a task to complete "in the Lord" (4:17). Finally, exemplifying the third usage, the fact that those who follow Jesus are united with him serves as the basis for moral action, as in the exhortation "Wives, be subject to your husbands as is fitting in the Lord" (3:18), as well as for Christian identity and identification, as in the address "To the saints and faithful brothers in Christ at Colossae" (1:2; cf. also 4:7: "Tychicus . . . a beloved brother . . . and a fellow servant in the Lord").

The same language serves, in other words, to describe the life, identity, and ministries both of Christ and of those who follow him, precisely because those of the former are meant to be determinative in every way for the latter. In fact, the same interpenetration of identities can be described in opposite terms: "Christ in you, the hope of glory" (1:27); "Christ is all and in all" (3:11; cf. 3:15-16). Such language attempts to convey, on the one hand, the theological magnitude of the believers' inclusion in the accomplishment of Christ, and, on the other, the fact that the power of Christ is actively at work in them (so 1:29; 3:16-17).

To return to the statement in 3:3, then, the phrase "with Christ in God" suggests the interchangeability of the concepts "in Christ," "with Christ," and "in God" (so 1 Thess 1:1; 2 Thess 1:1). That believers are depicted as being, in effect, enthroned with Christ simply represents a logical extension of the Pauline concept of their inclusion "in Christ."

But exhortations to heavenly-mindedness notwithstanding, the full scope of this vision and its implications for followers of Jesus remain partially veiled. For the full disclosure and implementation of this vision awaits the final and glorious revelation of Christ (so Phil 3:20-21). So here in Col 3:4, Paul declares: "When Christ who is your life is revealed, then [and, we might add, not until then] you also will be revealed with him in glory." As was the case earlier in the Colossian letter, affirmation of the believers' present experience of the transcendent is balanced and tempered by the realization that they cannot evade the obligations and encumbrances of the temporal realm.

Section B.1: Death (3:5-11)

According to the moral and theological vision of Colossians, as noted earlier, believers in Christ are not called on to "crucify" the flesh through asceticism, for Christ has already been crucified and believers with him.

Yet in seeming contradiction, Paul now urges Christians at Colossae to "put to death . . . whatever in you is earthly: fornication, impurity, passion, evil desire, and greed" (3:5). Two observations are in order. The first, as already indicated, is that Paul's emphases on divine initiative and a believer's incorporation into the transcendent Christ do not absolve Christians from moral responsibility. On the contrary, they reestablish moral responsibility at a more profound level. For in sharp contrast to ascetic prohibitions and "matters of food and drink or of observing festivals, new moons, or Sabbaths" (2:16, 20-21), this vision of discipleship articulates such weightier issues of moral conduct and motivation as "fornication, impurity, passion, . . . anger, wrath, malice, slander, and abusive language" (2:5, 8).

One is reminded of similar clarifications of the ethical imperative in the Sermon on the Mount — as, for example, Jesus' statement about lust in Matt 5:27-28 ("You have heard that it was said, 'You shall not commit adultery.' But I say to you that everyone who looks at a woman with lust has already committed adultery with her in his heart") and his excoriation of certain types of scribal fastidiousness in Matt 23:23 ("You tithe mint, dill, and cummin, but have neglected the weightier matters of the law: justice and mercy and faith"). Thus inclusion *in* Christ, which is fully a matter of divine initiative and accomplishment, still demands ethical conformity *to* Christ.

The second observation is that Paul here seems to be describing a decisive turning from error to obedience — which probably accounts for the aorist imperatives in 3:5, 8, 12, and 14 — rather than a continuous moral endeavor — as would be suggested by the use of present imperatives. Such a reading suits the usual proposal that the language of robing and disrobing refers to baptismal ritual, whether or not a reference to actual baptismal garments is intended (cf. Lohse, *Colossians* 141-42). And such an understanding is further strengthened by the syntax of verses 9-10, which clearly indicate an antecedent reorientation of one's moral vision at the time of baptism: "Do not lie to one another, seeing that you *have stripped off* the old self with its practices and *have clothed yourselves* with the new self" (cf. O'Brien, *Colossians* 189). Discipleship, in other words, consists of living out more fully the consequences of identification with and submission to the death and resurrection of Christ (cf. 2:20; 3:1).

The remaining verses of this section (vv 10-11), in fact, anticipate the argument of 3:12-17, for they speak not of what believers "put off" in accordance with their death in Christ, but of what they assume or "put on" in keeping with his resurrection. Here Paul returns to his earlier theme of God's image in Christ being mirrored or reproduced in the lives of Christ's followers (cf. O'Brien, *Colossians* 191-92; cf. 1:15-20). He explains that the "new self," which is theirs by virtue of their inclusion in Christ's resurrection, is "being renewed in knowledge according to the image of its creator" (3:10; cf. 2 Cor 3:18). Again, the present tense and passive voice are all-important, for the disciples are "being renewed [*anakainoumenon*]" by God — not by their own religious endeavors — in an ongoing process of transformation, as "the new humanity, already existing in Christ, is progressively actualized in the Christian Church" (Moule, *Colossians* 120; cf. Lohse, *Colossians* 145-46).

In this simple interplay of syntax, the mutual responsibilities of God and of believers in the outworking of Christian discipleship, as well as something of a timetable, are revealed. For contrary to what the Colossians have apparently come to believe, it is God who consistently takes the initiative in their lives of discipleship: previously, in the historical death and resurrection of Jesus; presently, in conforming the followers of Jesus to the divine image. Believers' own responsibilities lie, first of all, in a pivotal (and, for them, past) acceptance of Christ's identification with them, and then in their ongoing acknowledgment of Christ's determinative shaping of their lives and identities.

Section B.2: Resurrection (3:12-17)

As Paul lays out the practical dimensions of resurrection in 3:12-17, the concept of conformity to the divine image comes into clearer focus. Even as the disciples are to "put off" all that is carnal and "of the earth" (3:5), so they must "clothe" themselves with all that is characteristic of their new, divinely ordered life: compassion, kindness, humility, meekness, patience, love, and peace (3:12-15). In context, it appears that Paul is exhorting the Colossian Christians to be conformed to the essential qualities of the divine character (cf. O'Brien, *Colossians* 198-201).

Two passages from Exodus regarding the character of God seem to have been inscribed on the heart of the Jewish people throughout all their history. The first is Exod 33:19: "I will be gracious to whom I will be gracious, and I will have mercy on whom I will have mercy." The second, Exod 34:6-7: "The Lord, the Lord, a God merciful and gracious, slow to anger and abounding in steadfast love and faithfulness, keeping steadfast love for the thousandth generation, forgiving iniquity and transgression and sin, yet by no means clearing the guilty." Some indication of the influence that these passages exercised may be found, for example, in such widely varying contexts as Pss 86:15; 103:8; Joel 2:13; Jonah 4:2; Neh 9:17; Rom 9:15-18; and 4 Ezra 7:132-139. While far from an exhaustive list, the instances cited suffice to demonstrate that the qualities extolled in Exodus 33 and 34 served as standard descriptions of the divine character for generation upon generation of God's people.

Although verbal echoing of these Old Testament texts in Colossians is limited to a single term (LXX Exod 34:6: *oiktirmōn*, "merciful, compassionate"; Col 3:12: *oiktirmou*, "heartfelt compassion"), the conceptual similarities between these two lists of moral qualities are sufficient to suggest that, in exhorting the believers at Colossae to be conformed to the image of God, Paul urges them to reflect the divine character in their dealings with one another. Indeed, this premise is borne out by the remainder of the passage:

> Just as the Lord has forgiven you, so you also must forgive. . . . Let the peace of Christ arbitrate in your hearts. . . . Let the word of Christ dwell in you richly. . . . And whatever you do, in word or deed, do everything in the name of the Lord Jesus, giving thanks to God the Father through him (3:13-16).

In each of the above exhortations, either the example or the present ministrations of God and Christ provide the impetus for the believers' own godly conduct. Furthermore, their life of Christian discipleship is repeatedly said to consist of conformity to the work of God, either within them or in their midst — as is only fitting if the very nature and character of God, as revealed in Christ, provides their inspiration (so 1 Cor 2:9-13, 16; Phil 2:5).

5. Discipleship in Christian Community:
The Household Code and the Greetings (3:18–4:18)

The remainder of the Colossian letter is addressed either to particular social situations (the "household code," 3:18–4:6) or to specific individuals within the Christian community (the greetings, 4:7-18). As such, these sections serve as "test cases" and illustrations of the life of faithful discipleship.

In speaking of the social structures of his day, Paul indicates that following Jesus is of relevance to areas of universal human concern. His instructions do not advocate social revolution (cf. 4:5-6). Rather, he proposes a transformation from within of the existing structures. In contrast to a preoccupation with highly specific rituals of religious observance, as was threatening believers at Colossae, Paul adopts a form of moral instruction (the *Haustafel,* or "household code") that was derived, via Hellenized Judaism, from Stoic thought, in order to articulate a christocentric contribution to matters of contemporary ethical concern (cf. O'Brien, *Colossians* 215-18; Lincoln and Wedderburn, *Later Pauline Letters,* 20-22, for comparative materials). In one sense, the content of his admonitions is not new. Plutarch or Seneca, for example, might similarly have admonished wives to be submissive and children to be obedient. But Paul adds the distinctive qualifier: "as is fitting *in the Lord*" (3:18), "for this is your acceptable duty *in the Lord*" (3:20; cf. Lohse, *Colossians* 154-57).

Moral conduct for followers of Jesus, as we have noted, is determined in every case in the letter to the Colossians by union with Christ and by the obligation to conform to his will and person that such a relationship entails. Here again in 3:18–4:6 the conduct of believers — of husbands and wives, of fathers and children, of masters and slaves — is to be shaped by the conduct and character of their Lord. Although in 3:19 the implications for husbands to love their wives is not fully spelled out, the parallel passage in Eph 5:25-33 expresses more of the full scope of Paul's admonition and sets out its rationale: husbands are to sacrifice themselves as Christ sacrificed himself (vv 25-27), caring for their wives as they do their own bodies, just as Christ cares for his body, the church (vv 28-30). No less audacious are the assertions that Christian slaves are to serve their heavenly Lord, who will recompense their labor in a way that their earthly bondage does not allow (4:22-24) and that there is a heavenly Lord to whom earthly lords and masters will themselves have to answer (4:1; cf. 1 Cor 7:22).

In each instance, it is essential to note that Paul is not so much setting forth rules for conduct as insisting on the expression of a new reality. Accordingly, the admonition of 3:17, which introduces the "household code," is much more than a simple literary transition between sections of parenesis: "Do everything in the name of the Lord Jesus." In fact, it articulates the very essence of moral conduct for the believer (O'Brien, *Colossians* 218-19).

The letter to the Colossians concludes, as was typical of a first-century letter, with a series of personal greetings and a personal subscription in 4:7-18. Precisely because of their personal nature, these greetings offer a fascinating glimpse into the character and characteristics of this early community of Christian believers. It becomes evident, for example, not only that they are to pray for each other (4:2, 12), but that Paul, too, needs the prayers of the community in order to fulfill his ministry (v 3). The dealings that the writer, bearers, and recipients of this letter have with one another serve to encourage (v 8), comfort (v 11), affirm (vv 9, 13), and exhort (v 17). Even their suffering is shared to some extent (v 18; cf. 1:24). All of this testifies to the closeness and significance of their community relations, an example that can serve as a salutary corrective to the excessive individualism of our present age.

6. Conclusions

In one sense, it is not difficult to see how the Colossian error arose, for it aptly expresses the problematic nature of Christian discipleship in a postresurrection context. From one point of view, it would not be unreasonable to conclude that following a risen and exalted Lord should lead to preoccupation with the transcendent realm and to an accompanying denigration of the temporal. Against such a possibility, Paul insists on the enduring relevance of the whole of Christ's ministry in all its temporal and cosmological dimensions. Discipleship is balanced, as it were, between the equal yet competing theological exigencies of (1) the past and the future (the earthly ministry of Jesus vis-à-vis Christ's future manifestation) and (2) the mundane and the transcendent (personal and communal ethical obligations vis-à-vis visionary mysticism).

Particular aspects of Christ's ministry are applied to particular misconceptions. Insofar as they are identified with his death — with its victory over sin — believers in Christ are set free from ascetic observances and moral bondage. Insofar as they are included in his resurrection, they need acknowledge the authority of no other spiritual power, for they have already been granted entrance to the heavenly realm. But insofar as they still await the return of Christ, their initiation into heavenly mysteries by no means obviates the need for ethical endeavor, endurance, and even suffering.

Christian discipleship, according to Colossians, does not consist merely of gaining correct understanding or of adopting correct behavior, much as it includes both. Rather, continued "following" of Christ consists of continually "being renewed" (3:10), as a matter of divine initiative, in matters of orthodoxy and orthopraxis alike. The all-important goal of such renewal is gradual conformity to the complete "image" both of God and of humanity as represented by Christ. This is precisely what it means for believers to be "in Christ" or to experience, as the memorable wording of 1:27 states it: "Christ in you, the hope of glory."

Selected Bibliography

Bandstra, A. J. *The Law and the Elements of the World.* Kampen: Kok, 1964.

Best, E. *One Body in Christ: A Study in the Relationship of the Church to Christ in the Epistles of the Apostle Paul.* London: SPCK, 1955.

Caird, G. B. *Paul's Letters from Prison (Ephesians, Philippians, Colossians, Philemon).* Oxford: Oxford University Press, 1976.

————. *Principalities and Powers: A Study in Pauline Theology.* Oxford: Clarendon, 1956.

Collins, J. J. *The Apocalyptic Imagination: An Introduction to the Jewish Matrix of Christianity.* New York: Crossroad, 1984.

Francis, F. O., and W. A. Meeks, eds. *Conflict at Colossae: A Problem in the Interpretation of Early Christianity, Illustrated by Selected Modern Studies.* Missoula: Scholars, 1973.

Hanson, P. D. *The Dawn of Apocalyptic: The Historical and Sociological Roots of Jewish Apocalyptic Eschatology.* Philadelphia: Fortress, 1975.

Lincoln, A. T., and A. J. M. Wedderburn. *The Theology of the Later Pauline Letters.* Cambridge: Cambridge University Press, 1993.

Lohse, E. *A Commentary on the Epistles to the Colossians and to Philemon,* tr. W. R. Poehlmann and R. J. Karris. Hermeneia, Philadelphia: Fortress, 1971.

Moule, C. F. D. *The Epistles of Paul the Apostle to the Colossians and to Philemon.* Cambridge: Cambridge University Press, 1957.

O'Brien, P. T. *Colossians, Philemon.* Word Biblical Commentary, Waco: Word, 1975.

Rowland, C. "Apocalyptic Visions and the Exaltation of Christ in the Letter to the Colossians," *Journal for the Study of the New Testament* 19 (1983) 73-83.

Sappington, T. J. *Revelation and Redemption at Colossae.* Sheffield: JSOT, 1991.

Schweizer, E. *Lordship and Discipleship.* London: SCM, 1960.

Segal, A. F. "Heavenly Ascent in Hellenistic Judaism, Early Christianity and their Environment," in *Aufstieg und Niedergang der römischen Welt,* ed. H. Temporini and W. Haase. Berlin/New York: de Gruyter, 1972. II.23.2, 1333-94.

Wright, N. T. "Poetry and Theology in Colossians 1.15-20," *New Testament Studies* 36 (1990) 444-68.

Standing Before the Moral Claim of God: Discipleship in Hebrews

WILLIAM L. LANE

Hebrews is a sermon rooted in life. It conforms to a homiletical form that emerged in the social world of Hellenistic Judaism, where synagogue preaching sought to actualize traditional Scripture for a community in a nontraditional environment. The writer of Hebrews adapted this form in order to confirm the values and commitments of a group of Christians who were experiencing social ostracism and alienation. Recent research has done much to vindicate and refine the definition of Hebrews as a sermon or homily (see Lane, *Hebrews* lxix-lxxiv, for a summary of recent scholarship).

Recognizing the oral, sermonic character of Hebrews permits important features of its style and literary structure to receive the attention they deserve. The writer skillfully conveys the impression that he is present with the assembled group and is actually delivering the sermon he has prepared. In the homily proper (1:1–13:21) he studiously avoids any reference to actions like writing or reading, which would emphasize the geographical distance that separates him from the group he is addressing. Instead, he stresses the actions of speaking and listening appropriate to persons in conversation, and he identifies himself with his audience in a direct way (e.g., 2:5; 5:11; 6:9; 8:1; 9:5; 11:32). Moreover, throughout the sermon he assumes a conversational tone in order to diminish the sense of the distance that separates him from his audience and that makes writing necessary. He conceives of his work as speech.

He crafted the written text for the ear, not the eye, to convey a sense of structure and development. So by appealing to the dynamic relationship of speaking and listening, he is able to establish a sense of presence with his audience.

Hebrews is a sensitive pastoral response to the sagging faith of older and tired individuals who were in danger of relinquishing their Christian commitment. The homily throbs with an awareness of the privilege and cost of discipleship. The writer's intention is to strengthen the community in the face of a new crisis. He warns them of the judgment of God that they will incur if they waver in their commitment to Jesus. Exhortations to covenant fidelity and to perseverance are grounded in a fresh understanding of the significance of Jesus and his sacrifice. As high-priestly Son of God in solidarity with the human family in the particularity of the new people of God, Jesus is the supreme exemplar of faithfulness to God and patient endurance. His sacrificial death has secured for his people unlimited access to God and the assurance of divine help that arrives at the right times (cf. 4:15-16).

Evidence of extended and thoughtful reflection on the subject of Christian discipleship can be found throughout Hebrews. Hebrews is, in fact, a sermon on the cost of discipleship. The parts of Hebrews discussed in this chapter have been selected because they expose both strands of an early Christian tradition concerning discipleship and the perspectives characteristic of Hebrews. They are not meant to be exhaustive, but representative of the pattern of discipleship to which the community found itself called once more.

1. A Strong Encouragement to Faithful Discipleship: 2:10-18

In the hortatory section of 2:1-4 it is apparent that the addressees of Hebrews had shown a tendency to drift from their moorings — even to display a reckless lack of concern for the Christian message they had received. There is no indication in those verses, however, why they were being distracted from their commitment. It is only in the course of reflecting on the appropriateness of the incarnation and death of the Son of God in 2:10-18 that, for the first time, there is a suggestion that allegiance to Jesus is costly. For allegiance to Jesus exposed the community to testing (v 18). In fact, those addressed found themselves in a situation that was sufficiently serious to induce paralysis through the fear of death (v 15).

The circumstances that warranted such language remain unspecified. But as the address unfolds there are more pointed allusions to factors that precipitated the crisis of faith within the congregation. The presentation of Jesus as "champion" (v 10) and "high priest" (v 17) in this unit of material is highly significant, for it may be assumed that these christological constructs reflect a sensitivity to the situation being addressed. It is imperative, therefore, that these titles be interpreted from the perspectives offered within the immediate context. Thus interpreted, they, too, shed a measure of light on the situation of the addressees and the historical setting for the address.

The dominant concept of 2:10-18 is the solidarity of the Son of God with his people. This solidarity is affirmed in the statement that the one who makes people holy and those who are made holy are from the same family (v 11), as well as in the supporting citations from Ps 22:22 and Isa 8:17-18 (vv 12-13). The "brothers and sisters" *(adelphoi mou)* of the psalmist comprised "the congregation of the faithful" with whom Jesus lifts his voice in singing the praises of God. They are those who trust the Lord, the spiritual remnant concerning whom Isaiah had so much to say. They were represented in the writer's day by Jesus and by all who responded to his call to discipleship.

The divine Son identified himself with his people in order to die for them. This is affirmed generally in verse 9, where the phrase "that he might taste death for everyone" suggests that Jesus' death was for the benefit of others. The nature of the benefit derived from his death, however, remains unspecified there. But verses 10-16 clarify that the death of Jesus opened the way for others to participate in the glory of God, with that participation being the result of deliverance from enslavement to the devil and the removal of the fear of death. Jesus' acceptance of the mode of existence common to all persons and his identification with the community of faith constituted a pledge of the glorification of the human family in the particularity of the people of God.

Within this setting, Jesus is presented as both champion (v 10) and high priest (v 17). Drawing on the motif of individual, representative combat, the portrayal of Jesus as the champion or protagonist of an oppressed people addresses a word of comfort and encouragement to Christians in crisis. The depiction of Jesus as champion points beyond the immediate crisis of the community to the triumph that already has been secured for the people of God. The element of triumphalism in the metaphor complements the theology of glory expressed in verse 10. Champion christology provides a fresh interpretation of the incarnation from the perspective of the tradition that God or Jesus is the champion who rescues those enslaved by the prince of death (cf. Isa 49:24-26; Luke 11:21-22; see Lane, *Hebrews* 56-57, 60-63). The sober reminder that the champion overcame his adversary through death (vv 14-15) exhibits the costly character of the grace of God extended to the community through the Son (v 9).

This fruitful approach of champion christology, however, is not sustained beyond verse 16. For with verses 17-18 the writer prepares to lead his hearers directly into the body of the discourse, which is devoted to the exposition of Jesus as high priest and sacrifice. Common to the constructs of both champion christology and high priest christology are the elements of representation and solidarity with a particular people. The presentation of Jesus throughout verses 10-18 provides assurance that the exalted Son continues to identify himself with the oppressed people of God, who are being exposed to humiliation and testing in a hostile world.

This note of identification finds particular expression in verse 11, where the writer declares that Jesus does not hesitate to recognize those who have been consecrated to the service of God as his brothers and sisters. The formulation "he is not ashamed to call them brothers and sisters" openly declares Jesus' commitment to his disciples. This affirmation provides the encouragement needed by the hearers and prepares them for the subsequent declaration that "God is not ashamed to be called their God" in 11:16, where the context is distinctly covenantal.

The image of the family is appropriate in this context. Because the divine Son identifies himself with the covenantal family, he is able to achieve in others the perfect consecration to God that he himself embodies. The close connection of verse 11 with the preceding verse further suggests that the occasion when Jesus is not ashamed to call others "brothers and sisters" is the parousia, when God will lead many sons and daughters to glory. The declaration anticipates the eschatological entrance of the redeemed community into the heavenly world to come, and so constitutes a strong encouragement to faithful discipleship.

2. A Serious Call to Persevering Discipleship: 3:7-19

A major theme in Hebrews is that Christians are the people of God who, like the generation in the desert, experience the tensions of an interim existence between redemption and rest, between promise and fulfillment. The tragic failure of the desert generation to attain the goal of their redemption calls attention to a pattern of response to God's voice that must not be emulated (cf. 3:7–4:13). That fact was already recognized in Ps 95:7b-11 and was reiterated whenever Psalm 95 was used liturgically in a synagogue or church to summon a congregation to worship. The plea, "Today, if you hear his voice, do not harden your hearts, as in the rebellion," was intended to bring the memory of Israel at Kadesh before the people as a sober reminder that each generation has the awesome responsibility of standing before the moral claim of God. "Today" signals a fresh moment of biography and history, which is always conditioned by the response of obedience or disobedience, of faith or unbelief.

The writer of Hebrews quotes Psalm 95 in 3:7-11 to extend to his hearers a serious call to persevering discipleship. It was imperative that their partnership with Christ be affirmed by unfaltering adherence to the basic stance acknowledged in their baptismal confession (v 14). The demand for fidelity and endurance is supported by the promise of rest (cf. 4:1-11). But the writer goes on to urge mutual care and concern for every member of the community to ensure that no one responds inappropriately to the voice of God (vv 12-13).

The psalmist had posed the issue of response to God in terms of the response of the desert generation at Kadesh. And this understanding controls the interpretation of Psalm 95 in Hebrews as well. For the writer of Hebrews compares Christian existence, not to a long period of wandering in the desert, but to the situation of those who were on the verge of attaining what God had promised when they arrived at Kadesh. The eschatological conviction of the writer is that Christians stand in a comparable situation with respect to entrance into God's rest. The basis of the comparison between Israel at Kadesh and the Christian community addressed is the unresolved tension of standing before the promise of God in a moment conditioned by peril. This is the setting for persevering discipleship.

The fundamental failure of the desert generation was their refusal to believe that God was actually present among them, directing them through his word. Refusing to acknowledge God's presence and voice, they forfeited the possibility of entrance into God's rest. In calling attention to their fate, the writer warns the community not to lose faith in the presence of God with them that is celebrated whenever the word of God is read or the gospel tradition is proclaimed.

Especially in 3:7-19, typological exegesis entails the use of historical memory to nurture and formulate eschatological faith. The alternatives of blessing and curse that confronted Israel at Kadesh were conditioned on faith or unbelief in response to the promise of God. The refusal to believe God excluded Israel from participation in the realization of the promise. So in 3:7-19 the community is summoned to recognize the peril of refusing to believe God. The condition for the fulfillment of the divine promise remains active faith, expressed through obedience and Christian confession (cf. 3:6b, 14; 4:14). This is the hallmark of responsible Christian discipleship.

3. A Paradigm for Responsible Discipleship: 10:19-39

In the development of 10:19-39, a sharp warning concerning apostasy in verses 26-31 is followed by strong encouragement in verses 32-35. The wisdom of the writer in addressing his addressees pastorally is evident from the fact that he makes their own past experience of responsible discipleship the paradigm for their present situation and immediate future. He wants them to subject their present experience as Christians to fresh scrutiny in the light of their past stance of firm commitment. So by pointing the community to the past as well as to the future, the writer seeks to strengthen their Christian resolve for the present.

In verses 32-35 the writer counters an unhealthy attitude among the addressees by setting forth the community's past courageous stance of commitment under adverse circumstances as the model for their continuing boldness now. Drawing on a primitive Christian tradition designed to strengthen believers in a crisis of persecution, the writer applies that tradition to the experience of his addressees in order to encourage them to emulate their own earlier, splendid example.

The oratorical imperative "remember" in verse 32 is a call for reflection. For contemplation of the events that clustered around an earlier crisis of persecution and loss should not only revive that experience in their memories but also alter their present lifestyle. That those earlier events had been the direct result of their commitment to Christian discipleship is indicated by the participial phrase, "after you had received the light." The reference is to the saving illumination of their hearts and minds that was mediated through the preaching of the gospel (cf. 6:4: "those who have once-for-all been brought into the light").

The significant fact of the community's experience in that earlier period is stated in the phrase "you endured a hard contest with sufferings" (v 32b). From the beginning, therefore, suffering had been part of the addressees' Christian experience. The word "contest" *(athlēsis)* was originally used of the intense efforts of athletes in a sports arena (cf. Polybius 5.64.6; 7.10.2-4; 27.9.7, 11). Here, however, it is used metaphorically for persecution. Yet there is no suggestion in the immediate context, nor elsewhere in Hebrews (cf. 12:4), of the later Christian use of this term for martyrdom (e.g., *Passion of Andrew* 15, which speaks of "the day of the contest of the holy apostle Andrew"). For the writer of Hebrews, the image of enduring a contest was an acceptable way of giving a constructive interpretation to the experience of abuse.

The details in verses 33-34a serve to clarify the character of those earlier sufferings endured. The contrasting statements ("sometimes . . . and on other occasions") introduce an inverted parallelism that has significant implications for the interpretation of the details:

A "Sometimes you were publicly exposed to ridicule, both by insults and persecutions;
    B on other occasions you showed solidarity with those who were treated in this way;
    B' for, in fact, you shared the sufferings of those in prison;
A' and cheerfully accepted the seizure of your property."

This carefully structured recital of past indignities suggests that some of the congregation had been exposed to ridicule and persecution and were defenseless against seizure of their property (A/A'). Others in the fellowship had identified themselves with the hardships of these believers, sharing the sufferings of those who had been imprisoned by the civil authorities (B/B'). Thus the first group, it seems, had experienced not only verbal and physical abuse, but also imprisonment and the loss of property, whereas the other members of the community expressed solidarity with those who had borne the brunt of these sufferings.

A strong sense of community characterized the congregation in that earlier period, as seems evident from the parallel clauses in verses 33b-34a. Those who had not been affected personally by the hostility to which some members had been exposed openly identified themselves with their Christian brothers and sisters. They displayed genuine empathy with those in prison by visiting them, feeding them, and, undoubtedly, actively seeking their release (cf. Lucian, *Death of Peregrinus* 12-13, for each of these activities on behalf of an imprisoned Christian). Such involvement was not without cost, as both relatives and friends of Jews who were persecuted in the anti-Semitic riots of Alexandria in A.D. 38 discovered (cf. Philo, *Against Flaccus* 9, 10). The solidarity displayed by the addressees during that critical period demonstrated that their commitment to Christian discipleship was genuine.

The group publicly exposed to ridicule (v 33a) had also endured the seizure of their property (v 34b). It is not certain whether this was the result of official judicial actions of magistrates, who could impose heavy fines or confiscate property for suspected infractions (cf. Philo, *Against Flaccus* 10), or whether the allusion is to the looting of houses after their owners were imprisoned or removed (cf. Philo, *Against Flaccus* 56: "Their enemies overran the houses now left vacant and began to loot them, dividing up the contents like spoils of war"). Whatever the precise circumstances, the Christians cheerfully accepted their losses because they were persuaded that they had "better and permanent possessions" (v 34c). This persuasion was the basis of their endurance of "the hard contest with sufferings."

The strong confidence of the early Christians that they possessed "better and permanent possessions" in the transcendent heavenly world that Jesus had opened to them was the dominant factor that permitted them to develop a proper perspective on the deprivations they had endured. And this is the perspective that must be recaptured by the men and women addressed by the writer of Hebrews if they are to maintain steadfast commitment to Christ when confronted with a new and more severe crisis. Boldness and endurance are set out in verses 35-36 as the hallmarks of Christian discipleship in a hostile society.

The reason that the community has need of endurance is clarified by the citation of Hab 2:3-4 in verses 37-38. For the time of patiently waiting for the consummation of God's redemptive plan is not yet over. Furthermore, the community of faith continues to find itself exposed to alienation and social ostracism in society. Thus, sustained boldness and endurance are required of believers as they wait for the fulfillment of God's promise.

The posture of expectant waiting and fidelity that the members of the congregation must exhibit is set out in Hab 2:3b-4. The writer of Hebrews has modified his Greek text in three significant ways for the purposes of his argument in this section. First, he has sharpened the messianic interpretation of the text by adding the masculine article to the participle "coming," thereby creating the messianic title "the Coming One" (cf. Matt 3:11; 11:3 [par. Luke 7:19]; 21:9). The statement "The Coming One will come" refers to Christ at his parousia. The oracle, therefore, serves to affirm the absolute certainty and imminence of Christ's eschatological coming:

> A little longer,
> the Coming One will come;
> he will not delay.

Second, the writer has inverted the clauses of Hab. 2:4 so that the subject of the conditional phrase, "if he draws back," is no longer the expected deliverer, but the Christian who awaits the advent of the Coming One. The inversion is clearly the work of the writer of Hebrews, for it finds no support in the manuscript tradition of the LXX. It serves to fix the meaning of "my righteous one" in verse 38a beyond doubt. For now the "righteous one" is the disciple who demonstrates faithfulness to God — particularly as that person moves toward the goal of life, eschatologically understood. Conversely, the one who draws back in verse 38b is the disciple who loses sight of the goal.

In verse 37 it is the accountability of God that is at stake. He will keep his promise; the eschatological coming of Christ is certain. In verse 38, however, there is a shift in focus to the accountability of the disciple, who must demonstrate faithfulness in the face of hardships, suffering, and, perhaps, an unanticipated delay of the parousia.

Third, the writer has placed an adversative "but" (*kai* understood adversatively) before the clause "if he draws back" in verse 38b. This adversative is not a part of the biblical oracle, but a simple connective that separates the antithetical clauses of Hab. 2:4. The resultant form of the text describes alternative modes of conduct in a period marked by stress and hostility. The person whom God approves ("my righteous one") is the disciple who attains to life with God by faithfulness; the person whom God rejects is the disciple who withdraws from the covenant community (v 25!).

With these three textual modifications, the prophet's oracle is made to support the writer's call to boldness and endurance in verses 35-36 — which usage, it should be noted, corresponds to the original function of the passage in Habakkuk. The freedom with which the writer has reconstructed the oracle reflects something of the importance that he attaches to it. And his understanding of the oracle is clear from the use he makes of it in verse 39, which summarizes the preceding argument and brings the biblical text into the experience of his addressees: "But we are not those who shrink back and are destroyed, but those who believe and are saved." The emphatic "we" at the beginning of his statement identifies the writer with his addressees as the company of those faithful disciples who exhibit loyalty to Christ in the world.

The interpretation of Hab. 2:4 is carried forward by the dynamic tension developed in verse 39 between "withdrawal" *(hypostolē)* and "faithfulness" *(pistis)*. The noun *hypostolē* is a rare word that occurs only here in the New Testament. It derives its meaning from the verb *hypostellein* ("draw back," "withdraw"), which is used in the quotation of Hab 2:4 in verse 38. The verb reflects a lack of steadfastness and unreliability based on timidity. And so the noun carries the connotations of a state of "shrinking back" or "timidity."

Such withdrawal — such shrinking back in timidity — was for the writer of Hebrews equivalent to turning away from the living God (cf. 3:12) and deliberate persistence in sin (as in 10:26). The act of drawing back from loyalty to Christ distinguishes those who fail to attain the promised eternal life from those who, through faith and steadfast endurance, inherit what has been promised (v 36; cf. 6:12).

Conversely, "faithfulness" connotes persistent steadfastness. It is closely allied to the stance of "boldness" and "endurance" commended in verses 35-36. It reflects the stability of those who maintain their firm confidence in God's word of promise, despite adversity and disappointment.

The outcome of these radically different responses is posed rigorously in verse 39 by means of parallel result clauses: "leading to destruction *(eis apōleian)* . . . culminating in the acquisition of life *(eis peripoiēsin psychēs)*." The concomitant event of the approaching Day of the Lord (v 25) and the parousia of the Coming One (v 37) is judgment. For some disciples this event will bring vindication and the great reward of life. For others, however, it will result in destruction because of their inappropriate response of timid withdrawal.

This sharp contrast between vindication and ruin suggests that the presupposition underlying the preceding argument is that of God's covenant with his people. Obedience to the stipulations of the covenant carried the promise of blessing and life, whereas disobedience only invited the imposition of the curse-sanction of death (cf. Deut 30:15-20). And it must also be noted that the antithesis here in verse 39 between destruction and the acquisition of life recapitulates the writer's discussion of apostasy in 6:4-8 — where his reference to blessing and curse in verses 7-8 is also an allusion to the covenant.

The nature of the writer's response to the men and women he addresses confirms the specifically pastoral character of the exhortation (or parenesis) that he gives, in which he closely identifies himself with his audience. The severity with which he writes of apostasy and of the destructive lifestyle of those former disciples who deserted the community expresses his anguish and compassionate concern that Christians not be subverted by a form of worldliness that would separate them from Christ and from one another (cf. Mark 8:35-37).

4. A Paradigm for Heroic Discipleship: 12:1-4

The categorization in 10:39 of Christians as those who have faith and so acquire life invites a clarification of the dynamic nature of faith. So in 11:1-40 faith is spoken of as a quality of response to God — a response that celebrates the reality of promised blessings and the objective certainty of events announced but not yet seen (v 1). And that characterization is then substantiated throughout the rest of chapter 11 (esp. vv 4-38) by a catalogue of persons and events viewed from the perspective of faith in action (cf. Lane, *Hebrews* 314-95). This demonstration of the effective power of faith under the old covenant verifies the character and possibilities of faith for the Christian community.

The writer of Hebrews seems to have recognized, however, that an appeal for Christian endurance cannot finally be based just on an exposition of faithfulness to God under the old covenant. There can be an appropriate Christian response to such an appeal only in the light of the struggle and triumph of Christ himself. For Christians are to find in Jesus, whose death on the cross displayed both faithfulness and patient endurance (cf. 12:2-3), the supreme example of persevering faith. It is, in fact, Jesus' endurance of hostility from those who were blind to both God's redemptive design and their own advantage that provides a paradigm for the community of faith whenever it encounters hostility from society.

The extended periodic sentence in 12:1-2 develops the metaphor of an athletic contest in a stadium or an arena. It offers encouragement for Christian perseverance in faith and obedience toward the prescribed goal. Believers are encouraged by the certainty of being surrounded by "a host of witnesses." These "witnesses" are the men and women named in chapter 11, who have received acknowledgment from God because of the constancy of their faith (11:2, 4, 5, 39). They figure in Scripture as witnesses to the character and validity of committed faithfulness, and their lives provide evidence for subsequent generations of the possibilities of faith. Among those earlier exemplars of faith are people who exhibited patient endurance in their particular adverse situations (11:35b-38).

A "witness" in New Testament parlance is never merely a passive spectator, but always an active participant who confirms and attests the truth by his or her confession. The tendency to associate the term *martys*, or "witness," with martyrdom is strengthened by the account of the persecuted and martyred exemplars of faith in 11:35b-38. The emphasis in 12:1 falls on what Christians see in the host of witnesses under the old covenant rather than on what they see in Christians living in the period of the new covenant. And the appeal to these examples of old covenant piety is designed to inspire heroic Christian discipleship.

Contemplation of Jesus, however, offers a second — and paramount — encouragement to loyal Christian discipleship. The appeal in 12:2 is for a concentrated attention that turns away from all distractions, with eyes focused only on the person of Jesus. The use of the simple personal name "Jesus" shows that the accent is on his humanity, and especially on his endurance of the pain, humiliation, and disgrace of the cross. Concentrated attention on the person of Jesus and his redemptive accomplishment on behalf of the new people of God, in fact, typifies the fundamental challenge of Hebrews.

Here at the beginning of chapter 12, Jesus is designated as "the champion in the exercise of faith and the one who brought faith to complete expression, who . . . endured a cross" (v 2b). The pregnant expression "he endured a cross" is not used elsewhere in Hebrews to designate the crucifixion of Jesus. The writer appears to have used it here, however, to emphasize that Jesus demonstrated the endurance of faith to which every Christian disciple is called. The same lexical root is used in verses 1 and 2, but with differing nuances. In verse 1 the noun "endurance" *(hypomonē)* carries the nuance of active exertion against all weariness, while in verse 2 the verb "endure" *(hypomenein)* suggests a more passive toleration of a degrading experience. The expression in verse 2 treats the death of Jesus not so much as a redemptive event (as in 1:3), but as an ordeal that was inflicted through the active opposition of sinners (cf. v 3). It places Jesus' death under the specific modality of the harsh reality of crucifixion in antiquity.

The circumstantial clause "disdaining the shame" in verse 2c recalls an ancient formula of execution: "Lictor, go bind his hands, veil his head, hang him on the tree of shame" (Cicero, *Pro Rabirio* 13; Livy 1.26.6-7). It reflects the universal response of antiquity toward the horrific nature of crucifixion, and it underscores Christ's utter humiliation in dying so ignominiously — like a slave or common criminal — in torment on a cross. In the death of Jesus, God identified himself with an extreme expression of human wretchedness, which Jesus endured as the representative of fallen humanity.

Yet to "scorn" or "disdain" acquires in verse 2 also a positive meaning: "be brave" or "be unafraid of" an experience in spite of its painful character. The note of "shame" in this verse prepares the audience for the pastoral appeal in 13:12-13 to identify themselves with Jesus, "bearing his shame." Behind the writer's formulation may be heard Jesus' passion predictions in the Synoptic tradition and his call to his disciples to follow him in cross-bearing (e.g., Mark 8:31, 34 par.).

The parenetic purpose in evoking the endurance of Jesus in his passion is made explicit in verse 3. Being well aware of the disheartened condition of his addressees and concerned that they might relinquish their discipleship (cf. 10:32-35), the writer invites the members of the congregation to compare their experience with that of Jesus. For Jesus endured hostile opposition from sinners. And the fact that he endured such hostility has pointed relevance for the writer's addressees. In the past they had experienced hostile opposition (10:32-34), and it was reasonable to expect that they would encounter hostility again (10:35-39; 13:13).

The writer's reference to hostile opposition endured from sinners is a sober reminder that crucifixion was a form of punishment in which the caprice and sadism of the executioners was given free expression. The indignities that Jesus suffered satisfied a primitive lust for revenge and exposed the sadistic cruelty of those involved. In the expression "such active opposition," the qualifying term underscores the depth of the hostility that Jesus endured. It may also be an allusion to the immediate situation confronting the addressees.

The pastoral intention of the exhortation in the first part of verse 3 ("Consider him who endured such opposition from sinners") is made explicit by the purpose clause in the latter part of that verse: "so that you may not become weary and lose heart." The writer was deeply concerned that the men and women he addressed would become weary with the necessity of maintaining their Christian confession in a climate of hostility. Jesus had not allowed the hostile opposition of sinners to wear him down, but had triumphed over it. The tendency of the community, however, was to become fatigued. Their courage and readiness to identify themselves with Jesus faltered. In an attempt to avoid suffering, they could easily fall. Consideration of Jesus emphasizes the element of struggle and the patient endurance required. The exhortation addressed a weakening of resolve and a failure of nerve on the part of some of the persons addressed in the writer's homily.

In the transitional sentence in verse 4, the writer directs his addressees to reflect on their own experience of hostile opposition. Jesus' experience of triumph through suffering provides perspective on the sufferings actually endured by the community (cf. 10:32-34). The pointed observation "you have not resisted to the point of bloodshed" can be understood figuratively to mean "you still have not done your utmost." The expression is drawn from the games, in which the most dangerous contest was the armed boxing match. Boxing was the supreme test in the pentathlon, and bloody wounds were commonplace. According to the writer's contemporary, the Stoic philosopher Seneca "the younger" (ca. 4 B.C.–A.D. 65), the true athlete was the man who "saw his own blood" (Letter 13 in *L. Annaei Senecae ad Lucillum epistula moral*, ed. O. Heuse [Leipzig: Teubner, 1914] 24). So in the immediate context the allusion is to the violent death of Jesus, who endured crucifixion (12:2). But the writer's point is that Jesus had to suffer more degrading shame and deeper hostility than anything yet endured by the community. And on this understanding, the writer's intention is to say

216

that the community had not yet given the fullest measure in their struggle against sin.

An alternative proposal finds in verse 4 a reference to bloody persecution. The writer's declaration, then, would amount to a statement of fact — that is, that though his addressees had endured persecution in the form of insults, imprisonment, and the loss of property (10:32-34), they had not yet been exposed to the ignominy of martyrdom. As one group of believers within a larger network of Christians (13:17, 24), they had escaped an ordeal involving bloodshed. Understood in this way, the text would reflect on the relationship between a congregation of Christian believers and hostile public authorities: none of the Christians had yet died a martyr's death. And that the writer of Hebrews commonly compares the situation of his audience with that of Jesus strongly favors this alternative interpretation.

Set in the context established by 12:2-3, the writer's observation in verse 4 has a shaming function. The addressees are told that their sufferings are insignificant in comparison with those endured by Jesus, for his sufferings were both quantitatively and qualitatively greater than theirs. Yet the members of the congregation addressed were weary and disheartened. So they are summoned to a firm resolve to contend for faith, regardless of the cost.

Christians are, therefore, at least to a certain degree, engaged in the same struggle that Jesus was. They must not regard themselves as exempt from the ordeal of faith that was endured by the witnesses who preceded them (11:35b-38; 12:1) and by Jesus himself (12:2-3). There is a cost to true discipleship. And while others may be considered exemplars of faith, Jesus himself is the ultimate paradigm of heroic discipleship.

5. Discipleship as the Emulation of Exemplary Faith: 13:7

The addressees of Hebrews are admonished in 13:7 to continue to remember their former leaders, who are characterized as preachers of the word of God. The expression "leaders" (a substantival participle in the Greek), which is applied collectively to the leadership of the church, is not a technical term, but broadly descriptive of the role that certain people played in the life of the community from its inception. They may be characterized as charismatically endowed persons, whose authority derived from the word they proclaimed. The formulation "who spoke the word of God to you" indicates that the leaders were a link in the chain of tradition that accounted for the reliable transmission of the message of salvation to the audience (cf. 2:3-4).

Those leaders, we may assume, were now deceased. For as those who "spoke the word of God," their preaching belonged to the community's past. It is probable that the community had been formed in response to the word they proclaimed, and, conversely, that it was on the basis of their preaching that they were elevated to leadership roles. They were, therefore, looked back to as the original leaders or founding personalities of the community.

The members of the congregation addressed are to continue to remember their former leaders because of the example of their forward-looking faith (giving to "faith" the same meaning here as in 11:1-2). These former leaders retained authority for the community because their faith was validated by the solid accomplishment of their lives (v 7b). In the clause "considering the accomplishment of their conduct," the accent falls on the wholesome result of these leaders' daily behavior. A firmness of faith characterized the exemplary conduct of these leaders throughout their lives. Moreover, the quality of their faith aligned them with the exemplars of faith under the old covenant, whose faithfulness is celebrated in 11:4-38. So the steadfast faithfulness of the community's deceased leaders set the standard that those who responded to their preaching must now emulate.

Although the writer of Hebrews does not use the noun "disciple" or the verb "follow" that evidently appeared in the Synoptic tradition, a discipleship motif is introduced with the call to emulate the exemplary faith of the addressees' former leaders. In the context of verse 7, emulation of their faith will be reflected in firm adherence to the word that they proclaimed and a ready alignment with the conduct that they modeled. This represents a perspective on discipleship that is distinctive to Hebrews. For in Hebrews, discipleship involves imitating past exemplars of faithfulness (cf. 6:12, where the call to "imitate" is first introduced).

6. Discipleship as the Emulation of Jesus: 13:12-14

Heb 13:10-16 is a cohesive unit characterized by sustained argumentation. It provides an example of hortatory exposition. The basis of the argumentation is the exposition of Scripture. The intent of the passage, however, is clearly parenetic.

The emphatic assertion in verse 10a, "We have an altar," is the determining thesis of the passage, which is elaborated and established in the christological argument in verses 11-12. The writer has not previously used the term "altar" (or "place of sacrifice") with reference to the death of Jesus. Nevertheless, the term can be so interpreted on the analogy of its sustained use with reference to the high-priestly office of Christ in chapters 8–10 (cf. 8:1-5; 9:11-14, 24-26; 10:11-12). The allusion to Golgotha in verse 12 indicates that the reference to an "altar" is anchored in history, and so is to be seen as used metaphorically for the event of the sacrificial death of Jesus "outside the city gate" (cf. 12:2). Thus the content of the confession "We have an altar" is the grace of God that has been disclosed in history through Jesus' death on Golgotha. For Jesus' sacrificial death on the cross not only fulfilled the intention of the levitical arrangement, but it also superseded that cultic arrangement by accomplishing the consecration that the cult of Israel called for but could not effect.

The factual basis of the gospel comes to expression in verse 12 in "outside the city gate" and "he suffered death." It was Roman practice to perform executions beyond the inhabited areas of towns or cities (Artemidorus, *Dreams* 2.53; Plautus, *Soldier* 359-60). Furthermore, in Jewish circles an execution "outside the city gate" involved the shame of exclusion from the sacred precincts (cf. 12:2: "disdaining the shame [of crucifixion]"). Thus the writer's juxtaposition of "outside the city gate" with "he suffered death" brings out an element of shame that is not in the verb itself. Indeed, the fact that Jesus died as one rejected by his people gives added poignancy to his death. For Jesus was repudiated by his own people, and his death appeared to seal his rejection as final. It was as an outcast that Jesus offered his sacrifice to God.

The parenetic intention of the argument in verses 10-12, however, is made explicit when the writer in verse 13 draws the inference to which his argument leads: "So then, let us go out to him outside the camp, bearing the shame he bore." The appeal is an adaptation of the call to discipleship in terms of cross-bearing, which was rooted in the Synoptic tradition (cf. Mark 8:34; Matt 10:38; 16:24; Luke 14:27). Thus Jesus' action in going "outside the gate" (v 12) set a precedent for others to follow. And so now the task of the community is to emulate Jesus, leaving behind the security, congeniality, and respectability of the sacred enclosure, risking the reproach that fell on him.

Discipleship in this context means being directed by the course of Jesus' life. It entails exposure to shame and the severance of social ties (cf. Matt 10:37-38; Luke 14:26-27). It is affirmed in the acceptance of reproach for one's Christian commitment. The allusion to Golgotha in verse 12 implies following Jesus on his way to the cross, with the path of discipleship being marked out as one of patient endurance of suffering. Furthermore, it must be noted that the distinctive understanding of discipleship that comes to expression in verse 13 appears to be informed by a pre-Synoptic strand of the Jesus tradition concerning the conditions for discipleship, particularly as it has been preserved by the evangelist Luke.

Concurrently, "going out" to Jesus "outside the camp" reaffirms a commitment to be the pilgrim people of God, who leave behind the security of the familiar in order to respond to the call of God on their lives. For the writer of Hebrews, Jesus' disciples are those who follow Jesus not only on the way to the cross here and now, but ultimately to the final goal of their Christian pilgrimage: the future heavenly city (v 14). Conversely, the certainty that the transcendent city of God has been promised to those who respond to his call is, for the writer, the sufficient ground of discipleship. So with these distinctive nuances, the concept of discipleship that was evidently enshrined in the pre-Synoptic tradition has been transposed for the situation of a second generation Christian community. What the writer of Hebrews does, in effect, is to argue that the course and goal of Jesus' life provide the pattern for breaking loose from the grip of fear and lethargy in which every second generation group of believers tends to live.

7. A Matter of Pastoral Strategy

The writer of Hebrews was convinced that adherence to the confession of Jesus that the community had made was of critical importance because it would determine salvation or absolute loss (3:12-15; 6:4-8; 10:26-31, 35-39; 12:14-17, 25-29). His concern was not simply that the members of the community would return to the synagogue, but that they would turn away from God altogether (cf. 3:12-13). So he brings the witness of the Old Testament to bear on considerations that were crucial to the self-understanding of the community — to matters that had to do with priesthood, covenant, and sacrifice. In each case, the writer is creative in his selection of biblical texts to be brought before the community. No other writer in the New Testament cites Ps 95:7-11; Ps 110:4; Jer 31:31-34; or Ps 40:6-8. These texts establish a context for appreciating the validity of the Christian message and the importance of Christian discipleship.

Because he was persuaded that these matters must be decided on the basis of the word that God had spoken in Scripture and through his Son, the writer brought before the community biblical texts that demonstrated that God had announced a new arrangement to provide purgation for a defiled people and access into the divine presence. That announcement set out the importance of the priestly ministry of Jesus and his sacrifice, by which the new covenant had been inaugurated. And it is on this basis of the unique priestly ministry and sacrifice of Jesus that the writer calls the new covenant community to the worship of God (4:15-16; 7:24-25; 9:11-28; 10:19-25; 12:14, 18-29; 13:15-16). This represents a different perspective from that of any other writer in the New Testament.

The writer appreciated the historical and theological differences between Jewish Christianity and Judaism (see Lane, *Hebrews* cxxv-cxxxv). He clearly believed that God had acted decisively in Jesus to accomplish salvation and to create the people of the new covenant. Only from such an eschatological perspective could he speak of God's final word, of the coming of the new that made the old obsolete, or of the incarnation of the Son of God. These convictions lay the basis for the writer's distinctive reading of Scripture and for his significant teaching about discipleship as response to the moral claim of God.

Yet the writer also fully recognized that God had been at work in the old covenant. God's decisive action in Jesus, in fact, occurred within the context of divine intervention in the life of Israel. Thus the word that God spoke in the past continued to be invested with divine authority, in spite of the fact that it was fragmentary and partial (1:1). It remained normative for both the writer and his addressees (2:1-4; 3:7–4:13).

A line of redemptive continuity is traced out by the writer — a line that extends from the event of God speaking at Sinai to the event of God speaking at that moment (12:18-29). Through all of redemptive history the character of God has remained unchanged. Thus, like Israel of old at Sinai, the Christian community stands before God who is a consuming fire (12:25-29). Greater covenant privilege simply implies greater covenant responsibility. The writer, therefore, calls the men and women of the new covenant to a costly identification with Jesus (13:12-14), whose sacrificial ministry was the culmination of God's old covenant with Israel. He does not, however, set aside Jewish identity and tradition or the authority of the biblical text for the new covenant community.

The pastoral strategy adopted in Hebrews was designed to stir the members of a Jewish Christian congregation to recognize that they could not turn back the hands of the clock or deny their Christian understanding and experience. They must hold firmly to their Christian confession.

8. Epilogue

Hebrews has acquired a reputation for being formidable to understand and remote from the world in which we now live. Consequently, it has been neglected in the liturgy and preaching of the churches, in the curricula of seminaries, and in the devotional reading of the laity. There has been no dearth of commentaries, dissertations, and articles on Hebrews. Still, Hebrews tends to remain unappreciated in the classroom, the pulpit, and the pew.

Ironically, Hebrews is a call for ultimate certainty and ultimate commitment to Jesus. James Olthuis once described Hebrews as a "certitudinal book" — that is, it concerns itself with the issue of certainty by confronting ultimate questions about life and death with ultimate realities. Its presentation of the way in which God responds to the human family — as the One who speaks, creates, covenants, pledges, calls, and commits himself to his people — is intended to breathe new life into men and women who suffer a failure of nerve because they live in an insecure, anxiety-provoking society.

Hebrews is, in fact, a gift of God, as is all of Scripture. It is a gift to be particularly appreciated whenever God's people find themselves prone to discouragement, confronted by hostility, or distracted for whatever reason. It is a crucial document whenever the church concerns itself with patterns of discipleship for responding to the culture and situation of its day — for responding to a culture and situation not unlike the one addressed in the homily itself, though with some shifts of detail. Its importance lies in its call for unwavering commitment to God, who continues to speak decisively in his Son and through Scripture to a generation that needs to be resensitized to the voice of the living God.

Discipleship in Hebrews is an essential aspect of devotion to God. It consists in imitating past exemplars of faithfulness to God and in a readiness to be directed by the course of Jesus' life. It entails exposure to shame, the severance of social ties, and patient endurance of suffering. The appropriate response to the complete commitment of God to his people, expressed in the promise "I will never fail you; I will never forsake you" (13:5), is confident, committed discipleship, regardless of the cost. Like God's people of old, Christians continue to stand before the moral claim of God!

Selected Bibliograpy

Attridge, H. W. *A Commentary on the Epistle to the Hebrews.* Hermeneia, Philadelphia: Fortress, 1989.

Barth, M. "The Old Testament in Hebrews: An Essay in Biblical Hermeneutics," in *Current Issues in New Testament Interpretation: Essays in Honor of O. A. Piper,* ed. W. Klassen and G. F. Snyder. New York: Harper and Row, 1962, 53-76.

Brown, R. "Pilgrimage in Faith: The Christian Life in Hebrews," *Southwestern Journal of Theology* 28 (1985) 28-35.

Bruce, F. F. *The Epistle to the Hebrews.* New International Commentary on the New Testament, revised edition, Grand Rapids: Eerdmans, 1990.

Ellingworth, P. *Commentary on Hebrews.* New International Greek Testament Commentary, Grand Rapids: Eerdmans, 1993.

Hession, R. *From Shadow to Substance: The Rediscovery of the Inner Message of the Epistle to the Hebrews, Centered around the Words "Let Us Go On."* Grand Rapids: Zondervan, 1977.

Jewett, R. *Letter to Pilgrims: A Commentary on the Epistle to the Hebrews.* New York: Pilgrim, 1981.

Johnson, W. G. "The Pilgrimage Motif in the Book of Hebrews," *Journal of Biblical Literature* 97 (1978) 239-51.

Jones, P. R. "The Figure of Moses as a Heuristic Device for Understanding the Pastoral Intent of Hebrews," *Review and Expositor* 76 (1978) 95-107.

Käsemann, E. *The Wandering People of God: An Investigation of the Letter to the Hebrews.* Minneapolis: Augsburg, 1984.

Lane, W. L. *Hebrews.* Word Biblical Commentary, Dallas: Word, 1991.

————. *Hebrews: A Call to Commitment.* Peabody: Hendrickson, 1987.

Lewis, T. W. "'. . . And If He Shrinks Back' (Heb. X.38b)," *New Testament Studies* 22 (1975-76) 88-94.

Manson, W. *The Epistle to the Hebrews.* London: Hodder and Stoughton, 1951.

Peterson, D. G. *Hebrews and Perfection: An Examination of the Concept of Perfection in the "Epistle to the Hebrews."* Cambridge: Cambridge University Press, 1982.

Controlling the Tongue and the Wallet: Discipleship in James

PETER H. DAVIDS

The letter of James is another New Testament writing that never uses the terms "disciple" or "discipleship." Yet "to ask about discipleship in James," as Luke Johnson points out, "is really to ask about the shape of Christian existence" ("Friendship" 166). So when discipleship is defined as "the shape of Christian existence" or an appropriate lifestyle for a follower of Jesus of Nazareth, it should then be seen that James has much to say on the topic. What follows here, therefore, is a presentation of the pattern of an authentic Christian existence or lifestyle as portrayed in the letter attributed to "James, a servant of God and of the Lord Jesus Christ" (1:1a).

Elsewhere we have argued that the Letter of James is composed of traditions stemming from James, the brother of Jesus (possibly even from Jesus himself), which were edited sometime during the 60s of the first century in Palestine to form an instructional letter or epistle (Davids, *James; idem,* "Epistle of James" 3622-45; cf. Martin, *James*). It is addressed "to the twelve tribes scattered among the nations" (1:1b), which probably means to Jewish Christian believers living in the Diaspora — although the author may well have viewed all believers in Jesus as part of the renewed Israel, and so be speaking of the whole church in Jewish Christian terms.

James, it is true, contains no discussion of circumcision. Nor does it refer to any other religious practice of Judaism, though the call to charity coheres with Jewish concerns generally. The lack of reference to distinctively Jewish rites and practices, however, is just what one would expect of a work written in the Jewish Christian community, where such matters were assumed rather than discussed. Furthermore, since the writing is more of a tractate than a letter, James is probably to be seen as reflecting more the concerns and tensions of the community where it originated than the particular problems or issues of its addressees.

With respect to the letter's relations with the wider church, it is evident that its author had some contact with Pauline thought, though probably not a direct knowledge of Paul's letters. It is impossible to determine when this contact may have occurred, due to the edited nature of the writing. All that can be said is that since the type of Pauline thought referred to in James is a distortion of Paul's actual teaching (see below), such contact could have come about early in Paul's teaching just as well as later in his more fully developed thought.

In taking up a consideration of the Letter of James, we also need to remember that the whole work consists of only five chapters, with a total of only one hundred eight verses. Its scope is nothing like that of Hebrews or Revelation, let alone of the Pauline corpus, the Johannine corpus, or Luke's two volumes. In James, therefore, we are evidently dealing with only a small portion of an author's thought and values. And while the context for Christian discipleship (or Christian "existence" or "lifestyle") may be assumed to have remained basically the same wherever and whenever the topic was discussed by our author, we cannot be sure that the specific concerns of this letter would have received the same emphasis at another point in the community's life or that other concerns might not have loomed larger over time. Nonetheless, with the setting described above and this caveat in mind, we can now turn to the picture of discipleship in the Letter of James itself.

1. The Context of Discipleship

The first issue to confront the reader of James is the context in which discipleship takes place. For apart from an appreciation of the teaching about the Christian life in James' letter and of the circumstances of James' community, one cannot determine what James is teaching about Christian discipleship. Five matters in particular need to be observed with respect to this context.

226

Jesus as Lord

James was written in a Christian community. One would, therefore, expect that belief in Jesus as Lord was an important part of the letter's context. The term "lord" *(kyrios)* appears ten times in the letter. But only in 1:1 and 2:1 does it clearly refer to Jesus, though it is probable that 5:14-15 also uses the term for Jesus. These few occurrences, however, are enough to identify the book as a Christian work.

Yet James's conception of Jesus as Lord is deeper than just the confession of Christ's lordship. An analysis of the letter indicates that there are a minimum of thirty-six parallels with the teaching of Jesus, twenty-five of them with the Sermon on the Mount (or, better, with the "Q" tradition now embodied in the Sermon on the Mount; cf. Davids, *James* 47-48; Deppe, *Sayings of Jesus;* Witherington, *Jesus the Sage* 236-47). This count does not even consider the possibility that some sayings in James, such as 3:18, may be otherwise unknown sayings of Jesus (and so among the "agrapha") quoted anonymously, just as 5:12 cites the tradition ("Q" ?) behind Matt 5:34-37. Given that there are only one hundred eight verses in the letter, this large number of parallels suggests close contact with the teaching of Jesus — especially when one compares James with Paul. In other words, it would be fair to say that James appears to be largely an application of the teaching of Jesus to a Jewish Christian church situation.

James, then, gives shape to the confession "Jesus is Lord" by rooting Christian ethical teaching in the church's tradition of the teaching of Jesus. For James, this confession means that the teaching of Jesus directs the life and work of the church. In fact, this teaching is so well known that it is rarely cited (and then not by name), but instead is merely alluded to (cf. Davids, "Jesus and James" 63-84; *idem,* "Gospels" 75-100).

Another way of expressing belief in Jesus as Lord appears in the polar opposition set out in 4:4 between "the world" — that is, that "system of meaning and values which excludes God from consideration" (so Johnson) — and God. The believer is called on to choose single-minded commitment to God rather than being "double-minded" and trying to "have it both ways" (1:8; 4:8). But what is clear from James's degree of use of the Jesus tradition, as well as his two or three explicit references to Jesus as Lord, is that the "system of meaning and values" that he wants his readers to adopt appears in the teaching of Jesus, who exists as the "glorious Lord" of the church.

Apocalyptic Expectations

Another part of the context for understanding the teaching of James is the letter's apocalyptic expectations. More than one definition of the term "apocalyptic" exists. For our purposes, however, we will here speak of an apocalyptic mind-set as a revelatory perspective that expresses both a belief in the inbreaking of divine revelation and a belief in the approaching end of the age. When this perspective is expressed in literary form, these beliefs become a spatial axis (an otherworldly journey or messenger) and a temporal axis (a journey through time) respectively.

As to genre, James is not an apocalyptic writing. It is not a revelatory book. Nor does it have much of a spatial axis, for its author does not go on otherworldly journeys. James does, however, show apocalyptic belief, for he is aware of otherworldly regions: of what the Lord of hosts hears (5:4), of how demons react (2:19, which, like *1 Enoch*, could indicate an awareness of events in the "underworld"), and of how those wrongly "condemned and murdered" by "the rich" now accuse those same rich in heaven (5:6; cf. Rev. 6:9-10; on this interpretation of 5:6, see Davids, *James* 180). And James does express a clear temporal axis in that its author is aware of future events, particularly future judgment. He knows that "the Judge is at the door" and that "the coming of the Lord" is near (5:7-8). He vividly portrays the punishment that is about to fall on the rich (5:1-5), though he is less vivid in his descriptions of the blessedness of the faithful — speaking of their reward only in terms of a "crown of life" (1:12) and a promised kingdom (2:5).

As noted above, such features do not make James an apocalyptic writing. But they are, nonetheless, still significant for an understanding of the letter, because they show that James moves in an atmosphere of apocalyptic expectations. The end of the age is near; the Judge is approaching. The dualistic tension between the values of God and the values of this world will soon be expressed in the differing fates of those who love God and those who are "the rich." Furthermore, James's parenesis (ethical exhortation) functions in much the same way as does the parenesis of the Johannine Apocalypse. That is, James calls for endurance in a situation of persecution because the reward of those who remain faithful is sure, while the doom of the wicked is approaching — however secure they may appear to be in the present.

While some believers of James's community may have died (cf. 2:6; 5:6), the level of persecution appears to be more that of insult and economic oppression than the "fiery trials" anticipated by 1 Peter or the martyrdom referred to in Revelation. Still, suffering is no less real to those enduring it, even if not as bad as that experienced by others. And suffering sets a context that calls for an endurance based on an expectation of the eschatological end, a waiting for the apocalyptic consummation, when the rich will "get theirs" and the faithful will receive "a crown of life" (1:12; cf. Rev 2:10).

Wisdom Assumptions

Wisdom teaching forms another part of the context of James. It is not only that James refers to wisdom in two passages and to the Holy Spirit in none — or that James refers to wisdom similarly to how Paul refers to the Spirit (the "fruit of wisdom" in 3:13-18 being roughly parallel to "the fruit of the Spirit" in Gal 5:22-23) — that causes one to be alerted to the letter's wisdom assumptions. More significant is the fact that the two themes of the letter parallel important themes and concerns of the wisdom tradition. The first of these is the theme of wealth and poverty. This is, of course, a theme that is extensively discussed in the Wisdom literature, though James's attitudes reflect more the mediation of this teaching to him through the Jesus tradition. The second of these wisdom themes is the ethics of speech, exhortation to listen, to control one's tongue, to be slow to anger, and to avoid conflicts. Words are powerful, and a person's words and deeds should match. These two themes, in fact, are major themes of the wisdom writings of antiquity, whether of the ancient Near East generally, the Jewish Scriptures, or the writings of Second Temple Judaism (cf. Baker, *Personal Speech-Ethics*).

Other features found in ancient Wisdom literature also show up in James — for example, the pithy saying (the *mashal*), the use of similes (such as the descriptions of the tongue in ch. 3), and hyperbolic speech. The teaching of James is not couched in the careful language of legal parlance, but in the strong antitheses of Wisdom. Furthermore, like Proverbs and other Wisdom literature, the statements of James often appear disconnected. Deeper analysis, however, shows that it is held together both by various literary structures and by dialectical antitheses — and so, like Proverbs and other Wisdom literature, must be seen as a highly structured writing.

In the past, the wisdom features of James were thought to deny the presence of any structure and of any apocalyptic elements in the letter. Martin Dibelius's commentary on James, for example, focused on the wisdom features and ended up viewing James as only a collection of parenetic sayings — by which he meant, only a collection of rather stock treatments of various moral subjects strung together without any necessary inner connections. New Testament scholarship today, however, has increasingly viewed such an analysis as simplistic.

It is not only unwise, but also false, to propose an either-or approach to the question of prophetic or apocalyptic features in a Jewish Christian writing or to say that such a work has either prophetic or wisdom features but not both, as if these generic styles did not swirl around together in Jewish and Christian communities. So while in James prophetism, for example, dominates in such a passage as 5:1-6, even there we see a focus on wealth and an effort to point out a lack of prudent action in the light of the true situation: these matters are prophetically discerned, but are also themes highlighted in ancient Wisdom literature. Wisdom in James, therefore, cannot be separated from a prophetic-apocalyptic style. Rather, the wisdom assumptions evident in the letter point to a body of literature and an attitude that informed its composition.

Communal Concern

Discipleship in James is rooted in the Christian community. The work is addressed to "my brothers" (adelphoi mou), a designation that indicates that community members were viewed as members of an extended family. Furthermore, the conflicts dealt with in the letter are those that occur in a Christian community, whether discrimination against other members (2:1-13) or "wars and fighting" among members (4:1-10). The only time that people outside the community are named, in fact, is when "the rich" are castigated.

Admittedly, it is somewhat difficult to tell in 1:9-11 where "the rich" are located, whether within or outside the community — though the idea that they are ephemeral (as in vv 10-11) does not sound like a description of a community member. In 2:1-13, however, they are clearly outside the community, since they blaspheme the name of Christ (2:7). So the address to the rich in 5:1-6 is probably to be taken as a prophetic condemnation suited more for the benefit of the community listening in on what is said than of rich landlords themselves, who may never hear it. In none of the places where the rich are referred to or addressed is the term "brothers" *(adelphoi)* used. It may be implied in 1:10 from the parallel with 1:9, but not necessarily, particularly if the community assumed that "rich" indicated someone outside the community. At any rate, in chapters 2 and 5 it is clear that "the rich" are not in any way members of the Christian community.

Our point here is that in James we are given not an ethic for the world but an ethic for the Christian community — that is, a discipleship ethic. The values of a Christian ethic contrast with the values of the world, that is, of "the rich." Paul also tended to focus his ethic on the Christian community, believing, in principle, that one was not to try to discipline those outside the Christian community (cf. 1 Cor 5:12, a principle that Paul applies in 1 Cor 7:12-16). Unlike Paul, however, James never explains why he focuses on the Christian community. So we are left to wonder: Has persecution forced a separation from the outside world? Did apocalyptic dualism require a focus on the community of those who love God? Or did James simply view the Christian community as an example to that world? What is clear in all this, however, is that James addresses the Christian community rather than trying to reform society around him.

External Opposition

As we have seen, the context for the issues addressed in James includes external opposition to the Christian community. In 1:2 apocalyptic assumptions are brought to bear on the "various trials" experienced in the community in the call for an inner joy due to anticipated reward. At first the reader is left to guess what is meant by "various trials." "Trial" *(peirasmos)* may connote something external to an individual, such as persecution or deprivation, or something internal, such as desire. But as early as 1:9-11 we are introduced to the contrast between the poor community member and the rich person. And while it may be grammatically possible in this passage to understand the rich person as someone within the community, this is, as noted above, somewhat unlikely in the context of the entire letter. So very early in James it becomes evident that external opposition to the community comes from "the rich."

In the second half of the first chapter, the reader is turned inward. And other than noting that there could be some reason for the anger mentioned in verses 19-20, no further conflicts from an external source appear until chapter two.

In 2:5-7, however, the agents of external conflict appear quite clearly. Here it is "the rich" who "oppress" and "drag into court" the believers, that is, those who are "the poor." Furthermore, "the rich" "slander the good name" of Jesus. So while discrimination within the community is the problem dealt with in verses 1-4, verses 5-7 clearly identify the source of external opposition as "the rich."

Conflict is also mentioned in chapters 3 and 4, though here it is said to exist among the community's own members. No group within the community is singled out as the offending party. There are no false teachers or interlopers, as one finds in some of the Pauline letters. Instead, there is internal competition within the Christian community, with that community being otherwise undifferentiated. The only cause described is that of "desires" at work within the individuals, which is the same internal cause described in the second half of chapter 1.

In chapter 5, however, a clearly external group of people is again spoken of. Merchants within the community are addressed in 4:13-17, but they are not described as "rich" (though they evidently have enough capital to engage in trade) or as doing anything harmful to other community members (unless their failing to "do good" in verse 17 implies a failure to give charitably). The same cannot be said, however, for the group addressed in 5:1-6, because here again we meet "the rich," who are even more roundly condemned than in chapters 1 and 2.

Here in chapter 5 the rich are primarily involved not in legal procedures against the community (as in 2:6) but in the oppression of the laborers who harvest their crops. These poor workers cry out to God for fair wages, while the rich live in wanton luxury. The section ends with a possible reference to judicial oppression (5:6) — assuming, of course, that "the righteous" refers to laborers with a righteous claim against the rich. It is not clear, however, whether these righteous persons are killed by being executed or by being denied the wages they need to sustain them. Most likely the latter is in view, given the context of the whole section.

Throughout the whole letter, therefore, only one group appears in opposition to the community. This group is identified as "the rich." While there were conflicts among the Christians themselves, these appear to have been not struggles among clearly defined groups so much as a general unrest and lack of charity.

While James clearly draws much of his material from the Old Testament prophetic denunciations of the rich, he evidently does so because that language is useful in his own historical context. Historically, the picture he draws fits that of the church in Palestine in the decades preceding the Roman-Jewish war of A.D. 66-70. The country was run by wealthy elites who were hostile to the Jewish Christians, and believers in Jesus were mostly poor. Many of the wealthy elites were landowners whose estates were farmed by hired laborers, not slaves (as would have been the case elsewhere in the Mediterranean world). The oppression felt by the Jewish Christians was mostly economic, though, it seems, "the rich" were not above shaming the Christians for their beliefs, perhaps in part to influence the judges in legal disputes. As the elite group of the day, they expressed the values of their society, which James refers to as "the world." So beyond their actual oppression of believers in Jesus, James views their values as fundamentally opposed to those of God. And it is this context that forms a large part of the social setting for James's teaching on Christian discipleship.

2. The Discipleship of the Wallet

The most obvious area of discipleship in James is that of the wallet. While the subject of wealth could take up all the rest of our discussion of discipleship in the letter, we must use it only as a significant starting point for our study.

The Danger of Wealth

James does not reject the material world per se. Yet wealth is not good news for him. It is a source of spiritual danger. This outlook on wealth may not be immediately obvious, but it does become clear when one examines the letter.

One danger of wealth is the illusion of permanence that it gives. In 1:9-11 "the rich" are exhorted to rejoice in "being brought low." This is the opposite of what is said to the poor. It is also the opposite of the behavior expected of the rich, who normally rejoice in the security of their wealth and the prestige that it brings them in the community, if it is acquired honorably. James's point is that the wealth of the rich — even their very existence itself — is temporary: "In the midst of a busy life [the rich] will wither away." So it is better to be brought low, for then one is in a position to view reality aright.

Another danger of wealth is mentioned in 2:1-4: the potential to cause divisions within the community of believers. The scene pictured is that of a church court. And though the situation depicted is perhaps hypothetical and somewhat hyperbolic, the point is that the church may be tempted to take into account the disparity of wealth among its members and to express a prejudice in favor of wealthier persons. In so doing, the church will itself begin to act like its own rich persecutors. In effect, it will become so corrupt that it will begin to persecute its own members.

A third danger of wealth appears in 4:1-3. Here wealth actually possessed is not the problem. The problem is desire for wealth — what the rabbis would term the evil *yetzer*, or evil impulse, in a human being (cf. 1 Tim 6:10). This desire creates conflict in the community and corrupts the prayers of the believers, for believers no longer seek to serve God but serve their own desires and so do not receive answers to their prayers. Desire, in fact, has become an idol.

A fourth danger of wealth is named in 4:13-17. Here the merchants in the community are depicted as forgetting God by thinking only in terms of financial gain. There is no hint of dishonorable activity on their part. Nonetheless, they are advised to take the will of God into account in their dealings. Does James mean that they are to consult God before laying their plans? Or does he imply that God has already revealed all that they need to know and that therefore they know the good that they should do (cf. v 17), which is to give to the poor? Whatever the case, the merchants within the church are depicted as being focused not on giving but on gaining. Their value system is that of the world (cf. v 4). They forget how quickly their life and wealth can disappear. Normal business has blinded them to the good that they can do with their wealth.

A fifth danger of wealth is found in 5:1-6. Here wealth is seen as blinding its possessors to the eschatological hour. They live in luxury as on a "day of slaughter" when fresh meat is available (v 5), but are unaware that the "day" is really God's "day of slaughter" — as referred to generally in the Old Testament, but more specifically in *1 Enoch* 94:9

234

as a day of "death," "darkness," and "great judgment." The rich, in fact, are approaching the day of judgment, when their wealth will "eat their flesh." So unaware are they of the eschatological times that they oppress their laborers, whose cry has risen to "the Lord of hosts" — a title well known from Isaiah's judgment oracles. They even condemn "the righteous," who are either other Christians or laborers who have a righteous claim against them, or both. These people are blind indeed!

The Dignity of the Poor

James never refers to the rich positively. By contrast, the poor are given dignity. Poor believers are to rejoice in their "exaltation" (1:9). That is, they are to see their dignity from God's point of view. Likewise, James asks, "Has not God chosen the poor in the world to be rich in faith and to be heirs of the kingdom that he has promised to those who love him?" (2:5). The problem with discrimination on the basis of wealth is that it fails to view the poor through God's eyes. In reality, however, God has chosen the poor to be "rich in faith" and "heirs of the kingdom." So in 5:4 oppressed laborers are said to have the ear of God, while in 5:6 the oppressed poor are probably those referred to as "the righteous." Throughout the letter, therefore, James speaks regarding the dignity of the poor (cf. Maynard-Reid, *Poverty and Wealth*).

It is not that James is simply speaking about the actual "piety of the poor" (i.e., an *Armenfrömigkeit*). Rather, he exhorts believers in the family of God *(adelphoi)* who are poor to rejoice in their exaltation. The poor are those who are "rich in faith" and who "love [God]." Such a perspective on poverty, James exhorts, is to be that which guides the community member. And it is the perspective of Christian discipleship.

James, however, has nothing to say about the poor who lack faith and who do not love God, for they are outside of the community of believers and so outside his field of vision. While the oppressed laborers of chapter 5 could be any Jewish peasants in Palestine, they are described as people who pray. In the context of the letter, therefore, especially if 5:7-11 addresses the same group, it is poor community members who are in view. It is these poor believers, and not just any poor people, who have the dignity of having been chosen by God to receive the kingdom.

The Calls to Patient Endurance and Sharing

Proper attitudes toward wealth and the poor (as cited above) are to shape the response of the community to which James speaks. This response is twofold.

First, there is the call to patient endurance in the midst of trials (1:2-4; 5:7-11). Believers cannot control their oppressors, but they can show endurance supported by prayer (5:13). This gives practical expression to their perception of their own dignity. They endure with eschatological joy — not because they enjoy suffering, but because they can see beyond the oppression to the revelation of their true status by the Judge who is "at the door" (5:9).

Second, there is the call to sharing. James's definition of pure piety is, among other things, "to care for orphans and widows in their distress" (1:27). Likewise, the homily in 2:14-26 stresses the importance of works of charity. The illustration about destitute Christian brothers or sisters that begins the homily illustrates lack of charity, and both examples cited in the homily (Abraham and Rahab) are Old Testament individuals who were known in Jewish tradition for their acts of charity (cf. Ward, "Works of Abraham"). And what James says about the lack of such works is very strong: a faith that lacks deeds of charity is worthless. This is repeated three times in the homily, forming its underlying structure (2:14, 17, 26). Thus sharing is not an optional part of Christian discipleship; persons who withhold the sharing of their goods with the poor show that they have not been grasped by the faith at all, though they may know all of its propositions (2:18-19).

This perception is reinforced by 4:13-17, if our interpretation of this passage is correct. Here merchants are said to be in danger of "fading away" like the rich (cf. 1:10-11) because they are not doing the good that they know to do. Again, the call to charity in this passage is not optional. The centrality of such deeds has already been implied in 1:22-25, where hearing must be coupled with doing for it to be of any value. Now in 4:17 charity is the difference between living in sin and proper behavior.

For James, then, Christians deal with the danger of wealth by giving it away. In this way the believer recognizes the dignity of the poor and accepts an eschatological perspective that shows that one has not merely heard about God, but has a truly saving faith.

3. The Discipleship of the Tongue

If the wallet forms the external dimension of discipleship in James, the tongue forms its internal dimension. When dealing with James's teaching regarding the tongue, however, one needs to exercise some caution, for there was a fairly standard set of themes or *topoi* with respect to the tongue in the speech ethics of antiquity. James's letter, in fact, sets out very little in the way of original instruction regarding the tongue. Yet the fact that the use of the tongue is one of the two major themes in the letter suggests that this subject must have been significant in the community to whom James wrote.

A community under external pressure tends to have various internal "seams" opened. A family unit that lives in relative harmony during good times, for example, may break down into bickering subunits when economic difficulties or other hardships hit it. The "seams" that could be covered over when there was no external pressure are revealed by such pressure. Larger communities, as well, show the same tendency. Thus given the "various trials" experienced by the community, it is not surprising to read of internal difficulties and to have James bringing out traditional teaching on the tongue.

The Tongue as a Danger

James begins dealing with this internal matter by stating that the tongue is dangerous. First, it can express anger, which does not produce God's righteousness or justice (1:19-20). It is important to note that James is not speaking here about the emotion of anger, which is relatively uncontrollable, but the expression of anger, especially in speech. And because of this focus, it is *listening* that forms the opposite of both speaking and anger. Speaking apparently gets in the way of understanding and so leads to anger. In fact, an angry person is one who speaks without listening. According to 1:26, therefore, the first part of true piety is control of the tongue.

Second, the tongue can be used to criticize other community members, so leading to community disharmony. This topic is taken up several times in the letter, in 3:9-12; 4:11-12; and 5:9. James's point in all of these passages is that the misuse of the tongue insults God — either by taking his place as Judge or by attacking someone made in his image — and thus puts one in danger of eschatological judgment.

Third, the tongue is relatively uncontrollable. James begins his discussion of taming the tongue in 3:1-12 by stating that not many should become teachers and so open themselves to the severer judgment that teachers receive. He goes on to make two points in his illustrations in chapter three: on the one hand, the tongue can control the body, while, on the other, it cannot itself be controlled. It is in speech that we humans most readily see the evil that is within us. And James traces this evil back to "Gehenna" (3:6), a statement that prepares for the call to "resist the devil" in 4:7. In addition, James describes the influences that control the tongue in three other ways: "not-wisdom-from-above," meaning a "wisdom" from "below" that is "demonic" (3:15); "desires" from within (4:1-2, taking "kill" in v 2 as metaphorical, in keeping with wisdom speech); and the "devil" (4:7). Ultimately, of course, all of these expressions are interconnected. And they serve to put discipleship into a cosmic context, with the devil and his agents pitted against other forces within the members of the community.

The Tongue as a Blessing

When talking about the tongue, James follows Proverbs and the Wisdom tradition generally in focusing on *control* of the tongue. Nevertheless, he also says some positive things about the tongue.

First, while "not many" should become teachers (3:1), the tongue can be used quite positively in teaching. James's whole letter, in fact, comprises wisdom teaching and is the work of a teacher. Furthermore, the purpose statement of the letter in 5:19-20 speaks of the value of turning "sinners from the error of their ways," which is a function of teaching. Therefore, when properly used, the tongue can have a positive value indeed.

Second, the tongue can be used to bless God (3:9). The only references to worship in the whole letter appear in 3:9 and 5:13. Yet these statements indicate the positive value of speech. Related to this is the suggestion that the tongue can be also used in repentance (4:9).

Third, the tongue can be used to ask God for the wisdom necessary to live a righteous life. Wisdom should be requested of God (1:5), for true wisdom comes from above (3:17). And when James says in 1:17, "Every good and perfect gift is from above, coming down from the Father of lights," he is most likely thinking of wisdom as God's main "good gift." Such wisdom will help the believer become "mature and complete, lacking in nothing" (1:4). Moreover, such wisdom will manifest itself in a virtuous lifestyle, as set out in 3:17-18: "But the wisdom from above is first pure, then peaceable, gentle, willing to yield, full of mercy and good fruits, without a trace of partiality or hypocrisy. And a harvest of righteousness is sown in peace for those who make peace."

Noting the connection of wisdom to the above catalogue of virtues, one cannot help but notice that wisdom in James functions much the same as the Holy Spirit does in Paul (cf. Gal 5:22-25). Thus there are two forces opposing one another: God or wisdom from above versus the devil or demonic wisdom or human desire (the evil *yetzer*). Humans are not passive receptors of these opposing forces, but are called on to take an active stance in favor of God in the inherent tension. While it is true that no one can control the tongue (3:8), one can use the tongue to repent of "adultery" (4:4) and to ask God for wisdom. The result will be the reception of wisdom and the flight of the devil (4:7-10). Discipleship, therefore, is active participation on the side of God.

The Use of the Tongue in Prayer

Having just noted that one of the positive uses of the tongue is to ask God for wisdom, we may observe that the theme of prayer appears three times in the letter. In 1:5-8, the readers are enjoined to ask for wisdom, and that injunction includes two major points. On the one hand, because he is generous, there is no reason to imagine that God would not grant wisdom to the petitioner. On the other hand, human beings must exercise faith rather than doubt. The verb translated "doubt" *(diakrinein)* normally means "make a discrimination," "judge," or "discern." In some passages, however, it carries the idea of trying to discern if something is true or can be trusted (e.g., Matt 21:21; Mark 11:23; Acts 10:20; Rom 4:20; 14:23; Jude 22). In many of these passages it is used in contrast with the noun "belief" *(pistis)* or the verb "believe" *(pisteuein)*.

The issue at hand when dealing with 1:6, "When one asks [God], one must believe and not doubt," is: What is the object of faith or doubt? In Rom 4:20 Paul says that Abraham's faith was in the promise of God, and so faith or doubt would have focused on that promise. In Acts 10:20, where the Spirit tells Peter "Do not hesitate to go with them [the three men sent by Cornelius]," one must supply the object of possible doubt. In all the other passages, however, the object of both faith and doubt seems to be God himself. Therefore, the essential point for prayer is: Can petitioners commit themselves to God, or will they waver in their trust? James calls for unwavering trust in God, for the doubter is not only unstable but also will not receive anything from the Lord (1:7-8).

In James's second passage on prayer, 4:2-3, he points out that the reason believers lack what they want is because they struggle and fight rather than ask God. Furthermore, his readers' prayers remain unanswered because their requests are motivated by their own "desires," that is, the evil *yetzer*. James goes on to accuse his readers of "adultery," thereby paralleling their situation with that of Israel in going after idols rather than being faithful to God. In 1:14-15 the same idea of "desire" appears (though under a different term), and it is contrasted with the God who gives without changing character (1:17). Thus though the term "faith" is not used, desire is contrasted with commitment to God. In this sense desire is a form of "doubt."

The third passage on prayer is 5:13-18, which does explicitly mention faith. Three prayer situations are described. In the first (v 13a), persecution is in view (balancing the trials mentioned in 1:2), and believers are told to pray for endurance. In the second (v 13b), a time of joy is envisioned, and prayer becomes songs of praise to God. In the third (vv 14-16), someone is described as ill enough that the elders must be called to pray for that person. The elders are instructed to anoint the person with oil (following the apostolic example in Mark 6:13, which is probably an acted prayer), with the promise that their "prayer of faith" will result in God's healing.

This action of the elders is then held up in verse 16 as a model for the general practice of the congregation. Then the call to trust God is reinforced in verses 17-18 by the example of Elijah, whose prayers had enormous consequences even though he was a human being "just like us." No mistrust of God or doubt is mentioned in this passage, but such is implicit as the opposite to the prayer of faith and the example of Elijah.

For James, therefore, Christian discipleship is a matter of absolute trust in God. Whether one is asking for wisdom, for daily needs, or for healing, it all amounts to the same thing: trust in God or faith versus mistrust, doubt, or desire. A "this-worldly" orientation will not receive anything other than judgment from God.

4. Discipleship in James vis-à-vis the Rest of the New Testament

There are two major dimensions to the idea of trust in God. One is patient endurance, which shows itself in a controlled tongue and faith-filled prayer. The other is a generous heart (like God's), which shows itself in valuing the poor, distrust of money, and acts of generosity. How do these characteristics of discipleship compare with the rest of the New Testament?

James and Jesus

It is clear that the teachings of the Letter of James are extremely close to the ethic of Jesus, especially as that ethic is portrayed in the Lukan tradition (Davids, "James and Jesus"). Not only are there similar apocalyptic contexts, but there is the same distrust of wealth and the same call to charity. True, the Jesus tradition does not include as much about speech ethics as James does. But what it does include, particularly in condemning anger, is quite similar. Furthermore, the Jesus tradition also has a call to endurance. In fact, Matthew 10 shows the same combination of enduring persecution while healing disease that Jas 5:13-16 does.

There are several differences, however, between James and the Jesus tradition. First, there is the obvious difference that James is in the form of a letter or epistle and the Gospels are not. The difference in genre means that James does not teach through narrative portrayals as the Gospels do. Second, though the Gospels were written within Christian communities and speak to their respective communities, they still remain Gospels. And as Gospels, they set out the foundational narratives of the Christian church and do not frequently refer to unfaithfulness within the various Christian communities, whereas James functions pastorally in an endeavor to correct such unfaithfulness as he sees in his community. Thus James has a significantly different tone — though not one that is entirely different from some of the statements of Jesus in the Gospels that are directed to the Pharisees.

When we read James, then, we are reading basic instruction in discipleship. We are looking at a community that started on the way of Christian discipleship some time ago, but has been worn down by

241

low-grade persecution. Seams in the community are opening up; charity is drying up. So James returns to the teaching of Jesus and reapplies it to his community. This time, however, the proclamation of the teaching of Jesus is not the fresh good news that it was when first announced to the author's addressees, but an encouraging and a corrective word to bring them back to their former level of faithfulness.

James and Paul

When it comes to a comparison of James and Paul, there are also similarities and differences. Like Paul, James is concerned with correcting problems in the Christian community. Unlike Paul's letters, however, James's letter betrays no problem in the community with the author's authority, nor is there any discernible problem regarding Jew-Gentile relations.

The major issue when comparing James and Paul is that of the place of "works" in the Christian life (cf. Davids, "James and Paul"). One of Paul's basic concerns was whether Christian discipleship implied that one should first become a Jew. Thus the "works" that concerned him were the "works of the law" (especially circumcision, but also sabbath-observance, festival-keeping, and dietary rules). The "faith" that interested him was usually expressed as a commitment to Jesus as Lord. And the *dikaiosynē* (we use the Greek term purposefully since James and Paul use it with different meanings) he was concerned about was the "justification" of sinners.

James, however, approaches matters from an entirely different perspective, especially in one critical passage, 2:14-26. The works that James is concerned about must be interpreted as "charity toward the poor." Paul also addresses this subject in Gal 2:10 ("All they asked was that we should continue to remember the poor, which was actually what I was eager to do"), but he does not use the term "works" in speaking of it. Similarly, the "faith" that James refers to in 2:19 (unlike other places in his letter) is the orthodox confession of the *Shema*, that "there is one God" (Deut 6:4), which does not even mention Jesus, much less show a commitment to him as Lord. The *Shema* is probably cited by James because Jews viewed it as Abraham's discovery, and so it served as an example of the faith of Abraham. And the *dikaiosynē* that James refers to is a "declaration of approval" by God.

It is not that James had no contact with Pauline thought. The phraseology refuted in 2:14-26 is close enough to Paul's language that it is likely that it does, in fact, echo Paul's teaching. At the same time, while some of the terminology and the citation of Gen 15:6 are shared with Paul, there is no real correspondence of content. Common terms are used with different meanings. It appears likely, therefore, that in James's Jewish Christian community the Pauline problem of Jew-Gentile relationships was not a factor. Instead, it seems that some individuals were using the Pauline conceptions of faith and works to evidence their orthodox confession, but without showing their Christian discipleship by such concrete acts as giving to the poor. For these individuals, faith and works were entirely separate matters, with orthodox confession being the criterion for salvation. But James will not accept any confession of faith without hard evidence of Christian love in action.

Since Paul's context was different, he confronted different issues regarding discipleship. Yet on two issues they overlap. When he discusses giving, Paul speaks quite carefully because he must avoid both the issue of the tithe as a mark of the Jew and the issue of his own support (1 Corinthians 9; 2 Corinthians 8–9; Philippians 4). However, in 1 Corinthians 5–6, when he confronts individuals who appear to have separated faith from ethics, his response is much the same as James's. For Paul confession of Jesus as Lord implies behavioral consequences. Therefore, he can describe people who live in ways that are contradictory to such a confession as not inheriting the kingdom of God (cf. 1 Cor 6:9-11; Gal 5:19-21).

James never evidences any concern about his own support by the church or the problem that the demand for Christian charity could be viewed as a demand stemming from the Law (as some rabbinic sayings would later demonstrate). What he does in his context, rather, is the same as what Paul does in his context: James refuses to allow Christians to break the connection between commitment to Jesus and an appropriate Christian lifestyle. Likewise, on matters having to do with the use of the tongue (including slander and community conflict) and anger, James and Paul are fully at one.

5. James and Ministry Today

Given the shape of James's teaching on discipleship, what implications can be drawn for Christian ministry today? Even as we ask the question we are forced to make a great hermeneutical leap in moving from a relatively distant culture to our own. This is not the place to enter into a full hermeneutical discussion of how to apply principles from one time and culture to another. But as a minimum one can argue that the following contributions to the modern discussion of discipleship can be drawn from James.

The Teaching of Jesus Is Relevant to Christian Ministry

The letter of James shows us a pastor at work using materials that have been mined from the Jesus tradition (from what is often termed the "Q" tradition) and applying those teachings to his church. As such, the letter is a reminder that Christian discipleship is based on submission to "our glorious Lord Jesus Christ," and so must be conditioned constantly by Jesus' teaching. If we read the Gospels as community products giving the forms of the foundational narrative that shaped particular Christian communities, we must also read the Letter of James as applying that same story in another form to a particular Christian community. While the parts of the teaching of Jesus that are most relevant to particular readers may change and while the nature of the application may be influenced by differing cultures, the principle of applying Jesus' teaching to the life of the church is surely important for Christian ministry. Discipleship is, therefore, first of all a following of Jesus.

Christian Life Means Total Commitment to God

Humanity's perspective on life is not the same as God's. Human values are not God's values. How the world views "the rich" and "the poor" is not necessarily how God views people. There is a danger, not simply that believers will totally adopt the stances of their respective cultures, but that they will try to maintain a "both-and" position of partial commitment to God and partial commitment to some of the world's values for their lives. James speaks against this, calling for people to make a clear decision, for one can serve only one master. People who adopt a lifestyle of worldly values while mouthing orthodox confessions are only deceiving themselves. Those who try to grasp both the world

244

and God will lose both. As Kierkegaard said, "Purity of heart is to will one thing." Therefore, the church needs to examine its valuation of wealth and of speech to make sure that in both it agrees with God's valuation.

Christian Faith Can Thrive in a Context of Suffering

Suffering, by which is meant here external pressure, is often viewed as a threat to faith. James encourages his readers, however, to understand that faith can thrive in such a context. The danger is that believers may attempt to secure their future rather than trust God for their future. That is, if individuals begin to doubt the goodness of God, they will cease to endure and, instead, will struggle with other believers for status in the world or in the Christian community.

Pastoral care needs to bring Christians back again and again to the character of God and to encourage them to draw on "the wisdom from above."

Christian Faith Is Rooted in a Community Perspective

James speaks to the individualism of the modern age, which stresses introspective analysis. More particularly, however, James warns today's church against an individualism that emphasizes concern for the salvation of one's own soul over against a community perspective. James points out that the church is a community, and that it is only as the community sticks together that it will be the kind of counterculture that it is called to be. It is not to be a community full of strife and struggle for status, but a community marked by peace and forgiveness.

In terms of ministry, such a view calls on the church to look favorably on those who build community, not on the "rugged individualists" who build their own careers. It also calls on members of the church to care for one another, as is evident in the admonitions about prayer in 5:14-16. The community, of course, is not perfect, and so there will be times of confrontation and the need for repentance. In 4:7-12 James sets out a proper type of confrontation ("resist the devil"), and calls on the church to repent and submit to God.

Christian Faith Cannot Be Divorced from Caring Acts

If the church is to demonstrate its faith, that faith cannot be divorced from caring acts. The church has often focused on outward profession of creed or doctrinal statement, but all too often ignored deeds — so long, of course, as certain (often sexual) moral codes were not breached. James calls for a deeper analysis of what it means to be a "Christian family" and what it means to connect faith to works. In particular he addresses the "mammon spirit" that tends to separate the wallet from Christian devotion and to set up economic security as a parallel and alternative god. While the specific forms in which the orphan, the widow, and the needy appear today may be different than in James's day, we are still confronted with economic prejudice and a separation of discipleship from the wallet. Until the church addresses this, it has not heard the message of James. Nor has it grasped the truth that faith that does not lead to works is dead indeed.

Selected Bibliography

Baker, W. R. *Personal Speech-Ethics in the Epistle of James.* Tübingen: Mohr, 1995.

Chester, A., and R. P. Martin. *The Theology of the Letters of James, Peter, and Jude.* Cambridge: Cambridge University Press, 1994.

Davids, P. H. *A Commentary on the Epistle of James.* New International Greek Testament Commentary, Grand Rapids: Eerdmans, 1982.

———. "The Epistle of James in Modern Discussion," in *Aufstieg und Niedergang der Römischen Welt* II.25.5, ed. W. Haase and H. Temporini. Berlin: De Gruyter, 1988, 3622-45.

———. "The Gospels and Jewish Tradition," in *Studies of History and Tradition in the Four Gospels,* ed. R. T. France and D. Wenham. Sheffield: JSOT Press, 1980, 75-100.

———. "James and Jesus," in *The Jesus Tradition outside the Gospels,* ed. D. Wenham. Sheffield: JSOT Press, 1984, 63-84.

———. "James and Paul," in *Dictionary of Paul and His Letters,* ed. G. F. Hawthorne, R. P. Martin, and D. G. Reid. Downers Grove: InterVarsity, 1993, 457-61.

Deppe, D. B. *The Sayings of Jesus in the Epistle of James.* Chelsea: Bookcrafters, 1989.

Dibelius, M. *A Commentary on the Epistle of James.* Hermeneia, Philadelphia: Fortress, 1976.

Johnson, L. T. "Friendship with the World/Friendship with God: A Study of Discipleship in James," in *Discipleship in the New Testament,* ed. F. F. Segovia. Philadelphia: Fortress, 1985, 166-83.

Laws, S. *The Epistle of James.* Harper's New Testament Commentary, San Francisco: Harper and Row, 1980.

Martin, R. P. *James.* Word Biblical Commentary, Waco: Word, 1988.

Maynard-Reid, P. U. *Poverty and Wealth in James.* Maryknoll: Orbis, 1987.

Mayor, J. B. *The Epistle of St. James.* London: Macmillan, 1892.

Ward, R. B. "The Works of Abraham: James 2:14-26," *Harvard Theological Review* 61 (1968) 283-90.

Witherington, B. *Jesus the Sage: The Pilgrimage of Wisdom.* Minneapolis: Fortress, 1994, 236-47.

Going to Heaven with Jesus:
From 1 Peter to Pilgrim's Progress

J. RAMSEY MICHAELS

The hope of popular religion, in distinction from that of biblical Christianity, is "going to heaven when we die." In the New Testament, however, only Jesus is explicitly said to have "gone to heaven" — once in the book of Acts at his ascension (Acts 1:11; cf. Luke 24:51) and once in 1 Pet 3:22 ("having gone to heaven, with angels and authorities and powers subject to him"). Yet there is at least some basis in the New Testament for the notion of "going to heaven" as the reward of those who trust in Jesus.

In some texts, this has already happened. According to Eph 2:6, for example, God has "raised us up with Christ and seated us with him in the heavenly realms." But other texts (without using "going to heaven" terminology) place the experience in the future. Thus, for example, Jesus tells Peter in the Fourth Gospel: "Where I am going you cannot follow me now, but you will follow later" (13:36). And then he says to all the disciples: "In my Father's house are many dwellings; if there were not, would I have told you that I go to prepare a place for you? And if I go and prepare a place for you, I will come again and take you to myself, so that where I am, you too may be" (14:2-3). Earlier he has said, "Let anyone who serves me follow me, and where I am there my servant will be" (12:26). And at the end of that Gospel, Jesus explicitly commands Peter: "Follow me" (21:22).

It is not necessary to assume that the author of 1 Peter knew John's Gospel to suspect that such Johannine texts may have had an impact on the portrayal of Christian discipleship in 1 Peter. Even in the Synoptic tradition, Jesus called Peter and his friends by the lake with the words, "Come with me, and I will make you fish for people" (Mark 1:17 par.). If Peter wrote 1 Peter, he would have remembered Jesus' call "Come with me"; and if he did not, those who made him the letter's implied author would likely have seen the connection.

1. The Great Journey

The difficulty with popular religion's hope of "going to heaven when we die" is not with the notion of "going to heaven," but with the qualifying clause "when we die." For in the New Testament the journey to heaven begins not at death but at the moment a person is called to discipleship.

The theme of salvation as a journey to heaven is implicit in the Fourth Gospel — possibly, as well, in Jesus' choice of an itinerant ministry for at least part of his time on earth. It dominates Hebrews from beginning to end and also comes to expression in 1 Peter. No New Testament letter, in fact, emphasizes Christian discipleship and the journey to heaven motif more than 1 Peter. And in 1 Peter that discipleship is depicted as only the beginning of such a journey.

John Bunyan's classic *Pilgrim's Progress* has immortalized the theme of discipleship as a journey to heaven for generations of Christians in England and throughout the world. The impact of the thought and language of Hebrews is evident on almost every page of both *Pilgrim's Progress* and Bunyan's *Grace Abounding to the Chief of Sinners*. But the influence of 1 Peter on these writings is — though subtle — no less real.

Almost at the beginning of *Pilgrim's Progress*, Christian tells Obstinate "I seek an inheritance, incorruptible, undefiled, and that fadeth not away; and it is laid up in Heaven, and fast there, to be bestowed at the time appointed, on them that diligently seek it. Read it so, if you will, in my book" (*Pilgrim's Progress* 54; cf. 1 Pet 1:4). That Bunyan knew 1 Peter well is evident already from his speeches in his own defense on the occasion of his trial and imprisonment (*Grace Abounding* 85-110). For example, in those speeches he argued: "It was a mercy to suffer upon so good an account: for we might have been apprehended as thieves or murderers, or for other wickedness; but blessed be God it was not so, but we suffer as Christians for well doing: and we had better be the persecuted, than the persecutors, etc." (*ibid.* 89; cf. 1 Pet 2:19-20; 3:17; 4:15-16); and: "I said . . . that I was to submit to the King as supreme, also to the governors, as to them that are sent by him" (*ibid.* 104; cf. 1 Pet 2:13). And when asked where he got his authority, Bunyan answered: "I said, by that in the first epistle of Peter, the fourth chapter, the eleventh verse. . . . As every man hath received the gift, even so let him minister the same unto another, as good stewards of the manifold grace of God: if any man speak, let him speak as the oracles of God, etc." (*ibid.* 98). Bunyan found in 1 Peter the marching orders for his journey to heaven — not only for telling his imaginative story of Pilgrim's progress, but also for his defense before the court when called on to give "an accounting of the hope that is yours" (cf. 1 Pet 3:15, which Bunyan did not explicitly quote).

We have used Bunyan's classic allegory not as proof that discipleship is a central theme of 1 Peter, but simply as a useful point of comparison and contrast. Bunyan, of course, was a precritical interpreter of the New Testament. But no study of Christian discipleship — even one focused on the New Testament writings themselves — is complete without some attention to this classic work. Its application to 1 Peter, however, is limited by the fact that Christian's pilgrimage was not explicitly an "imitation of Christ." Nonetheless, the parallels are both real and informative and so will be highlighted in the course of our discussion below.

2. Pilgrimage and Growth in 1 Peter 1–2

The biblical basis for Bunyan's depiction of a believer's pilgrimage toward an incorruptible inheritance in heaven is to be found in 1 Pet 1:3-9, which begins with Peter's programmatic announcement that God "in his great mercy gave us new birth by raising Jesus Christ from the dead" (v 3). By virtue of their rebirth, Christian believers (like "Christian" in Bunyan's allegory) are pointed toward the future. They not only have "a living hope" and an inheritance, but they look toward "a salvation about to be revealed at the last day" (v 5). This salvation is not so much something that will come to them as something to which they must go. It is the future "goal" or "outcome" (*telos*) of their faith (v 9).

In 1 Peter, therefore, "faith" is not "belief," but "faithfulness" through the "various ordeals" of the present (vv 5-6, 9). Tested and proven faithfulness will be exchanged for "praise, glory, and honor at the time when Jesus Christ is revealed" (v 7). Salvation in 1 Peter is not an inevitable future reward for which one passively waits. Rather, it springs from present circumstances, however difficult, and one's obedient response to those circumstances (cf. Malina, "Christ and Time," who distinguishes in Mediterranean culture between a "forthcoming" future that arises out of present circumstances and a more distant "imaginary" future). Thus salvation in 1 Peter stands at the end of a journey — that is, at the end of our journey of discipleship as Christians.

The journey metaphor is latent also in 1:13-21 in Peter's reference to the holy "conduct" *(anastrophē)* required of Christian believers (v 15). And it also underlies his concern that believers "live out" or "spend" *(anastraphēte)* the time of their "sojourn" or "pilgrimage" *(paroikia)* in reverent fear toward the God they call Father (v 17).

In chapter 2 the metaphor changes, but only slightly. Here Peter urges his readers to "grow up to salvation now that you have tasted that the Lord is good" (vv 2-3). Whether it is seen as the end of a journey or as the result of a growth process, "salvation" or "vindication" is something toward which we are moving, not something for which we are merely waiting. Christians in 1 Peter are not only "a chosen race, the King's priesthood, a holy nation," but they are, above all, "a people destined for vindication" *(laos eis peripoiēsin, v 9)*. The phrase "a people destined for vindication" echoes Isa 43:21 (LXX). But Peter, with the use of the preposition *eis* in the sense of "to," "for," or "destined for," gives to the Old Testament statement a distinctly future orientation — which such translations as "God's own people" (NRSV) or "a people belonging to God" (NIV) do not do justice to, being based more on the language of Isaiah (see also Exod 19:5) than on that of 1 Peter itself (cf. Michaels, *1 Peter* 109-10).

Christians are also a people called out of darkness to God's "marvelous light" (v 9b). The "marvelous light" in 1 Peter is probably future rather than present, just as the "eternal glory" of 5:10 to which believers are similarly "called" is future (cf. *1 Clement* 36:2, written from Rome a few decades later: "through him our darkened and foolish understanding blossoms toward the light"). In 1 Peter, "marvelous light" and "eternal glory" are alternate expressions for the vindication or salvation to which believers will come at the last day (the "yonder shining light" in

Pilgrim's Progress 53 is different: Bunyan's marginal note interprets it rather as "the Word").

The journey metaphor continues in the second half of chapter 2, beginning with the address in v 11: "Dear friends, I appeal to you as aliens and strangers" *(hōs paroikous kai parepidēmous)*. Peter's language here echoes the identification of his addressees at the very beginning of his letter as "a chosen people, living as strangers in the diaspora" *(eklektois parepidēmois diasporas,* 1:1). He further tells them in 2:12 to "make sure your conduct [*anastrophē*] among the Gentiles is good, so that in a case where they accuse you of doing wrong they may, from observing your good works, glorify God on the day of visitation." His words here recall those in 1:15 and 17, which refer to the lives of believers as a "sojourn" (*paroikia,* v 17) and to the necessity of holiness in their "conduct" or "course of life" (using the same word, *anastrophē,* v 15).

John Elliott has argued that the language of sojourn and alienation in 1 Peter is not metaphorical, but that the letter was written to communities that were actually homeless or displaced in a sociological sense in the Roman Empire (*Home for the Homeless* 21-58). Elliott's view, however, though widely discussed, has not gained general acceptance (see the review by P. J. Achtemeier in the *Journal of Biblical Literature* 103 [1984] 130-33; also Martin, *Metaphor and Composition* 142-43; Chin, "Heavenly Home for the Homeless"). There is now, in fact, wide agreement among scholars that "alienation" or "homelessness" was not a sociological given for the addressees of 1 Peter but a result of their conversion to Christianity. And the same is true of the "journey" on which the addressees found themselves — that is, it stemmed not from their sociological situation but from their conversion to Christ. Yet that journey is not exactly a journey to a "heavenly home," as in some traditional formulations, for heaven is not their home, and the heavenly Jesus is a savior whom they have never seen (cf. v 8). Their journey is more like that of Bunyan's Christian — from a home in the "City of Destruction" to "Mount Sion," or "the Celestial City," a place they have never been (cf. *Pilgrim's Progress* 68, 72, 90, 102, *passim*).

3. Following Jesus to the Cross and Beyond: 2:21-25

Peter's words on discipleship in 2:21-25, which form the centerpiece of his teaching, are embedded in his advice to household servants (vv

18-25) and linked explicitly for the first time in the letter to the life of Jesus (so vv 21-23). Here in this section Peter stands squarely in the tradition of these words of Jesus in Mark's Gospel: "Those who would come after me must deny themselves and take up their cross and follow me. For those who want to save their lives will lose them, and those who lose their lives for my sake and the gospel's will find them" (Mark 8:34-35 par.).

Having accented "faith" as "faithfulness" in chapter 1, Peter now adopts "follow" rather than "believe" (or "trust") as his controlling command. For following, unlike faith or believing, is a notion not easily intellectualized. It represents not merely confession or the acceptance of a message, but action — gathering into one Paul's notion of justifying faith and James's appeal for good deeds. So here 1 Peter reads like a letter Paul might have written if he had paid closer attention to Jesus' teaching in the Synoptic tradition, or one that Mark, Matthew, or Luke might have written if they had adopted the letter form.

Peter introduces his appeal to Jesus' example with "Christ also suffered [*kai Christos epathen*] for you" (v 21a). The statement does not refer to Christ's redemptive death on the cross, which Peter does not mention until verse 24, for it is followed immediately by these explanatory words: "leaving you an example, that you might follow in his footsteps" (v 21b). Therefore, the reference to Christ having suffered "for you" *(hyper hymōn)* must be taken in the sense of "leaving you an example" (cf. Michaels, *1 Peter* 134 and 143 for fuller discussion; alternatively, see Goppelt, *I Peter* 201f.). "Example" *(hypogrammon),* a word found only here in the New Testament, was used elsewhere in the Greek world of both a letter of the alphabet written out for a child to copy and a moral example — the latter especially in later Christianity, often in dependence on 1 Peter itself (cf. Michaels, *1 Peter* 144).

Discipleship in 1 Peter, as in most of the other New Testament writings, involves suffering. But what was it about Jesus' suffering that made it worthy of imitation? Surely not its redemptive character. For Christian disciples are not called to bear the sins of the world or even of one another. Rather, what made Christ's suffering a fitting example was that it was undeserved or unjust suffering. He suffered for doing good, not for doing evil. And in his suffering he kept on doing good: "He committed no sin, nor was deceit ever found on his lips. He was insulted, but he would never insult in return; when he suffered, he never threatened" (2:22-23).

In chapter 3 Peter will explicitly command his readers: "Do not return evil for evil, or insult for insult, but on the contrary, bless — because to this you were called" (v 9). The last clause of this command echoes a similar expression in 2:21a, "for to this you were called" *(eis touto gar eklēthēte)*, which closely links the two passages. Thus discipleship in 1 Peter is emphatically a matter of "calling" (cf. Elliott, "Backward and Forward" 195). And if in the long run disciples are called to "marvelous light" or "eternal glory," in the short run they are called to the way of Jesus, a way characterized by nonresistance and nonretaliation.

Yet Peter, unlike the apostle Paul, never holds himself up as an example to be imitated. His own personal history, which was well known, probably made such a thing impossible. For Peter not only refused three times to follow Jesus to the cross, but at Jesus' arrest failed to practice nonretaliation (cf. John 18:10). The thrust of 1 Peter, therefore, both for its original addressees and for readers today, is that Peter learned from his mistakes.

Contrary to much that has been written on 1 Peter, the call to discipleship in this letter is not a call to suffering, as if suffering in itself were something good. Rather, it is a call to do good — and, furthermore, to do good even in the presence of undeserved suffering, like that faced by Jesus. Just as the metaphors of alienation and displacement should not be taken literally (*contra* Elliott), neither should the journey metaphor. The call to discipleship — or to the doing of good in the face of undeserved suffering — is not a call to embark on a literal journey, like Jesus' call to Peter and his companions by the Sea of Galilee. 1 Peter is not calling anyone to a radically itinerant ministry or lifestyle.

Rather, Peter's call to follow in the footsteps of Jesus Christ appears in the context of certain fairly stable social relationships in the Roman Empire: citizens in relation to governing authorities (2:13-17), slaves in relation to slave owners (2:18-25), and wives and husbands in relation to each other (3:1-7). The "journey" of which 1 Peter speaks is nothing other than the natural course of a person's life *(anastrophē)*. It is not a journey that "gets anywhere" in a physical or geographical sense. Subjects of the emperor remain his subjects, slaves remain slaves, and wives and husbands stay married to each other. Their journey is not one that can be mapped out or plotted any more than Christian's journey to "Mount Sion" in *Pilgrim's Progress* can be plotted. As Stanley Fish has pointed out, when Christian and Faithful reach the town of Vanity, with its Vanity Fair, they are, for all practical purposes, still in the place from which they started, the City of Destruction (Fish, "Progress"). And, as is often noted, Part I of Bunyan's classic ends with the grim reminder that "there was a way to Hell, even from the Gates of Heaven, as well as from the City of Destruction" (*Pilgrim's Progress* 217).

Still, in the setting of social relationships in an ungodly empire, Peter sees Christian believers moving in the footsteps of Jesus toward the "inheritance reserved in heaven for you," or the "salvation about to be revealed at the last day" (1:4-5). It is no accident that the call to discipleship in 2:21-25 emerges specifically out of a section outlining the responsibilities of Christian slaves or household servants in 2:18-20. Up to this point, Peter has maintained a basic optimism about the safety of Christians generally within Roman society. Local magistrates are committed "to punish wrongdoers and commend those who do good deeds" (2:14). Consequently, if Christians do good, they will "put to silence the ignorance of the foolish" (2:15). This is Peter's expectation in the short run. Yet both he and his readers seem to know of household situations where justice does not always prevail. Slaves were more likely than others to face unjust suffering, and Peter seems to regard their experience as a precursor of what is in store for the Christian community as a whole.

It is difficult to tell where Peter's advice to household servants leaves off and his more general call to Christian discipleship begins. The generalizing process seems to start already in verse 19: "For it is grace when someone [perhaps a slave, or perhaps not] puts up with afflictions out of a conscious commitment to God." Probably the reference to being "beaten" in verse 20 still has slaves primarily in view, yet nothing there or in verses 21-25 can be limited to them (cf. Michaels, *1 Peter* 135, 141). Clearly, when Peter says "for to this you were called" (v 21a), he is no longer addressing slaves in particular but Christian believers generally (cf. again 3:9).

Peter's use of servants or slaves to represent the Christian community as a whole may have been occasioned, in part, by the early Christian identification of the "servant" of Isaiah 53 with Jesus of Nazareth, for he draws on that tradition explicitly in verse 22: "He committed no sin, nor was deceit ever found in his mouth" (cf. Isa 53:9b). Yet Peter, it seems, was not bothered by the theological difficulty — even impossibility — of sinful human beings following the example of someone who was divine and sinless. On the contrary, having compared Jesus earlier to a "faultless and flawless lamb" (1:19), Peter now emphasizes the sinlessness of Jesus even in the face of the most severe provocation. The example to be followed is Jesus, and that precisely in his sinlessness!

Peter is not teaching "perfectionism" as a lofty or abstract theological ideal. Rather, he is making a direct, almost naive, appeal to break with sin and "do good." He has no interest in debating whether or not such a break is possible. The practical thrust of his argument is "Just do it!"

To a surprising degree "doing" in 1 Peter is understood as "speaking," whether in the case of Jesus himself or on the part of those who want to be his disciples. In Peter's Isaiah quotation, the statement that Jesus "committed no sin" is immediately expanded with "nor was deceit ever found in his mouth" (v 22). A whole sentence, in fact, is given over to commenting on Jesus' sinlessness in matters of speech: "He was insulted, but he would never insult in return; when he suffered, he never threatened" (v 23a).

Threats were common in the martyrdoms of antiquity, both in early Judaism and in early Christianity. These were not just the tormentors' threats against the martyrs but also counterthreats by the martyrs themselves against those who made them suffer. For example, seven Jews being tortured to death by the Greek tyrant Antiochus IV ("Epiphanes") said: "You seek to terrify us with your threat of death by torture. . . . But you, because of your foul murder, will suffer at the hand of divine justice the everlasting torment by fire you deserve" (4 Maccabees 9:5-9; cf. 2 Maccabees 7:17, 19, 31, 34-36; 4 Maccabees 10:11; *Martyrdom of Polycarp* 11:2; *Martyrdom of Perpetua and Felicitas* 18:8; see Michaels, *1 Peter* 146). Peter's claim is that Jesus resorted to no such threats. Instead, he silently left his tormentors "in the hands of him who judges justly" (v 23b), thereby, in effect, consigning them to whatever God in his justice had in store for them (cf. Paul in Rom 12:19). The point is not that Peter (or Jesus) viewed the final judgment differently than did the Maccabean or early Christian martyrs (cf. 1:17; 3:16-17; 4:5, 17-18), but simply that Jesus kept quiet about the punishment that awaited those who would put him to death and persecute his followers (cf. Michaels, *1 Peter* 147).

Peter builds simultaneously on the tradition of Isa 53:7 that the servant was as silent as a lamb in his sufferings and on the tradition of the Gospels that Jesus was silent before his accusers. Yet Peter never says explicitly that Jesus was silent, only that he refrained from insults and threats. The attitude that Peter desires for a follower of Jesus varies according to circumstances. For there are times when silence is appropriate (3:1) and other times when Jesus' followers must be ready to speak (3:15; 4:10-11). But it is always right to bless rather than curse (3:9) and to "stop the tongue from evil and the lips from speaking deceit" (3:10, using the words of Psalm 34).

Why this emphasis on speech, more than action, as the way in which both Jesus and his followers "do good"? Probably because the abuse to which the addressees of the letter were being subjected was, so far, largely verbal in nature. They either had been or could expect to be "accused" (*katalalousin*, 2:12; *katalaleisthe*, 3:16), "denounced" (*hoi epēreazontes*, 3:16), and "ridiculed" (*oneidizesthe*, 4:14) for their Christian faith. When Peter tells them to "put to silence the ignorance of the foolish" (2:15), he is referring to ignorant and foolish talk. The "persecution" that they faced was — at least for the moment — a matter of words, not of the sword or instruments of torture. Yet that was no small thing. In the world of the Bible, words matter. Words can destroy a person — if not one's enemies, then certainly oneself!

Jesus refused to be drawn into a war of words with his tormentors, and Peter wants to make sure that the same is true of Jesus' disciples. He could have endorsed Jesus' pronouncement that "people will give account in the day of judgment for every idle word they speak, for by your words you will be justified and by your words you will be condemned" (Matt 12:36-37). And he would have applauded the principle laid down in James: "Those who are never at fault in what they say are perfect, and able to keep their whole body under control" (Jas 3:2).

The key to Peter's call for sinlessness in word, and so in actions, lies in his abrupt transition from Jesus as example in 2:21-23 to Jesus as redeemer in 2:24. For having held up Jesus' behavior in the face of unjust suffering as a model for Christian behavior in verses 21-23, he continues in verse 24: "He himself carried our sins in his body to the cross, so that we, having parted with those sins, might live for what is right." The change from "you" and "your" in verses 20-21 (also v 18) to "we" and "our" in verse 24 marks a shift to a distinctly confessional formulation in verse 24 of the common early Christian belief in salvation through Christ's death.

1 Peter cuts through all the modern debates over whether the cross of Christ is an example of self-giving love or a divinely appointed means

of reconciliation and redemption. Without question, it is both in this letter — with the two aspects not in tension. Each, in fact, requires the other. Christians can put sin behind them and follow in Jesus' footsteps only because they have been redeemed by his death. Discipleship, therefore, demands more than a passive acceptance of the saving benefits of that death. It is nothing less than active participation in Jesus' death and all that led up to it.

What exactly did Jesus' death accomplish according to 1 Peter? Clearly, it is understood as a sacrificial or redemptive death, for Jesus' blood cleanses from the guilt of sin (cf. 1:2, 19). But it is more! The meaning of 2:24 is not that Jesus bore the guilt of humanity's sins in his body on the cross, but that he carried humanity's sins in his body to the cross and left them there. He is more than a passive sacrificial victim. If not quite the Great High Priest of Hebrews, he is still in 1 Peter the active sin-bearer and destroyer of sins. He did not simply atone for sins so that people could go on sinning and then continually be forgiven. Rather, he quite literally took sins away, just as John the Baptist said he would in the Fourth Gospel: "Look, the lamb of God who takes away the sin of the world" (John 1:29; cf. 1 John 3:5).

What happens to the believer's sins according to Peter is what happened to Christian's sins in Bunyan's allegorical classic:

> He ran thus till he came at a place somewhat ascending; and upon that place stood a Cross, and a little below in the bottom, a sepulchre. So I saw in my dream, that just as Christian came up with the Cross, his burden loosed from off his shoulders, and fell from off his back; and began to tumble, and so continued to do till it came to the mouth of the sepulchre, where it fell in, and I saw it no more (*Pilgrim's Progress*, 81-82).

In a similar way, disciples of Jesus in 1 Peter have "parted with" their sins so as to "live for what is right" (v 24). Christ himself "finished with sin" when he suffered (4:1; cf. Heb 9:28). And those who would be his disciples must arm themselves "with the same resolve" so as to live the rest of their lives "no longer for human impulses but to do the will of God" (4:1-2; cf. Michaels, *1 Peter* 225-28).

Clearly, Peter's standards for discipleship border on perfectionism. Yet it is not a perfectionism divorced from reality. He knows that the kind of "realism" that begins by recounting the inevitability of sin and failure in the lives of Christians is not going to make an impact — either by word or by example — on a hostile society. He is encouraged by the fact that his addressees have already made a decisive break with their past (1:18, 22-23; 4:3-4), and he dares to hope that their resistance to "the impulses that once drove you in your ignorance" will continue (1:14; 2:1, 11).

Like another early Christian perfectionist, the author of 1 John, Peter probably knows: "If we claim to be without sin, we deceive ourselves and the truth is not in us. If we confess our sins, he is faithful and just and will forgive us our sins and purify us from all unrighteousness" (1 John 1:8-9). Peter never quite says that. Yet he does urge his readers to "remain constant in your love for each other, for love covers many sins" (4:8). Only in a communal setting of mutual love and forgiveness, he knows, is it possible to realize the ideal of following in Jesus' footsteps by putting sin away and doing good for the rest of our lives.

The great journey, however, does not stop with the cross. When Christian in *Pilgrim's Progress* left his burden of sin at the cross, his journey had little more than begun. Jesus' journey, too, led past the cross to the resurrection, and finally to heaven.

In his call in 2:21-25 to follow in Jesus' footsteps, Peter presupposes the resurrection of Jesus, though without mentioning it explicitly. He concludes his reflection on Christ's death with "by his wounding you have been healed" (v 24b, borrowing the language of Isa 53:5b). And he continues by reminding his readers once more of the circumstances of their conversion: "For you were going astray like sheep, but you have returned now to the Shepherd and Guardian of your souls" (v 25). They are in the Shepherd's care not as sheep placidly safe within the fold, but as sheep who will follow the Shepherd wherever he leads. Their experience recalls that of Jesus' disciples in Mark's Gospel in a situation that the historical Peter would have remembered very well, when Jesus told his disciples that the Scripture "I will strike the shepherd, and the sheep will be scattered" (Zech 13:7) was about to be fulfilled — adding that "after I am risen, I will lead you into Galilee" (Mark 14:27-28; cf. 16:7).

Jesus' resurrection is mentioned in the Markan text, but only briefly as the presupposition of the main promise: that Jesus, the stricken Shepherd, will return and continue to do what a shepherd does — that is, lead his flock to that which God has in store for them (Mark 14:28; cf. John 10:15-18). In 1 Pet 2:24-25, however, the resurrection of Jesus is not mentioned at all. In verse 24, Jesus "carried our sins in his body to the cross"; in verse 25 he is suddenly alive again, welcoming converts from the Gentile world as "Shepherd and Guardian of your souls." At most, the resurrection is implied in the notion that Christian believers have virtually died to their sins in order to "live for what is right" (v 24b). The resurrection of Jesus, which was explicit earlier in 1:3, 21 and will be again in 3:21, is here in 2:21-25 assumed as a given. The cross is only the beginning. The "Shepherd and Guardian" of the disciples has to be a risen Shepherd in order for their real pilgrimage — that is, their journey to heaven — to begin (cf. Heb 13:20-21).

4. Following Jesus to God in Heaven: 3:18-22

If 2:21-25 is the centerpiece and core of Peter's teaching on discipleship, it is not quite the whole of it (as it appears to be, for example, in Elliott's "Backward and Forward"). For in 3:18-22 Jesus' resurrection becomes explicit. And once again the expression "for Christ also" *(hoti kai Christos)* introduces an appeal to Jesus' example (v 18; cf. 2:21), with, again, the point of comparison being that Jesus suffered for doing good ("a just man on behalf of the unjust"), even as his followers are called to do.

This section, 3:18-22, follows 3:13-17, where Peter concluded that "it is better to suffer for doing good, if God should require it, than for doing evil" — or, as Bunyan put it, "we had better be the persecuted, than the persecutors" (*Grace Abounding* 89; cf. Michaels, "Eschatology" 398-400; *idem, 1 Peter* 191-92). And in this section Jesus' suffering is presented as the model for the suffering of his disciples. Again, however, it is not that their suffering, like his, is redemptive; rather, it is that their suffering, like his, is unjust and undeserved, so that, like him, they will be vindicated.

The purpose of Jesus' suffering goes beyond setting an example. His intention in going to the cross was "to bring you to God" (v 18) — not simply to faith and hope in God (as in 1:21), but to God himself in heaven (cf. Michaels, *1 Peter* 203). The realization of this purpose lies in the future. Christians have already "come to him, the living Stone" (2:4), and have "turned now to the Shepherd and Guardian of your souls" (2:25). But "the living Stone" or "Shepherd and Guardian" is Jesus Christ, not God the Father. Christ is not the goal but the way. Thus, even though he is not yet visible to them (1:8; 5:4), Christ the Shepherd is leading his followers to God in heaven as a true Shepherd should. And so coming to God is a process still going on.

It is in 3:18-22 that Peter again speaks explicitly of the resurrection of Jesus. For Jesus was not only "put to death in the flesh" but also "made alive in the Spirit" (v 18b), and "in that state" as risen Lord he "has gone to heaven" (v 22). The three verbs "put to death," "made alive," and "gone to heaven" share a common ending in Greek *(-theis)* and seem to have belonged to an early confessional source from which Peter is quoting (cf. Michaels, *1 Peter* 197-200). Peter develops in these verses, in particular, the notion that Christ "has gone to heaven" as a consequence of his resurrection, and he elaborates in some detail what that journey to heaven involved. Just as there is a uniqueness to the death of Jesus that is not shared by those who follow in his footsteps, so there is a uniqueness to his journey to heaven that is not to be shared by those who follow him. Christ in his risen state announced final victory over the evil and unclean spirits he had confronted in the course of his ministry. Peter places the origin of these spirits in the time of Noah, in the story of the illicit union between angels and humans found in Gen 6:1-4 (cf. Michaels, *1 Peter* 207-10; *idem, Biblical Themes* 70-74).

This proclamation, like Christ's redemptive death, was "once for all" (*hapax*, v 18). It is not reenacted in the experience of Jesus' disciples. Yet they are its beneficiaries, just as they are of his death. And they participate in the victory he announced. For if Jesus encountered "disobedient spirits" in the course of his journey to heaven, his disciples will encounter those who "disobey the word" (2:8; 3:1) or are "disobedient to the gospel of God" (4:17) in the course of theirs. Peter is confident that because of Christ's victory, such troublemakers will either be won over by the conduct of Jesus' disciples (3:1) so as to "glorify God on the day of visitation" (2:12) or be "put to shame" on that same day of judgment (2:8; 3:16; 4:17). Either way, Jesus' disciples will be vindicated against their enemies on earth just as surely and decisively as Christ was vindicated against the "disobedient spirits" from the time of Noah. The triumph of Jesus' disciples is assured because the Risen One, in whose steps they follow, is now at God's right hand in heaven, "with angels and authorities and powers subject to him" (v 22).

5. Following Jesus in Enemy Territory: 5:6-11

Victory assured is not the same as victory already won. A century after 1 Peter, a Christian Gnostic from Egypt was so taken with the notion

261

of a disciple's participation in Christ's victorious journey to heaven that he wrote "We suffered with him, and we rose with him, and we went to heaven with him" (*Treatise on the Resurrection* 45.25-28; cf. B. Layton, *The Gnostic Treatise on Resurrection from Nag Hammadi* [Missoula: Scholars, 1979] 17). Both the author of this document and Peter seem to have drawn on the same traditional formulation: "put to death — made alive — gone to heaven." But 1 Peter is not quite so explicit as the *Treatise* about the disciples' identification with Christ in his journey. Consequently, he never states or implies that our journey is over. Even in the wake of Jesus' proclamation to the spirits and his enthronement in heaven, Peter still sounds the warning a chapter and a half later, in 5:8: "Pay attention! Wake up! Your enemy, the devil, is on the prowl like a roaring lion ready to devour his prey."

Christ's journey is complete. But ours goes on! And while it does, the devil still stalks the earth to devour us. We need only think of the many snares and conflicts that faced Christian in Bunyan's allegorical account, notably his combat with Apollyon in the Valley of Humiliation (*Pilgrim's Progress* 102-6). At the end Christian gives thanks "to him that hath delivered me out of the mouth of the lion, to him that did help me against Apollyon" (*ibid.* 106; cf. 2 Tim 4:17). In 1 Peter, sufferings and struggles must continue "for a little while" against the devil's rage (1:6; 5:10). "Resist him," Peter urges, "firm in faith, knowing that your brothers and sisters throughout the world are undergoing the same kind of sufferings" (5:9). Peter's words here match those of James, who wrote: "Resist the devil and he will flee from you" (Jas 4:7); also those of Paul: "Put on the full armor of God so that you may stand against the tricks of the devil. . . . Wear the full armor of God so as to resist in the evil day, and when you have done all this, to stand" (Eph 6:11, 13).

All such texts raise the question of how one should resist the devil while practicing nonretaliation toward the devil's human agents. 1 Peter has consistently presented nonretaliation both as the way of Jesus in his passion (2:22-23) and as the way of true discipleship (3:9). Paul cautioned that "our warfare is not against flesh and blood, but against the rulers, against the authorities, against the world powers of this darkness, against the spiritual forces of evil in heavenly places" (Eph 6:12). And Jesus, when he warned his disciples "not to resist the evil one" (Matt 5:39), made it clear by the illustrations he used (vv 39-42) that he was referring not to the devil but to specific human enemies, whom his disciples were required to love (vv 43-48). The consistent testimony of the New Testament, therefore, is that resisting the devil and resisting human antagonists are not the same thing (see Michaels, *Biblical Themes* 76-77).

This is the difference between Christian discipleship, as Peter views it, and religious fanaticism. Religious fanatics see evil only outside themselves, never within. Religious fanaticism begins when a group — simplistically and without qualification — identifies its enemies with the devil and then proceeds to understand the biblical call to resist evil as a call to violence. 1 Peter never makes that mistake. In a warning strikingly appropriate to certain militant "Christian" groups today, Peter writes: "None of you must suffer as a murderer, or a thief, or any sort of criminal, or even as a busybody. But if you suffer for being a Christian, don't be ashamed, only glorify God in this matter" (4:15-16).

To Peter, the devil is "on the prowl like a roaring lion" — not merely in the threat of persecution from enemies, but in the danger that Christian believers themselves will deny or compromise their faith under pressure. To be "devoured" or "swallowed" by the devil is not to be slandered, persecuted, or even killed by enemies or governing authorities. Rather, it is to give up one's faith and abandon the journey (cf. the story of a second-century female martyr named Biblis in Euse-bius, *Ecclesiastical History* 5.1.25, where being "devoured" or "swallowed" is not martyrdom but apostasy). No one is ever "swallowed" against one's will. Peter learned this lesson well from his own attempts to fight against evil, both external and within. And so he taught that true disciples resist the devil not by hostile or subversive action against anyone, but simply by trusting God.

The exhortation in 5:9, "Resist him [the devil], firm in faith," is one in which the second clause interprets the first. To resist the devil is a corollary of the exhortations of 5:6-7: "Humble yourselves under the mighty hand of God, and when it is time he will lift you up. All your anxiety throw on him, for he cares about you." James links these two exhortations in the same way: "Submit yourselves, therefore, to God. Resist the devil and he will run from you" (Jas 4:7). The two commands, therefore, amount to the same thing. For Peter, the only way to fight evil is to do good. Like Paul in Rom 12:19, he wants his readers not to be "overcome with evil," but to "overcome evil with good." This is the key to the completion of their journey to heaven with Jesus.

6. Following Jesus in Community

A disturbing feature of *Pilgrim's Progress* has always been the abrupt manner in which Christian leaves his wife and children behind to embark on his sacred journey. "So I saw in my dream," Bunyan writes, "that the man began to run. Now he had not run far from his own door, but his wife and children perceiving it began to cry after him to return. But the man put his fingers in his ears, and ran on crying, 'Life, life, eternal life.' So he looked not behind him, but fled towards the middle of the plain" (*Pilgrim's Progress* 53). Although precedent for such action can be found in the Gospels (Luke 14:26; 18:29), Christian's single-minded concern about his own salvation has left a bad taste with many readers of Bunyan's classic through the centuries. Even Mr. Worldly-Wiseman asks him "Hast thou a wife and children?" and is told "Yes, but I am so laden with this burden that I cannot take that pleasure in them as formerly: methinks, I am as if I had none" (*ibid.* 60). Later, a good woman named Charity questions him at some length about the matter, and Christian's answers seem to reflect Bunyan's personal struggles over the issue (*ibid.* 96-97). At the end of Part I, however, Charity vindicates him by concluding that "if thy wife and children have been offended with thee, for this they thereby show themselves to be implacable to good; and thou hast delivered thy soul from their blood" (*ibid.* 97). Part I of Bunyan's great allegory, therefore, is the story of Christian's heroic, largely individual, pilgrimage from the City of Destruction to Mount Sion. He has his companions, Faithful and Hopeful, and there is a certain amount of male bonding. But for the most part the path of discipleship for him is itinerant and lonely (cf. Stranahan, "Bunyan and Hebrews" 288).

All this changes in Part II, however, where Christian's wife Christiana, with her children, belatedly follows the tracks of her husband's pilgrimage. There is irony in her sad recollection of "how she did harden her heart against all his entreaties, and loving persuasions [of her and her sons] to go with him" (*Pilgrim's Progress* 235). This reinforces the perspective of Part I, but actually the reverse was true in Part I: Christian had stopped his ears and hardened his heart against her cries. Yet whatever her motivation, Christiana and her sons and her friend Mercy are drawn into the pilgrimage. They retrace Christian's journey, and discipleship for Bunyan now becomes a life lived in community. As Roger Sharrock observes, Part II of *Pilgrim's Progress* is a different book, a bustling social novel. . . . The interest has shifted from the lonely epic of the individual to the problems of the small urban community of Nonconformists: problems of mixed marriages, the need for cohesion, and the difficulty certain members have (Fearing, Feeble-mind) in fitting into the life of the church. Bunyan had now been many years an administrator and a pastor of souls. . . . As most novelists do, he has passed from an autobiographical first novel to an external, more calculated subject ("Introduction" to *Pilgrim's Progress* 24).

Similarly, Peter in his brief letter makes room for community in Christian discipleship, though without the need of second thoughts or a sequel. Baptism, a practice of the Christian community that is ignored in Part I of *Pilgrim's Progress* but mentioned in Part II (*ibid.* 267-68, 402 n. 32), is thoroughly at home in 1 Peter (3:21). And as noted earlier, the call to follow in Jesus' footsteps appears in the context of stable households: slaves do not go off and leave their masters; wives do not leave their husbands, nor husbands their wives. The entire letter is a directive to Christians in Asia Minor on behalf of "your brothers and sisters throughout the world" (5:9). If they have a responsibility to show "reverence toward God" and "respect for everyone" (including the emperor), they have an equal responsibility to show "love for the family of believers" (2:17). No one is on the journey to heaven alone. The very purpose of the new life that is theirs in Christ is "for pure love for God's family" so that they might "love one another unremittingly from the heart" (1:22).

The household was in Rome's eyes an institution intended to support the authority of the state and the emperor. Roman philosophers viewed households as the very fabric of the empire, just as families today are widely viewed as the key to the moral strength of a nation. Peter saw the family — potentially, at least — as an island of godliness in a godless society. Yet Peter also knew that the household was more often a mission field, where belief confronted unbelief, than a place of prayer and ministry based on a common faith. Most slaves did not have Christian masters, and many wives did not have Christian husbands.

If the Romans wanted the household to be the empire in miniature, Peter saw the possibility of it becoming the church in miniature. It seldom did so because too often the husband was not a believer. Yet when husband and wife are believers — and husbands treat their wives

265

as "co-heirs of the grace of life" — Peter is confident that their "prayers will not be hindered" (3:7). In such instances, the family becomes a model for the worshiping and ministering congregations. As such, it becomes the vehicle of "the grace of life" prophesied long ago (1:10) and soon to be brought about in its fullness "when Jesus Christ is revealed" (1:13).

In two other places in his letter (4:7-11 and 5:1-5) Peter speaks of discipleship in community, though not in the sense of the natural ties of a family but in relation to what we commonly call the "church" (the Greek term *ekklēsia*, however, never appears in 1 Peter). In these passages, too, the notion of "grace" *(charis)* is central (4:10; 5:5).

The first of these passages, 4:7-11, is governed by Peter's conviction that "the end of all things is near" (v 7). Its emphasis is on equality and mutuality. All Christian disciples have love "for each other" (v 8), practice hospitality "toward one another" (v 9), and minister in various ways "to each other" (v 10). Love is the governing principle, and mutual hospitality and ministry are simply the concrete expressions of mutual love. Each disciple in the community has received a "gift" *(charisma)* from God, and Peter wants them all to use their gifts "as good managers of God's diversified grace" *(charis,* v 10), whether their gifts be those of speech or of service (v 11). By his repetition of the word "God," Peter reminds them that God is at the end of the journey they have undertaken. The end is near, and God stands ready to judge (cf. 4:5). The grace they have is God's grace; those who speak bring words from God; those who serve do so out of God's strength. And everything is done so that God may be glorified.

The second passage, 5:1-5, reads something like the household codes of 2:18-25 and 3:1-7. "Elders" and "younger ones" could be members of a household just as easily as members of a congregation. The only difference is that Peter begins here not (as in 2:18 and 3:1) with those considered subservient, but with those in positions of leadership. 4:7-11 was based on a sense that "the end of all things is near" (4:7), and the directive to elders is based on a similarly urgent belief that "it is time for judgment to begin with the household of God" (4:17). Beginning with the household of God meant beginning with the elders of the church (cf. Ezek 9:6; see Michaels, *1 Peter* 271, 277), and so Peter addresses them first (5:1-4).

In contrast to 4:7-11, distinctions here are made on the basis of seniority. Peter's apparent assumption is that some of the Asian congregations are ruled by elders and some are not. He appeals to the elders with the authority of "an elder myself, a witness to the sufferings of Christ, and a sharer as well in the glory to be revealed" (5:1). Drawing on the imagery of Christ as the Shepherd of the flock that follows him in his journey to heaven, he calls on the elders to "shepherd the flock of God that is in your care" (v 2), so that "when the Chief Shepherd appears you will receive the unfading crown of glory" (v 4). Peter also urges the elders to be "examples" *(typoi)* to the flock (v 3b). But this is as close as he comes to making anyone other than Jesus the model for Christian discipleship. Since he is one of the elders (v 1), he includes himself as an "example" of sorts. Still, his strong admonition about "not lording it over your congregations" (v 3a; cf. Mark 10:42) places the accent not on the persons of the elders themselves (or on Peter himself) as moral examples, but on their humility, servanthood, and accountability to Christ (v 4).

After a brief word urging those who are "younger" in the congregation (v 5a) to defer to the elders' authority (as slaves defer to their masters or wives to husbands), Peter comes back finally to his characteristic emphasis on mutuality: "All of you, with each other, then, clothe yourselves with humility, for God opposes the arrogant, but gives grace [*charis*] to the humble" (v 5b; cf. 4:7-11). He then sums up his call to discipleship with words echoing the teaching of Jesus: "So humble yourselves under the mighty hand of God, and when it is time, he will lift you up" (5:6; cf. Luke 14:11; 18:14b; Matt 23:12).

The key to following Jesus in the doing of good is the same for the community as for the individual — that is, submission to God. In the community, submission to God implies submission as well to one's believing companions, who are also pilgrims on the heavenly journey. Disciples love one another, help one another, forgive one another. Only in community, 1 Peter teaches, is it possible to follow in the path that Jesus walked alone.

Selected Bibliography

Best, E. "I Peter and the Gospel Tradition," *New Testament Studies* 16 (1969) 95-113.

Bunyan, J. *The Pilgrim's Progress* and *Grace Abounding to the Chief of Sinners.* London: Penguin Books, 1987.

Chin, M. "A Heavenly Home for the Homeless: Aliens and Strangers in 1 Peter," *Tyndale Bulletin* 42 (1991) 96-112.

Elliott, J. H. "Backward and Forward 'In His Steps': Following Jesus from Rome to Raymond and Beyond. The Tradition, Redaction, and Reception of 1 Peter 2:18-25," in *Discipleship in the New Testament*, ed. F. F. Segovia. Philadelphia: Fortress, 1985, 184-208.

————. *A Home for the Homeless: A Sociological Exegesis of 1 Peter, Its Situation and Strategy.* Philadelphia: Fortress, 1981.

Fish, S. "Progress in *The Pilgrim's Progress*," in *Self-Consuming Artifacts: The Experience of Seventeenth-Century Literature.* Berkeley: University of California, 1972, 224-64.

Goppelt, L. *A Commentary on I Peter.* Grand Rapids: Eerdmans, 1993.

Gundry, R. H. "Further Verba on 'Verba Christi' in First Peter," *Biblica* 55 (1974) 211-32.

————. " 'Verba Christi' in 1 Peter: Their Implications Concerning the Authorship of 1 Peter and the Authenticity of the Gospel Tradition," *New Testament Studies* 13 (1967) 336-50.

Malina, B. J. "Christ and Time: Swiss or Mediterranean?" *Catholic Biblical Quarterly* 51 (1989) 1-31.

Martin, T. W. *Metaphor and Composition in 1 Peter.* Society of Biblical Literature Dissertation Series 131; Atlanta: Scholars, 1992.

Michaels, J. R. "Eschatology in 1 Peter iii.17," *New Testament Studies* 13 (1967) 394-401.

————. *1 Peter.* Word Biblical Commentary, Waco: Word, 1988.

————. *Word Biblical Themes: 1 Peter.* Dallas: Word, 1989.

Stranahan, B. P. "Bunyan and the Epistle to the Hebrews: His Source for the Idea of Pilgrimage in *The Pilgrim's Progress*," *Studies in Philology* 79 (1982) 272-96.

van Unnik, W. C. "The Teaching of Good Works in 1 Peter," *New Testament Studies* 1 (1954) 92-110.

Following the Lamb:
Discipleship in the Apocalypse

DAVID E. AUNE

Throughout the history of Christianity there have been, and continue to be, countless situations in which the followers of Christ have experienced various forms of opposition and hostility resulting not only in physical and emotional suffering, but even death. The Apocalypse of John was written at the end of the first century or the very beginning of the second century A.D. in response to one such situation of hostility against Christians, whether real or anticipated. The author portrays Rome and its emperors as the willing accomplices of Satan who try in vain to destroy the people of God. The three series of eschatological plagues depicted in the book — the seven seals in 6:1–8:1; the seven bowls in 8:2–11:19; the seven trumpets in 15:1–16:21 — are presented as divine punishments directed at those responsible for the persecution of God's people (cf. 6:12-17; 16:5-6; 18:4-8). The persecutors become the persecuted, and when the enemies of God and his people are finally conquered in decisive eschatological battles (19:11-21; 20:7-10), the last judgment takes place (20:11-14), followed by the triumphal appearance of the New Jerusalem on a transformed earth.

Until recently it has generally been accepted that the Johannine Apocalypse arose in the context of the persecution of the Christian church by the Roman emperor Domitian (A.D. 81-96). That was the explicit view of Eusebius of Caesarea, an early third-century Christian historian (*Ecclesiastical History* 3.17; 4.26.5-11), which was repeated by

269

other third- and fourth-century Christian authors. Of late, however, studies have shown that much of Domitian's negative reputation is undeserved and that no persecution was sponsored by that emperor against Christians, whether officially or unofficially. Two possible ways of relating this new information to the interpretation of the Apocalypse of John, therefore, are open: the author of this writing perceived a degree of anti-Christian hostility that did not conform to actual experience, or, more probably, the persecution reflected in the Apocalypse was the result of sporadic local opposition to Christianity, which sometimes ended tragically — as in the case of Antipas of Pergamum (cf. 2:13), who is the only martyr specifically mentioned in the entire book.

John of Patmos, the author-editor of the Apocalypse, was centrally concerned with Christian discipleship, which he explored in a variety of ways against the dark background of anti-Christian sentiment in the Roman province of Asia at the end of the first century A.D. It was his view, given the existing or imminent social and political situation of the Christians of Anatolia, that death was the almost inevitable consequence for those who remained faithful to the demands of the word of God and were faithful to Jesus.

The theme of discipleship in the Apocalypse of John has two focal points: the present and the future. Present and future are related in the Apocalypse not only in the general sense that the present will soon become the future, but in the more specific sense that the future will be qualitatively *different* from the present. It is for this kind of future that theologians in the early nineteenth century coined the term *eschatology*.

The emphasis on discipleship in the present is concentrated in 1:1–3:22 and 22:10-21, sections which frame the book and deal primarily with the historical situation of the seven Christian congregations to whom John addressed his prophetic book. The future or eschatological dimensions of discipleship, however, are the focus of 4:1–22:9, the main part of the book, which deals with the unfolding eschatological plan of God for the world. The present and future dimensions of discipleship are closely related in the Apocalypse, with discipleship in the future being based on discipleship in the present.

An exhaustive study of discipleship in the Apocalypse of John is not possible in this short chapter. One passage and two groups of passages are, however, crucial, and need to be treated here. The single passage is 14:1-5, which speaks of the 144,000 and is centrally important for an understanding of how the author views the nature of Christian discipleship. One group of passages speak of "victory," with that victory being presented as possible only through apparent defeat and death. The other group of passages are those that have to do with obedience to the commands of God and witnessing to the salvific significance of Jesus.

1. Characteristics of Discipleship in 14:1-5

Rev 14:1-5 narrates an eschatological scene in which John sees a vision of the Lamb standing on Mount Zion with 144,000 people who have the name of the Lamb and of God written on their foreheads. Down through the centuries, readers of the Apocalypse have puzzled over the identification of the 144,000. The number is obviously symbolic, not literal. But does this group represent Jewish Christians (cf. 7:4-8), or an elite group of Christians such as the martyrs, or the entire people of God? While it seems logical to identify them with the 144,000 mentioned in 7:4, there is a strong grammatical argument that stands in the way of such an equation. For in 7:4 the Greek phrase behind the number 144,000 lacks a definite article, indicating that the author there was introducing an unknown entity to his audience. But when the number 144,000 is next mentioned here in 14:1, it also lacks the definite article — thereby suggesting that the author did not regard this group as being identical with the group mentioned in 7:4. The 144,000 are mentioned again in 14:3, and this time with the "anaphoric" definite article, so called because it "refers back" to the previous mention of the 144,000 in 14:1.

Another interpretive problem is whether the scene takes place on earth or in heaven — that is, is "Zion" to be understood literally of the earthly Jerusalem or metaphorically of heaven (cf. Gal 4:26; Heb 12:22; *5 Ezra* 2:42-48; *Targum of Isaiah* 24:23; 31:4)? Early Jewish apocalyptic traditions depict the Messiah on Mount Zion, where he will annihilate the enemies of Israel, which have gathered there for battle (e.g., 4 Ezra 13:33-36; *2 Baruch* 40:1-3; cf. Isa 40:9-11). The original readers, who were familiar with Jewish apocalyptic expectations, would probably have connected the 144,000 celibate males who stood with the Lamb on Mount Zion with the eschatological army gathered to repulse the onslaught of the heathen nations. What the author of the Apocalypse appears to have done with this traditional eschatological scenario is to use it in a metaphorical way, as did the author of Hebrews (12:22), so that the earthly struggle of the people of God is juxtaposed on a scene of their heavenly triumph. On such a reading of 14:1-5, the 144,000 are depicted as prepared to do battle and win, but the notion of "victory" means that they (like their Lord) must be killed. So while the Lamb is not literally in their midst, he will be in their midst in the heavenly Mount Zion when they have conquered the Beast by laying down their lives (as in 7:9-17 and 15:2-4). This way of reading the passage will be reinforced in the following discussion.

John of Patmos provides his readers with a threefold characterization of the 144,000 in 14:4-5, each introduced by the stereotypical phrase "these [are]" — with each of these characterizations being important for an understanding of the author's view of Christian discipleship: First, "*these are those* who have not polluted themselves with women, for they are chaste." Second, "*these are those* who follow the Lamb where he would go." Third, "*these are those* who have been redeemed from humanity, the firstfruits for God and the Lamb, and in their mouth no lie was found; they are blameless." Each of these characterizations requires elaboration in what follows.

Discipleship and Celibacy

The first characterization of the 144,000 focuses on their sexual asceticism: "These are those who have not polluted themselves with women, for they are chaste [*parthenoi*]" (14:4a). The contrast between the 144,000 and the "polluting" influence of women indicates that they are all males. The notion that men can be polluted by women is offensive in modern Western societies, since it not only implies a superior status for males, but also suggests that women are sources of impurity and so constitute a constant danger for males. This viewpoint, which is frequently found in Third World countries, was not, however, uncommon in antiquity. For example, in the Mishnah, which was codified about A.D. 200 by Rabbi Judah the Prince, women are considered a necessary evil because procreation is impossible without them. Yet they are also viewed as a major source of ritual impurity for their rabbinic spouses, whose lives revolved about the central concern of ritual purity. The term "pollution" as it is used in the Mishnah, of course, has to do primarily with ritual purity rather than moral purity, though the two were not always distinguished.

The context for this emphasis in Rev 14:4 on sexual purity or virginity (the term *parthenoi*, which we have translated "chaste," literally means "[male] virgins," a term rarely applied to males) is one of discipleship. As such, it points the reader to the discipleship sayings of the Synoptic Gospels, some of which emphasize sexual asceticism — particularly those of Luke's Gospel. In Mark 10:29, seven types of renunciation are mentioned for disciples of Jesus: home, brothers, sisters, mother, father, children, and fields. All seven are repeated in Matt 19:29, but they are reduced to five in Luke 18:29, with the interesting addition of *wives:* house, wife, brothers, parents, and children — though Geza Vermes argues that "house" in Mark 10:29 and Matt 19:29 is synonymous with "wife," since in vernacular Aramaic "one belonging to his house" is the wife of the owner (*Jesus the Jew* [New York: Macmillan, 1973] 246, note 79).

More expressly, in the Q passage in Luke 14:26-27, *wives* are also included in a list of things that the followers of Jesus must "hate," though wives are not mentioned in the parallels in Matt 10:37-38 or *Gospel of Thomas* 53. In the Q parable of the Great Supper (Luke 14:15-24; Matt 22:1-14), only Luke includes recent marriage as an excuse not to attend the banquet, thereby giving marriage a negative connotation (marriage is not mentioned as an excuse in the parallel in *Gospel of Thomas* 64). According to Matt 19:12, there are three types of eunuchs, eunuchs by birth (i.e., males born without normal sexual organs), those made eunuchs (i.e., emasculated males), and "those who have made themselves eunuchs for the sake of the Kingdom of Heaven" (through either self-emasculation or, more probably, voluntary celibacy). The Lukan version of the question about the resurrection (Mark 12:18-27; Matt 22:23-33; Luke 20:27-40) emphasizes celibacy, the "angelic life," for those who will be accounted worthy to attain to the age to come and the resurrection (Luke 20:34-36). And a definite correlation between discipleship and sexual abstinence characterizes the various apocryphal *Acts of the Apostles* that originated in Asia Minor in ca. A.D. 175-225.

We must ask whether the virginity of the 144,000 should be understood literally or metaphorically, though it is a thorny issue. The metaphorical interpretation of virginity in this passage has been motivated, in part, by the modern Protestant rejection of celibacy as a legitimate expression of moral or religious virtue. It is also facilitated by the fact that in the Old Testament unchastity is a frequent metaphor for the act of turning away from the true worship of God and embracing the idolatrous worship of idols (cf. Jer 3:2; 13:27; Ezek 16:15-58; 23:1-49; 43:7; Hos 5:4; 6:10). Perhaps here, too, virginity is a metaphor for faithfulness to God.

Another possible interpretation is linked with the apocalyptic expectation of an attack on Zion or Jerusalem in the eschaton by heathen armies. The 144,000, who are gathered around the Lamb on Mount Zion, may represent the eschatological army of the Messiah (cf. 20:9). From this perspective their celibacy could be understood within the context of the requirement for temporary sexual abstinence demanded of participants in a holy war as prescribed in the Old Testament (cf. 1 Sam 21:4-5; 2 Sam 11:11-12; Deut 23:9-14). In the Qumran community, which flourished from the mid-second century B.C. until it was destroyed by the Romans in A.D. 68, there was a close link between the celibacy apparently practiced by the community and holy war theology (1QM [War Scroll] 7:3-6; cf. Philo, *Apology* 11.14-17; Pliny, *Natural History* 5.15; Josephus, *War* 2.120-21).

Following the Lamb

The 144,000 are further characterized in 14:4b as "those who follow [*hoi akolouthentes*] the Lamb wherever he would go." The unusual metaphor of the Lamb who is also Shepherd, presupposed here, is expressed explicitly in 7:17: "The Lamb in the midst of the throne will shepherd [*poimanei*] them and guide them to springs of living water." The title "Lamb," in this context, is used in place of the more conventional early Jewish metaphor of the Messiah as the Shepherd of the eschatological people of God (cf. *Psalms of Solomon* 17; *Fragmentary Targum* on Exod 12:42; see also Isa 40:11; Ezek 34:23). The connection between "Messiah" and "Shepherd" lies in the fact that the term *Messiah*, "anointed one," originated as a designation for the king of Israel or Judah, while the term "Shepherd" was a stock metaphor for "king" (cf. 2 Sam 7:7; Isa 44:28; Jer 3:15; 10:21; 25:34-36; Mic 5:4; Nah 3:18). The figure of a shepherd is used of Jesus several times in the New Testament (cf. Matt 15:24; 25:32; Mark 14:27-28 = Matt 26:31-32; Luke 19:10; John 10:2, 11, 12, 14; Heb 13:20; 1 Pet 2:25).

Of central interest here is the use of the verb "follow" *(akolouthein)*. In the New Testament this verb occurs primarily in the Gospels (seventy of seventy-nine occurrences). It has two literal meanings: "follow" in the sense of "go behind" and "follow" in the sense of "accompany." By figurative extension, it also means "be a disciple of," in the sense of adhering to the teachings or instructions of a leader and promoting the cause of that leader. It is striking that this figurative meaning of "follow" is found in the New Testament only in the four Gospels and in Rev 14:4.

Furthermore, the phrase "where he would go" in 14:4 suggests that the 144,000 follow the Lamb regardless of the cost — with that Lamb depicted in the Apocalypse as the one who was slaughtered and who thereby ransomed people for God (5:9, 12; 13:8). And one implication of true discipleship in the canonical Gospels is the possibility of dying for one's adherence to Jesus (cf. Matt 10:38 = Luke 14:27; Mark 8:34-35 = Matt 16:24-25 = Luke 9:23-24; Luke 17:33; John 12:25-26; 1 Pet 2:21; Rev 12:11). Furthermore, following the Lamb wherever he goes includes the necessity of forsaking everything, including normal marital relationships (see above).

The phrase "those who follow the Lamb wherever he would go [*hoi akolouthentes tǭ arniǭ hopou an hypagǭ*]" appears, therefore, to be modeled on Gospel traditions that speak of discipleship, particularly the introduction to the Q saying in Luke 9:57-58 (= Matt 8:19-20): "As they were going along the road a man said to him [Jesus], 'I will follow you wherever you go.'" This phrase probably indicates the early existence of a very simple, yet potentially profound, generic conception of discipleship — that is, that those who are Jesus' disciples "follow Jesus wherever he goes."

Such a conception of discipleship reappears in the second century in *Acts of Paul* 25, where Thecla, a female follower of Paul, says to him: "I will shave my head and follow you wherever you go." The same phrase, probably alluding to Rev 14:4, occurs in a letter of the churches of Lyons and Vienne (from the mid-second century A.D.), where it is said of the Christian martyr Vettius Epagathus that "he was and is a true disciple of Christ, following the Lamb wherever he goes" (preserved in Eusebius, *Ecclesiastical History* 5.1.10).

Similarly worded sayings occur in the Fourth Gospel. In John 13:36 Jesus is reported to have said: "Where I go you are unable to follow [*akolouthēsai*] me now, but you will follow me later." Here discipleship clearly means following Jesus to death (cf. 21:18-19). John 13:36 is thematically linked to 12:26: "If any one serves me, he must follow [*akoloutheitē*] me; and where I am there shall my servant be also." Finally, in John 14:3 Jesus speaks of the eventual reward for disciples who follow him to death: "Where I am you may be also. And you know the way I am going." These Johannine passages, it appears, provide versions of the tradition found in Rev 14:4, though without the latter's apocalyptic features. According to this tradition true discipleship means following Jesus to the death, with the promise of then sharing Jesus' relationship with the Father.

Firstfruits for God and the Lamb

The third clause that describes the 144,000 is found in 14:5 and consists of three characteristics, the first and last of which are closely related: "These are those who have been redeemed from humanity, the first-fruits [*aparchē*] for God and the Lamb. In their mouth no lie was found. They are blameless." The term "firstfruits" *(aparchē)* is usually explained as a metaphor drawn from the sacrificial language of the Old Testament, where it refers to the first and best portion of agricultural produce, which represents the entire crop and is ritually presented to God (cf. Exod 23:19; 34:22; Lev 23:9-14; Num 28:26-27; Deut 16:9-12). Though the Hebrew terms for "firstfruits" are never applied to individual people or animals in the Old Testament (the term "first-born" being used instead), in the New Testament "firstfruits" *(aparchē)* is always used metaphorically, often of people. In Rom 16:5, for example, Paul speaks of Epaenetus as "the firstfruits of Asia" — that is, just as the firstfruits of the wheat, barley, or grape harvest represented the entire harvest, so Epaenetus represented the first of many converts to Christianity from Asia Minor (cf. 1 Cor 16:15; 2 Thess 2:13; Jas 1:18). This may suggest that the 144,000, numerous as they were, are but the first of a much larger number of faithful Christians.

But the number 144,000 is obviously symbolic. It probably represents the complete number of the people of God: the twelve tribes of Israel times the twelve apostles ($12 \times 12 = 144$) times 1,000 (representing completeness, totality, and perfection) $= 144,000$. So if the number 144,000 represents the complete number of the people of God on earth, construing the metaphorical significance of the "firstfruits" as the first and best of an even larger number hardly seems to be on the right track.

It is generally overlooked that sacrificial or cultic terms meaning "firstfruits" are even more common in the cultures of the Greco-Roman world than in the Old Testament and early Judaism. The Greek term *aparchiai* and the Latin term *primitiae,* both meaning "firstfruits," refer to animal as well as vegetable sacrifices and offerings (cf. Herodotus 4.71; Sophocles, *Trachiniae* 183, 761; Thucydides 3.85; Isocrates, *Archidamus* 96). More directly relevant, however, is the fact that the phrase "firstfruits consisting of people" *(aparchē anthrōpōn)* was used of human beings (sometimes captives) who were actual offerings presented to the gods, who then either became temple servants or were freed (cf. Plutarch, *Theseus* 16.2; *Quaestiones Graecae* 298f.; *De Pythiae oraculis* 402a; Diodorus Siculus 4.66).

Against this Greco-Roman background, the 144,000 of Rev 14:1-5 can be regarded not as the first and best representatives of a larger number, but rather as actual sacrificial offerings to God and the Lamb. That they are designated in verse 5 as "blameless" *(amōmos),* a term often used of flawless sacrificial victims (cf. Exod 29:1; Lev 1:3; 4:3; 5:15; 22:21; Ezek 43:22-23; Philo, *Legum Allegoriae* 1.50; Heb 9:14; 1 Pet 1:19), suggests that they are themselves destined to be sacrificial victims — that is, through martyrdom. And that "no lie was found in their mouth" (14:4b; cf. Zeph 3:13, where the phrase is applied to the remnant of Israel) does not mean simply that they were honest, but rather that they refused to acknowledge the claims of the Beast on their lives and chose to remain faithful to God and to the Lamb (cf. 14:9, 11; 15:2).

In the Old Testament and early Judaism an extremely large vocabulary was devoted to the notions of deceit and treachery, suggesting that lying (along with idolatry, murder, and sexual immorality) was considered one of the major vices. Paradoxically, there is not a single law in the Old Testament that forbids lying generally, though there are injunctions against bearing false witness and perjury (Exod 20:16; Lev 19:12; Prov 21:28). In the Old Testament, God is associated with truth and idolatry is associated with lying, and by the late Second Temple period this was transposed into the association of God with truth and Satan with lying (cf. 1QS [Manual of Discipline] 4:9; 10:22; John 8:41-47; Rom 3:4; Titus 1:22).

2. The Paradoxical Meaning of Victory

In Revelation 5, one of the most dramatic scenes of the Apocalypse, the universal quest for someone worthy to open the scroll sealed with seven seals ends with the introduction of "the Lion of the tribe of Judah" by one of the twenty-four elders. In that introduction, "the Lion of the tribe of Judah" is also called "the Branch of David, who has conquered [enikēsen] and can open the scroll" (v 5), using descriptive titles that were clearly drawn from traditional designations of the Davidic Messiah. Paradoxically, however, when John looks more closely at this figure, what he actually sees is "a Lamb standing as though slaughtered" (v 6). Then in the hymnic section that follows, the reader learns that the reason the Lamb alone is worthy to open the sealed scroll is that he was slaughtered and by that sacrificial act has ransomed people for God from all parts of the world (v 9). Thus it is the *death* of Jesus (under the metaphor of the Lamb) that is understood as his *victory* — which is a theological conception very close to the statement attributed to Jesus in John 16:33: "I have conquered [enikēka] the world."

This dual presentation of the salvific function of Jesus as the crucified Messiah, which has been aptly called the irony of kingship through crucifixion, is not unique to the Apocalypse but of central theological significance in other major sections of the New Testament as well (e.g., 1 Cor 1:23-24). Martin Luther designated these two complementary aspects of the work of Christ as the *theologia crucis* ("theology of the cross") and the *theologia gloriae* ("theology of glory"). The atoning death of Christ, conceptualized as conflict resulting in victory, reflects the classic idea of the atonement, according to which Christ fought against and triumphed over all the evil powers in the world, under whom human beings were in bondage and suffering — and so decisively triumphing over those powers, he reconciled the world to God.

The victory achieved by Jesus through suffering and death becomes a central paradigm for discipleship in the Apocalypse. This correlation between the experience of Jesus and the demands of discipleship is made explicit in the final words to the church of Laodicea in 3:21: "As for the one who conquers [ho nikōn], I will authorize that one to sit with me on my throne, just as I conquered [enikēsa] and sat with my Father on his throne." And like this conclusion of the proclamation to Laodicea (3:14-22), each of the other six proclamations to the churches of Roman Asia concludes with a promise to "the one who conquers" (2:7, 11, 17, 26-28; 3:5, 12).

A more oblique way of correlating the death of Jesus with the victory of Christians is articulated in the context of the hymn of rejoicing in 12:11: "They conquered [*enikēsan*] him [Satan] through the blood of the Lamb and by the word of their testimony, and they did not love their lives to the point of death." The verb "conquer, be victorious" *(nikan)* occurs seventeen times in the Apocalypse. When the exalted Jesus is the subject of this verb (as in 3:21 and 5:5), it means that he conquered *through death*. And it means precisely the same thing where it is used (eleven times) elsewhere in the Apocalypse of Christians, explicitly in 12:11 and implicitly in eight other places (2:7, 11, 17, 26; 3:5, 12, 21 [twice]). Likewise, the theme of martyrs "conquering" *(nikan)* their besiegers and torturers by nobly facing suffering and death appears in 4 Macc 6:10: "And like a noble athlete the old man, while being beaten, was victorious [*enika*] over his torturers" (see also 7:4b; 9:6, 30; 11:20; 16:14; 17:15). In 4 Macc 1:11, in a summary passage, it is said that "by their endurance [*hypomonē*] they [the Jewish martyrs] conquered [*nikēsantes*] the tyrant."

3. The Commands of God and the Witness to Jesus

At the conclusion of the narrative about the Woman, the Child, and the Dragon in Revelation 12, the Dragon (= Satan) is enraged because his attempts to destroy the Woman (here representing the people of God) have been unsuccessful. He then turns his anger toward the offspring or seed of the Woman (representing Christians), who are described as "those who keep the commands of God [*tōn tēroutōn tas entolas tou theou*] and maintain the witness of Jesus [*echontōn tēn martyrian Iēsou*]" (v 17). A close parallel occurs in an abrupt parenetic exhortation in 14:12: "This indicates that the perseverance of God's people involves keeping the commands of God [*hoi tērountes tas entolas tou theou*] and the faith of Jesus [*tēn pistin Iēsou*]." These statements constitute a remarkable definition of Christian faith in which the validity of the traditional commands of God (i.e., the Torah), understood from a Christian perspective, is seen as *complementary* rather than antithetical to the requirements of "the witness of Jesus" or "the faith of Jesus." Furthermore, both of these sayings, as well as their parallels elsewhere in the Apocalypse, occur in contexts of persecution.

279

It is not completely clear, however, what each of these statements really means (we have translated them literally to reveal their ambiguity). Should the "commandments of God" be understood to refer in a restricted way to the Decalogue, or more generally to the Torah? Furthermore, does the phrase focus on either the ceremonial or the ethical requirements of the Decalogue, or does it have in mind the entire Torah? And what is the "witness" or "testimony" of Jesus? Does it refer to the witness borne *by* Jesus (taking "of Jesus" as a subjective genitive), or is it the witness or testimony of Christians *about* Jesus that is in view (taking "of Jesus" as an objective genitive)?

There is a striking parallel to these two statements in 12:17 and 14:12 in 1QpHab [the Qumran commentary on Habakkuk] 8:1-3: "Its interpretation pertains to *all the doers of the Law* in the House of Judah, whom God will rescue from the House of Judgment for their tribulation and *their fidelity to the Teacher of Righteousness*." Here the phrase "the doers of the Law" corresponds to "those who keep the commands of God" in Rev 12:17 and 14:12, while "their fidelity to the Teacher of Righteousness" corresponds to "the witness of Jesus" in 12:17 and "the faith of Jesus" in 14:12. This parallel suggests that the latter phrase should be construed as an objective genitive, that is, as "faith in Jesus" or (more probably) "faithfulness to Jesus."

In Jewish martyrological literature, adherence to the commands of God is one of the major reasons that martyrs give for their willingness to suffer and die rather than compromise their faith (cf. 1 Macc 1:60-63; 2 Macc 7:1-3; 3 Macc 1:23; 4 Macc 5:16-17, 29; 6:18; 7:8; 9:1-2; pseudo-Philo, *Biblical Antiquities* 38:2). In such contexts, "obeying the commands of God" refers primarily to sociological markers of Jewish identity, including circumcision, dietary laws, Sabbath observance, and avoidance of any participation in pagan sacrificial rituals (cf. Dan 3:3-18; 1 Macc 1:60-63). In early Christianity, on the other hand, "keep the commandments of God" (e.g., *Barnabas* 4:11) came to have a very particular meaning — that is, the *ethical* as opposed to ceremonial commands of the Torah. Thus while for early Judaism the Law included the entire Torah, for early Christian authors the central part of the law was the second table of the Decalogue, its ethical commandments, and the love command.

In the New Testament and other early Christian literature, the phrase "keep the commandments" occurs quite frequently (e.g., Matt 19:17; John 14:15, 21; 15:10; 1 John 2:3; 3:22, 24; 5:3; Hermas, *Mandates*

7.7.5; 12.3.4; 12.6.3; *Similitudes* 5.1.5; 5.3.3), almost always in a positive sense. Paul also speaks quite positively of "obeying the commandments of God" (1 Cor 7:19) — though he excludes circumcision, which is certainly part of the Torah, unless his focus was on the ethical rather than on the ceremonial laws (cf. Rom 7:8; 13:8-9). And even though the ethical requirements of the Torah may be thought to play a negative theological role (e.g., Rom 7:7-11), in general they are regarded in an overwhelmingly positive light in early Christianity as the revealed will of God (cf. Rom 7:12). Paul's negative perception of "the works of the law" was, in fact, sometimes — though not entirely (cf. Rom 3:20; 7:7-25) — restricted to the distinctive socioreligious markers of Judaism: circumcision, food regulations, and Sabbath observance.

There was a tendency in early Christian thought, beginning with Jesus himself, to see the whole Law as encapsulated in either the two commands to love God and to love one's neighbor (Mark 12:28-31 = Matt 22:36-40; *Didache* 1:2; Justin, *Dialogue* 93.2; Theophilus, *Ad Autolycum* 2.34), or in the single command to love one's neighbor (Rom 13:9-10; Gal 5:14; Jas 2:8). This tendency to summarize the Law under a single rubric or two was also prevalent in Judaism. The command to love one's neighbor was, of course, not part of the Decalogue, but derived from Lev 19:18 (cf. Lev 19:33-34; Deut 10:19). This love command took on a significant theological role in the New Testament (1 Thess 4:9; Rom 13:8-10). So in the context of these considerations, it is probable that "keeping the commandments of God" in Rev 12:18 and 14:12 should be regarded as referring exclusively to the *ethical* requirements of the Torah.

The phrases "the witness of Jesus" (12:17) and "the faith of Jesus" (14:12) can be construed in a number of ways. In 20:4 the martyrs are clearly referred to in a similar way: "those who had been beheaded because of their witness to Jesus and because of the word of God." Here, as in 12:17 and 14:12, the relationship of these Christians to both Jesus and God is described in a very particular way. The phrase "the word of God" is doubtless a more general designation for "the commandments of God," and refers to the will of God revealed in the Torah. A closely related text is in 6:9, where John sees the souls of those slain "because of the word of God and because of the witness [*martyrian*] which they bore." Here the absence of the qualifying genitive "of Jesus," which is present in the other parallels in the Apocalypse, indicates that "witness" *(martyria)* refers to the witness expressed in word and deed borne by those faithful Christians who experienced martyrdom.

281

There are several expressions in the Apocalypse, which are set out in similar couplets, that contain variations of this phrase:

1:2 Who bore witness to the message from God,
that is, the witness borne by Jesus [tēn martyrian Iēsou Christou]
1:9 Because of the word of God
and my witness to Jesus [tēn martyrian Iēsou].
6:9 Because of the word of God
and because of the witness which they bore.
20:4 Because of their witness to Jesus [tēn martyrian Iēsou]
and because of the word of God.

Two additional parallel couplets contain just one of the lines of the parallels listed above:

12:17 Who keep the commandments of God
and maintain their witness to Jesus [tēn martyrian Iēsou].
19:10 Who maintain the witness to Jesus [tēn martyrian Iēsou].
For the witness to Jesus is the spirit of prophecy.

So while the Greek phrase tēn martyrian Iēsou, literally, "the witness of Jesus," can be an objective genitive, and therefore translated "the witness about Jesus" or "the witness to Jesus," it can also be translated as a subjective genitive — that is, "the witness borne by Jesus."

There are several instances in the Apocalypse where a genitive dependent on "witness" (martyria) should be construed as a subjective genitive (e.g., 1:2; 11:17; 12:11; cf. 6:9), but there are other instances where it seems contextually appropriate to construe the genitive as an objective genitive (e.g., 12:17; 14:12; 17:6; 19:10 [twice]; 20:4). More specifically, the phrase "the witness of Jesus" (martyria Iēsou) occurs five times in the Apocalypse (1:2, 9; 12:17; 19:10; 20:4), and only in 1:2 does it appear appropriate to translate the phrase as a subjective genitive — and there "the witness borne by Jesus" appears to be identical with the contents of the prophetic book that John has written.

In the other occurrences of the phrase "the testimony/witness of Jesus" (martyria Iēsou), it is the testimony or witness of Jesus that is in view — presumably referring to the testimony that Jesus maintained during his trial (cf. Matt 27:11-14; Mark 15:1-5; Luke 23:1-12; John 18:19-24, 33-38), which can be characterized as either evasive answers (except for Mark 14:62), silence, or profound response (cf. John 18:33-38). Furthermore, construing "witness" *(martyria)* as a subjective genitive would mean that it would be one of the very few references to the historical Jesus in the Apocalypse (along with 1:5; 2:8; 5:6; 11:8). Finally, since the statements found in 6:9; 11:7; 12:11; and 17:6 all unambiguously emphasize the fact that the testimony is born by Christians, the focus of that testimony must be the salvific significance of Jesus.

4. Concluding Observations

Without treating the subject of discipleship in the Apocalypse of John in any exhaustive fashion, we have attempted to focus on three important groups of texts that deal with this theme. Rev 14:1-5 is a centrally important text for understanding the author's views on the nature of Christian discipleship. Christians who have given their allegiance to God and are consequently symbolically and indelibly marked with the name of God and of the Lamb on their foreheads "follow the Lamb wherever he goes." In the context this does not refer to green pastures and springs of water (as in 7:17) but rather to a willingness to suffer and die as a consequence of faithfulness to God and the Lamb. Just as this language of discipleship has been turned into a metaphor for death, so the designations "firstfruits for God and the Lamb" and "blameless" (14:5) underscore the sacrificial calling of these faithful followers of the Lamb.

Paradoxically, the term "victory" in the Apocalypse is an ironical term, for it refers to a victory achieved through apparent defeat and death. The exalted Jesus is paradigmatic for Christian disciples. But the victory he has achieved is based on the sacrificial death that he experienced (5:9), and so those who conquer as he conquered will be rewarded by sitting with him on his throne (3:21).

Finally, John's view of a Christian disciple is of one who is obedient to the commands of God (by which the ethical commands of the second table of the Decalogue are likely in view) and witnesses to the salvific significance of Jesus. There is no dichotomy here between law and grace — a Pauline theological problem that is remarkably absent from the Johannine Apocalypse. Rather, obedience to the will of God as mediated by the Torah is considered complementary to the demands of faith in Christ.

Selected Bibliography

Bruce, F. F. "The Spirit in the Apocalypse," in *Christ and Spirit in the New Testament: Studies in Honour of C. F. D. Moule*, ed. B. Lindars and S. Smalley. Cambridge: Cambridge University Press, 1973, 333-34.

Collins, T. *Apocalypse 22:6-21 as the Focal Point of Moral Teaching and Exhortation in the Apocalypse.* Rome: Pontificia Universitas Gregoriana, 1986.

Dehandschutter, B. "The Meaning of Witness in the Apocalypse," in *L'Apocalypse johannique et l'Apocalyptique dans le Nouveau Testament.* Leuven: Leuven University Press, 1980, 283-88.

Jeske, R. L. "Spirit and Community in the Johannine Apocalypse," *New Testament Studies* 31 (1985) 452-66.

Lampe, G. W. H., "The Testimony of Jesus is the Spirit of Prophecy (Rev. 19,10)," in *The New Testament Age: Essays in Honor of Bo Reicke*, ed. W. Weinreich. Macon: Mercer University Press, 1984, 2.245-58.

Mazzaferri, F. "*Marturia Iēsou* Revisited," *Bible Translator* 39 (1988) 114-22.

Schüssler Fiorenza, E. "The Followers of the Lamb: Visionary Rhetoric and Social-Political Situation," in *Discipleship in the New Testament*, ed. F. F. Segovia. Philadelphia: Fortress, 1985, 144-65.

Trites, A. A. *The New Testament Concept of Witness.* Cambridge: Cambridge University Press, 1977.

Vassiliadis, P. "The Translation of *Marturia Iēsou* in Revelation," *Bible Translator* 36 (1985) 129-34.

Index of Subjects

Abraham, 148
Anger, 237, 241
Antipas of Pergamum, 270
Antisthenes, 145
Aphrodite, 106
Apocalyptic writings, 148-49, 228-29
Apostasy, 208, 213
Apostles, 56, 59, 79
Apostolic Decree, 105
Aristotle, 3, 33, 145
Artemidorus, 219
Ascension of Jesus, 60
Asceticism, 181, 189, 191-93
Augustus, 105

Baptism, 11, 26, 40, 44
    of Jesus, 26, 58
    as a sacrament, 196, 265
"Bear fruit," 90
Beatitudes, 60-62
"Believe," 84-85
Beloved Disciple, 57, 83, 87-89, 92
Biblis, 263
Branch of David, 278
"Brothers," 72-73

Cabirus cult, 105, 108

Cato, 104
Celibacy, 272-74
Character of God, 197-98
Christ, see Messiah, Jesus Christ
Chrysippus, 146
Cicero, 215
Circumcision, 225, 242
Cleanthes, 146, 172
Colotes, 147
Commands of God, 279-83
Commands of Jesus, 90-91
Conformity to Christ, 151-55,
    see also "In Christ," Identification
    with Christ
Controversy stories, 10, 18-19
Cost of discipleship, 60, 63-64,
    207-13, 216-17, 219-20
Covenant, 101-03, 108, 112, 116, 118,
    213, 221-22
Creation, 186
Criticism, 237
Cross, 25, 38, 40, 43-44, 64, 69-70, 73,
    88, 131, 215, 218, 257-58, see also
    Jesus Christ, death of
Crowds, 31, 35, 43, 63
Crucifixion, 11, 25, 83, 85, 88, 91,

285

Inheritance, 255
Isis, 106
Isocrates, 121, 277
Israel, 101-03, 108, 112, 221, 225

James and Jesus, 241-42
James and Paul, 226, 242-43
Jesus Christ
death of, 11-12, 14, 25, 60, 130-31,
150-53, 190-92, 195-97, 205,
215, 218, 278, *see also* Cross,
Crucifixion, Suffering of Jesus
resurrection of, 26-27, 39-40, 60,
83, 85, 150-51, 192-94, 197-98,
259-62
as champion, 205-06, 214-15
as example of discipleship, 25-27,
127-37, 166-72, 213-20, 252-61
as firstborn, 186
as high priest, 205, 221
as Lord, 227, 244
as redeemer, 257-58
Jewish leaders, 31, 35, 43
"Jews, the," 79-83
Johannine community, 79-80, 85, 88,
93-96
Johannine letters, 78, 93-96
John the Baptist
in Matthew, 32, 183
in Luke, 57-58, 61
in John, 56, 79-80, 82-83
Joseph of Arimathea, 21, 32, 56, 84
Josephus, 2, 105, 149-50
Judas, 32, 56, 79
Judgment, 228
Julian laws, 105
Juridical language, 144, 152,
158-59, 161
Juvenal, 105

"Keep," 92
Kingdom, 10, 14-15, 38-39, 45, 57, 63,
66, 74, 243, 273
"Know," 84-85, 95

Lamb (of God), 79, 258, 271, 274-79
Light and darkness, 89, 95, 100

Lion of the tribe of Judah, 278
Livy, 215
Lord's Supper, 11, 26
Love, 46, 90-91, 94-96, 115
Love of Christ, 130-31
Lucian, 210

Marcus Aurelius, 167
Marriage, 14-15
Martha and Mary, 83-84
Mary Magdalene, 32, 83
Mary, mother of Jesus, 88
Messiah/Christ, 37, 79-81, 84-85, 95,
224
Mission, 90-92
Mission of the church, 53-54, 75
Moses, 148
Mount Zion, 271-72, 274
Mystery religions, 147, 151
Mystical language, 144, 151-52, 161
Mystical union with Christ, 188-89,
194, *see also* "In Christ"

Narrative criticism, 31, 33-35, 41, 47
Nazareth pericope, 58, 71
Nicodemus, 82, 84, 88

Olivet Discourse, 15
"144,000," 2, 4, 270-77
Ovid, 105

Parables, 15, 55, 64-67
Parousia/return of Christ, 90, 100,
113, 206, 211
Passion narratives
in Mark, 20-21
in Luke, 51, 67-70
in John, 50
Passion predictions
in Mark, 11-15
in Luke, 55, 65
Patrons/benefactors, 114-15
Pattern, 120
Paul, 98-202
in Acts, 52, 73
companion of Luke, 53
as example of discipleship, 121-24,
137-39, 172-74, 176-77

Index of Modern Authors

Index of Scripture and Other Ancient References

301

12:25-29	220	2:8	281	5:19-20	238
13:5	223	2:14	236		
13:7	121, 217-18	2:14-26	236, 242-43	**1 Peter**	
13:10-16	218-19	2:17	236	1:1	252
13:12-13	215	2:18-19	236	1:2	258
13:12-14	218-20, 222	2:19	228, 242	1:3	260
13:13	215	2:26	236	1:3-9	250-51
13:15-16	221	3:1	238	1:4	249
13:17	217	3:1-12	229, 238	1:4-5	255
13:20	274	3:2	257	1:6	262
13:20-21	260	3:6	238	1:8	260
13:24	217	3:8	239	1:10	266
		3:9	238	1:13	266
James		3:9-12	237	1:13-21	251
1:1	225	3:13-18	229	1:14	259
1:2	231, 240	3:15	238	1:15	252
1:2-4	236	3:17	238	1:17	252, 256
1:4	239	3:17-18	239	1:18	259
1:5	238	4:1-2	238	1:19	256, 258, 277
1:5-8	239	4:1-3	234	1:21	260
1:6	239	4:1-10	230	1:22	265
1:7-8	240	4:2-3	240	1:22-23	259
1:8	227	4:4	227, 239	2:1	259
1:9	235	4:7	238, 262, 263	2:1-10	251-52
1:9-11	230-31, 233-34	4:7-10	239	2:4	260
1:10-11	236	4:7-12	245	2:8	260
1:12	228, 229	4:8	227	2:11	259
1:14-15	240	4:9	238	2:11-20	252
1:17	238, 240	4:11-12	237	2:12	257, 260
1:18	276	4:13-17	232, 234, 236	2:13	250
1:19-20	237	4:17	236	2:13-17	254
1:19-27	232	5:1-5	228	2:15	257
1:20	150, 158	5:1-6	230-31, 232-33, 234	2:17	265
1:22-25	236			2:18	257
1:26	237	5:4	228, 235	2:18-25	254-55, 266
1:27	236	5:6	228, 235	2:19-20	250
2:1-4	234	5:7-8	228	2:21	254, 275
2:1-13	230	5:7-11	235, 236	2:21-23	257
2:1-26	231	5:9	237	2:21-25	252-53, 259-60
2:5	228, 235	5:13	236, 238	2:22-23	256, 262
2:5-7	232	5:13-18	240, 241	2:24	257, 258
2:6	232	5:14-16	245	2:25	260, 274

306